World Military Guide
United States of America

Compiled by
Kiera Mccune

Scribbles

Year of Publication 2018

ISBN : 9789352979059

Book Published by

Scribbles

(An Imprint of Alpha Editions)

email - alphaedis@gmail.com

Produced by: PediaPress GmbH
Limburg an der Lahn
Germany
http://pediapress.com/

The content within this book was generated collaboratively by volunteers. Please be advised that nothing found here has necessarily been reviewed by people with the expertise required to provide you with complete, accurate or reliable information. Some information in this book may be misleading or simply wrong. Alpha Editions and PediaPress does not guarantee the validity of the information found here. If you need specific advice (for example, medical, legal, financial, or risk management) please seek a professional who is licensed or knowledgeable in that area.

Sources, licenses and contributors of the articles and images are listed in the section entitled "References". Parts of the books may be licensed under the GNU Free Documentation License. A copy of this license is included in the section entitled "GNU Free Documentation License"

The views and characters expressed in the book are those of the contributors and his/her imagination and do not represent the views of the Publisher.

Contents

Articles   1

Introduction   1
    United States Armed Forces 1

History   23
    Military history of the United States 23

Organizational Structure   63
    Organizational structure of the United States Department of Defense   63

Military Budget   81
    Military budget of the United States 81

Deployments   103
    United States military deployments 103

Women in Military   107
    Women in the United States Army 107
    Women in the United States Marines 113
    Women in the United States Navy 118
    Women in the United States Air Force 149
    Women in the United States Coast Guard 154

Five Star Rank   157
    Five-star rank 157

Unified Combatant Commands   **173**

   Unified combatant command 173

   United States Africa Command 187

   United States Central Command 202

   United States European Command 214

   United States Indo-Pacific Command 229

   United States Northern Command 243

   United States Southern Command 249

   United States Cyber Command 267

   United States Special Operations Command 274

   United States Strategic Command 309

   United States Transportation Command 319

Appendix   **333**

   References 333

   Article Sources and Contributors 348

   Image Sources, Licenses and Contributors 351

Article Licenses   **361**

Index   **363**

Introduction

United States Armed Forces

United States Armed Forces	
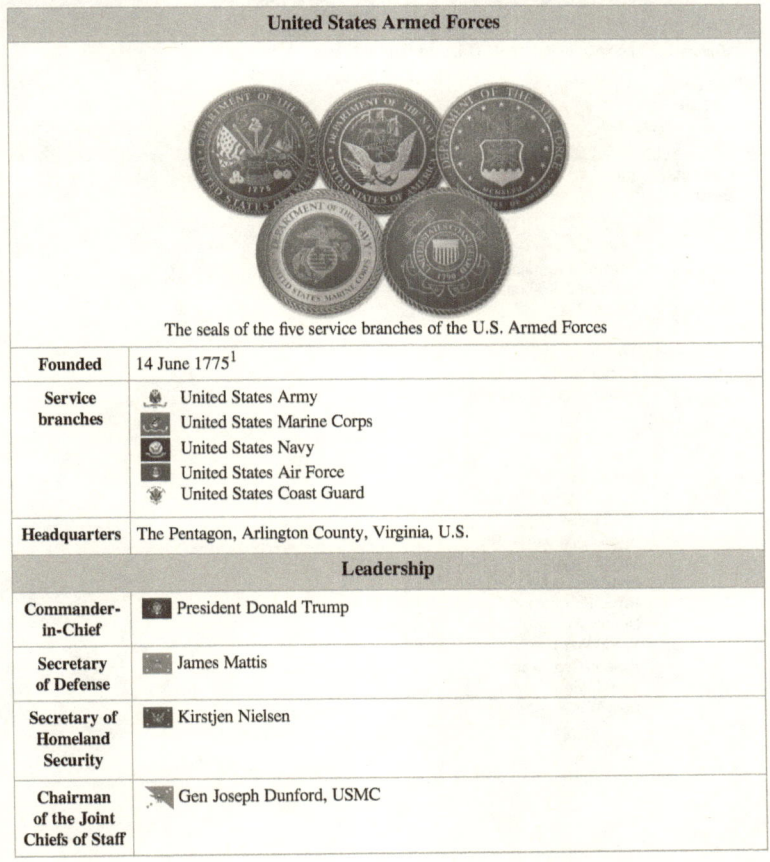 The seals of the five service branches of the U.S. Armed Forces	
Founded	14 June 1775[1]
Service branches	United States Army United States Marine Corps United States Navy United States Air Force United States Coast Guard
Headquarters	The Pentagon, Arlington County, Virginia, U.S.
Leadership	
Commander-in-Chief	President Donald Trump
Secretary of Defense	James Mattis
Secretary of Homeland Security	Kirstjen Nielsen
Chairman of the Joint Chiefs of Staff	Gen Joseph Dunford, USMC

Vice Chairman of the Joint Chiefs of Staff	Gen Paul J. Selva, USAF
Senior Enlisted Advisor to the Chairman	CSM John W. Troxell, USA
Manpower	
Military age	17 with parental consent, 18 for voluntary service. Maximum age for first-time enlistment is 35 for the Army, 28 for the Marine Corps, 34 for the Navy, 39 for the Air Force and 27 for the Coast Guard.
Active personnel	1,281,900 (ranked 3rd)
Reserve personnel	811,000
Expenditures	
Budget	US$610 billion (2017) (ranked 1st)
Percent of GDP	3.1% (2017)
Industry	
Domestic suppliers	List
Related articles	
History	American Revolutionary War Whiskey Rebellion Indian Wars Barbary Wars War of 1812 Patriot War Mexican–American War Utah War Cortina Troubles Reform War American Civil War • New York City draft riots Las Cuevas War Spanish–American War Banana Wars Philippine–American War Boxer Rebellion Border War World War I Russian Civil War World War II Cold War

	- Puerto Rican Nationalist Revolts
- Korean War
- 1958 Lebanon crisis
- Dominican Civil War
- Bay of Pigs Invasion
- Cuban Missile Crisis
- Vietnam War
- Korean DMZ Conflict
- Operation Eagle Claw
- Multinational Force Lebanon
- Invasion of Grenada
- Operation Golden Pheasant
- Invasion of Panama

Persian Gulf War
Somali Civil War
- Operation Gothic Serpent
- Battle of Mogadishu

Bosnian War
- Operation Deliberate Force
- Operation Deny Flight

Kosovo War
- Operation Allied Force

Global War on Terrorism
- Operation Enduring Freedom
  - War in Afghanistan
  - Philippines
  - Horn of Africa
  - Trans Sahara
- Iraq War
- War in North-West Pakistan

Military deployment after Hurricane Katrina
Pakistan–United States skirmishes
Intervention against ISIL Other |
| Ranks | Army
- Army officer
- Army warrant officer
- Army enlisted

Marine Corps
- Marine Corps officer
- Marine Corps warrant officer
- Marine Corps enlisted

Navy
- Navy officer
- Navy warrant officer
- Navy enlisted

Air Force
- Air Force officer
- Air Force enlisted

Coast Guard
- Coast Guard officer
- Coast Guard warrant officer
- Coast Guard enlisted |

The **United States Armed Forces**[2] are the military forces of the United States of America. It consists of the Army, Marine Corps, Navy, Air Force, and Coast Guard. The President of the United States is the Commander-in-Chief of the U.S. Armed Forces and forms military policy with the U.S. Department of Defense (DoD) and U.S. Department of Homeland Security (DHS), both federal executive departments, acting as the principal organs by which military policy is carried out. All five armed services are among the seven uniformed services of the United States.[3]

From the time of its inception, the U.S. Armed Forces played a decisive role in the history of the United States. A sense of national unity and identity was forged as a result of victory in the First Barbary War and the Second Barbary War. Even so, the founders of the United States were suspicious of a permanent military force. It played a critical role in the American Civil War, continuing to serve as the armed forces of the United States, although a number of its officers resigned to join the military of the Confederate States. The National Security Act of 1947, adopted following World War II and during the Cold War's onset, created the modern U.S. military framework. The Act established the National Military Establishment, headed by the Secretary of Defense; and created the Department of the Air Force and the National Security Council. It was amended in 1949, renaming the National Military Establishment the Department of Defense, and merged the cabinet-level Department of the Army, Department of the Navy, and Department of the Air Force, into the Department of Defense.

The U.S. Armed Forces are one of the largest militaries in terms of the number of personnel. It draws its personnel from a large pool of paid volunteers. Although conscription has been used in the past in various times of both war and peace, it has not been used since 1972, but the Selective Service System retains the power to conscript males, and requires that all male citizens and residents residing in the U.S. between the ages of 18–25 register with the service.

As of 2017, the U.S. spends about US$610 billion annually to fund its military forces and Overseas Contingency Operations. Put together, the U.S. constitutes roughly 40 percent of the world's military expenditures. The U.S. Armed Forces has significant capabilities in both defense and power projection due to its large budget, resulting in advanced and powerful technologies which enables a widespread deployment of the force around the world, including around 800 military bases outside the United States. The U.S. Air Force is the world's largest air force, the U.S. Navy is the world's largest navy by tonnage, and the U.S. Navy and the U.S. Marine Corps combined are the world's second largest air arm.

History

The history of the U.S. Armed Forces dates to 14 June 1775, with the creation of the Continental Army, even before the Declaration of Independence marked the establishment of the United States. The Continental Navy, established on 13 October 1775, and Continental Marines, established on 10

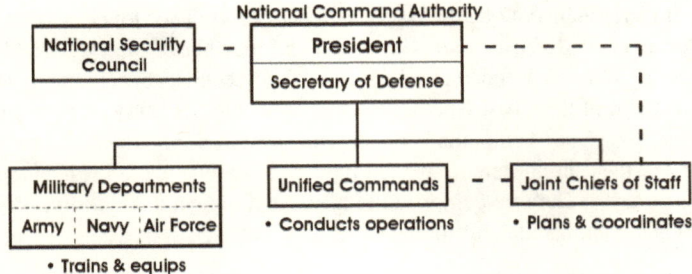

Figure 1: *Structure of the National Command Authority*

November 1775, were created in close succession by the Second Continental Congress in order to defend the new nation against the British Empire in the American Revolutionary War.

These forces demobilized in 1784 after the Treaty of Paris ended the War for Independence. The Congress of the Confederation created the current United States Army on 3 June 1784. The United States Congress created the current United States Navy on 27 March 1794 and the current United States Marine Corps on 11 July 1798. All three services trace their origins to their respective Continental predecessors. The 1787 adoption of the Constitution gave the Congress the power to "raise and support armies", to "provide and maintain a navy" and to "make rules for the government and regulation of the land and naval forces", as well as the power to declare war. The President is the U.S. Armed Forces' commander-in-chief.

The United States Coast Guard traces its origin to the founding of the Revenue Cutter Service on 4 August 1790 which merged with the United States Life-Saving Service on 28 January 1915 to establish the Coast Guard. The United States Air Force was established as an independent service on 18 September 1947; it traces its origin to the formation of the Aeronautical Division, U.S. Signal Corps, which was formed 1 August 1907 and was part of the Army Air Forces before becoming an independent service as per the National Security Act of 1947.

Command structure

Command over the U.S. Armed Forces is established in the Constitution. The sole power of command is vested in the President by Article II as Commander-in-Chief. The Constitution also allows for the creation of "executive Departments" headed by "principal officers" whose opinion the President can require.

This allowance in the Constitution formed the basis for creation of the Department of Defense in 1947 by the National Security Act. The DoD is headed by the Secretary of Defense, who is a civilian and member of the Cabinet. The Defense Secretary is second in the U.S. Armed Forces chain of command, with the exception of the Coast Guard, which is under the Secretary of Homeland Security, and is just below the President and serves as the principal assistant to the President in all defense-related matters.[4] Together, the President and the Secretary of Defense comprise the National Command Authority, which by law is the ultimate lawful source of military orders.[5]

To coordinate military strategy with political affairs, the President has a National Security Council headed by the National Security Advisor. The collective body has only advisory power to the President, but several of the members who statutorily comprise the council (the Secretary of State, the Secretary of Energy and the Secretary of Defense) possess executive authority over their own departments.

Just as the President, the Secretary of Defense, and the Secretary of Homeland Security, are in charge of the entire military establishment, maintaining civilian control of the military, so too are each of the Defense Department's constitutive military departments headed by civilians. The four DoD branches are organized into three departments, each with civilian heads. The Department of the Army is headed by the Secretary of the Army, the Department of the Navy is headed by the Secretary of the Navy and the Department of the Air Force is headed by the Secretary of the Air Force. The Marine Corps is organized under the Department of the Navy, however it is still considered a separate and equal service. The Coast Guard is under the Department of Homeland Security and receives its operational orders from the Secretary of Homeland Security. However, the Coast Guard may be transferred to the Department of the Navy by the President or Congress during a time of war, thereby placing it within the DoD.[6]

The President, Secretary of Defense and other senior executive officials are advised by a seven-member Joint Chiefs of Staff, which is headed by the Chairman of the Joint Chiefs of Staff, the highest-ranking officer in the United States military and the Vice Chairman of the Joint Chiefs of Staff. The rest of the body is composed of the heads of each of the DoD's service branches (the Chief of Staff of the Army, the Chief of Naval Operations, the Commandant of the Marine Corps and the Chief of Staff of the Air Force) as well as the Chief of the National Guard Bureau. Although commanding one of the five military branches, the Commandant of the Coast Guard is not a member of the Joint Chiefs of Staff. Despite being composed of the highest-ranking officers in each of the respective branches, the Joint Chiefs of Staff does not possess

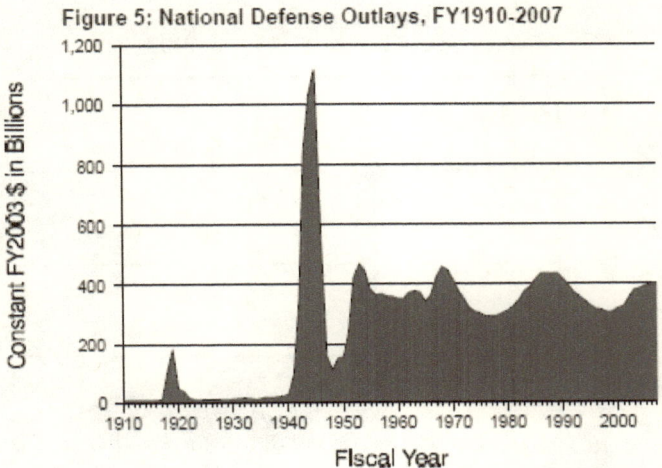

Figure 2: *U.S. military spending from 1910 to 2007, adjusted for inflation to 2003 dollars; the large spike represents World War II spending.*

operational command authority. Rather, the Goldwater-Nichols Act charges them only with advisory power.

All of the branches work together during operations and joint missions in Unified Combatant Commands, under the authority of the Secretary of Defense with the typical exception of the Coast Guard. Each of the Unified Combatant Commands is headed by a Combatant Commander, a senior commissioned officer who exercises supreme command authority per 10 U.S.C. § 164[7] over all of the forces, regardless of branch, within his geographical or functional command. By statute, the chain of command flows from the President to the Secretary of Defense to each of the Combatant Commanders. In practice, the Chairman of the Joint Chiefs of Staff often acts as an intermediary between the Secretary of Defense and the Combatant Commanders.

Budget

The United States has the world's largest military budget. In the fiscal year 2016, $580.3 billion in funding were enacted for the DoD and for "Overseas Contingency Operations" in the War on Terrorism. Outside of direct DoD spending, the United States spends another $218 to $262 billion each year on other defense-related programs, such as Veterans Affairs, Homeland Security, nuclear weapons maintenance and DoD.

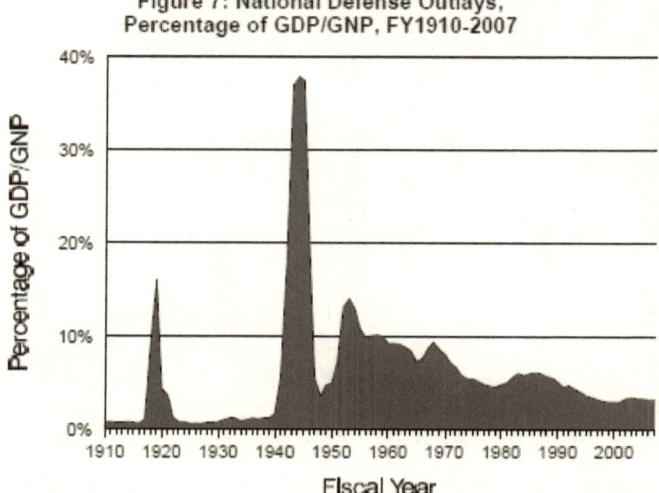

Figure 3: *American defense spending by GDP percentage 1910 to 2007*

By military department, $146.9 billion was allocated for the Department of the Army, $168.8 billion for the Department of the Navy, $161.8 billion for the Department of the Air Force and $102.8 billion for DoD-wide spending. By function, $138.6 billion was requested for personnel, $244.4 billion for operations and maintenance, $118.9 billion for procurement, $69.0 billion for research and development, $1.3 billion for revolving and management funds, $6.9 billion for military construction and $1.3 billion for family housing.

Personnel

The projected active duty end strength in the armed forces for fiscal year 2017 was 1,281,900 servicemembers, with an additional 801,200 people in the seven reserve components. It is an all-volunteer military, but conscription through the Selective Service System can be enacted at the President's request and Congress' approval. All males ages 18 through 25 who are living in the United States are required to register with the Selective Service for a potential future draft.

The U.S. Armed Forces is the world's third largest military, after the Chinese's People's Liberation Army and the Indian Armed Forces, and has troops deployed around the globe.

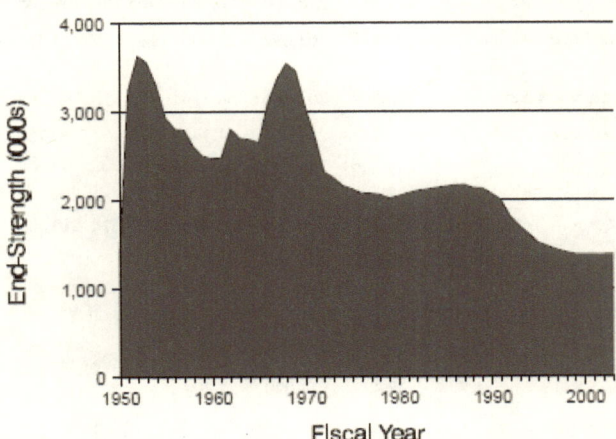

Figure 4: *Active duty U.S. military personnel from 1950 to 2003; the two peaks correspond to the Korean War and the Vietnam War.*

As in most militaries, members of the U.S. Armed Forces hold a rank, either that of officer, warrant officer or enlisted, to determine seniority and eligibility for promotion. Those who have served are known as veterans. Rank names may be different between services, but they are matched to each other by their corresponding paygrade.[8] Officers who hold the same rank or paygrade are distinguished by their date of rank to determine seniority, while officers who serve in certain positions of office of importance set by law, outrank all other officers in active duty of the same rank and paygrade, regardless of their date of rank. Currently, only one in four persons in the United States of the proper age meet the moral, academic and physical standards for military service.[9]

Personnel by service

February 2018 Demographic Reports and end strengths for reserve components.

Component	Military	Enlisted	Officer	Male	Female	Civilian
United States Army	471,513	376,206	90,785	465,784	69,345	299,644
United States Marine Corps	184,427	163,092	21,335	181,845	15,551	20,484
United States Navy	325,802	267,286	54,114	265,852	62,168	179,293
United States Air Force	323,222	258,015	61,144	270,462	50,750	174,754
United States Coast Guard	42,042	32,782	8,239			
Total Active	**1,347,106**	**1,137,916**	**236,826**	**1,219,510**	**210,485**	*681,232*
Army National Guard of the United States	336,879	291,865	45,014			
United States Army Reserve	190,699	153,064	37,635			
United States Marine Corps Reserve	38,473	34,079	4,394			
United States Navy Reserve	57,650	43,596	14,054			
Air National Guard of the United States	106,549	91,274	15,275			
United States Air Force Reserve	68,216	54,658	13,558			
United States Coast Guard Reserve	6,142	5,086	1,056			
Total Reserves	**807,562**	**673,622**	**130,986**			
Other DoD personnel						108,833

Personnel stationing

Overseas

As of 31 December 2010, U.S. Armed Forces troops were stationed in 150 countries; the number of non-contingent deployments per country ranges from 1 in Suriname to over 50,000 in Germany. Some of the largest deployments are: 103,700 in Afghanistan, 52,440 in Germany *(see list)*, 35,688 in Japan (USFJ), 28,500 in South Korea (USFK), 9,660 in Italy and 9,015 in the United Kingdom. These numbers change frequently due to the regular recall and deployment of units.

Altogether, 77,917 military personnel are located in Europe, 141 in the former Soviet Union, 47,236 in East Asia and the Pacific, 3,362 in North Africa, the Near East and South Asia, 1,355 in sub-Saharan Africa and 1,941 in the Western Hemisphere excluding the United States itself.

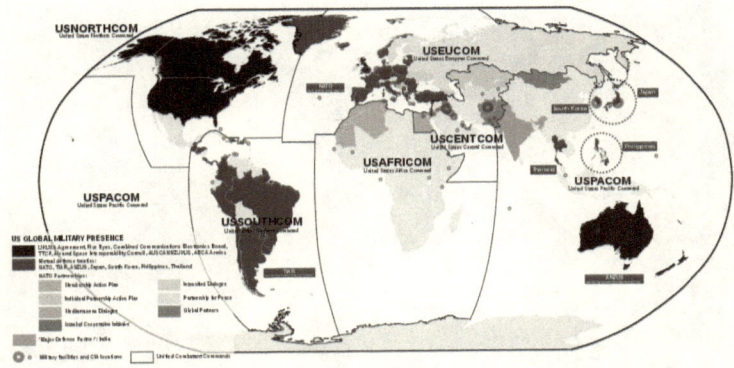

Figure 5: *U.S. global military presence*

Domestic

Including U.S. territories and ships afloat within territorial waters As of 31 December 2009, a total of 1,137,568 personnel were on active duty within the United States and its territories (including 84,461 afloat). The vast majority (941,629 personnel) were stationed at bases within the contiguous United States. There were an additional 37,245 in Hawaii and 20,450 in Alaska while 84,461 were at sea, 2,972 in Guam and 179 in Puerto Rico.

Types of personnel

Enlisted

Prospective service members are often recruited from high school or college, the target age ranges being 18–35 in the Army, 18–28 in the Marine Corps, 18–34 in the Navy, 18–39 in the Air Force and 18–27 (up to age 32 if qualified for attending guaranteed "A" school) in the Coast Guard. With the permission of a parent or guardian, applicants can enlist at age 17 and participate in the Delayed Entry Program (DEP), in which the applicant is given the opportunity to participate in locally sponsored military activities, which can range from sports to competitions led by recruiters or other military liaisons (each recruiting station's DEP varies).

After enlistment, new recruits undergo basic training (also known as "boot camp" in the Marine Corps, Navy and Coast Guard), followed by schooling in their primary Military Occupational Specialty (MOS), rating and Air Force Specialty Code (AFSC) at any of the numerous training facilities around the United States. Each branch conducts basic training differently. The Marine

Figure 6: *Service members of the U.S. Armed Forces at an American football event: (left to right) U.S. Marine Corps, U.S. Air Force, U.S. Navy and U.S. Army personnel*

Corps send all non-infantry MOS's to an infantry skills course known as Marine Combat Training prior to their technical schools. Air Force Basic Military Training graduates attend Technical Training and are awarded their Air Force Specialty Code (AFSC) at the apprentice (3) skill level. All Army recruits undergo Basic Combat Training (BCT), followed by Advanced Individual Training (AIT), with the exceptions of cavalry scouts, infantry, armor, combat engineers and military police recruits who go to One Station Unit Training (OSUT), which combines BCT and AIT. The Navy sends its recruits to Recruit Training and then to "A" schools to earn a rating. The Coast Guard's recruits attend basic training and follow with an "A" school to earn a rating.

Initially, recruits without higher education or college degrees will hold the pay grade of E-1 and will be elevated to E-2 usually soon after basic training. Different services have different incentive programs for enlistees, such as higher initial ranks for college credit, being an Eagle Scout and referring friends who go on to enlist as well. Participation in DEP is one way recruits can achieve rank before their departure to basic training.

There are several different authorized pay grade advancement requirements in each junior-enlisted rank category (E-1 to E-3), which differ by service. Enlistees in the Army can attain the initial pay grade of E-4 (specialist) with a four-year degree, but the highest initial pay grade is usually E-3 (members of the Army Band program can expect to enter service at the grade of E-4). Promotion through the junior enlisted ranks occurs after serving for a specified number of years (which can be waived by the soldier's chain of command), a specified level of technical proficiency or maintenance of good conduct. Promotion can be denied with reason.

Non-commissioned and petty officers

With very few exceptions, becoming a non-commissioned officer (NCO) or petty officer in the U.S. Armed Forces is accomplished by progression through the lower enlisted ranks. However, unlike promotion through the lower enlisted tier, promotion to NCO is generally competitive. NCO ranks begin at E-4 or E-5, depending upon service and are generally attained between three and six years of service. Junior NCOs function as first-line supervisors and squad leaders, training the junior enlisted in their duties and guiding their career advancement.

While considered part of the non-commissioned officer corps by law, senior non-commissioned officers (SNCOs) referred to as chief petty officers in the Navy and Coast Guard, or staff non-commissioned officers in the Marine Corps, perform duties more focused on leadership rather than technical expertise. Promotion to the SNCO ranks, E-7 through E-9 (E-6 through E-9 in the Marine Corps) is highly competitive. Personnel totals at the pay grades of E-8 and E-9 are limited by federal law to 2.5 percent and 1 percent of a service's enlisted force, respectively. SNCOs act as leaders of small units and as staff. Some SNCOs manage programs at headquarters level and a select few wield responsibility at the highest levels of the military structure. Most unit commanders have a SNCO as an enlisted advisor. All SNCOs are expected to mentor junior commissioned officers as well as the enlisted in their duty sections. The typical enlistee can expect to attain SNCO rank after 10 to 16 years of service.

Each of the five services employs a single Senior Enlisted Advisor at departmental level. This individual is the highest ranking enlisted member within that respective service and functions as the chief advisor to the service secretary, service chief and Congress on matters concerning the enlisted force. These individuals carry responsibilities and protocol requirements equivalent to three-star general or flag officers. They are as follows:

- Senior Enlisted Advisor to the Chairman
- Sergeant Major of the Army
- Sergeant Major of the Marine Corps
- Master Chief Petty Officer of the Navy
- Chief Master Sergeant of the Air Force
- Master Chief Petty Officer of the Coast Guard

Warrant officers

Additionally, all services except for the Air Force have an active warrant officer corps. Above the rank of warrant Officer One, these officers may also be commissioned, but usually serve in a more technical and specialized role within units. More recently, they can also serve in more traditional leadership roles associated with the more recognizable officer corps. With one notable exception (Army helicopter and fixed-wing pilots), these officers ordinarily have already been in the military often serving in senior NCO positions in the field in which they later serve as a warrant officer as a technical expert. Most Army pilots have served some enlisted time. It is also possible to enlist, complete basic training, go directly to the Warrant Officer Candidate School at Fort Rucker, Alabama and then on to flight school.

Warrant officers in the U.S. military garner the same customs and courtesies as commissioned officers. They may attend the officer's club, receive a command and are saluted by junior warrant officers and all enlisted service members.

The Air Force ceased to grant warrants in 1959 when the enlisted grades of E-8 and E-9 were created. Most non-flying duties performed by warrant officers in other services are instead performed by senior NCOs in the Air Force.

Commissioned officers

Officers receive a commission in one of the branches of the U.S. Armed Forces through one of the following routes.

- Service academies (United States Military Academy (Army), United States Naval Academy, United States Air Force Academy, United States Coast Guard Academy and the United States Merchant Marine Academy)
- Reserve Officers' Training Corps (ROTC)
- Officer Candidate School (OCS) (Officer Training School (OTS) in the Air Force): this can be through active-duty schools, or through state-run schools in the case of the Army National Guard.
- Direct commission: civilians who have special skills that are critical to sustaining military operations and supporting troops may receive direct commissions. These officers occupy leadership positions in law, medicine, dentistry, pharmacy, intelligence, supply-logistics-transportation, engineering, public affairs, chaplain, oceanography and others.
- Battlefield commission: under certain conditions, enlisted personnel who have skills that separate them from their peers can become officers by direct commissioning of a commander so authorized to grant them. This type of commission is rarely granted and is reserved only for the most exceptional enlisted personnel; it is done on an *ad hoc* basis, typically only in wartime. No direct battlefield commissions have been awarded

since the Vietnam War. The Navy and Air Force do not employ this commissioning path.
- Limited Duty Officer: due to the highly technical nature of some officer billets, the Marine Corps, Navy and Coast Guard employ a system of promoting proven senior enlisted members to the ranks of commissioned officers. They fill a need that is similar to, but distinct from that filled by warrant officers (to the point where their accession is through the same school). While warrant officers remain technical experts, LDOs take on the role of a generalist, like that of officers commissioned through more traditional sources. LDOs are limited, not by their authority, but by the types of billets they are allowed to fill. However, in recent times they have come to be used more and more like their more-traditional counterparts.

Officers receive a commission assigning them to the officer corps from the President with the Senate's consent. To accept this commission, all officers must take an oath of office.

Through their careers, officers usually will receive further training at one or a number of the many staff colleges.

Company grade officers in pay grades O-1 through O-3 (known as "junior" officers in the Navy and Coast Guard) function as leaders of smaller units or sections of a unit, typically with an experienced SNCO (or CPO in the Navy and Coast Guard) assistant and mentor.

Field grade officers in pay grades O-4 through O-6 (known as "senior" officers in the Navy and Coast Guard) lead significantly larger and more complex operations, with gradually more competitive promotion requirements.

General officers, (known as flag officers in the Navy and Coast Guard) serve at the highest levels and oversee major portions of the military mission.

Five-star ranking

These are ranks of the highest honor and responsibility in the U.S. Armed Forces, but they are almost never given during peacetime and only a very small number of officers during wartime have held a five-star rank:

- General of the Army
- Fleet Admiral
- General of the Air Force

No corresponding rank exists for the Marine Corps or the Coast Guard. As with three- and four-star ranks, Congress is the approving authority for a five-star rank confirmation.

The rank of General of the Armies is considered senior to General of the Army, but was never held by active duty officers at the same time as persons who held the rank of General of the Army. It has been held by two people: John J. Pershing who received the rank in 1919 after World War I and George Washington who received it posthumously in 1976 as part of the American Bicentennial celebrations. Pershing, appointed to General of the Armies in active duty status for life, was still alive at the time of the first five-star appointments during World War II and was thereby acknowledged as superior in grade by seniority to any World War II–era Generals of the Army. George Washington's appointment by Public Law 94-479 to General of the Armies of the United States was established by law as having "rank and precedence over all other grades of the Army, past or present", making him not only superior to Pershing, but superior to any grade in the Army in perpetuity.

In the Navy, the rank of Admiral of the Navy theoretically corresponds to that of General of the Armies, though it was never held by active-duty officers at the same time as persons who held the rank of Fleet Admiral. George Dewey is the only person to have ever held this rank. After the establishment of the rank of Fleet Admiral in 1944, the Department of the Navy specified that the rank of Fleet Admiral was to be junior to the rank of Admiral of the Navy. However, since Dewey died in 1917 before the establishment of the rank of Fleet Admiral, the six-star rank has not been totally confirmed.

Women in the military

The Woman's Army Auxiliary Corps was established in the United States in 1942. Women saw combat during World War II, first as nurses in the Pearl Harbor attacks on 7 December 1941. The Woman's Naval Reserve, Marine Corps Women's Reserve and Women Airforce Service Pilots (WASPs) were also created during this conflict. In 1944, WACs arrived in the Pacific and landed in Normandy on D-Day. During the war, 67 Army nurses and 16 Navy nurses were captured and spent three years as Japanese prisoners of war. There were 350,000 American women who served during World War II and 16 were killed in action. In total, they gained over 1,500 medals, citations and commendations. Virginia Hall, serving with the Office of Strategic Services, received the second-highest U.S. combat award, the Distinguished Service Cross, for action behind enemy lines in France.

After World War II, demobilization led to the vast majority of serving women being returned to civilian life. Law 625, The Women's Armed Services Act of

Figure 7: *From 2005, the first all female C-130 Hercules crew to fly a combat mission for the U.S. Air Force*

1948, was signed by President Truman, allowing women to serve in the U.S. Armed Forces in fully integrated units during peace time, with only the WAC remaining a separate female unit. During the Korean War of 1950–1953, many women served in the Mobile Army Surgical Hospitals, with women serving in Korea numbering 120,000 Wikipedia:Accuracy dispute#Disputed statementduring the conflict. During the Vietnam War, 600 women served in the country as part of the Air Force, along with 500 members of the WAC and over 6,000 medical personnel and support staff. The Ordnance Corps began accepting female missile technicians in 1974 and female crewmembers and officers were accepted into Field Artillery missile units.

In 1974, the first six women naval aviators earned their wings as Navy pilots. The Congressionally mandated prohibition on women in combat places limitations on the pilots' advancement, but at least two retired as captains. In 1989, Captain Linda L. Bray, 29, became the first woman to command American soldiers in battle during the invasion of Panama. The 1991 Gulf War proved to be the pivotal time for the role of women in the U.S. Armed Forces to come to the attention of the world media; there are many reports of women engaging enemy forces during the conflict.

In the 2000s, women can serve on U.S. combat ships, including in command roles. They are permitted to serve on submarines. Women can fly military

Figure 8: *Sergeant Leigh Ann Hester, awarded the Silver Star for direct combat*

aircraft and make up 2% of all pilots in the U.S. Military. In 2003, Major Kim Campbell was awarded the Distinguished Flying Cross for landing her combat damaged A-10 Thunderbolt II with no hydraulic control and only one functional engine after being struck by hostile fire over Baghdad.

On 3 December 2015, U.S. Defense Secretary Ashton Carter announced that all military combat jobs would become available to women. This gave women access to the roughly 10% of military jobs which were previously closed off due to their combat nature. The decision gave military services until January 2016 to seek exceptions to the rule if they believe that certain jobs, such as machine gunners, should be restricted to men only. These restrictions were due in part to prior studies which stated that mixed gender units are less capable in combat. Physical requirements for all jobs remained unchanged, though. Many women believe this will allow for them to improve their positions in the military, since most high-ranking officers start in combat positions. Since women are now available to work in any position in the military, female entry into the draft has been proposed.

Sergeant Leigh Ann Hester became the first woman to receive the Silver Star, the third-highest U.S. decoration for valor, for direct participation in combat. In Afghanistan, Monica Lin Brown was presented the Silver Star for shielding wounded soldiers with her body. In March 2012, the U.S. military had two women, Ann E. Dunwoody and Janet C. Wolfenbarger, with the rank of four-star general. In 2016, Air Force General Lori Robinson became the first female officer to command a major Unified Combatant Command (USNORTHCOM) in the history of the United States Armed Forces.

Despite concerns of a gender gap, all personnel both men and women at the same rank and time of service are compensated the same rate across all branches.

A study conducted by the RAND Corporation also suggests that women who make the military their career see an improved rate of promotion, as they climb through the military ranks at a faster rate.

Order of precedence

Under current Department of Defense regulation, the various components of the U.S. Armed Forces have a set order of seniority. Examples of the use of this system include the display of service flags, placement of Soldiers, Marines, Sailors, Airmen and Coast Guardsmen in formation, etc. When the Coast Guard shall operate as part of the Department of the Navy, United States Coast Guard Academy cadets, the United States Coast Guard and the Coast Guard Reserve shall take precedence after United States Naval Academy midshipmen; the United States Navy; and Navy Reserve, respectively.[10]

- Cadets, U.S. Military Academy
- Midshipmen, U.S. Naval Academy
- Cadets, U.S. Coast Guard Academy (when part of the Department of the Navy)
- Cadets, U.S. Air Force Academy
- Cadets, U.S. Coast Guard Academy (when part of the Department of Homeland Security)
- Midshipmen, U.S. Merchant Marine Academy
- United States Army
- United States Marine Corps
- United States Navy
- United States Coast Guard (when part of the Department of the Navy)
- United States Air Force
- United States Coast Guard (when part of Department of the Homeland Security)
- Army National Guard of the United States
- United States Army Reserve
- United States Marine Corps Reserve
- United States Navy Reserve

- United States Coast Guard Reserve (when part of the Department of the Navy)
- Air National Guard of the United States
- United States Air Force Reserve
- United States Coast Guard Reserve (when part of the Department of Homeland Security)
- Other training and auxiliary organizations of the Army, Marine Corps, Merchant Marine, Civil Air Patrol and Coast Guard Auxiliary, as in the preceding order. The CAP was constituted through the Administrative Order 9 of 1 December 1941 and operated under the U.S. Army Air Forces during World War II. The CAP became the official civilian auxiliary of the newly independent USAF with the enactment of Public Law 80-557 on 26 May 1948.

Note: While the U.S. Navy is older than the Marine Corps,[11] the Marine Corps takes precedence due to previous inconsistencies in the Navy's birth date. The Marine Corps has recognized its observed birth date on a more consistent basis. The Second Continental Congress is considered to have established the Navy on 13 October 1775 by authorizing the purchase of ships, but did not actually pass the "Rules for the Regulation of the Navy of the United Colonies" until 27 November 1775. The Marine Corps was established by act of said Congress on 10 November 1775. The Navy did not officially recognize 13 October 1775 as its birth date until 1972, when then–Chief of Naval Operations Admiral Elmo Zumwalt authorized it to be observed as such.

External links

 Wikimedia Commons has media related to *Military of the United States*.

 Wikiquote has quotations related to: *United States Armed Forces*

- Official U.S. Department of Defense website[12]
- Global Security on U.S. Military Operations[13]
- Department of Defense regulation detailing Order of precedence: DoD Directive 1005.8, 31 October 1977[14] and also in law at Title 10, United States Code, Section 133.
- Army regulation detailing Order of Precedence: AR 840-10, 1 November 1998[15]

- Marine Corps regulation on Order of Precedence: NAVMC 2691, Marine Corps Drill and Ceremonies Manual, Part II, Ceremonies, Chapter 12-1[16].
- Navy regulation detailing Order of Precedence: U.S. Navy Regulations, Chapter 12, Flags, Pennants, Honors, Ceremonies and Customs[17].
- Air Force regulation detailing Order of Precedence: [[Category:All articles with dead external links[18]]Wikipedia:Link rot AFMAN 36-2203, Drill and Ceremonies, 3 June 1996, Chapter 7, Section A].

History

Military history of the United States

Military History of the United States	
Founded	Continental Army – 14 June 1775
Service branches	United States Army United States Marine Corps United States Navy United States Air Force United States Coast Guard
Head-quarters	The Pentagon, Arlington County, Virginia, U.S.
Related articles	
History	

The **military history of the United States** spans a period of over two centuries. During those years, the United States evolved from a new nation fighting Great Britain for independence (1775–1783), through the monumental American Civil War (1861–1865) and, after collaborating in triumph during World War II (1941–1945), to the world's sole remaining superpower from the late 20th century to present.[19]

The Continental Congress in 1775 established the Continental Army, Continental Navy, and Continental Marines and named General George Washington its commander. This newly formed military, along with state militia forces, the French Army and Navy, and the Spanish Navy defeated the British in 1781. The new Constitution in 1789 made the president the commander in chief, with authority for the Congress to levy taxes, make the laws, and declare war.[20]

As of 2017, the U.S. Armed Forces consists of the Army, Marine Corps, Navy and Air Force, all under the command of the United States Department of Defense. There also is the United States Coast Guard, which is controlled by the Department of Homeland Security.

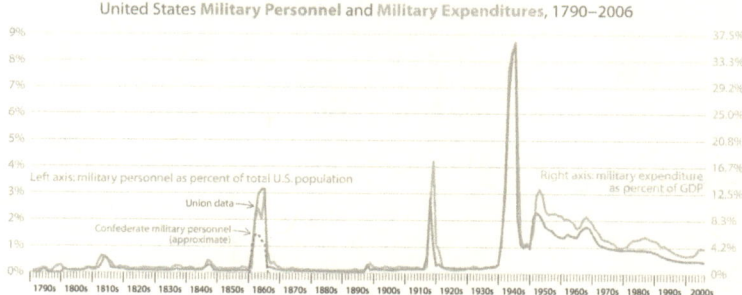

Figure 9: *U.S. military personnel and expenditures, 1790–2006. Personnel is shown in orange (left axis); expenditures are in teal (right axis). The two axes are scaled to visually align for World War II, thus showing the difference between the cost per soldier before and after President Dwight D. Eisenhower's "New Look" policy of the mid-1950s.*

The President of the United States is the commander-in-chief, and exercises the authority through the Secretary of Defense and the Chairman of the Joint Chiefs of Staff, which supervises combat operations. Governors have control of each state's Army and Air National Guard units for limited purposes. The president has the ability to federalize National Guard units, bringing them under the sole control of the Department of Defense.[21]

Colonial wars (1620–1774)

The beginning of the United States military lies in civilian frontier settlers, armed for hunting and basic survival in the wilderness. These were organized into local militias for small military operations, mostly against Native American tribes but also to resist possible raids by the small military forces of neighboring European colonies. They relied on the British regular Army and Navy for any serious military operation.[22]

In major operations outside the locality involved, the militia was not employed as a fighting force. Instead the colony asked for (and paid) volunteers, many of whom were also militia members.[23]

In the early years of the British colonization of North America, military action in the thirteen colonies that would become the United States were the result of conflicts with Native Americans, such as in the Pequot War of 1637, King Philip's War in 1675, the Yamasee War in 1715 and Father Rale's War in 1722.

Figure 10: *In 1763, the indigenous tribes of Pontiac's Confederacy lay siege to Fort Detroit, a British fort on the American frontier.*

Beginning in 1689, the colonies became involved in a series of wars between Great Britain and France for control of North America, the most important of which were Queen Anne's War, in which the British conquered French colony Acadia, and the final French and Indian War (1754–63) when Britain was victorious over all the French colonies in North America. This final war was to give thousands of colonists, including Virginia colonel George Washington, military experience which they put to use during the American Revolutionary War.[24]

War of Jenkins' Ear (1739–48)

In the struggle for control of North America, the contest between Great Britain and France was the vital one, the conflict with Spain, a declining power, important but secondary. This latter conflict reached its height in the "War of Jenkins Ear," a prelude to the War of Austrian Succession, which began in 1739 and pitted the British and their American colonists against the Spanish.

In the colonies the war involved a seesaw struggle between the Spanish in Florida and the West Indies and the English colonists in South Carolina and Georgia. Its most notable episode, however, was a British expedition mounted in Jamaica against Cartagena, the main port of the Spanish colony in Colombia. The mainland colonies furnished a regiment to participate in the assault as British Regulars under British command. The expedition ended in disaster, resulting from climate, disease, and the bungling of British commanders,

Figure 11: *The Siege of Yorktown was the decisive battle of the American Revolutionary War. The battle was the last major land engagement in the war, with the British Army's defeat at Yorktown prompting the British to negotiate an end to the conflict.*

and only about 600 of over 3,000 Americans who participated ever returned to their homes.

War of Independence (1775–83)

Ongoing political tensions between Great Britain and the thirteen colonies reached a crisis in 1774 when the British placed the province of Massachusetts under martial law after the Patriots protested taxes they regarded as a violation of their constitutional rights as Englishmen. When shooting began at Lexington and Concord in April 1775, militia units from across New England rushed to Boston and bottled up the British in the city. The Continental Congress appointed George Washington as commander-in-chief of the newly created Continental Army, which was augmented throughout the war by colonial militia. In addition to the Army, Congress also created the Continental Navy and Continental Marines He drove the British out of Boston but in late summer 1776 they returned to New York and nearly captured Washington's army. Meanwhile, the revolutionaries expelled British officials from the 13 states, and declared themselves an independent nation on 4 July 1776.[25]

Figure 12: *Washington's surprise crossing of the Delaware River in December 1776 was a major comeback after the loss of New York City; his army defeated the British in two battles and recaptured New Jersey.*

The British, for their part, lacked both a unified command and a clear strategy for winning. With the use of the Royal Navy, the British were able to capture coastal cities, but control of the countryside eluded them. A British sortie from Canada in 1777 ended with the disastrous surrender of a British army at Saratoga. With the coming in 1777 of General von Steuben, the training and discipline along Prussian lines began, and the Continental Army began to evolve into a modern force. France and Spain then entered the war against Great Britain as Allies of the US, ending its naval advantage and escalating the conflict into a world war. The Netherlands later joined France, and the British were outnumbered on land and sea in a world war, as they had no major allies apart from Indian tribes, Loyalists and Hessians.

A shift in focus to the southern American states in 1779 resulted in a string of victories for the British, but General Nathanael Greene engaged in guerrilla warfare and prevented them from making strategic headway. The main British army was surrounded by Washington's American and French forces at Yorktown in 1781, as the French fleet blocked a rescue by the Royal Navy. The British then sued for peace.

George Washington

General George Washington (1732–99) proved an excellent organizer and administrator, who worked successfully with Congress and the state governors, selecting and mentoring his senior officers, supporting and training his troops, and maintaining an idealistic Republican Army. His biggest challenge was logistics, since neither Congress nor the states had the funding to provide adequately for the equipment, munitions, clothing, paychecks, or even the food supply of the soldiers. As a battlefield tactician Washington was often outmaneuvered by his British counterparts. As a strategist, however, he had a better idea of how to win the war than they did. The British sent four invasion armies. Washington's strategy forced the first army out of Boston in 1776, and was responsible for the surrender of the second and third armies at Saratoga (1777) and Yorktown (1781). He limited the British control to New York and a few places while keeping Patriot control of the great majority of the population. The Loyalists, on whom the British had relied too heavily, comprised about 20% of the population but were never well organized. As the war ended, Washington watched proudly as the final British army quietly sailed out of New York City in November 1783, taking the Loyalist leadership with them. Washington astonished the world when, instead of seizing power, he retired quietly to his farm in Virginia.[26,27]

Patriots had a strong distrust of a permanent "standing army", so the Continental Army was quickly demobilized, with land grants to veterans. General Washington, who throughout the war deferred to elected officials, averted a potential coup d'état and resigned as commander-in-chief after the war, establishing a tradition of civil control of the U.S. military.

Early national period (1783–1812)

Following the American Revolutionary War, the United States faced potential military conflict on the high seas as well as on the western frontier. The United States was a minor military power during this time, having only a modest army, marine corps, and navy. A traditional distrust of standing armies, combined with faith in the abilities of local militia, precluded the development of well-trained units and a professional officer corps. Jeffersonian leaders preferred a small army and navy, fearing that a large military establishment would involve the United States in excessive foreign wars, and potentially allow a domestic tyrant to seize power.[28]

In the Treaty of Paris after the Revolution, the British had ceded the lands between the Appalachian Mountains and the Mississippi River to the United States, without consulting the Shawnee, Cherokee, Choctaw and other smaller tribes who lived there. Because many of the tribes had fought as allies of the British, the United States compelled tribal leaders to sign away lands in postwar treaties, and began dividing these lands for settlement. This provoked a war in the Northwest Territory in which the U.S. forces performed poorly; the Battle

Figure 13: *The Battle of Fallen Timbers was a decisive battle in the Northwest Indian War, where American forces defeated the tribes of the Western Confederacy.*

of the Wabash in 1791 was the most severe defeat ever suffered by the United States at the hands of American Indians. President Washington dispatched a newly trained army to the region led by General Anthony Wayne, which decisively defeated the Indian confederacy at the Battle of Fallen Timbers in 1794.[29]

When revolutionary France declared war on Great Britain in 1793, the United States sought to remain neutral, but the Jay Treaty, which was favorable to Great Britain, angered the French government, which viewed it as a violation of the 1778 Treaty of Alliance. French privateers began to seize U.S. vessels, which led to an undeclared "Quasi-War" between the two nations. Fought at sea from 1798 to 1800, the United States won a string of victories in the Caribbean. George Washington was called out of retirement to head a "provisional army" in case of invasion by France, but President John Adams managed to negotiate a truce, in which France agreed to terminate the prior alliance and cease its attacks.[30]

Barbary Wars

The Berbers along the Barbary Coast (modern day Libya) sent pirates to capture merchant ships and hold the crews for ransom. The U.S. paid protection money until 1801, when President Thomas Jefferson refused to pay and sent in

Figure 14: *Stephen Decatur boarding the Tripolitan gunboat, 3 August 1804, the First Barbary War*

the Navy to challenge the Barbary States, the First Barbary War followed. After the U.S.S. *Philadelphia* was captured in 1803, Lieutenant Stephen Decatur led a raid which successfully burned the captured ship, preventing Tripoli from using or selling it. In 1805, after William Eaton captured the city of Derna, Tripoli agreed to a peace treaty. The other Barbary states continued to raid U.S. shipping, until the Second Barbary War in 1815 ended the practice.[31]

War of 1812

By far the largest military action in which the United States engaged during this era was the War of 1812.[32] With Britain locked in a major war with Napoleon's France, its policy was to block American shipments to France. The United States sought to remain neutral while pursuing overseas trade. Britain cut the trade and impressed seamen on American ships into the Royal Navy, despite intense protests. Britain supported an Indian insurrection in the American Midwest, with the goal of creating an Indian state there that would block American expansion. The United States finally declared war on the United Kingdom in 1812, the first time the U.S. had officially declared war. Not hopeful of defeating the Royal Navy, the U.S. attacked the British Empire by invading British Canada, hoping to use captured territory as a bargaining

Figure 15: *"We have met the enemy and they are ours." Commodore Oliver Hazard Perry's victory on Lake Erie in 1813 was an important battle in the War of 1812.*

chip. The invasion of Canada was a debacle, though concurrent wars with Native Americans on the western front (Tecumseh's War and the Creek War) were more successful. After defeating Napoleon in 1814, Britain sent large veteran armies to invade New York, raid Washington and capture the key control of the Mississippi River at New Orleans. The New York invasion was a fiasco after the much larger British army retreated to Canada. The raiders succeeded in the burning of Washington on 25 August 1814, but were repulsed in their Chesapeake Bay Campaign at the Battle of Baltimore and the British commander killed. The major invasion in Louisiana was stopped by a one-sided military battle that killed the top three British generals and thousands of soldiers. The winners were the commanding general of the Battle of New Orleans, Major General Andrew Jackson, who became president and the Americans who basked in a victory over a much more powerful nation. The peace treaty proved successful, and the U.S. and Britain never again went to war. The losers were the Indians, who never gained the independent territory in the Midwest promised by Britain.[33]

Figure 16: *American forces storming Chapultepec Castle during the Mexican–American War.*

War with Mexico (1846–48)

With the rapid expansion of the farming population, Democrats looked to the west for new lands, an idea which became known as "Manifest Destiny." In the Texas Revolution (1835–36), the settlers declared independence and defeated the Mexican army, but Mexico was determined to reconquer the lost province and threatened war with the U.S. if it annexed Texas. The U.S., much larger and more powerful, did annex Texas in 1845 and war broke out in 1846 over boundary issues.[34]

In the Mexican–American War 1846–48, the U.S. Army under Generals Zachary Taylor and Winfield Scott and others, invaded and after a series of victorious battles (and no major defeats) seized New Mexico and California, and also blockaded the coast, invaded northern Mexico, and invaded central Mexico, capturing the national capital. The peace terms involved American purchase of the area from California to New Mexico for $10 million.[35]

American Civil War (1861–65)

Long-building tensions between the Northern and Southern States over slavery suddenly reached a climax after the 1860 election of Abraham Lincoln of the new anti-slavery Republican Party as U.S. President. Southern states seceded from the U.S. and formed a separate Confederacy. Within the Confederate

Figure 17: *Dead soldiers lie where they fell at Antietam, the bloodiest day in American history. Abraham Lincoln issued the Emancipation Proclamation after this battle.*

states, many U.S. forts with garrisons still loyal to the Union were cut off. Fighting started in 1861 when Fort Sumter was fired upon.[36]

The American Civil War caught both sides unprepared. Neither the North's small standing army nor the South's scattered state militias were capable of winning a civil war. Both sides raced to raise armies—larger than any U.S. forces before—first with repeated calls for volunteers, but eventually resorting to unpopular large-scale conscription for the first time in U.S. history.

The North initially sought a quick victory by trying to capture the Confederate capital at Richmond, Virginia, not far from the U.S. capital at Washington, D.C. The South hoped to win by getting Britain and France to intervene, or else by exhausting the North's willingness to fight. The Confederates under General Robert E. Lee skillfully and tenaciously defended their capital until the very end, while the North struggled to find any general to match.

As the fighting between the two capitals stalled, the North found more success in campaigns elsewhere, using rivers, railroads, and the seas to help move and supply their larger forces, putting a stranglehold on the South—the Anaconda Plan. The war spilled across the continent, and even to the high seas. After four years of appallingly bloody conflict, with more casualties than all other U.S. wars combined, the North's larger population and industrial might slowly

Figure 18: *The Battle of Gettysburg involved the largest number of casualties of the entire war.*

ground the South down. The resources and economy of the South were ruined, while the North's factories and economy prospered filling government wartime contracts.

The American Civil War is sometimes called the "first modern war" due to the mobilization and destruction of the civilian base—total war—and due to by many technical military innovations involving railroads, telegraphs, rifles, trench warfare, and ironclad warships with turret guns.[37]

Post-Civil War era (1865–1917)

Indian Wars (1865–91)

After the Civil War, population expansion, railroad construction, and the disappearance of the buffalo herds heightened military tensions on the Great Plains. Several tribes, especially the Sioux and Comanche, fiercely resisted confinement to reservations. The main role of the Army was to keep indigenous peoples on reservations and to end their wars against settlers and each other, William Tecumseh Sherman and Philip Sheridan were in charge. A famous victory for the Plains Nations was the Battle of the Little Big Horn in 1876, when Col. George Armstrong Custer and two hundred plus members of the 7th Cavalry were killed by a force consisting of Native Americans from the

Figure 19: *American forces led by George Custer suffered a major defeat against the Sioux in the Battle of Little Bighorn.*

Figure 20: *Charge by the Rough Riders during the Battle of San Juan Hill.*

Lakota, Northern Cheyenne, and Arapaho nations. The last significant conflict came in 1891.[38]

Figure 21: *American soldiers in Manila during the Philippine–American War.*

Spanish–American War (1898)

The Spanish–American War was a short decisive war marked by quick, overwhelming American victories at sea and on land against Spain. The Navy was well-prepared and won laurels, even as politicians tried (and failed) to have it redeployed to defend East Coast cities against potential threats from the feeble Spanish fleet.[39] The Army performed well in combat in Cuba. However, it was too oriented to small posts in the West and not as well-prepared for an overseas conflict.[40] It relied on volunteers and state militia units, which faced logistical, training and food problems in the staging areas in Florida.[41] The United States freed Cuba (after an occupation by the U.S. Army). By the peace treaty Spain ceded to the United States its colonies of Puerto Rico, Guam, and the Philippines. The Navy set up coaling stations there and in Hawaii (which voluntarily joined the U.S. in 1898). The U.S. Navy now had a major forward presence across the Pacific and (with the lease of Guantánamo Bay Naval Base in Cuba) a major base in the Caribbean guarding the approaches to the Gulf Coast and the Panama Canal.[42]

To win its first colonies, the U.S. had lost 385 KIA (369 Army, 10 Navy, 6 Marines); 1,662 WIA (1,594 Army, 47 Navy, 21 Marines); and 2,061 dead of disease in the combat zones (a total of 5,403 died of disease at all locations, including stateside posts). Total Spanish combat deaths in action against U.S. forces were about 900.[43]

Figure 22: *The Great White Fleet at the Straits of Magellan. The fleet set out to make friendly visits to other countries, and showcase America's naval power to the world.*

Philippine–American War (1899–1902)

The Philippine–American War (1899–1902) was an armed conflict between a group of Filipino revolutionaries and the American forces following the ceding of the Philippines to the United States after the defeat of Spanish forces in the Battle of Manila. The Army sent in 100,000 soldiers (mostly from the National Guard) under General Elwell Otis. Defeated in the field and losing its capital in March 1899, the poorly armed and poorly led rebels broke into armed bands. The insurgency collapsed in March 1901 when the leader Emilio Aguinaldo was captured by General Frederick Funston and his Macabebe allies. Casualties included 1,037 Americans killed in action and 3,340 who died from disease; 20,000 rebels were killed.[44]

Modernization

The Navy was modernized in the 1880s, and by the 1890s had adopted the naval power strategy of Captain Alfred Thayer Mahan—as indeed did every major navy. The old sailing ships were replaced by modern steel battleships, bringing them in line with the navies of Britain and Germany. In 1907, most of the Navy's battleships, with several support vessels, dubbed the Great White Fleet, were featured in a 14-month circumnavigation of the world. Ordered by President Theodore Roosevelt, it was a mission designed to demonstrate the Navy's capability to extend to the global theater.[45]

Secretary of War Elihu Root (1899–1904) led the modernization of the Army. His goal of a uniformed chief of staff as general manager and a European-type general staff for planning was stymied by General Nelson A. Miles but did succeed in enlarging West Point and establishing the U.S. Army War College as well as the General Staff. Root changed the procedures for promotions and organized schools for the special branches of the service. He also devised the principle of rotating officers from staff to line. Root was concerned about the Army's role in governing the new territories acquired in 1898 and worked out the procedures for turning Cuba over to the Cubans, and wrote the charter of government for the Philippines.[46]

Rear Admiral Bradley A. Fiske was at the vanguard of new technology in naval guns and gunnery, thanks to his innovations in fire control 1890–1910. He immediately grasped the potential for air power, and called for the development of a torpedo plane. Fiske, as aide for operations in 1913–15 to Assistant Secretary Franklin D. Roosevelt, proposed a radical reorganization of the Navy to make it a war-fighting instrument. Fiske wanted to centralize authority in a chief of naval operations and an expert staff that would develop new strategies, oversee the construction of a larger fleet, coordinate war planning including force structure, mobilization plans, and industrial base, and ensure that the US Navy possessed the best possible war machines. Eventually, the Navy adopted his reforms and by 1915 started to reorganize for possible involvement in the World War then underway.[47]

Banana Wars (1898–1935)

"Banana Wars" is an informal term for the minor intervention in Latin America from 1898 until 1934. These include military presence in Cuba, Panama with the Panama Canal Zone, Haiti (1915–1935), Dominican Republic (1916–1924) and Nicaragua (1912–1925) & (1926–1933). The U.S. Marine Corps began to specialize in long-term military occupation of these countries, primarily to safeguard customs revenues which were the cause of local civil wars.[48]

Hispaniola

Banditry and guerrilla resistance was endemic throughout the period of occupation. U.S. Marine losses in the Dominican Republic, 1916–22, totaled 17 killed, 54 dead of disease, 55 wounded (from a peak strength of 3,000). The Marines inflicted about 1,000 Dominican casualties.[49] The most serious insurgencies occurred in Haiti, where some 5,000 rough mountaineers of the north, called Cacos, rebelled in 1915–17, losing 200 killed, to Marine losses of 3 KIA, 18 WIA, of 2,029 deployed. In 1918, the Cacos, angered by the

Figure 23: *William Allen Rogers' cartoon depicting Theodore Roosevelt's Big Stick policy. The enforcement of this policy in Latin America led to several U.S. interventions in the region, referred to as the Banana Wars.*

Marine-enforced practice of corvée (forced labor), followed the leadership of Charlemagne Peralte and Benoit Batraville into rebellion again, against the 1,500-man 1st Marine Brigade and the 2,700-man Haitian Gendarmerie. The rebellion lasted for more than 19 months, October 17, 1918–May 19, 1920. Both Caco leaders were killed in battle, along with at least 2,004 of their men. The Marines lost 28 slain in action and the Gendarmerie lost 70 killed.

Moro Rebellion (1899–1913)

The Moro Rebellion was an armed insurgency between Muslim Filipino tribes in the southern Philippines between 1899 and 1913. Pacification was never complete as sporadic antigovernment insurgency continues into the 21st century, with American advisors helping the Philippine government forces.[50]

Mexico (1910–19)

The Mexican Revolution involved a civil war with hundreds of thousands of deaths and large numbers fleeing combat zones. Tens of thousands fled to the U.S. President Wilson sent U.S. forces to occupy the Mexican city of Veracruz

Figure 24: *American and Mexican soldiers guarding the border in Ambos Nogales during the Border War.*

for six months in 1914. It was designed to show the U.S. was keenly interested in the civil war and would not tolerate attacks on Americans, especially the 9 April 1914, "Tampico Affair", which involved the arrest of American sailors by soldiers of the regime of Mexican President Victoriano Huerta.[51] In early 1916 Pancho Villa a Mexican general ordered 500 soldiers on a murderous raid on the American city of Columbus New Mexico, with the goal of robbing banks to fund his army.[52]

The German Secret Service encouraged Pancho Villa in his attacks to involve the United States in an intervention in Mexico which would distract the United States from its growing involvement in the war and divert aid from Europe to support the intervention.[53] Wilson called up the state militias (National Guard) and sent them and the U.S. Army under General John J. Pershing to punish Villa in the Pancho Villa Expedition. Villa fled, with the Americans in pursuit deep into Mexico, thereby arousing Mexican nationalism. By early 1917 President Venustiano Carranza had contained Villa and secured the border, so Wilson ordered Pershing to withdraw.[54,55]

Figure 25: *The American Expeditionary Force marches in France, 1918.*

World War I (1917–18)

The United States originally wished to remain neutral when World War I broke out in August 1914. However, it insisted on its right as a neutral party to immunity from German submarine attack, even though its ships carried food and raw materials to Britain. In 1917 the Germans resumed submarine attacks, knowing that it would lead to American entry. When the United States declared war in early April 1917, the United States Army was still small by European standards (most of which had conscription) and mobilization would take at least a year. Meanwhile, the United States continued to provide supplies and money to Britain and France, and initiated the first peacetime draft.[56] Industrial mobilization took longer than expected, so divisions were sent to Europe without equipment, relying instead on the British and French to supply them.[57]

By summer 1918, a million American soldiers, or "doughboys" as they were often called, of the American Expeditionary Force (AEF) were in Europe, serving on the Western Front under the command of General John Pershing, with 25,000 more arriving every week. The failure of the German Army's Spring Offensive exhausted its manpower reserves and they were unable to launch new offensives. The Imperial German Navy and home front then revolted and a new German government signed a conditional surrender, the Armistice, ending the war on the Western Front on 11 November 1918.[58]

Figure 26: *The Washington Naval Conference was an arms control conference that sought to limit naval armaments amongst the world's powers.*

Russian Revolution (1918–19)

The so-called Polar Bear Expedition was the involvement of 5,000 U.S. troops, during the Russian Revolution, in blocking the Bolsheviks in Arkhangelsk, Russia as part of the greater Allied military expedition in the Russian Civil War.[59]

1920s: Naval disarmament

The U.S. sponsored a major world conference to limit the naval armaments of world powers, including the U.S., Britain, Japan, and France, plus smaller nations.[60] Secretary of State Charles Evans Hughes made the key proposal of each country to reduce its number of warships by a formula that was accepted. The conference enabled the great powers to reduce their navies and avoid conflict in the Pacific. The treaties remained in effect for ten years, but were not renewed as tensions escalated.

1930s: Neutrality Acts

After the costly U.S. involvement in World War I, isolationism grew within the nation. Congress refused membership in the League of Nations, particularly due to Article X of the League's charter. Pursuant to Article X, the charter would have required by contract the United States Military to intervene if a member of the League were attacked; this prompted the United States Senate to vehemently oppose the Treaty of Versailles. Isolationism further grew after the events of the Nye Committee, which investigated corrupt military spending and fueled the *Merchants of death* argument, thus increasing anti-war opinions.

In response to the growing turmoil in Europe and Asia, the gradually more restrictive Neutrality Acts were passed, which were intended to prevent the U.S. from supporting either side in a war. President Franklin D. Roosevelt sought to support Britain, however, and in 1940 signed the Lend-Lease Act, which permitted an expansion of the "cash and carry" arms trade to develop with Britain, which controlled the Atlantic sea lanes.

Roosevelt favored the Navy (he was in effective charge in World War I), and used relief programs such as the PWA to support Navy yards and build warships. For example, in 1933 he authorized $238 million in PWA funds for thirty-two new ships. The Army Air Corps received only $11 million, which barely covered replacements and allowed no expansion.[61]

Due to the underlying pressure against military involvement by both citizens and politicians, the United States was reluctant to intervene in any overseas conflicts. The involvement that the United States had toward the Japanese Invasion of Manchuria in 1931 only extended as far as non-recognition. Other events such as Benito Mussolini's Italian Conquest of Ethiopia went ignored by the U.S. along with the League of Nations being unable to act upon the usage of chemical weapons by the Italian fascists.[62] No official involvement was waged during the Spanish Civil War and the Second Sino-Japanese War, though both wars utilized loopholes for U.S. involvement, such as volunteering and using British ships as a middleman for delivering provisions (since the Neutrality Acts only specified American ships). This, along with Roosevelt's Quarantine Speech, produced mixed opinions among Americans that were still anxious about military involvement. Non-interventionists were mainly constituent in the Republican Party, but other Democratic politicians, such as Louis Ludlow, attempted to pass bills to compromise and even amend the United States Constitution for the purpose of calling for public Referendum to decide military involvement in cases that do not immediately follow an attack on the United States. This amendment was introduced many times, but failed to gain enough support, including opposition even by Roosevelt.

Figure 27: *The explosion aboard the USS Arizona during the attack on Pearl Harbor.*

The overall neglect for military involvement eventually resulted in appeasement in the early stages of World War II, at the distress of Roosevelt (who wanted to continue cash-and-carry for the European theatres and the Pacific). After being rebuffed by Congress for attempting to reinstate cash-and-carry for the European theatres, Roosevelt eventually won the favor of restoring the arms trade with belligerent nations after Germany's invasion of Poland, which is said by many to have fixed the United States economy. Total involvement in the war began after the Attack on Pearl Harbor, where isolationism began to cede.

World War II (1941–45)

Starting in 1940 (18 months before Pearl Harbor), the nation mobilized, giving high priority to air power. American involvement in World War II in 1940–41 was limited to providing war material and financial support to Britain, the Soviet Union, and the Republic of China. The U.S. entered officially on 8 December 1941 following the Japanese attack on Pearl Harbor, Hawaii. Japanese forces soon seized American, Dutch, and British possessions across the Pacific and Southeast Asia, except for Australia, which became a main American forward base along with Hawaii.

Figure 28: *General of the Army MacArthur signs on behalf of the Allies*

The loss of eight battleships and 2,403 Americans at Pearl Harbor forced the U.S. to rely on its remaining aircraft carriers, which won a major victory over Japan at Midway just six months into the war, and on its growing submarine fleet. The Navy and Marine Corps followed this up with an island hopping campaign across the central and south Pacific in 1943–45, reaching the outskirts of Japan in the Battle of Okinawa. During 1942 and 1943, the U.S. deployed millions of men and thousands of planes and tanks to the UK, beginning with the strategic bombing of Nazi Germany and occupied Europe and leading up to the Allied invasions of occupied North Africa in November 1942, Sicily and Italy in 1943, France in 1944, and the invasion of Germany in 1945, parallel with the Soviet invasion from the east. That led to the surrender of Nazi Germany in May 1945. While the final European Axis Powers were defeated within a year of Operation Overlord, the fighting in Central Europe was especially bloody for the United States, with more US military deaths occurring in Germany than in any other country during the war.[63]

In the Pacific, the U.S. experienced much success in naval campaigns during 1944, but bloody battles at Iwo Jima and Okinawa in 1945 led the U.S. to look for a way to end the war with minimal loss of American lives. The U.S. used atomic bombs on Hiroshima and Nagasaki to destroy the Japanese war effort and to shock the Japanese leadership, which quickly caused the surrender of Japan. Following the dropping of atomic bombs on Hiroshima and Nagasaki,

Japan surrendered to the Allied forces on 15 August 1945, ending 35 years of Japanese occupation of Korean Peninsula. American forces under General John R. Hodge arrived at the southern part of the Korean Peninsula on 8 September 1945, while the Soviet Army and some Korean Communists had stationed themselves in the northern part of the Korean Peninsula.

The United States was able to mobilize quickly, eventually becoming the dominant military power in most theaters of the war (excepting only eastern Europe), and the industrial might of the U.S. economy became a major factor in the Allies' mobilization of resources. Strategic and tactical lessons learned by the U.S., such as the importance of air superiority and the dominance of the aircraft carrier in naval actions, continue to guide U.S. military doctrine into the 21st century.

World War II holds a special place in the American psyche as the country's greatest triumph, and the U.S. military personnel of World War II are frequently referred to as "the Greatest Generation." Over 16 million served (about 11% of the population), and over 400,000 died during the war. The U.S. emerged as one of the two undisputed superpowers along with the Soviet Union, and unlike the Soviet Union, the U.S. homeland was virtually untouched by the ravages of war. During and following World War II, the United States and Britain developed an increasingly strong defense and intelligence relationship. Manifestations of this include extensive basing of U.S. forces in the UK, shared intelligence, shared military technology (e.g. nuclear technology), and shared procurement.

Cold War era (1945–91)

Following World War II, the United States emerged as a global superpower vis-a-vis the Soviet Union in the Cold War. In this period of some forty years, the United States provided foreign military aid and direct involvement in proxy wars against the Soviet Union. It was the principal foreign actor in the Korean War and Vietnam War during this era. Nuclear weapons were held in ready by the United States under a concept of mutually assured destruction with the Soviet Union.

Postwar military reorganization (1947)

The National Security Act of 1947, meeting the need for a military reorganization to complement the U.S. superpower role, combined and replaced the former Department of the Navy and War Department with a single cabinet-level Department of Defense. The act also created the National Security Council, the Central Intelligence Agency, and the Air Force.

Figure 29: *American beachhead during the Battle of Inchon*

Korean War (1950–53)

The Korean War was a conflict between the United States and its United Nations allies and the communist powers under influence of the Soviet Union (also a UN member nation) and the People's Republic of China (which later also gained UN membership). The principal combatants were North and South Korea. Principal allies of South Korea included the United States, Canada, Australia, the United Kingdom, although many other nations sent troops under the aegis of the United Nations. Allies of North Korea included the People's Republic of China, which supplied military forces, and the Soviet Union, which supplied combat advisors and aircraft pilots, as well as arms, for the Chinese and North Korean troops.[64]

The war started badly for the US and UN. North Korean forces struck massively in the summer of 1950 and nearly drove the outnumbered US and ROK defenders into the sea. However the United Nations intervened, naming Douglas MacArthur commander of its forces, and UN-US-ROK forces held a perimeter around Pusan, gaining time for reinforcement. MacArthur, in a bold but risky move, ordered an amphibious invasion well behind the front lines at Inchon, cutting off and routing the North Koreans and quickly crossing the 38th Parallel into North Korea. As UN forces continued to advance toward the Yalu River on the border with Communist China, the Chinese crossed the

Figure 30: *Several hundred Marines were sent to Lebanon during the 1958 crisis to bolster the pro-Western government.*

Yalu River in October and launched a series of surprise attacks that sent the UN forces reeling back across the 38th Parallel. Truman originally wanted a Rollback strategy to unify Korea; after the Chinese successes he settled for a Containment policy to split the country.[65] MacArthur argued for rollback but was fired by President Harry Truman after disputes over the conduct of the war. Peace negotiations dragged on for two years until President Dwight D. Eisenhower threatened China with nuclear weapons; an armistice was quickly reached with the two Koreas remaining divided at the 38th parallel. North and South Korea are still today in a state of war, having never signed a peace treaty, and American forces remain stationed in South Korea as part of American foreign policy.[66]

Lebanon crisis of 1958

In the Lebanon crisis of 1958 that threatened civil war, Operation Blue Bat deployed several hundred Marines to bolster the pro-Western Lebanese government from 15 July to 25 October 1958.

Figure 31: *Formation of Bell UH-1 Iroquois ca. 1966*

Dominican Intervention

On 28 April 1965, 400 Marines were landed in Santo Domingo to evacuate the American Embassy and foreign nationals after dissident Dominican armed forces attempted to overthrow the ruling civilian junta. By mid-May, peak strength of 23,850 U.S. soldiers, Marines, and Airmen were in the Dominican Republic and some 38 naval ships were positioned offshore. They evacuated nearly 6,500 men, women, and children of 46 nations, and distributed more than 8 million tons of food.

The intervention cost the U.S. 27 KIA and 172 WIA. Another 20 Americans died from non-hostile causes; 111 were seriously injured. Ten of the KIA were Marines; 13 were from the 82nd Airborne. Among the 2,850 Dominican dead were 325 National Police officers and 500 members of the armed forces. An estimated 600 rebels were killed. Civilians accounted for the remainder.

Vietnam War (1964–75)

The Vietnam War was a war fought between 1955 and 1975 on the ground in South Vietnam and bordering areas of Cambodia and Laos (*see* Secret War) and in the strategic bombing (*see* Operation Rolling Thunder) of North Vietnam. American advisors came in the late 1950s to help the RVN (Republic of Vietnam) combat Communist insurgents known as "Viet Cong." Major American military involvement began in 1964, after Congress provided President

Figure 32: *United States Embassy following the Tet Offensive*

Lyndon B. Johnson with blanket approval for presidential use of force in the Gulf of Tonkin Resolution.[67]

Fighting on one side was a coalition of forces including the Republic of Vietnam (South Vietnam or the "RVN"), the United States, supplemented by South Korea, Thailand, Australia, New Zealand, and the Philippines. The allies fought against the North Vietnamese Army (NVA) as well as the National Liberation Front (NLF, also known as Viet communists Viet Cong), or "VC", a guerrilla force within South Vietnam. The NVA received substantial military and economic aid from the Soviet Union and China, turning Vietnam into a proxy war.[68]

The military history of the American side of the war involved different strategies over the years.[69] The bombing campaigns of the Air Force were tightly controlled by the White House for political reasons, and until 1972 avoided the main Northern cities of Hanoi and Haiphong and concentrated on bombing jungle supply trails, especially the Ho Chi Minh Trail.[70] The most controversial Army commander was William Westmoreland whose strategy involved systematic defeat of all enemy forces in the field, despite heavy American casualties that alienated public opinion back home.[71]

The U.S. framed the war as part of its policy of containment of Communism in south Asia, but American forces were frustrated by an inability to engage the enemy in decisive battles, corruption and incompetence in the Army of the Republic of Vietnam, and ever increasing protests at home. The Tet Offensive in 1968, although a major military defeat for the NLF with half their forces eliminated, marked the psychological turning point in the war. With President Richard M. Nixon opposed to containment and more interested in achieving détente with both the Soviet Union and China, American policy shifted to "Vietnamization," – providing very large supplies of arms and letting the Vietnamese fight it out themselves. After more than 57,000 dead and many more wounded, American forces withdrew in 1973 with no clear victory, and in 1975 South Vietnam was finally conquered by communist North Vietnam and unified.[72]

Memories and lessons from the war are still a major factor in American politics. One side views the war as a necessary part of the Containment policy, which allowed the enemy to choose the time and place of warfare. Others note the U.S. made major strategic gains as the Communists were defeated in Indonesia, and by 1972 both Moscow and Beijing were competing for American support, at the expense of their allies in Hanoi. Critics see the conflict as a "quagmire"—an endless waste of American blood and treasure in a conflict that did not concern US interests. Fears of another quagmire have been major factors in foreign policy debates ever since.[73] The draft became extremely unpopular, and President Nixon ended it in 1973,[74] forcing the military (the Army especially) to rely entirely upon volunteers. That raised the issue of how well the professional military reflected overall American society and values; the soldiers typically took the position that their service represented the highest and best American values.[75]

Grenada

In October, 1983, a power struggle in Grenada, which had installed a communist-leaning government, led to increased tensions in the region. Neighboring nations asked the U.S. to intervene. The invasion was a hurriedly devised grouping of paratroopers, Marines, Rangers, and special operations forces in Operation Urgent Fury. Over a thousand Americans quickly seized the entire island, taking hundreds of military and civilian prisoners, especially Cubans, who were building a large military airstrip.[76,77]

Beirut

In 1983 fighting between Palestinian refugees and Lebanese factions reignited that nation's long-running civil war. A UN agreement brought an international force of peacekeepers to occupy Beirut and guarantee security. US Marines landed in August 1982 along with Italian and French forces. On 23 October 1983, a suicide bomber driving a truck filled with 6 tons of TNT crashed

Figure 33: *In 1983, American forces, assisted by the Caribbean Peace Force, invaded the island nation of Grenada.*

through a fence and destroyed the Marine barracks, killing 241 Marines; seconds later, a second bomber leveled a French barracks, killing 58. Subsequently, the US Navy engaged in bombing of militia positions inside Lebanon. While US President Ronald Reagan was initially defiant, political pressure at home eventually forced the withdrawal of the Marines in February 1984.[78]

Libya

Code-named "Operation *El Dorado Canyon*", comprised the joint United States Air Force, Navy, and Marine Corps air-strikes against Libya on 15 April 1986. The attack was carried out in response to the 1986 Berlin discotheque bombing, and resulted in the killing of 45 officers and 15 civilians.

Panama

On 20 December 1989 the United States invaded Panama, mainly from U.S. bases within the then-Canal Zone, to oust dictator and international drug trafficker Manuel Noriega. American forces quickly overwhelmed the Panamanian Defense Forces, Noriega was captured on 3 January 1990 and imprisoned in the U.S. and a new government was installed.[79]

Figure 34: *In 1986, the USAF conducted air strikes against Libya, in retaliation for the West Berlin discotheque bombing.*

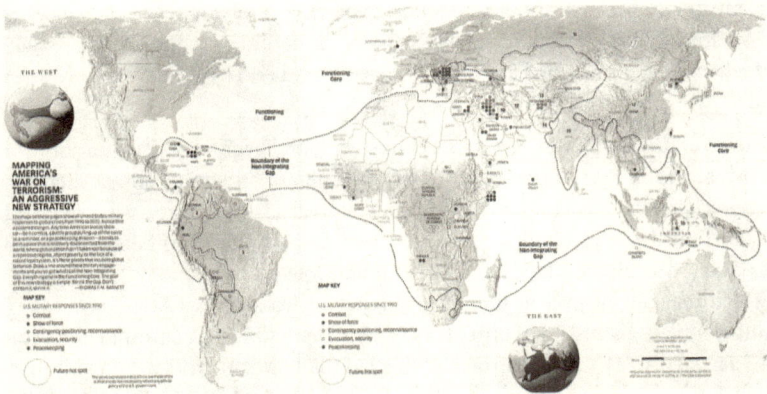

Figure 35: *U.S. military engagements 1990–2002*

Post–Cold War era (1991–2001)

Persian Gulf War (1990–91)

The Persian Gulf War was a conflict between Iraq and a coalition force of 34 nations led by the United States. The lead up to the war began with the Iraqi invasion of Kuwait in August 1990 which was met with immediate economic sanctions by the United Nations against Iraq. The coalition commenced hostilities in January 1991, resulting in a decisive victory for the U.S. led coalition forces, which drove Iraqi forces out of Kuwait with minimal coalition deaths. Despite the low death toll, over 180,000 US veterans would later be classified as "permanently disabled" according to the US Department of Veterans Affairs (see Gulf War Syndrome). The main battles were aerial and ground combat within Iraq, Kuwait and bordering areas of Saudi Arabia. Land combat did not expand outside of the immediate Iraq/Kuwait/Saudi border region, although the coalition bombed cities and strategic targets across Iraq, and Iraq fired missiles on Israeli and Saudi cities.[80]

Before the war, many observers believed the US and its allies could win but might suffer substantial casualties (certainly more than any conflict since Vietnam), and that the tank battles across the harsh desert might rival those of North Africa during World War II. After nearly 50 years of proxy wars, and constant fears of another war in Europe between NATO and the Warsaw Pact, some thought the Persian Gulf War might finally answer the question of which military philosophy would have reigned supreme. Iraqi forces were battle-hardened after 8 years of war with Iran, and they were well equipped with late model Soviet tanks and jet fighters, but the antiaircraft weapons were crippled; in comparison, the US had no large-scale combat experience since its withdrawal from Vietnam nearly 20 years earlier, and major changes in US doctrine, equipment and technology since then had never been tested under fire.

However, the battle was one-sided almost from the beginning. The reasons for this are the subject of continuing study by military strategists and academics. There is general agreement that US technological superiority was a crucial factor but the speed and scale of the Iraqi collapse has also been attributed to poor strategic and tactical leadership and low morale among Iraqi troops, which resulted from a history of incompetent leadership. After devastating initial strikes against Iraqi air defenses and command and control facilities on 17 January 1991, coalition forces achieved total air superiority almost immediately. The Iraqi air force was destroyed within a few days, with some planes fleeing to Iran, where they were interned for the duration of the conflict. The overwhelming technological advantages of the US, such as stealth aircraft and infrared sights, quickly turned the air war into a "turkey shoot". The heat signature of any tank which started its engine made an easy target. Air defense radars were quickly destroyed by radar-seeking missiles fired from wild weasel aircraft. Grainy video clips, shot from the nose cameras of missiles as they aimed at impossibly small targets, were a staple of US news coverage and revealed to the world a new kind of war, compared by some to a video game. Over 6 weeks of relentless pounding by planes and helicopters, the Iraqi

Figure 36: *USS Wisconsin fires on Iraqi positions in Kuwait*

army was almost completely beaten but did not retreat, under orders from Iraqi President Saddam Hussein, and by the time the ground forces invaded on 24 February, many Iraqi troops quickly surrendered to forces much smaller than their own; in one instance, Iraqi forces attempted to surrender to a television camera crew that was advancing with coalition forces.

After just 100 hours of ground combat, and with all of Kuwait and much of southern Iraq under coalition control, US President George H. W. Bush ordered a cease-fire and negotiations began resulting in an agreement for cessation of hostilities. Some US politicians were disappointed by this move, believing Bush should have pressed on to Baghdad and removed Hussein from power; there is little doubt that coalition forces could have accomplished this if they had desired. Still, the political ramifications of removing Hussein would have broadened the scope of the conflict greatly, and many coalition nations refused to participate in such an action, believing it would create a power vacuum and destabilize the region.[81]

Following the Persian Gulf War, to protect minority populations, the US, Britain, and France declared and maintained no-fly zones in northern and southern Iraq, which the Iraqi military frequently tested. The no-fly zones persisted until the 2003 invasion of Iraq, although France withdrew from participation in patrolling the no-fly zones in 1996, citing a lack of humanitarian purpose for the operation.

Figure 37: *American soldiers taking fire during the Battle of Mogadishu. The battle led to the withdrawal of U.S. forces in Somalia, and the end of American support for UNOSOM II.*

Somalia

US troops participated in a UN peacekeeping mission in Somalia beginning in 1992. By 1993 the US troops were augmented with Rangers and special forces with the aim of capturing warlord Mohamed Farrah Aidid, whose forces had massacred peacekeepers from Pakistan. During a raid in downtown Mogadishu, US troops became trapped overnight by a general uprising in the Battle of Mogadishu. Eighteen American soldiers were killed, and a US television crew filmed graphic images of the body of one soldier being dragged through the streets by an angry mob. Somali guerrillas paid a staggering toll at an estimated 1,000–5,000 total casualties during the conflict. After much public disapproval, American forces were quickly withdrawn by President Bill Clinton. The incident profoundly affected US thinking about peacekeeping and intervention. The book *Black Hawk Down* was written about the battle, and was the basis for the later movie of the same name.[82]

Haiti

Operation Uphold Democracy (19 September 1994 – 31 March 1995) was an intervention designed to reinstate the elected President Jean-Bertrand Aristide, who was reported to have died in office during the bombing of the presidential palace. The operation was effectively authorized by the 31 July 1994 United Nations Security Council Resolution 940.[83]

Figure 38: *U.S. Army Special Forces and U.S. Air Force Combat Controllers on horseback in November 2001.*

Yugoslavia

During the war in Yugoslavia in the early 1990s, the US operated in Bosnia and Herzegovina as part of the NATO-led multinational implementation force (IFOR) in *Operation Joint Endeavour*. The USA was one of the NATO member countries who bombed Yugoslavia between 24 March and 9 June 1999 during the Kosovo War and later contributed to the multinational force KFOR.[84]

War on Terrorism (2001–present)

The War on Terrorism is a global effort by the governments of several countries (primarily the United States and its principal allies) to neutralize international terrorist groups (primarily Islamic Extremist terrorist groups, including al-Qaeda) and ensure that countries considered by the US and some of its allies to be *Rogue Nations* no longer support terrorist activities. It has been adopted primarily as a response to the September 11, 2001 attacks on the United States. Since 2001, terrorist motivated attacks upon service members have occurred in Arkansas and Texas.

Figure 39: *A Marine Corps M1 Abrams tank patrols a Baghdad street in April 2003.*

Afghanistan

The intervention in Afghanistan (Operation Enduring Freedom – Afghanistan) to depose that country's Taliban government and destroy training camps associated with al-Qaeda is understood to have been the opening, and in many ways defining, campaign of the broader War on Terrorism. The emphasis on Special Operations Forces (SOF), political negotiation with autonomous military units, and the use of proxy militaries marked a significant change from prior U.S. military approaches.[85]

Philippines

In January 2002, the U.S. sent more than 1,200 troops (later raised to 2,000) to assist the Armed Forces of the Philippines in combating terrorist groups linked to al-Qaida, such as Abu Sayyaf, under Operation Enduring Freedom – Philippines. Operations have taken place mostly in the Sulu Archipelago, where terrorists and other groups are active. The majority of troops provide logistics. However, there are special forces troops that are training and assisting in combat operations against the terrorist groups.

Iraq

After the lengthy Iraq disarmament crisis culminated with an American demand that Iraqi President Saddam Hussein leave Iraq, which was refused, a coalition led by the United States and the United Kingdom fought the Iraqi army in the 2003 invasion of Iraq. Approximately 250,000 United States troops, with support from 45,000 British, 2,000 Australian and 200 Polish combat forces, entered Iraq primarily through their staging area in Kuwait. (Turkey had refused to permit its territory to be used for an invasion from the north.) Coalition forces also supported Iraqi Kurdish militia, estimated to number upwards of 50,000. After approximately three weeks of fighting, Hussein and the Ba'ath Party were forcibly removed, followed by 9 years of military presence by the United States and the coalition fighting alongside the newly elected Iraqi government against various insurgent groups.

Syrian and Iraqi intervention

With the emergence of ISIL and its capture of large areas of Iraq and Syria, a number of crises resulted that sparked international attention. ISIL had perpetrated sectarian killings and war crimes in both Iraq and Syria. Gains made in the Iraq War were rolled back as Iraqi army units abandoned their posts. Cities were taken over by the terrorist group which enforced its brand of Sharia law. The kidnapping and decapitation of numerous Western journalists and aidworkers also garnered interest and outrage among Western powers. The US intervened with airstrikes in Iraq over ISIL held territories and assets in August, and in September a coalition of US and Middle Eastern powers initiated a bombing campaign in Syria aimed at degrading and destroying ISIL and Al-Nusra-held territory. By December 2017, ISIL had no remaining territory in Iraq, following the 2017 Western Iraq campaign. Airstrikes by US and Coalition forces have continued in Syria against the Assad government especially after the Douma chemical attack in 2018.

Libyan intervention

As a result of the Libyan Civil War, the United Nations enacted United Nations Security Council Resolution 1973, which imposed a no-fly zone over Libya, and the protection of civilians from the forces of Muammar Gaddafi. The United States, along with Britain, France and several other nations, committed a coalition force against Gaddafi's forces. On 19 March 2011, the first U.S. action was taken when 114 Tomahawk missiles launched by US and UK warships destroyed shoreline air defenses of the Gaddafi regime. The U.S. continued to play a major role in Operation Unified Protector, the NATO-directed mission that eventually incorporated all of the military coalition's actions in the theater. Throughout the conflict however, the U.S. maintained it was playing a supporting role only and was following the UN mandate to protect civilians, while the real conflict was between Gaddafi's loyalists and Libyan rebels fighting to depose him. During the conflict, American drones were also deployed.

Further reading

<templatestyles src="Template:Refbegin/styles.css" />

- Allison, William T., Jeffrey G. Grey, Janet G. Valentine. *American Military History: A Survey from Colonial Times to the Present* (2nd ed. 2012) 416pp
- Boyne, Walter J. *Beyond the Wild Blue: A History of the U.S. Air Force, 1947–2007* (2nd ed. 2007) 576 pp excerpt[86]
- Bradford, James C. (2003). *Atlas of American military history*[87]. Oxford University Press. ISBN 978-0-19-521661-5.
- Brown, Jerold E. (2001). *Historical Dictionary of the U.S. Army*[88]. Greenwood Publishing Group. ISBN 9780313293221.
- Chambers, John Whiteclay; Fred Anderson (1999). *The Oxford companion to American military history*[89]. Oxford University Press. ISBN 978-0-19-507198-6.
- Chambers, John Whiteclay and G. Kurt Piehler, eds. *Major Problems in American Military History: Documents and Essays* (1988) 408pp excerpts from primary and secondary sources table of contents[90]
- Crocker, III, H. W. (2007). *Don't Tread on Me: A 400-Year History of America at War*[91]. Random House Digital, Inc. ISBN 978-1-4000-5364-3.
- Hacker, Barton C.; Margaret Vining (2007). *American Military Technology: The Life Story of a Technology*[92]. JHU Press. ISBN 978-0-8018-8772-7.
- Hagan, Kenneth J. and Michael T. McMaster, eds. *In Peace and War: Interpretations of American Naval History* (2008), essays by scholars
- Howarth, Stephen (1999). *To Shining Sea: a History of the United States Navy, 1775–1998*[93]. Norman, OK: U of Oklahoma Press. ISBN 0-8061-3026-1.
- Hearn, Chester G. *Air Force: An Illustrated History: The U.S. Air Force from 1910 to the 21st Century* (2008) excerpt and text search[94]
- Isenberg, Michael T. *Shield of the Republic: The United States Navy in an Era of Cold War and Violent Peace 1945–1962* (1993)
- Lookingbill, Brad D. (2010). *American Military History*[95]. John Wiley and Sons. ISBN 978-1-4051-9052-7.
- Love, Robert W., Jr. (1992). *History of the U.S. Navy* 2 vol.

- Matloff, Maurice (1996). *American Military History: 1775–1902*[96]. Da Capo Press. ISBN 978-0-938289-70-8.; numerous editions;
- Matloff (1996). *American Military History: 1902–1996*[97]. Da Capo Press. ISBN 978-0-938289-71-5.; numerous editions
- Millett, Allan R. *Semper Fidelis: History of the United States Marine Corps* (1980) excerpt and text search[98]
- Millett, Allan R., Peter Maslowski and William B. Feis. *For the Common Defense: A Military History of the United States from 1607 to 2012* (3rd ed. 2013) excerpt and text search[99]
- Morris, James M., ed. *Readings in American Military History* (2003) 401pp articles by experts
- Moten, Matthew (2014). *Presidents and Their Generals: An American History of Command in War*[100]. Harvard UP.
- Muehlbauer, Matthew S., and David J. Ulbrich. *Ways of War: American Military History from the Colonial Era to the Twenty-First Century* (Routledge, 2013), 536pp; university textbook; online review[101]
- Stewart, Richard W. *American military history* (2 vol 2010); The current ROTC textbook
- Sweeney, Jerry K.; Kevin B. Byrne (2006). *A handbook of American military history*[102]. U of Nebraska Press. ISBN 978-0-8032-9337-3.
- Urwin, Gregory J. W. (1983). *The United States Cavalry: an illustrated history, 1776–1944*[103]. University of Oklahoma Press. ISBN 978-0-8061-3475-8.
- Utley, Robert M. (1984) *Frontier Regulars: The United States Army and the Indian, 1866–1891*
- Utley, Robert M. (2002) *Indian Wars*
- Williams, T. Harry (1960). *Americans at War: The Development of the American Military System*[104]. LSU Press. ISBN 978-0-8071-2474-1.
- U. S. Department of the Army (2001). *The Writing of American Military History: A Guide*[105]. The Minerva Group, Inc. ISBN 978-0-89875-350-9.
- Woodward, David R. *The American Army and the First World War* (Cambridge University Press, 2014). 484 pp. online review[106]

Historiography

- Grimsley, Mark. "The American military history master narrative: Three textbooks on the American military experience," *Journal of Military History* (2015) 79#3 pp 782–802; review of Allison, Millett, and Muehlbauer textbooks

External links

 Wikimedia Commons has media related to *Military history of the United States*.

- Website for *Ways of War: American Military History from the Colonial Era to the Twenty-First Century* By Muehlbauer and Ulbrich[107], with additional text, bibliographies and student aids
- United States Military Campaigns, Conflicts, Expeditions and Wars[108] Compiled by Larry Van Horn, U.S. Navy Retired
- *Military History wiki*[109]
- A Continent Divided: The U.S. – Mexico War[110], Center for Greater Southwestern Studies, the University of Texas at Arlington
- National Indian Wars Association[111]
- Instances of Use of United States Forces Abroad, 1798–1993[112] by U.S. Navy

Organizational Structure

Organizational structure of the United States Department of Defense

The **United States Department of Defense** (DoD) has a complex **organizational structure**. It includes the Army, Navy (the Marine Corps is a subset of the Navy), Air Force, the Unified combatant commands, U.S. elements of multinational commands (such as NATO and NORAD), as well as non-combat agencies such as the Defense Intelligence Agency and the National Security Agency. The DoD's annual budget was roughly US$496.1 billion in 2015. This figure is the base amount and does not include the $64.3 billion spent on "War/Non-War Supplementals". Including those items brings the total to $560.4 billion for 2015.

Civilian control over matters other than operations is exercised through the three service departments, the Department of the Army, the Department of the Navy (which includes the Marine Corps), and the Department of the Air Force. Each is led by a service secretary, who is below Cabinet rank.

In wartime, the Department has authority over the Coast Guard, which is under the control of the Department of Homeland Security (DHS) in peacetime. Prior to the creation of DHS, the Coast Guard was under the control of the Department of Transportation, and earlier under the Department of the Treasury. According to the U.S. Code, the Coast Guard is at all times considered one of the five armed services of the United States. During times of declared war (or by Congressional direction), the Coast Guard operates as a part of the Navy; this has not happened since World War II, but members have served in undeclared wars and conflicts since then while the service remained in its peacetime department.

Figure 40: *The Pentagon, headquarters of the United States Department of Defense.*

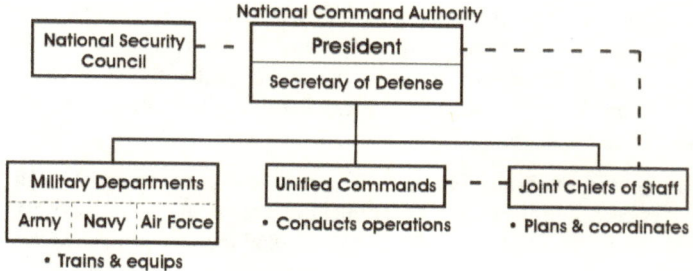

The Pentagon, in Arlington County, Virginia, across the Potomac River from Washington, D.C., is the Department's headquarters. The Department is protected by the Pentagon Force Protection Agency, which ensures law enforcement and security for the Pentagon and various other jurisdictions throughout the National Capital Region (NCR).

Chain of Command

The President of the United States is, according to the Constitution, the Commander-in-Chief of the U.S. Armed Forces and Chief Executive of the Federal Government. The Secretary of Defense is the "Principal Assistant to the President in all matters relating to the Department of Defense", and is vested with statutory authority (10 U.S.C. § 113[113]) to lead the Department and all of its component agencies, *including military command authority second only to the President.*

The President and the Secretary of Defense exercise authority and control of the Armed Forces through two distinct branches of the chain of command. One branch (10 U.S.C. § 162[114]) runs from the President, through the Secretary of Defense, to the Combatant Commanders for missions and forces assigned to their commands. The other branch, used for purposes other than operational direction of forces assigned to the combatant commands, runs from the President through the Secretary of Defense to the Secretaries of the Military Departments, i.e., the Secretary of the Army (10 U.S.C. § 3013[115]), the Secretary of the Navy (10 U.S.C. § 5013[116]), and the Secretary of the Air Force (10 U.S.C. § 8013[117]). The Military Departments, organized separately within the Department, operate under the authority, direction, and control of the Secretary of that Military Department. The Secretaries of the Military Departments exercise authority through their respective Service Chiefs (i.e., Chief of Staff of the Army, Commandant of the Marine Corps, Chief of Naval Operations, and Chief of Staff of the Air Force) over forces not assigned to a Combatant Command. The Service Chiefs, except as otherwise prescribed by law, perform their duties under the authority, direction, and control of the Secretaries of their respective Military Departments, to whom they are directly responsible.

In the Goldwater-Nichols Department of Defense Reorganization Act of 1986, Congress clarified the command line to the combatant commanders and preserved civilian control of the military. The Act states that the operational chain of command runs from the President to the Secretary of Defense to the Combatant Commanders. The Act permits the President to direct that communications pass through the Chairman of the Joint Chiefs of Staff from the Secretary of Defense, and to the Combatant Commanders. This authority places the Chairman in the communications chain. Further, the Act gives the Secretary of Defense wide latitude to assign the Chairman oversight responsibilities for the activities of the Combatant Commanders.

Civilian control

Article II Section 2 of the Constitution designates the President as "Commander in Chief" of the Army, Navy and state militias. The President exercises this supreme command authority through the civilian Secretary of Defense, who by federal law is the *head of the department*, has *authority direction, and control over the Department of Defense*, and is the *principal assistant to the*

President in all matters relating to the Department of Defense.[118] The Secretary's principal deputy is the equally civilian Deputy Secretary of Defense who is delegated full powers to act for the Secretary of Defense. The Office of the Secretary of Defense (OSD) is the Secretary and Deputy Secretary's civilian staff, which includes several Under Secretaries and Assistant Secretaries of Defense with functional oversight responsibilities. The Secretaries of the Military Departments (i.e. Secretary of the Army, Secretary of the Navy, and Secretary of the Air Force) are subordinate to the Secretary of Defense. They have the authority under Title 10 of the United States Code to *conduct all the affairs* of their respective departments (Department of the Army, Department of the Navy, and Department of the Air Force) within which the military services are organized.[119]

Historically, there have been challenges to civilian control. Most notably, during the Korean War, General Douglas MacArthur ignored civilian instructions regarding advancing troops toward the Yalu River, which triggered an introduction of massive forces from China. Also, on April 5, 1950, Representative Joseph William Martin, Jr., the Minority Leader of the United States House of Representatives, released copies of a letter from MacArthur critical of President Harry S. Truman's limited-war strategy to the press and read it aloud on the floor of the house. President Truman relieved MacArthur of command, and MacArthur then explored political options against Truman. The Revolt of the Admirals is another example in the same era of a challenge to civilian control.

DoD policies and directives protect the policy of civilian control by establishing strict limitations on the political activities of members of the military. For example, DoD Directive 1344.10 prohibits active-duty members of the military from running for office or making political appearances in uniform. However, enforcing this strict separation between the military and politics has been problematic. For example, over the years, many elected officials, including members of Congress, continued serving in the reserves while holding elected office. As another example, at a September 14, 2007, rally for Republican Presidential candidate John McCain in New Hampshire, seven on-duty uniformed Army personnel addressed the gathering. As another example, although DOD Directive 1344.10 prohibits political appearances by active-duty military members in uniform, Virginia Governor Bob McDonnell invited a uniformed Army Staff Sergeant to stand behind him during his televised Republican response to the 2010 State of the Union Address.

Components of the Department of Defense

	Program
Secretary of Defense	Deputy Secretary of Defense *Joint Improvised Explosive Device Defeat Organization
	Chief Management Officer
Acquisition and Sustainment Under Secretary of Defense for Acquisition and Sustainment Operational Test and Evaluation Directorate	Assistant Secretary of Defense (Acquisition) *Deputy Assistant Secretary of Defense (Manufacturing and Industrial Base Policy) *Deputy Assistant Secretary of Defense (Policy, Planning, Resources, and Performance) *Deputy Assistant Secretary of Defense (Warfare Systems Support) *Deputy Assistant Secretary of Defense (Defense Procurement) *Defense Acquisition University
	Assistant Secretary of Defense (Sustainment) *Deputy Assistant Secretary of Defense (Material Readiness) *Deputy Assistant Secretary of Defense (Program Support and Logistics Policy) *Deputy Assistant Secretary of Defense (Transportation Policy)
	Assistant Secretary of Defense (Nuclear, Chemical & Biological Defense Programs) *Deputy Assistant Secretary of Defense (Nuclear Matters) *Deputy Assistant Secretary of Defense (Chemical and Biological Defense Policy) *Deputy Assistant Secretary of Defense (Threat Reduction and Arms Control)
	Defense Logistics Agency
	Defense Contract Management Agency
	Defense Threat Reduction Agency
Research and Engineering Under Secretary of Defense for Research and Engineering	Deputy Under Secretary of Defense (Research and Engineering)
	Assistant Secretary of Defense (Research and Technology) *Deputy Assistant Secretary of Defense (Research and Technology Investment) *Deputy Assistant Secretary of Defense (Laboratories and Personnel)
	Assistant Secretary of Defense (Advanced Capabilities) *Deputy Assistant Secretary of Defense (Mission Engineering and Integration) *Deputy Assistant Secretary of Defense (Prototyping and Experimentation) *Defense Technical Information Center *Test Resource Management Center
	Defense Science Board
	Strategic Intelligence Analysis Cell
	Missile Defense Agency
	Defense Advanced Research Projects Agency
	DARPA

		Strategic Capabilities Office
		Defense Innovation Unit-Experimental
	Policy **Under Secretary of** **Defense for Policy**	Assistant Secretary of Defense (Strategy, Plans, and Capabilities) *Deputy Assistant Secretary of Defense (Strategy and Force Development) *Deputy Assistant Secretary of Defense (Plans) *Deputy Assistant Secretary of Defense (Nuclear and Missile Defense Policy) *Deputy Assistant Secretary of Defense (Security Cooperation)
		Assistant Secretary of Defense (International Security Affairs) *Deputy Assistant Secretary of Defense (African Affairs) *Deputy Assistant Secretary of Defense (Middle East) *Deputy Assistant Secretary of Defense (Europe and NATO) *Deputy Assistant Secretary of Defense (Russia, Ukraine, and Eurasia) *Secretary of Defense Representative in the United States Mission to NATO *Secretary of Defense Representative to the Organization for Security and Co-operation in Europe
		Assistant Secretary of Defense (Homeland Defense) and Global Strategic Affairs *Deputy Assistant Secretary of Defense (Cyber Policy) *Deputy Assistant Secretary of Defense (Space Policy) *Deputy Assistant Secretary of Defense (Countering Weapons of Mass Destruction) *Deputy Assistant Secretary of Homeland Defense Integration and Defense Support of Civil Authorities *Deputy Assistant Secretary of Defense (Defense Continuity and Mission Assurance)
		Assistant Secretary of Defense (Special Operations and Low-Intensity Conflict) *Deputy Assistant Secretary of Defense (Counternarcotics and Global Threats) *Deputy Assistant Secretary of Defense (Stability and Humanitarian Affairs) *Deputy Assistant Secretary of Defense (Special Operations and Combatting Terrorism)
		Assistant Secretary of Defense (Asian and Pacific Security Affairs) *Deputy Assistant Secretary of Defense (East Asia) *Deputy Assistant Secretary of Defense (South and Southeast Asia) *Deputy Assistant Secretary of Defense (Afghanistan, Pakistan, and Central Asia)
		Defense POW/MIA Accounting Agency
		Defense Security Cooperation Agency
		Defense Policy Board Advisory Committee
		Defense Prisoner of War/Missing Personnel Office
		Defense Technology Security Administration
	Comptroller **Under Secretary of** **Defense (Comptroller)**	Principal Deputy Under Secretary of Defense (Comptroller)
		Defense Contract Audit Agency

Organizational structure of the United States Department of Defense

		Defense Finance and Accounting Service
Personnel and Readiness **Under Secretary of** **Defense for Personnel** **and Readiness**		Principal Deputy Under Secretary of Defense (Personnel and Readiness) *Joint Advertising Marketing Research & Studies (JAMRS)
		Military Deputy to the Under Secretary of Defense (Personnel and Readiness) *Office of Diversity Management and Equal Opportunity **Defense Equal Opportunity Management Institute *Defense Suicide Prevention Office *Personnel Risk Reduction Office
		Assistant Secretary of Defense (Health Affairs) *Military Health System[120] **TRICARE Management Activity[121] *Deputy Assistant Secretary of Defense (Wounded Warrior Care & Transition Policy)
		Assistant Secretary of Defense (Manpower and Reserve Affairs) *Defense Commissary Agency *Department of Defense Education Activity **Department of Defense Dependents Schools *Deputy Assistant Secretary of Defense (Civilian Personnel Policy) *Deputy Assistant Secretary of Defense (Military Personnel Policy) *Deputy Assistant Secretary of Defense (Military Community and Family Policy) *Deputy Assistant Secretary of Defense (Readiness) *Office of Total Force Planning & Requirements *Transition to Veterans Program Office
		Defense Human Resources Activity
		DoD/VA Collaboration Office
		Uniformed Services University of the Health Sciences
		Office of the Chancellor for Education and Professional Development
Intelligence **Under Secretary of** **Defense for Intelligence**		Principal Deputy Under Secretary of Defense (Intelligence)
		Assistant Secretary of Defense for Networks and Information Integration *Defense Information Systems Agency
		Director for Defense Intelligence (Warfighter Support)
		Director for Defense Intelligence (Intelligence & Security)
		Director for Defense Intelligence (Technical Collection & Special Programs)
		Director for Defense Intelligence (Intelligence Strategy, Programs & Resources)
		Defense Security Service
		Defense Intelligence Agency
		National Geospatial-Intelligence Agency
		National Security Agency

	Central Security Service	
	National Reconnaissance Office	
Other	Assistant Secretary of Defense (Public Affairs) *Deputy Assistant Secretary of Defense (Internal Communications) *Defense Media Activity	
	Director of Administration and Management *Pentagon Force Protection Agency *Washington Headquarters Services	
	Director of Cost Assessment and Program Evaluation *Office of Net Assessment	
	General Counsel of Defense *Defense Legal Services Agency	

Defense Agencies

Defense Agencies are established as DoD Components by law, the President, or the Secretary of Defense to provide for the performance, on a DoD-wide basis, of a supply or service activity that is common to more than one Military Department when it is determined to be more effective, economical, or efficient to do so, pursuant to sections 101, 191(a), and 192 of Title 10 of the United States Code or when a responsibility or function is more appropriately assigned to a Defense Agency. Pursuant to section 191(b) Title 10, such organizations are designated as Defense Agencies. Each Defense Agency operates under the authority, direction, and control of the Secretary of Defense, through a Principal Staff Assistant in the Office of the Secretary of Defense.

Seal or Logo	Name	Acronym	Charter	Under the Authority of	Headquarters
DARPA	Defense Advanced Research Projects Agency	DARPA	DoDD 5134.10[122]	Under Secretary of Defense for Acquisition, Technology and Logistics	Arlington, VA
	Defense Commissary Agency	DeCA	DoDD 5105.55[123]	Under Secretary of Defense for Personnel and Readiness	Fort Lee, VA
	Defense Contract Audit Agency	DCAA	DoDD 5105.36[124]	Under Secretary of Defense (Comptroller)	Fort Belvoir, VA
	Defense Contract Management Agency	DCMA	DoDD 5105.64[125]	Under Secretary of Defense for Acquisition, Technology and Logistics	Fort Lee, VA
	Defense Finance and Accounting Service	DFAS	DoDD 5118.05[126]	Under Secretary of Defense (Comptroller)	Arlington, VA

Organizational structure of the United States Department of Defense

	Defense Information Systems Agency	DISA	DoDD 5105.19[127]	Assistant Secretary of Defense for Networks & Information Integration	Arlington, VA
	Defense Intelligence Agency	DIA	DoDD 5105.21[128]	Under Secretary of Defense for Intelligence	Joint Base Anacostia-Bolling, DC
	Defense Legal Services Agency	DLSA	DoDD 5145.04[129]	General Counsel of the Department of Defense	The Pentagon
	Defense Logistics Agency	DLA	DoDD 5105.22[130]	Under Secretary of Defense for Acquisition, Technology and Logistics	Fort Belvoir, VA
	Defense Security Cooperation Agency	DSCA	DoDD 5105.65[131]	Under Secretary of Defense for Policy	The Pentagon
	Defense Security Service	DSS	DoDD 5105.42[132]	Under Secretary of Defense for Intelligence	Alexandria, VA
	Defense Threat Reduction Agency	DTRA	DoDD 5105.62[133]	Under Secretary of Defense for Acquisition, Technology and Logistics	Fort Belvoir, VA
	Missile Defense Agency	MDA	DoDD 5134.09[134]	Under Secretary of Defense for Acquisition, Technology and Logistics	The Pentagon
	National Geospatial-Intelligence Agency	NGA	DoDD 5105.60[135]	Under Secretary of Defense for Intelligence	Springfield, VA
	National Reconnaissance Office	NRO	DoDD 5105.23[136]	Under Secretary of Defense for Intelligence	Chantilly, VA
	National Security Agency Central Security Service	NSA/CSS	DoDD 5100.20[137]	Under Secretary of Defense for Intelligence	Fort George G. Meade, MD
	Pentagon Force Protection Agency	PFPA	DoDD 5105.68[138]	Director of Administration and Management	The Pentagon

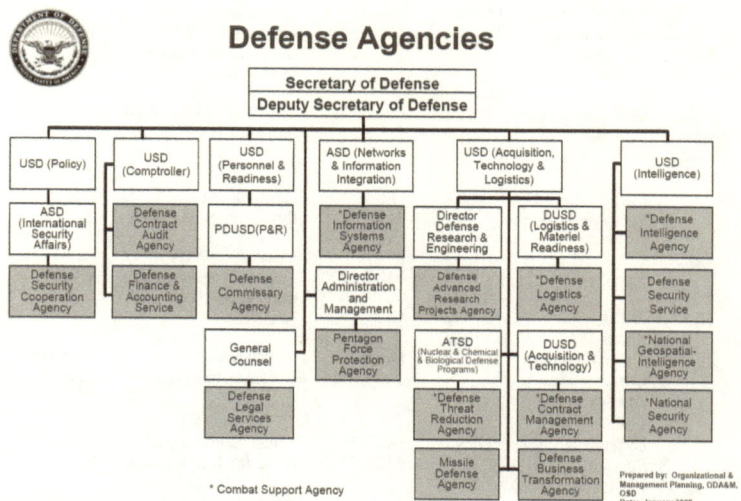

Figure 41: *Defense Agencies within the Department of Defense.*

Department of Defense Field Activities

Department of Defense Field Activities are established as DoD Components by law, the President, or the Secretary of Defense to provide for the performance, on a DoD-wide basis, of a supply or service activity that is common to more than one Military Department when it is determined to be more effective, economical, or efficient to do so, pursuant to sections 101, 191(a), and 192 of Title 10 of the United States Code. Pursuant to section 191(b) of Title 10, such organizations are designated as DoD Field Activities. Each DoD Field Activity operates under the authority, direction, and control of the Secretary of Defense, through a Principal Staff Assistant in the Office of the Secretary of Defense.

Seal or Logo	Name	Acronym	Charter	Under the Authority of	Headquarters
	Defense Media Activity	DMA	DoDD 5105.74[139]	Assistant Secretary of Defense for Public Affairs	Fort Meade, MD
	Defense POW/MIA Accounting Agency	DPAA	DoDD 5110.10[140]	Under Secretary of Defense for Policy	The Pentagon

	Defense Technical Information Center	DTIC	DoDD 5105.73[141]	Under Secretary of Defense for Acquisition, Technology and Logistics	Fort Belvoir, VA
	Defense Technology Security Administration	DTSA	DoDD 5105.72[142]	Under Secretary of Defense for Policy	The Pentagon
	Department of Defense Education Activity	DoDEA	DoDD 1342.20[143]	Principal Deputy Under Secretary of Defense for Personnel and Readiness	Arlington, VA
	Department of Defense Human Resources Activity	DoDHRA	DoDD 5100.87[144]	Under Secretary of Defense for Personnel and Readiness	Arlington, VA
	Department of Defense Test Resource Management Center	TRMC	DoDD 5105.71[145]	Under Secretary of Defense for Acquisition, Technology and Logistics	
	Office of Economic Adjustment	OEA	DoDD 3030.01[146]	Under Secretary of Defense for Acquisition, Technology and Logistics	Arlington, VA
	Washington Headquarters Services	WHS	DoDD 5110.04[147]	Director of Administration and Management	The Pentagon

Military Departments

Department of the Army

The Department of the Army includes all elements of the U.S. Army

- Secretary of the Army

Headquarters, Department of the Army

- Office of the Secretary of the Army
- Chief of Staff of the Army

Army Field Organizations

- Army Commands
- Army Component Commands
- Field Operating Agencies
- Direct Reporting Units

Department of the Navy

The Department of the Navy includes all elements of the U.S. Navy and the U.S. Marine Corps

- Secretary of the Navy

Navy Department

- Office of the Secretary of the Navy
- Office of the Chief of Naval Operations
- Headquarters Marine Corps (See also: Organization of the United States Marine Corps)

Department of the Air Force

The Department of the Air Force includes all elements of the U.S. Air Force

- Secretary of the Air Force

Headquarters Air Force

- Office of the Secretary of the Air Force
  - Under Secretary of the Air Force
- The Air Staff
  - Chief of Staff of the Air Force

Air Force Field Organizations

- Major Commands
- Direct Reporting Units
- Field Operating Agencies

Organization of the Joint Chiefs of Staff

- Chairman of the Joint Chiefs of Staff
  - Vice Chairman of the Joint Chiefs of Staff
    - Joint Requirements Oversight Council
  - Joint Chiefs of Staff
  - The Joint Staff
    - Director of the Joint Staff
      - DOM- Directorate of Management
      - J1 - Personnel and Manpower
      - J2 - Intelligence
      - J3 - Operations
        - National Military Command Center
        - Alternate National Military Command Center
        - National Airborne Operations Center

- J4 - Logistics
- J5 - Strategic Plans and Policy
- J6 - Command, Control, Communications and Computer Systems
- J7 - Operational Plans and Joint Force Development
- J8 - Force Structure, Resources, and Assessment
- National Defense University
  - College of International Security Affairs
  - Industrial College of the Armed Forces
  - Information Resources Management College
  - Joint Forces Staff College
  - National War College
- U.S. Delegation to the Inter-American Defense Board
- U.S. Delegation to the United Nations Military Staff Committee
- U.S. Representative at the NATO Military Committee
- U.S. Section, Joint Mexico-U.S. Defense Commission

Unified Combatant Commands

There are nine Unified Combatant Commands; six regional and three functional. Africa Command became initially operational in October 2007, while Joint Forces Command was officially disestablished on August 4, 2011.

Seal	Name	Acronym	Headquarters	Area of Responsibility	Other Role of CCDR
	United States Africa Command	AFRICOM	Kelley Barracks, Stuttgart, Germany; to be relocated to African continent or other location TBD	Africa excluding Egypt	
	United States Central Command	CENTCOM	MacDill Air Force Base, Florida	Egypt through the Persian Gulf region, into Central Asia, excluding Israel	
	United States European Command	EUCOM	Stuttgart, Germany	Europe, including Turkey, and Israel	Also Supreme Allied Commander Europe (SACEUR)
	United States Northern Command	NORTHCOM	Peterson Air Force Base, Colorado	North American homeland defense and coordinating homeland defense with federal and state civil authorities.	Also Commander of North American Aerospace Defense Command (NORAD) (bilateral U.S.-Canadian military command)

	United States Pacific Command	PACOM	Camp H. M. Smith, Oahu, Hawaii	The Asia-Pacific region including Hawaii.	
	United States Southern Command	SOUTH-COM	Miami, Florida	South, Central America and the surrounding waters	
	U.S. Special Operations Command	SOCOM	MacDill Air Force Base, Florida	Provides special operations for the Army, Marine Corps, Navy, and Air Force.	
	United States Strategic Command	STRATCOM	Offutt Air Force Base, Nebraska	Covers the strategic deterrent force and coordinates the use of space assets.	
	United States Transportation Command	TRANSCOM	Scott Air Force Base, Illinois	Covers global mobility of all military assets for all regional commands.	

The Geographic Commands

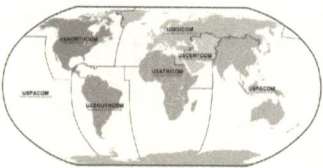

In 2007, a new geographical command for Africa was authorized. This proposed significant changes to the areas of responsibility for other adjacent geographical commands as shown in the accompanying graphic.

Office of the Inspector General of the Department of Defense

The Office of the Inspector General is an independent and objective unit within the Department of Defense that conducts and supervises audits and investigations relating to the programs and operations of the Department of Defense, pursuant to the responsibilities specified in title 5, U.S.C. Appendix and DoDD 5106.01[148].

- Inspector General of the Department of Defense
  - Defense Criminal Investigative Service

Figure 42: *Seal of the Inspector General.*

National Guard Bureau

The National Guard Bureau (NGB) is a joint activity of the Department of Defense. The Chief of the National Guard Bureau is a principal advisor to the Secretary of Defense, through the Chairman of the Joint Chiefs of Staff, on matters involving non-federalized National Guard forces, and other matters as determined by the Secretary of Defense. For NGB matters pertaining to the responsibilities of the Departments of the Army and Air Force in law or DoD policy, the Secretary of Defense normally exercises authority, direction, and control over the NGB through the Secretaries of the Army and the Air Force. The NGB is the focal point at the strategic level for National Guard matters that are not under the authority, direction, and control of the Secretaries of the Army or Air Force, including joint, interagency, and intergovernmental matters where the NGB acts through other DoD officials as specified in DoDD 5105.77[149].

- Chief of the National Guard Bureau

Figure 43: *Seal of the National Guard Bureau.*

Other

The United States Naval Observatory falls under the Chief of Naval Operations. In 2003 the National Communications System was moved to the Department of Homeland Security, but only for executive purposes; it still centralizes its activities within the Department of Defense, since the human resources required by NCS (example: Military Departments) still reside within the Department of Defense, or for retention of practical maintenance.

References

https://en.wikipedia.org/wiki/Commandant_of_the_Marine_Corps

Further reading

 Wikimedia Commons has media related to *United States Department of Defense*.

- Vego, Milan (1999). "Command and Control". In Chambers, John W. & Anderson, Fred. *The Oxford companion to American military history*[150]. Oxford University Press. pp. 165–167. ISBN 978-0-19-507198-6.

Military Budget

Military budget of the United States

The military budget is the portion of the discretionary United States federal budget allocated to the Department of Defense, or more broadly, the portion of the budget that goes to any military-related expenditures. The military budget pays the salaries, training, and health care of uniformed and civilian personnel, maintains arms, equipment and facilities, funds operations, and develops and buys new items. The budget funds four branches of the U.S. military: the Army, Marine Corps, Navy, and Air Force. In FY 2015, Pentagon and related spending totaled $598 billion, about 54% of the fiscal year 2015 U.S. discretionary budget. For FY 2017, President Obama proposed the base budget of $523.9 billion, which includes an increase of $2.2 billion over the FY 2016 enacted budget of $521.7 billion. For the FY 2019 president Donald Trump proposed an increase to the military to $681.1 billion.

For the period 2010-14, SIPRI found that the United States was the world's biggest exporter of major arms, accounting for 31 percent of global shares, followed by Russia with 27 percent. The USA delivered weapons to at least 94 recipients. The United States was also the world's eighth largest importer of major military equipment for the same period. The main imports were 19 transport aircraft from Italy; and equipment produced in the US under license—including 252 trainer aircraft of Swiss design, 223 light helicopters of German design and 10 maritime patrol aircraft of Spanish design.Wikipedia:Citation needed

Budget by year

The following is historical spending on defense from 1996-2015, spending for 2014-15 is estimated. The Defense Budget is shown in billions of dollars and total budget in trillions of dollars. The percentage of the total U.S. federal budget spent on defense is indicated in the third row, and change in defense spending from the previous year in the final row.

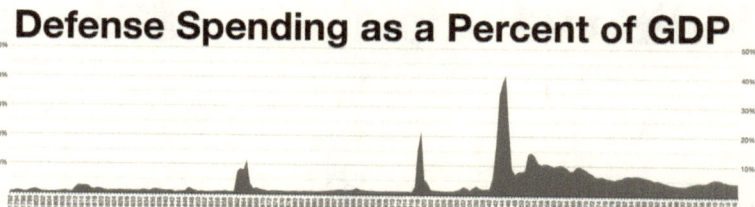

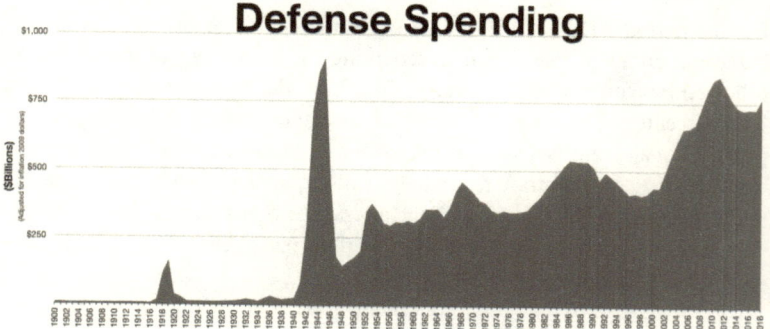

Decades	1990s						2000s										2010s					
Years	96	97	98	99	00	01	02	03	04	05	06	07	08	09	10	11	12	13	14	15
Defense Budget (Billions)	266	270	271	292	304	335	362	456	491	506	556	625	696	698	721	717	681	610	614	637
Total Budget (Trillions)	1.58	1.64	1.69	1.78	1.82	1.96	2.09	2.27	2.41	2.58	2.78	2.86	3.32	4.08	3.48	3.51	3.58	3.48	3.64	3.97
Defense Budget %	16.8	16.5	16.0	16.4	16.7	17.1	17.3	20.1	20.4	19.6	20.0	21.9	20.9	17.1	20.7	20.4	19.1	17.5	16.8	16.0
Defense Spending % Change	-0.1	+1.6	+0.2	+7.8	+4.0	+10.1	+8.2	+26.0	+7.6	+3.1	+10.0	+12.5	+11.3	+0.2	+3.4	-0.6	-5.0	-10.5	+0.6	+3.8

Budget for 2011

For the 2011 fiscal year, the president's base budget for the Department of Defense and spending on "overseas contingency operations" combine to bring the sum to US$664.84 billion.[151]

When the budget was signed into law on 28 October 2009, the final size of the Department of Defense's budget was $680 billion, $16 billion more than President Obama had requested. An additional $37 billion supplemental bill to support the wars in Iraq and Afghanistan was expected to pass in the spring of 2010, but has been delayed by the House of Representatives after passing the Senate.[152,153]

Emergency and supplemental spending

The recent military operations in Iraq and Afghanistan were largely funded through supplementary spending bills outside the federal budget, which are not included in the military budget figures listed below.[154] However, the wars in Iraq and Afghanistan were categorized as "overseas contingency operations" in the starting of the fiscal year 2010, and the budget is included in the federal budget.Wikipedia:Citation needed

By the end of 2008, the U.S. had spent approximately $900 billion in direct costs on the wars in Iraq and Afghanistan. The government also incurred indirect costs, which include interests on additional debt and incremental costs, financed by the Veterans Administration, of caring for more than 33,000 wounded. Some experts estimate the indirect costs will eventually exceed the direct costs.[155] As of June 2011, the total cost of the wars was approximately $1.3 trillion.

Military budget of the United States

By title

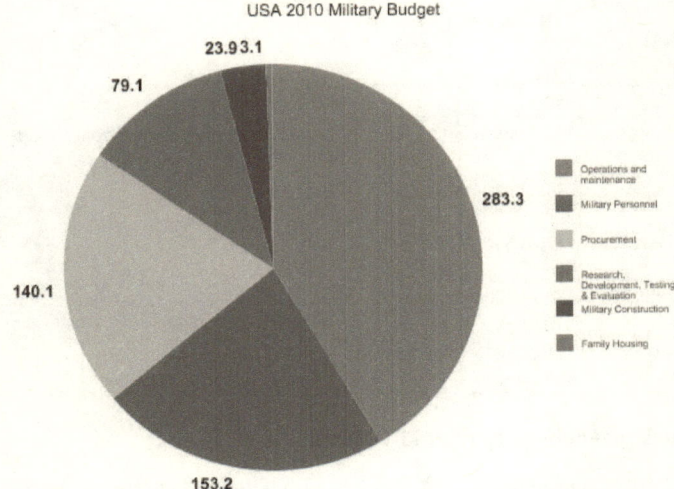

USA 2010 Military Budget

http://en.wikipedia.org/wiki/Military_budget_of_the_United_States

The federally budgeted (see below) military expenditure of the United States Department of Defense for fiscal year 2013 are as follows. While data is provided from the 2015 budget, data for 2014 and 2015 is estimated, and thus data is shown for the last year for which definite data exists (2013).

Components	Funding	Change, 2012 to 2013
Operations and maintenance	$258.277 billion	-9.9%
Military Personnel	$153.531 billion	-3.0%
Procurement	$97.757 billion	-17.4%
Research, Development, Testing & Evaluation	$63.347 billion	-12.1%
Military Construction	$8.069 billion	-29.0%
Family Housing	$1.483 billion	-12.2%
Other Miscellaneous Costs	$2.775 billion	-59.5%
Atomic energy defense activities	$17.424 billion	-4.8%
Defense-related activities	$7.433 billion	-3.8%
Total Spending	**$610.096 billion**	**-10.5%**

By entity

Entity	2010 Budget request	Percentage of Total	Notes
Army	$244.8 billion	31.8%	
Marine Corps	$40.6 billion	4%	Total Budget taken allotted from Department of Navy
Navy	$142.2 billion		excluding Marine Corps
Air Force	$170.6 billion	22%	
Defense Intelligence	$80.1 billion	3.3%	*Because of classified nature, budget is an estimate and may **not** be the actual figure*
Defense Wide Joint Activities	$118.7 billion	15.5%	

Programs spending more than $1.5 billion

The Department of Defense's FY 2011 $137.5 billion procurement and $77.2 billion RDT&E budget requests included several programs worth more than $1.5 billion.

Program	2011 Budget request[156]	Change, 2010 to 2011
F-35 Joint Strike Fighter	$11.4 billion	+2.1%
Missile Defense Agency (THAAD, Aegis, GMD, PAC-3)	$9.9 billion	+7.3%
Virginia class submarine	$5.4 billion	+28.0%
Brigade Combat Team Modernization	$3.2 billion	+21.8%
DDG 51 Burke-class Aegis Destroyer	$3.0 billion	+19.6%
P–8A Poseidon	$2.9 billion	−1.6%
V-22 Osprey	$2.8 billion	−6.5%
Carrier Replacement Program	$2.7 billion	+95.8%
F/A-18E/F Hornet	$2.0 billion	+17.4%
Predator and Reaper Unmanned Aerial System	$1.9 billion	+57.8%
Littoral combat ship	$1.8 billion	+12.5%
CVN Refueling and Complex Overhaul	$1.7 billion	−6.0%
Chemical Demilitarization	$1.6 billion	−7.0%
RQ-4 Global Hawk	$1.5 billion	+6.7%
Space-Based Infrared System	$1.5 billion	+54.0%

Other military-related expenditures

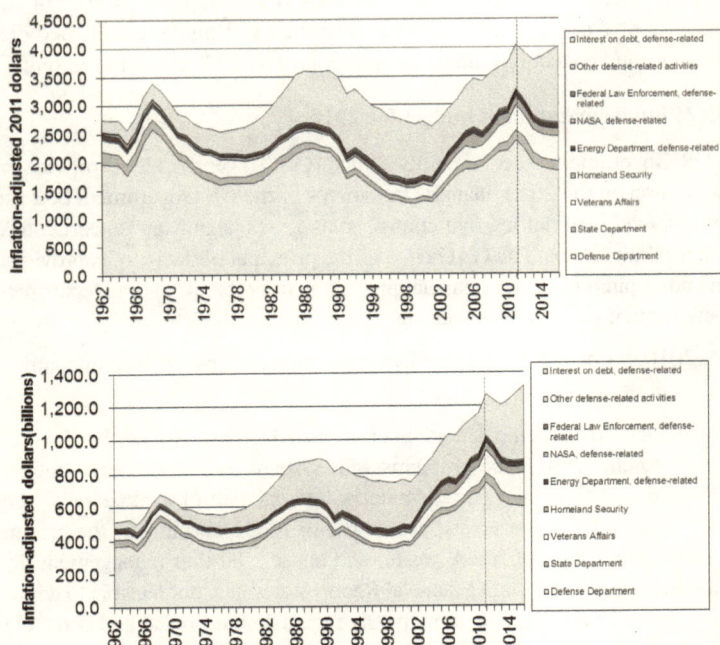

This does not include many military-related items that are outside of the Defense Department budget, such as nuclear weapons research, maintenance, cleanup, and production, which are in the Atomic Energy Defense Activities section,[157] Veterans Affairs, the Treasury Department's payments in pensions to military retirees and widows and their families, interest on debt incurred in past wars, or State Department financing of foreign arms sales and militarily-related development assistance. Neither does it include defense spending that is not military in nature, such as the Department of Homeland Security, counter-terrorism spending by the Federal Bureau of Investigation, and intelligence-gathering spending by NSA.

Audit of 2011 budget

Again in 2011, the GAO could not "render an opinion on the 2011 consolidated financial statements of the federal government", with a major obstacle again being "serious financial management problems at the Department of Defense (DOD) that made its financial statements unauditable".

In December 2011, the GAO found that "neither the Navy nor the Marine Corps have implemented effective processes for reconciling their FBWT." According to the GAO, "An agency's FBWT account is similar in concept to a corporate bank account. The difference is that instead of a cash balance, FBWT represents unexpended spending authority in appropriations." In addition, "As of April 2011, there were more than $22 billion unmatched disbursements and collections affecting more than 10,000 lines of accounting."

Audit of implementation of budget for 2010

The US Government Accountability Office (GAO) was unable to provide an audit opinion on the 2010 financial statements of the US Government because of 'widespread material internal control weaknesses, significant uncertainties, and other limitations'. The GAO cited as the principal obstacle to its provision of an audit opinion 'serious financial management problems at the Department of Defense that made its financial statements unauditable'.

In FY 2010, six out of thirty-three DoD reporting entities received unqualified audit opinions.

Chief financial officer and Under Secretary of Defense Robert F. Hale acknowledged enterprise-wide problems with systems and processes, while the DoD's Inspector General reported 'material internal control weaknesses ... that affect the safeguarding of assets, proper use of funds, and impair the prevention and identification of fraud, waste, and abuse'. Further management discussion in the FY 2010 DoD Financial Report states 'it is not feasible to deploy a vast number of accountants to manually reconcile our books' and concludes that 'although the financial statements are not auditable for FY 2010, the Department's financial managers are meeting warfighter needs'.

Budget for 2016

On February 9, 2016, the US Department of Defense under President Obama released a statement outlining the proposed 2016 and 2017 defense spending budgets that "[reflect] the priorities necessary for our force today and in the future to best serve and protect our nation in a rapidly changing security environment."

Budget by Appropriation

Components	Dollars In Billions
Military Personnel	138.6
Operation and Maintenance	244.4
Procurement	118.9
RDT&E	69.0
Revolving and Management Funds	1.3
Military Construction	6.9

Family Housing	1.3
Total	**580.3**

Budget by Military Departments

Departments	Dollars in Billions
Army	146.9
Navy	168.8
Air Force	161.8
Defense Wide	102.8
Total	**580.3**

Budget request for FY2019

In February 2018, the Pentagon requested $686 billion for FY 2019.

Budget request for FY2018

On March 16, 2017 President Trump submitted his request to Congress for $639 billion in military spending—$54 billion—which represents a 10 percent increase—for FY 2018 as well as $30 billion for FY2017 which ends in September. With a total federal budget of $3.9 trillion for FY2018, the increase in military spending would result in deep cuts to many other federal agencies and domestic programs, as well as the State Department. Trump had pledged to "rebuild" the military as part of his 2016 Presidential campaign.

In April 2017, journalist Scot J. Paltrow raised concerns about the increase in spending with the Pentagon's history of "faulty accounting".

On the 14th of July, H.R. 2810[158] the National Defense Authorization Act 2018 was passed by the U.S. House of Representatives 344 - 81, with 8 not voting. 60% of Democrats voted for this bill, which represented an 18% increase in defense spending. The Congress increased the budget to total 696 billion dollars.

Budget request for FY2017

The currently available budget request for 2017 was filed on February 9, 2016, under now former-President Barack Obama.

The press release of the proposal specifies the structure and goals for the Fiscal Year (FY) 2017 budget:

> *The FY 2017 budget reflects recent strategic threats and changes that have taken place in Asia, the Middle East and Europe. Russian aggression, terrorism by the Islamic State of Iraq and the Levant (ISIL) and others, and China's island building and claims of sovereignty in international waters all necessitate changes in our strategic outlook and in our operational commitments. Threats and actions originating in Iran and North Korea negatively affect our interests and our allies. These challenges have sharpened the focus of our planning and budgeting.*

The

DoD Base + OCO Budget
(Dollars in Billions)
Numbers may not add due to rounding

Budget by Appropriation	FY 2016 Enacted	FY 2017 Request	$ Change
Military Personnel	138.6	138.8	+0.3
Operation and Maintenance	244.4	250.9	+6.5
Procurement	118.9	112.1	-6.8
RDT&E	69.0	71.8	+2.8
Revolving and Management Funds	1.3	1.5	+0.2
Military Construction	6.9	6.3	-0.6
Family Housing	1.3	1.3	0.0
Total	580.3	582.7	+2.4

Budget by Military Departments	FY 2016 Enacted	FY 2017 Request	$ Change
Army	146.9	148.0	+1.1
Navy	168.8	164.9	-3.9
Air Force	161.8	166.9	+5.1
Defense-Wide	102.8	102.9	+0.1
Total	580.3	582.7	+2.4

Budget Request $582.7 Billion

proposal also includes a comparison of the 2016 and the proposed 2017 request amounts, a summary of acquisitions requested for 2017 and enacted in 2016, and provides in detail a breakdown of specific programs to be funded.

Investments

	FY 2016 Enacted	FY 2017 Request	Change
Aircraft and Related Systems	50.6	45.3	-5.3
C4I Systems	7.1	7.4	0.3
Ground Systems	9.9	9.8	-0.1
Missile Defense Programs	9.1	8.5	-0.6
Missiles and Munitions	12.7	13.9	1.2
Mission Support	52.9	52.4	-0.5
Science & Technology (S&T)	13.0	12.5	-0.5
Shipbuilding and Maritime Systems	27.5	27.0	-0.5
Space-Based Systems	7.0	7.1	0.1
Rescissions	-1.8	-	+1.8
Total	188	183.9	-4.1

Amounts are in $ billions.

Major acquisition programs

These are the top 25 DoD weapon programs described in detail:

		FY 2016		FY 2017	
		Qty	$	Qty	$
Aircraft					
F-35	Joint Strike Fighter	68	11.6	63	10.5
KC-46A	Tanker	12	3.0	15	3.3
P-8A	Poseidon	17	3.4	11	2.2
V-22	Osprey	20	1.6	16	1.5
E-2D AHE	Advanced Hawkeye	5	1.2	6	1.4
AH-64E	Apache Helicopter	64	1.4	52	1.1
C/HC/MC-130J	Hercules	29	2.4	14	1.3
UH-60	Black Hawk Helicopter	107	1.8	36	1.0
CH-53K	King Stallion Helicopter	–	0.6	2	0.8
MQ-4C	Triton	4	1.0	2	0.8
H-1 Upgrades	Bell Helicopter	29	0.9	24	0.8
NGJ	Next Generation Jammer Increment 1	–	0.4	–	0.6
CH-47F	Chinook Helicopter	39	1.1	22	0.7

Missile Defense/Missiles					
BMDS	Ballistic Missile Defense	–	7.7	–	6.9
Trident II	Trident II Missile Modifications	–	1.2	–	1.2
AMRAAM	Advanced Medium Range Air to Air Missile	429	0.7	419	0.7
Ships					
SSN 774	VIRGINIA Submarine	2	5.7	2	5.3
DDG 51	AEGIS Destroyer	2	4.4	2	3.5
CVN 78	FORD Aircraft Carrier	–	2.8	–	2.8
ORR	Ohio Replacement	–	1.4	–	1.9
LHA-6	Amphibious Assault Ship	–	0.5	1	1.6
LCS	Littoral Combat Ship	3	1.8	2	1.6
Space					
AEHF	Advanced Extremely High Frequency Satellite	–	0.6	–	0.9
EELV	Evolved Expendable Launch Vehicle	4	1.5	5	1.8
Trucks					
JLTV	Joint Light Tactical Vehicle	804	0.4	2,020	0.7

$ in billions, Qty being the number of items requested.

Science and Technology Program

This program's purpose is to "invest in and develop capabilities that advance the technical superiority of the U.S. Military to counter new and emerging threats." It has a budget of $12.5 billion, but is apart from the overall Research, Development, Test, and Evaluation (RDT&E) portfolio, which compromises $71.8 billion. Efforts funded apply to the Obama administration's refocusing of the US military to Asia, identifying investments to "sustain and advance [the] DoD's military dominance for the 21st century", counter the "technological advances of U.S. foes", and support Manufacturing Initiative institutes. A breakdown of the amounts provided, by tier of research, is provided:

Program	FY 2016 Request	FY 2016 Enacted	FY 2017 Request	Change (FY16 Enacted - FY17 Request)
Basic Research	2.1	2.3	2.1	-0.2
Applied Research	4.7	5.0	4.8	-0.2
Advanced Technology Development	5.5	5.7	5.6	-0.1
Total	**12.3**	**13.0**	**12.5**	**-0.5**

Total budget by department

Total Budget	FY 2016 Enacted	FY 2017 Request	Change
Army	146,928,044	148,033,950	+1,105,906
Navy	168,786,798	164,861,078	-3,925,720
Air Force	161,783,330	166,879,239	+5,095,909
Defense-Wide	102,801,512	102,927,320	+125,808
Total	580,299,684	582,701,587	+2,401,903

Amounts in Thousands of $USD

Total budget of military

Total Budget	FY 2016 Enacted	FY 2017 Request	Change
Military Personnel	138,552,886	138,831,498	+278,612
Operation and Maintenance	244,434,932	250,894,310	+6,459,378
Procurement	118,866,320	112,081,088	-6,785,232
RDT&E*	69,009,764	71,765,940	+2,756,176
Revolving and Management Funds	1,264,782	1,512,246	+247,464
Military Construction	6,909,712	6,296,653	-613,059
Family Housing	1,261,288	1,319,852	+58,564
Total	580,299,684	582,701,587	+2,401,903

*Research, Development, Test and Evaluation

Amounts in thousands of $USD

Funding of payments and benefits

This portion of the military budget comprises roughly one third to one half of the total defense budget, considering only military personnel or additionally including civilian personnel, respectively. These expenditures "will likely always be, the single largest expense category for the Department." Since 2001, military pay and benefits have increased by 85%, but remained roughly one third of the total budget due to an overall increased budget. Military pay remains at about the 70th percentile compared to the private sector to attract sufficient amounts of qualified personnel.

Military Pay and Benefits Funding	FY 2016 Enacted	FY 2017 Request
Military Personnel Appropriations	128.7	128.9
Medicare-Eligible Retiree Health Care Accruals	6.6	6.4
Defense Health Program	32.9	33.8
DoD Education Activity	3.1	2.9
Family Housing	1.3	1.3
Commissary Subsidy	1.4	1.2
Other Benefit Programs	3.5	3.4
Military Pay and Benefits Funding	177.5	177.9
Civilian Pay and Benefits Funding	71.8	72.9
Total Pay and Benefits Funding	**249.3**	**250.8**
DoD Base Budget Authority	521.7	523.9
Military Pay and Benefits as % of Budget	34.0%	34.0%
Total Pay and Benefits as % of Budget	**47.8%**	**47.9%**

Funding the military health system

The request for 2017 amounts to $48.8 billion. The system has 9.4 million beneficiaries, including active, retired, and eligible Reserve Component military personnel and their families, and dependent survivors.

Program	FY 2017 Request
Defense Health (DHP)	33.5
Military Personnel	8.6
Military Construction	0.3
Health Care Accrual	6.4
Unified Medical Budget	**48.8**

Support service contractors

The role of support service contractors has increased since 2001 and in 2007 payments for contractor services exceeded investments in equipment for the armed forces for the first time. In the 2010 budget, the support service contractors will be reduced from the current 39 percent of the workforce down to the pre-2001 level of 26 percent. In a Pentagon review of January 2011, service contractors were found to be "increasingly unaffordable."[159]

Military budget and total US federal spending

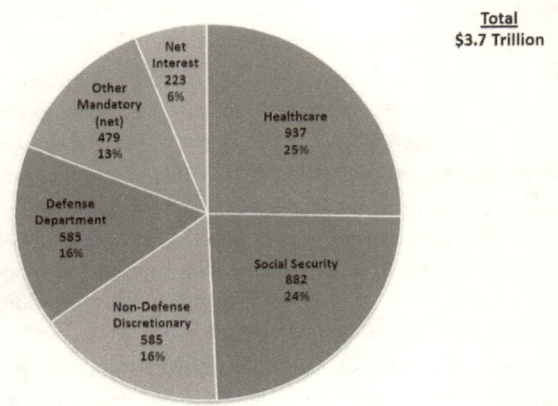

Source Data: CBO Historical Tables, March 2016

The U.S. Department of Defense budget accounted in fiscal year 2010 for about 19% of the United States federal budgeted expenditures and 28% of estimated tax revenues. Including non-DOD expenditures, military spending was approximately 28–38% of budgeted expenditures and 42–57% of estimated tax revenues.Wikipedia:Citation needed According to the Congressional Budget Office, defense spending grew 9% annually on average from fiscal year 2000–2009.

Because of constitutional limitations, military funding is appropriated in a discretionary spending account. (Such accounts permit government planners to have more flexibility to change spending each year, as opposed to mandatory spending accounts that mandate spending on programs in accordance with the law, outside of the budgetary process.) In recent years, discretionary spending as a whole has amounted to about one-third of total federal outlays.[160] Department of Defense spending's share of discretionary spending was 50.5% in 2003, and has risen to between 53% and 54% in recent years.

For FY 2010, Department of Defense spending amounts to 4.7% of GDP.[161] Because the U.S. GDP has grown over time, the military budget can rise in absolute terms while shrinking as a percentage of the GDP. For example, the Department of Defense budget is slated to be $664 billion in 2010 (including the cost of operations in Iraq and Afghanistan previously funded through supplementary budget legislation), higher than at any other point in American history, but still 1.1–1.4% lower as a percentage of GDP than the amount spent on military during the peak of Cold-War military spending in the late 1980s. Admiral Mike Mullen, former Chairman of the Joint Chiefs of Staff, has called four percent an "absolute floor".[162] This calculation does not take into account some other military-related non-DOD spending, such as Veterans Affairs, Homeland Security, and interest paid on debt incurred in past wars, which has increased even as a percentage of the national GDP.

In 2015, Pentagon and related spending totaled $598 billion. Military expenditures exceed the total amount of funds allocated to support social security, transportation, unemployment, labor, science, energy and the environment, international affairs, housing, veteran's benefits, medicare, education.

In addition, the United States will spend at least $179 billion over the fiscal years of 2010-2018 on its nuclear arsenal, averaging $20 billion per year. Despite President Barack Obama's attempts in the media to reduce the scope of the current nuclear arms race, the U.S. intends to spend an additional $1 trillion over the next 30 years modernizing its nuclear arsenal.

In September 2017 the United States Senate followed President Donald Trump's plan to expand military spending, which will boost spending to $700 billion, about 91.4% of which will be spent on maintaining the armed forces and primary Pentagon costs. Military spending is increasing regularly and more money is being spent every year on employee pay, operation and maintenance, and benefits including as health benefits. Methods to counteract rapidly increasing spending include shutting down bases, but that has been banned since an Obama administration Budget Act included a section that stopped just that.

Federal waste

As of September 2014, the Department of Defense was estimated to have "$857 million in excess parts and supplies". This figure has risen over the past years, and of the Pentagon waste that has been calculated, two figures are especially worth mentioning: the expenditure of "$150 million on private villas for a handful of Pentagon employees in Afghanistan and the procurement of the JLENS air-defense balloon" which, throughout the program's development over the past two decades, is estimated to have cost $2.7 billion. Also, it is important to note that the JLENS air-balloon still does not function properly.

One problem with military spending is waste that comes from poor cost estimation. The armed forces are seemingly unable to properly estimate costs, which ends up wasting billions of dollars annually. What is more, there are instances such as in the research and development department where costs are underestimated, which leads to a waste of a different kind: time. Without the appropriate resources, researchers cannot do their job adequately. What this can lead to is employees not working as efficiently as possible.

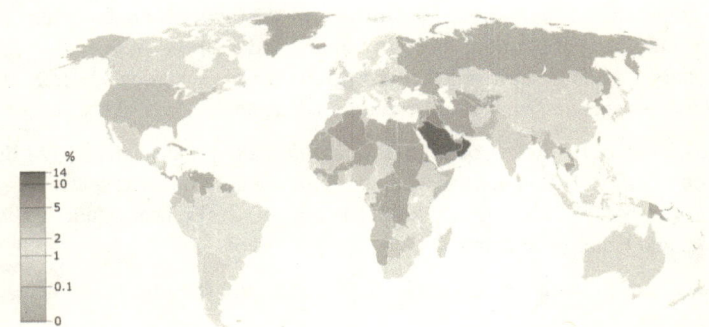

Figure 44: *Map of military expenditures as a percentage of GDP by country, 2015.*[163]

Comparison with other countries

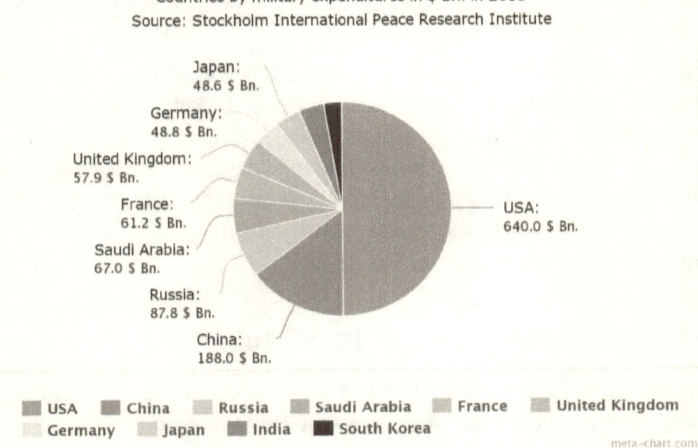

The United States spends more on their defense budget than China, Saudi Arabia, Russia, the United Kingdom, India, France, and Japan combined. The 2009 U.S. military budget accounts for approximately 40% of global arms spending. The 2012 budget is 6–7 times larger than the $106 billion military budget of China. The United States and its close allies are responsible for two-thirds to three-quarters of the world's military spending (of which, in turn, the U.S. is responsible for the majority). The US also maintains the largest number of military bases on foreign soil across the world. While there are no freestanding foreign bases permanently located in the United States, there are now around 800 U.S. bases in foreign countries. Military spending makes up nearly 16% percent of entire federal spending and approximately half of discretionary spending. In a general sense discretionary spending (defense and non-defense spending) makes up one-third of the annual federal budget.

In 2015, out of its budget of 1.11 trillion, the United States spent $598 billion on military. U.S. defense spending is equivalent to the next seven largest military budgets—India, the United Kingdom, Japan, France, Saudi Arabia, Russia, and China—combined.

In 2017, the U.S. military budget is 773.5 billion and is estimated to increase in the upcoming years.

In 2005, the United States spent 4.06% of its GDP on its military (considering only basic Department of Defense budget spending), more than France's 2.6% and less than Saudi Arabia's 10%.[information 2006] This is historically low for the United States since it peaked in 1944 at 37.8% of GDP (it reached the lowest point of 3.0% in 1999–2001). Even during the peak of the Vietnam War the percentage reached a high of 9.4% in 1968.

The US Military's budget has plateaued in 2009, but is still considerably larger than any other military power.

As compared with other countries, the United States spends billions more than its closest competitor, China, and more than the next 5 countries, China, Russia, Saudi Arabia, India, and France put together. Military spending is important to the Trump administration and it is unlikely that he has any reason to curb it. In addition, military spending is popular with 2017 House Speaker Paul Ryan, showing that U.S. military spending will continue to stay high as compared with other countries.

Past commentary on military budget

In 2009, Secretary of Defense Robert Gates wrote that the U.S. should adjust its priorities and spending to address the changing nature of threats in the world: "What all these potential adversaries—from terrorist cells to rogue nations to rising powers—have in common is that they have learned that it is unwise to confront the United States directly on conventional military terms. The United States cannot take its current dominance for granted and needs to invest in the programs, platforms, and personnel that will ensure that dominance's persistence. But it is also important to keep some perspective. As much as the U.S. Navy has shrunk since the end of the Cold War, for example, in terms of tonnage, its battle fleet is still larger than the next 13 navies combined—and 11 of those 13 navies are U.S. allies or partners." Secretary Gates announced some of his budget recommendations in April 2009.

According to a 2009 Congressional Research Service there was a discrepancy between a budget that is declining as a percentage of GDP while the responsibilities of the DoD have not decreased and additional pressures on the military budget have arisen due to broader missions in the post-9/11 world, dramatic increases in personnel and operating costs, and new requirements resulting from wartime lessons in the Iraq War and Operation Enduring Freedom.[164]

Expenses for fiscal years 2001 through 2010 were analyzed by Russell Rumbaugh, a retired Army officer and ex-CIA military analyst, in a report for the Stimson Center. Rumbaugh wrote: "Between 1981 and 1990, the Air Force bought 2,063 fighters. In contrast, between 2001 and 2010, it bought only 220. Yet between 2001 and 2010 the Air Force spent $38B of procurement funding just on fighter aircraft in inflation-adjusted dollars, compared with the $68B it spent between 1981 and 1990. In other words, the Air Force spent 55 percent as much money to get 10 percent as many fighters." As Adam Weinstein explained one of the report's findings: "Of the roughly $1 trillion spent on gadgetry since 9/11, 22 percent of it came from 'supplemental' war funding — annual outlays that are voted on separately from the regular defense budget."

Most of the $5 billion in budget "cuts" for 2013 that were mandated by Congress in 2012 really only shifted expenses from the general military budget to the Afghanistan war budget. Declaring that nearly 65,000 troops were temporary rather than part of the permanent forces resulted in the reallocation of $4 billion in existing expenses to this different budget.[165]

In May 2012, as part of Obama's East Asia "pivot", his 2013 national military request moved funding from the Army and Marines to favor the Navy, but the Congress has resisted this.[166]

Reports emerged in February 2014 that Secretary of Defense Chuck Hagel was planning to trim the defense budget by billions of dollars. The secretary in his first defense budget planned to limit pay rises, increase fees for healthcare benefits, freeze the pay of senior officers, and reduce military housing allowances. A reduction in the number of soldiers serving in the U.S. Army would reduce the size of the force to levels not seen since prior to the start of World War II.

In July 2014, American Enterprise Institute scholar Michael Auslin opined in the National Review that the Air Force needs to be fully funded as a priority, due to the air superiority, global airlift, and long-range strike capabilities it provides.

In January 2015 Defense Department published its internal study on how to save $125 billion on its military budget from 2016 to 2020 by renegotiating vendor contracts and pushing for stronger deals, and by offering workers early retirement and retraining.

2012 fiscal cliff

On 5 December 2012, the Department of Defense announced it was planning for automatic spending cuts, which include $500 billion and an additional $487 billion due to the 2011 Budget Control Act, due to the fiscal cliff. According to *Politico*, the Department of Defense declined to explain to the House of Representatives Appropriations Committee, which controls federal spending, what its plans were regarding the fiscal cliff planning.

This was after half a dozen defense experts either resigned from Congress or lost their reelection fights.

Lawrence Korb has noted that given recent trends military entitlements and personnel costs will take up the entire defense budget by 2039.

GAO audits

The Government Accountability Office was unable to provide an audit opinion on the 2010 financial statements of the U.S. government due to "widespread material internal control weaknesses, significant uncertainties, and other limitations." The GAO cited as the principal obstacle to its provision of an audit opinion "serious financial management problems at the Department of Defense that made its financial statements unauditable."

In Fiscal Year (FY) 2011, seven out of 33 DoD reporting entities received unqualified audit opinions. Under Secretary of Defense Robert F. Hale acknowledged enterprise-wide weaknesses with controls and systems. Further management discussion in the FY 2011 DoD Financial Report states "we are not able to deploy the vast numbers of accountants that would be required to reconcile our books manually". Congress has established a deadline of FY 2017 for the DoD to achieve audit readiness.

For FYs 1998-2010 the Department of Defense's financial statements were either unauditable or such that no audit opinion could be expressed. Several years behind other government agencies, the first results from an army of about 2,400 contracted DoD auditors are expected on November 15, 2018.[167]

Reform

In a statement of 6 January 2011 Defense Secretary Robert M. Gates stated: "This department simply cannot risk continuing down the same path – where our investment priorities, bureaucratic habits and lax attitude towards costs are increasingly divorced from the real threats of today, the growing perils of tomorrow and the nation's grim financial outlook." Gates has proposed a budget that, if approved by Congress, would reduce the costs of many DOD programs and policies, including reports, the IT infrastructure, fuel, weapon programs, DOD bureaucracies, and personnel.

The 2015 expenditure for Army research, development and acquisition changed from $32 billion projected in 2012 for FY15, to $21 billion for FY15 expected in 2014.[168]

External links

- US Government Defense Spending History with Charts - a www.usgovernmentspending.com briefing[169] (archived[170])

Deployments

United States military deployments

The **military of the United States is deployed** in more than 150 countries around the world, with approximately 170,000 of its active-duty personnel serving outside the United States and its territories.

Outside of active combat, US personnel are typically deployed as part of several peacekeeping missions, military attachés, or are part of embassy and consulate security. Nearly 40,000 are assigned to classified missions in locations that the US government refuses to disclose.

The following tables provide detail of various countries, listed by region, where US military are deployed. Countries with fewer than 100 personnel deployed are not specified. These numbers do not include any military or civilian contractors or dependents. Countries in which US military are engaged in combat operations are not included. The numbers are based on the most recent United States Department of Defense statistics as of March 31, 2018.

Americas

Jurisdiction	Total	Army	Navy	USMC	USAF	USCG
Contiguous United States	1,086,852	382,945	268,132	145,234	253,767	36,774
Alaska	19,907	10,740	50	20	7,140	1,957
Cuba (Guantanamo Bay)	831	144	533	148	0	6
Armed Forces Americas	811	0	811	0	0	0
Honduras	366	204	3	13	146	0
Puerto Rico	162	96	22	24	20	0

	Jurisdiction	Total	Army	Navy	USMC	USAF	USCG
	Greenland	149	0	0	0	149	0
	Canada	135	6	39	13	73	4
	other	685	167	150	262	75	31
	Total	1,109,898	394,302	269,740	145,714	261,370	38,772

East Asia and Southeast Asia

Jurisdiction	Total	Army	Navy	USMC	USAF	USCG
Japan	55,043	2,594	20,345	20,001	12,086	17
South Korea	24,915	16,413	309	247	7,945	1
Thailand	461	45	8	380	28	0
Singapore	196	9	160	4	16	7
Philippines	110	11	7	83	8	1
other	116	29	36	23	26	2
Total	80,841	19,101	20,865	20,738	20,109	28

Europe

Jurisdiction	Total	Army	Navy	USMC	USAF	USCG
Germany	34,821	20,435	412	1,236	12,727	11
Italy	12,766	4,289	3,905	372	4,198	2
United Kingdom	9,184	270	200	12	8,663	39
Spain	3,680	27	2,357	906	390	0
Armed Forces Europe	2,098	521	1,337	5	220	15
Belgium	896	617	42	5	231	1
Netherlands	402	124	30	2	215	31
Greece	388	9	358	1	20	0
Norway	330	32	5	259	34	0
Romania	257	7	79	157	14	0
Portugal	227	2	43	3	179	0
Hungary	208	6	144	0	58	0
Poland	147	36	80	4	27	0
other	227	83	36	29	76	3
Total	65,631	26,458	9,028	2,991	27,052	102

Figure 45: *US military bases in Germany in 2014*

Pacific Ocean

Jurisdiction	Total	Army	Navy	USMC	USAF	USCG
Hawaii	43,540	16,472	13,813	7,001	5,040	1,214
Guam	5,451	170	3,172	34	2,075	0
Armed Forces Pacific	1,845	0	998	847	0	0
Australia	228	35	62	46	85	0
other	33	19	5	3	6	0
Total	51,097	16,696	18,050	7,931	7,206	1,214

West Asia and North Africa

Jurisdiction	Total	Army	Navy	USMC	USAF	USCG
Bahrain	4,173	19	3,197	694	24	239
Kuwait	2,036	698	5	1,296	37	0
Turkey	1,623	133	6	3	1,481	0
Qatar	548	260	5	36	247	0
United Arab Emirates	403	32	11	270	90	0
Israel	348	18	6	309	15	0
Saudi Arabia	305	209	20	19	57	0
Egypt	274	231	18	1	24	0
other	218	42	17	126	33	0
Total	9,928	1,642	3,285	2,754	2,008	239

Sub-Saharan Africa, Central & South Asia, and Indian Ocean

Jurisdiction	Total	Army	Navy	USMC	USAF	USCG
British Indian Ocean Territory	292	0	253	0	39	0
Niger	194	3	0	188	3	0
other	670	135	36	399	99	1
Total	1,156	138	289	587	141	1

Unspecified

Jurisdiction	Total	Army	Navy	USMC	USAF	USCG
Overseas	6,292	132	3	4,225	1,124	808
Domestic	5,989	5,989	0	0	0	0
Total	12,281	6,121	3	4,225	1,124	808

External links

- Base Listing as of 2012[171] (2.86 MB)
- Deployment map 1969-2004 (PBS)[172]
- U.S. Military Deployment Interactive Global Map & Facts[173]

Women in Military

Women in the United States Army

There have been **women in the United States Army** since the Revolutionary War, and women continue to serve in it today. As of fiscal year 2014, women are approximately 14 percent of the active duty Army, 23 percent of the Army Reserve, and 16 percent of the Army National Guard.

History

Pre-World War I

A few women fought in the Army in the American Revolutionary War while disguised as men. Deborah Sampson fought until her sex was discovered and she was discharged, and Sally St. Clare died in the war. Anna Maria Lane joined her husband in the Army, and by the time of the Battle of Germantown, she was wearing men's clothes. According to the Virginia General Assembly, "in the revolutionary war, in the garb, and with the courage of a soldier, [Lane] performed extraordinary military services, and received a severe wound at the battle of Germantown."

The number of women in the Army in the American Civil War is estimated at between 400 and 750, although an accurate count is impossible because the women again had to disguise themselves as men.

The United States established the Army Nurse Corps as a permanent part of the Army in 1901; the Corps was all-female until 1955.

Figure 46: *Ann Dunwoody was the first female four-star general in the Army*

World War I

Approximately 21,000 women served in the Army Nurse Corps during World War I. In 1917 World War I Army nurses Edith Ayres and Helen Wood became the first female members of the U.S. military killed in the line of duty. They were killed on May 20, 1917, while with Base Hospital #12 aboard the USS Mongolia en route to France. The ship's crew fired the deck guns during a practice drill, and one of the guns exploded, spewing shell fragments across the deck and killing Nurse Ayres and her friend Nurse Helen Wood.

World War II and after until the Korean War

The Army established the Women's Army Auxiliary Corps in 1942, which was changed to the Women's Army Corps in 1943. Over 150,000 women served as WACs during World War II.

In 1943 Dr. Margaret Craighill became the first female doctor to become a commissioned officer in the Army Medical Corps.

The Angels of Bataan (also known as the "Angels of Bataan and Corregidor" and "The Battling Belles of Bataan"[174]) were the members of the Army Nurse Corps (and the Navy Nurse Corps) who were stationed in the Philippines at the outset of the Pacific War (a theatre of World War II) and served during

Figure 47: *US Army nurses line the rail of their vessel as it pulls into Greenock, Scotland in August 1944*

World War II's Battle of the Philippines (1941–42). When Bataan and Corregidor fell to the Japanese in 1942, 66 army nurses (and 11 Navy nurses and 1 nurse-anesthetist) were captured and imprisoned in and around Manila.[175] They continued to serve as a nursing unit throughout their status as prisoners of war.[176] After years of hardship, they were finally liberated in February 1945.

Slightly after the war, in 1947, Florence Blanchfield became the first woman to receive a military commission in the regular army.

Also in 1947, Johnnie Phelps, a member of the Women's Army Corps and a lesbian, was told by General Eisenhower, "It's come to my attention that there are lesbians in the WACs, we need to ferret them out...." Phelps replied, "If the General pleases, sir, I'll be happy to do that, but the first name on the list will be mine." Eisenhower's secretary added, "If the General pleases, sir, my name will be first and hers will be second." Phelps then told Eisenhower, "Sir, you're right, there are lesbians in the WACs – and if you want to replace all the file clerks, section commanders, drivers, every woman in the WAC detachment, I will be happy to make that list. But you must know, sir, that they are the most decorated group – there have been no illegal pregnancies, no AWOLs, no charges of misconduct." Eisenhower dropped the idea.

In 1948 the Women's Armed Services Integration Act gave women permanent status in the Regular and Reserve forces of the Army.

Korean War

Army women who had joined the Reserves following World War II were involuntarily recalled to active duty during the Korean War. Although no Women's Army Corps unit was sent to Korea, approximately a dozen WACs, including one officer, served in Seoul and Pusan in secretarial, translator, and administrative positions in 1952 and 1953. As well, many WACs served in support positions in Japan and other overseas locations. Over 500 Army nurses served in the combat zone and many more were assigned to large hospitals in Japan. One Army nurse died in a plane crash on her way to Korea on July 27, 1950, shortly after hostilities began.

Vietnam War

In 1967, during the Vietnam War, Public Law 90-130 was signed into law; it removed legal ceilings on women's promotions that had kept them out of the general and flag ranks, and dropped the two percent ceiling on officer and enlisted strengths for women in the armed forces. Women's Army Corps soldiers served in the Vietnam War; at their peak in 1970, WAC presence in Vietnam consisted of some 20 officers and 130 enlisted women.

During the war, Anna Mae Hays, Chief of the Army Nurse Corps, became the first U.S. female brigadier general on June 11, 1970. Minutes later, Elizabeth Hoisington, Director of the Women's Army Corps, became the second. An Army nurse (1st LT Sharon Ann Lane) was the only US military woman to die from enemy fire in Vietnam. Two other Army nurses were awarded the Soldier's Medal for heroism in Vietnam; one was African-American 1LT Diane Lindsay. She was cited for restraining a Vietnamese soldier patient, who had pulled a pin from a live grenade at the 95th Evacuation Hospital in Vietnam. 1LT Lindsay helped convince the soldier to relinquish a second grenade, avoiding additional casualties.

Women in the Army since 1972

Frontiero v. Richardson, 411 U.S. 677[177] (1973), was a landmark Supreme Court case[178] which decided that benefits given by the military to the family of service members cannot be given out differently because of sex.

West Point admitted its first 119 female cadets in 1976, after Congress authorized the admission of women to the federal service academies in 1975. Four years later 62 female cadets graduated, including the first two black female graduates, Joy Dallas and Priscilla "Pat" Walker Locke.[179] In 1989, Kristin

Figure 48: *A female soldier maintaining her 50-caliber machine gun before undertaking a mission in Afghanistan during 2006*

Baker became the first female First Captain (an effigy of her is now on display in the Museum), the highest ranking senior cadet at the academy. Rebecca Marier became the academy's first female valedictorian in 1995.

In 1978, the Women's Army Corps was disestablished and its members integrated into the regular Army.

The Gulf War involved the deployment of approximately 26,000 Army women. Two Army women were taken as POWs (Army Specialist Melissa Rathbun-Nealy and Maj. Rhonda Cornum).

Before the "Don't Ask Don't Tell" policy was enacted in 1993, lesbians and bisexual women (and gay men and bisexual men) were banned from serving in the military. In 1993 the "Don't Ask Don't Tell" policy was enacted, which mandated that the military could not ask servicemembers about their sexual orientation.[180,181] However, until the policy was ended in 2011 service members were still expelled from the military if they engaged in sexual conduct with a member of the same sex, stated that they were lesbian, gay, or bisexual, and/or married or attempted to marry someone of the same sex.[182]

On April 28, 1993, combat exclusion was lifted from aviation positions by Les Aspin, permitting women to serve in almost any aviation capacity.

In 1994, the Pentagon declared:

> *Service members are eligible to be assigned to all positions for which they are qualified, except that women shall be excluded from assignment to units below the brigade level whose primary mission is to engage in direct combat on the ground.*[183]

That policy also excluded women being assigned to certain organizations based upon proximity to direct combat or "collocation" as the policy specifically referred to it. According to the Army, collocation occurs when, "the position or unit routinely physically locates and remains with a military unit assigned a doctrinal mission to routinely engage in direct combat."

In 1996, the Aberdeen scandal, a military sexual assault scandal, which occurred at Aberdeen Proving Ground, a United States Army base in Maryland resulted in the Army bringing charges against 12 commissioned and non-commissioned male officers for sexual assault on female trainees under their command with someWikipedia:Manual of Style/Dates and numbers officers convicted.

American women in the Army served in the Afghanistan War from 2001 until 2014, and in the Iraq War from 2003 until 2011. In 2008, Ann Dunwoody became the first female four-star general in the Army; she was also the first in the military. In 2011, Patricia Horoho became the first female Army surgeon general.

In 2013, Defense Secretary Leon Panetta removed the military's ban on women serving in combat, overturning the 1994 rule. Panetta's decision gave the military services until January 2016 to seek special exceptions if they believed any positions must remain closed to women. The services had until May 2013 to draw up a plan for opening all units to women and until the end of 2015 to actually implement it.

In August 2015, Kristen Marie Griest and Shaye Lynne Haver became the first two women to graduate from the US Army Ranger School. In October 2015, Lisa Jaster became the third woman to graduate from this school, and the first one from the Army Reserves.

In September 2015, Ranger School was permanently opened to women.

In December 2015, Defense Secretary Ash Carter stated that starting in 2016 all combat jobs would open to women.

Brig. Gen. Diana Holland became West Point's first woman Commandant of Cadets in January 2016.[184]

In March 2016, Ash Carter approved final plans from military service branches and the U.S. Special Operations Command to open all combat jobs to women, and authorized the military to begin integrating female combat soldiers "right away."

In April 2016, Tammy Barnett became the first woman to enlist in the infantry in the U.S. Army, and Kristen Marie Griest became the first female infantry officer in the U.S. Army when the U.S. Army approved her request to transfer there from a military police unit.[185] In May 2016, Shelby Atkins became the first female U.S. Army noncommissioned officer to be granted the infantry military occupational specialty.

It was announced on June 30, 2016 that, beginning on that date, otherwise qualified United States service members could not any longer be discharged, denied reenlistment, involuntarily separated, or denied continuation of service because of being transgender (including but not limited to transgender women). Beginning on January 1, 2018, openly transgender people (including but not limited to transgender women) were allowed to join the military.

On October 26, 2016, ten women became the first female graduates from the United States Army's Infantry Basic Officer Leader's Course at Fort Benning, Georgia.

In 2017, eighteen women graduated from the United States Army's first gender-integrated infantry basic training for enlisted soldiers.

References

 Wikimedia Commons has media related to *Women in the United States Army*.

Women in the United States Marines

There have been **women in the United States Marines** since 1918, and women continue to serve in it today.

Figure 49: *Opha May Johnson was the first known woman to enlist in the Marines. She joined the Marine Corps Reserve in 1918, officially becoming the first female Marine.*

History

Prior to World War I

Lucy Brewer (or Eliza Bowen, or Louisa Baker) is the pen name of a writer who purported to be the first woman in the United States Marines, serving aboard the USS *Constitution* as a sharpshooter in the 1800s while pretending to be a man named George Baker.[186] Brewer's adventures were probably written by Nathaniel Hill Wright (1787–1824) or Wright's publisher, Nathaniel Coverly. No one by the name of Lucy Brewer (or that of her other pseudonyms, or that of her husband) can be found in historical records; in addition, it is highly unlikely a woman could have disguised herself for three years on the *Constitution*, as the crew had little to no privacy.[187] (For example, no toilet facilities or private quarters existed on the ship, and physical examinations were thorough in the Marines.) In addition, Brewer's book *The Female Marine*'s identifying details of the *Constitution*'s travels and battles are nearly verbatim to accounts published by the ship's commanders in contemporary newspapers.[187]

World War I

Opha May Johnson was the first known woman to enlist in the Marines. She joined the Marine Corps Reserve in 1918, during America's involvement in World War I, officially becoming the first female Marine. From then until the end of World War I, 305 women enlisted in the Marines.

World War II

The Marine Corps created the Marine Corps Women's Reserve in 1943, during America's involvement in World War II. Ruth Cheney Streeter was its first director. Over 20,000 women Marines served in World War II, in over 225 different specialties, filling 85 percent of the enlisted jobs at Headquarters Marine Corps and comprising one-half to two-thirds of the permanent personnel at major Marine Corps posts. However, it was not until after World War II, in 1948, that the Women's Armed Services Integration Act of 1948 gave women permanent status in the Regular and Reserve forces of the Marines.

Korean War

The Marine Corps Women's Reserve was mobilized in August 1950 for the Korean War, eventually reaching peak strength of 2,787 active-duty women Marines. Most women Marines served as part of the clerical and administrative staff.

Vietnam War

In 1967 Master Sergeant Barbara Dulinsky became the first female Marine to serve in a combat zone in Vietnam. At the peak of the Vietnam War, there were approximately 2,700 women Marines on active duty, serving both stateside and overseas.

Women in the Marines since 1972

Frontiero v. Richardson, 411 U.S. 677[188] (1973), was a landmark Supreme Court case[189] which decided that benefits given by the military to the family of service members cannot be given out differently because of sex.

Approximately one thousand women Marines were deployed for Operation Desert Storm (1990) and Operation Desert Shield (1990-1991).

In 1991 the Tailhook scandal occurred, in which Marine Corps (and Navy) aviators were accused of sexually assaulting 83 women (and 7 men) at the Tailhook convention in Las Vegas.

Figure 50: *Captain Elizabeth A. Okoreeh-Baah, the first female MV-22 Osprey pilot, stands on the flight line in Al Asad, Iraq after a combat operation on March 12, 2008.*

Before the "Don't Ask Don't Tell" policy was enacted in 1993, lesbians and bisexual women (and gay men and bisexual men) were banned from serving in the military. In 1993 the "Don't Ask Don't Tell" policy was enacted, which mandated that the military could not ask servicemembers about their sexual orientation.[190,191] However, until the policy was ended in 2011 service members were still expelled from the military if they engaged in sexual conduct with a member of the same sex, stated that they were lesbian, gay, or bisexual, and/or married or attempted to marry someone of the same sex.[192]

On April 28, 1993, combat exclusion was lifted from aviation positions by Les Aspin, permitting women to serve in almost any aviation capacity.

In 1994, the Pentagon declared:

Service members are eligible to be assigned to all positions for which they are qualified, except that women shall be excluded from assignment to units below the brigade level whose primary mission is to engage in direct combat on the ground.[193]

That policy also excluded women being assigned to certain organizations based upon proximity to direct combat or "collocation" as the policy specifically referred to it. According to the Army, collocation occurs when, "the position or unit routinely physically locates and remains with a military unit assigned a doctrinal mission to routinely engage in direct combat."

American women in the Marines served in the Afghanistan War from 2001 until 2014, and in the Iraq War from 2003 until 2011.

In 2013 Leon Panetta removed the military's ban on women serving in combat, overturning the 1994 rule. Panetta's decision gave the military services until January 2016 to seek special exceptions if they believed any positions must remain closed to women. The services had until May 2013 to draw up a plan for opening all units to women and until the end of 2015 to actually implement it. In 2015 Joseph Dunford, the commandant of the Marine Corps, recommended that women be excluded from competing for certain front-line combat jobs. That year a U.S. official confirmed that the Marine Corps had requested to keep some combat jobs open only to men. However, in December 2015, Defense Secretary Ash Carter stated that starting in 2016 all combat jobs would open to women. In March 2016, Ash Carter approved final plans from military service branches and the U.S. Special Operations Command to open all combat jobs to women, and authorized the military to begin integrating female combat soldiers "right away."

Also in 2016, a female lance corporal in the Marines requested a lateral move into an infantry "military occupational specialty," making her the first female Marine to sign up for the infantry.

It was announced on June 30, 2016 that, beginning on that date, otherwise qualified United States service members could not any longer be discharged, denied reenlistment, involuntarily separated, or denied continuation of service because of being transgender (including but not limited to transgender women). Beginning on January 1, 2018, openly transgender people (including but not limited to transgender women) were allowed to join the military.

In early 2017 a nude photo scandal occurred; initially it was reported that the scandal was contained to only the Marine Corps, but the scandal later involved the rest of the US military.

Also in 2017, Maria Daume, who was born in a Siberian prison and later adopted by Americans, became the first female Marine to join the infantry through the traditional entry-level training process.

Also in 2017, the first woman graduated from the infantry officer course of the Marine Corps; her name was not made public.

Also in 2017, Mariah Klenke became the first female officer to graduate from the Marines' Assault Amphibian Officer course.

Notes

 Wikimedia Commons has media related to *Women in the United States Marine Corps*.

Women in the United States Navy

FSailo

Many women have served in the United States Navy for over a century. Today, there are over 52,391 women serving on active duty in an array of traditional (administrative, medical, etc.) and non-traditional (aviation, combat systems, etc.) ratings or careers. Like their male counterparts, female sailors are expected to adhere to regulations specific to appearance, grooming, and health and fitness; however some differences exist for example in physical fitness tests due to performance and in relation to pregnancy and parenting provisions created to help support military families.

History

Pre-World War I

Women worked as nurses for the navy as early as the American Civil War. The United States Navy Nurse Corps was officially established in 1908; it was all-female until 1965. After the establishment of the Nurse Corps in 1908 by an Act of Congress, twenty women were selected as the first members and assigned to the Naval Medical School Hospital in Washington, D.C. However, the navy did not provide room or board for them, and so the nurses rented their own house and provided their own meals.[195] In time, the nurses would come to be known as "The Sacred Twenty" because they were the first women to serve formally as members of the Navy. The "Sacred Twenty" were Mary H. Du Bose; Adah M. Pendleton; Elizabeth M. Hewitt; Della V. Knight; Josephine Beatrice Bowman; Lenah H. Sutcliffe Higbee; Esther Voorhees Hasson, the first Superintendent of the Navy Nurse Corps, 1908–1911; Martha E. Pringle; Elizabeth J. Wells; Clare L. De Ceu.; Elizabeth Leonhardt; Estelle Hine; Ethel R. Parsons; Florence T. Milburn; Boniface T. Small; Victoria White; Isabelle Rose Roy; Margaret D. Murray; Sara B. Myer; and Sara M. Cox. The Nurse Corps gradually expanded to 160 on the eve of World War I. For a few months in 1913, Navy nurses saw their first shipboard service, aboard *Mayflower* and *Dolphin*.

Figure 51: *Admiral Michelle J. Howard was the first female four-star admiral in the U.S. Navy. She was also the armed forces' first African-American woman to achieve four stars.*[194]

World War I

The increased size of the United States Navy in support of World War I increased the need for clerical and administrative support. The U.S. Naval Reserve Act of 1916 permitted the enlistment of qualified "persons" for service; Secretary of the Navy Josephus Daniels asked, "Is there any law that says a Yeoman must be a man?" and was told there was not. Thus, the navy was able to induct its first female sailors into the U.S. Naval Reserve. The first woman to enlist in the U.S. Navy was Loretta Perfectus Walsh on 17 March 1917. She was also the first American active-duty navy woman, and the first woman allowed to serve as a woman in any of the United States armed forces, as anything other than as a nurse. Walsh subsequently became the first woman U.S. Navy petty officer when she was sworn in as Chief Yeoman on March 21, 1917. During World War I Navy women served around the continental U.S. and in France, Guam and Hawaii, mostly as Yeomen (F), but also as radio operators, electricians, draftsmen, pharmacists, photographers, telegraphers, fingerprint experts, chemists, torpedo assemblers and camouflage designers. Some black women served as Yeomen (F) and were the first black women to serve as enlisted members of the U.S. armed forces. These first black women to serve in the navy were 16 Yeomen (F)—the total would rise to 24[196]—from some of "Washington's elite black families" who "worked in the Muster Roll division at Washington's Navy Yard...." All women in the navy were released from active duty after the end of the war.

World War II

World War II again brought the need for additional personnel. This time the navy organized to recruit women into a separate women's auxiliary, labeled Women Appointed for Voluntary Emergency Service (WAVES). WAVES served in varied positions around the continental U.S. and in Hawaii. See WAVES.

Two groups of navy nurses were held prisoner by the Japanese in World War II. Chief Nurse Marion Olds and nurses Leona Jackson, Lorraine Christiansen, Virginia Fogerty and Doris Yetter were taken prisoner on Guam shortly after Pearl Harbor and transported to Japan. They were repatriated in August 1942, although the newspaper did not identify them as navy nurses. Chief Nurse Laura Cobb and her nurses, Mary Chapman, Bertha Evans, Helen Gorzelanski, Mary Harrington, Margaret Nash, Goldie O'Haver, Eldene Paige, Susie Pitcher, Dorothy Still and C. Edwina Todd (some of the "Angels of Bataan") were captured in 1942 and imprisoned in the Los Baños internment camp, where they continued to function as a nursing unit, until they were rescued by American forces in 1945. Other Los Baños prisoners later said: "We are absolutely certain that had it not been for these nurses many of us who are alive and well would have died."[197] The nurses were awarded the Bronze Star Medal by the army, a second award by the navy and the army's Distinguished Unit Badge. Ann Agnes Bernatitus, one of the Angels of Bataan, nearly became a POW; she was one of the last to escape Corregidor Island, via the USS *Spearfish*. Upon her return to the United States she became the first American to receive the Legion of Merit.

In 1943, Thelma Bendler Stern, an engineering draftsman, became the first woman assigned to perform duties aboard a United States Navy ship as part of her official responsibilities.

WAVES Recruiting posters

Korean War era

Women in the Naval Reserve were recalled along with their male counterparts for duty during the Korean War.

Vietnam War era

Nurses served aboard the hospital ship USS *Sanctuary*. Nine non-nurse navy women served in country; however no enlisted navy women were authorized.

Women in the navy since 1970

Major changes occurred for navy women in the 1970s. Alene Duerk became the first female admiral in the navy in 1972. In 1976 RADM Fran McKee became the first female unrestricted line officer appointed to flag rank. In 1978, Judge John Sirica ruled the law banning navy women from ships to be unconstitutional in the case *Owens v. Brown*. That year, Congress approved a change to Title 10 USC Section 6015 to permit the navy to assign women to fill sea duty billets on support and noncombatant ships. During the 1970s, women began to enter the surface warfare and aviation fields, gained access to officer accession programs previously open only to men, and started to screen for command opportunities ashore.

Figure 52: *U.S. Navy Rear Adm. Robin Braun, Commander, Navy Recruiting Command.*

In December 2015, Defense Secretary Ash Carter stated that starting in 2016 all combat jobs would open to women. In March 2016 Ash Carter approved final plans from military service branches and the U.S. Special Operations Command to open all combat jobs to women, and authorized the military to begin integrating female combat soldiers "right away."

Aviation

In 1972, Roseann Roberts became the first female helicopter plane captain in the navy.

In 1973 the Secretary of the Navy announced the authorization of naval aviation training for women. LTJG Judith Neuffer was the first woman selected for flight training. In 1974, the navy became the first service to graduate a woman pilot, LT Barbara Allen Rainey, followed closely by classmates Judith Neuffer, Ana Marie Fuqua, Rosemary Bryant Mariner, Jane Skiles O'Dea and Joellen Drag.

Women began attending Aviation Officer Candidate School (AOCS) in 1976.[198]

In 1979 the Naval Flight Officer (NFO) program opened to women.

Also in 1979, LT Lynn Spruill became the first woman naval aviator to obtain carrier qualification.

Benefits

Frontiero v. Richardson, 411 U.S. 677[199] (1973), was a landmark Supreme Court case[200] which decided that benefits given by the military to the family of service members cannot be given out differently because of sex.

Officer Accession Programs

The Reserve Officer Training Corps (ROTC) was opened to women in 1972 and the first woman was commissioned from a ROTC program in 1974. The Women Officer School (WOS), Newport, RI, was disestablished in 1973, and Officer Candidate School (OCS) training was integrated to support men and women. The United States Naval Academy, along with the other military academies, first accepted women in 1976 and commissioned its first female graduates in 1980. Women also began attending Aviation Officer Candidate School (AOCS) in 1976.

Submarines

On 29 April 2010, the Department of the Navy announced authorization of a policy change allowing women to begin serving on board navy submarines. The new policy and plan was set to begin with the integration of female Officers. A group of up to 24 female Officers (three Officers on each of eight different crews) were scheduled to enter the standard nuclear submarine training pipeline in July 2010 – and expected to report to submarine duty by late 2011 or early 2012. Integration of Enlisted females into submarine crews was expected to begin soon thereafter.[201] Initial candidates for female Submarine Officer positions were highly qualified selects from accession sources that include the Naval Academy, Naval Reserve Officers Training Corps, STA-21 program and Officer Candidate School, with transfers possible for those from other Unrestricted Line Officer communities. A group of up to eight female Supply Corps Officers was also expected to complete requisite training and begin submarine service in the same time frame.

Initial assignments for female submariners were on the blue and gold crews of selected guided-missile submarines (SSGNs) and ballistic-missile submarines (SSBNs). Two submarines of each type served as the inaugural vessels. The first group of U.S. female submariners completed nuclear power school and officially reported on board two ballistic and two guided missile submarines in November 2011. In 2012, it was announced that 2013 would be the first year for women to serve on U.S. attack submarines. On 22 June 2012, a sailor assigned to USS *Ohio* (SSGN-726) became the first female supply officer to qualify in U.S. submarines. Lt. Britta Christianson of *Ohio*'s Gold Crew received her Submarine Supply Corps "dolphins" from the Gold Crew Commanding Officer Capt. Rodney Mills during a brief ceremony at Puget Sound Naval Shipyard and Intermediate Maintenance Facility (PSNS & IMF).

On 5 December 2012, three sailors assigned to USS *Maine* (SSBN-741) and USS *Wyoming* (SSBN-742) became the first female unrestricted line officers to qualify in U.S. submarines. Lt. j.g. Jennifer Noonan [ROTC Cornell University], a native of Scituate MA, and Lt. j.g. Amber Cowan both of *Maine*'s Blue Crew, and Lt. j.g. Marquette Leveque, a native of Fort Collins, Colo., assigned to the Gold Crew of *Wyoming*, and received their submarine "dolphins" during separate ceremonies at Naval Base Kitsap-Bangor, Wash. and Naval Submarine Base Kings Bay, Ga. respectively. In 2013, Navy Secretary Ray Mabus said that the first women to join Virginia-class attack subs had been chosen: They were newly commissioned female officers scheduled to report to their subs in fiscal year 2015. In August 2016, Chief Petty Officer Dominique Saavedra became the first enlisted female sailor to earn her submarine qualification, and was assigned to USS *Michigan* (SSGN-727).

Surface warfare

In 1972 the pilot program for assignment of officers and enlisted women to ships was initiated on board USS *Sanctuary* (AH-17). In 1978 Congress approved a change to Title 10 USC Section 6015 to permit the navy to assign women to fill sea duty billets on support and noncombatant ships. The Surface Warfare community opened to women. In 1979, the first woman obtained her Surface Warfare Officer (SWO) qualification. In 1993, Congress approved women to serve on combat ships. There were about 33 women who were the first assigned to these sea billets.

Timeline of women in the United States Navy

Year	Event
1908	The Navy Nurse Corps was established; it was all-female until 1965.
1917	Secretary of the Navy Josephus Daniels announced that the navy would enlist women on 17 March.
1917	Loretta Perfectus Walsh became the first woman to enlist in the navy on 17 March.
1942	President Franklin D. Roosevelt signed the Public Law 689 creating the navy's women reserve program on 30 July 1942.

Year	Event
1942	Lieutenant Commander Mildred H. McAfee, USNR, director of the WAVES, became the navy's first female line officer.
1944	Lieutenant Harriet Ida Pickens and Ensign Frances Wills were commissioned as the first African-American female navy officers.
1944	Sue Dauser, the director of the Navy Nurse Corps, became the first female captain in the navy.[202]
1948	On 15 October 1948, the first eight women were commissioned in the regular Navy: Joy Bright Hancock, Winifred Quick Collins, Ann King, Frances Willoughby, Ellen Ford, Doris Cranmore, Doris Defenderfer, and Betty Rae Tennant took their oaths as naval officers.[203]
1959	Yeoman Anna Der-Vartanian was the first woman in the navy promoted to master chief petty officer, and the first woman in the armed services promoted to E-9.
1961	Lieutenant Charlene I. Suneson became the first line WAVES officer to be ordered to shipboard duty.[204]
1967	Public Law 90-130 was signed into law; it removed legal ceilings on women's promotions that had kept them out of the general and flag ranks, and dropped the two percent ceiling on officer and enlisted strengths for women in the armed forces.
1972	Roseanne Roberts becomes the first woman helicopter captain.
1972	Alene Duerk became the first female admiral in the navy.
1973	*Frontiero v. Richardson*, 411 U.S. 677[199] (1973), was a landmark Supreme Court case which decided that benefits given by the military to the family of service members cannot be given out differently because of sex.
1974	Lieutenant Junior Grade Barbara Ann (Allen) Rainey became the first navy woman to earn her wings on 22 February 1974.
1974	The first women were commissioned through NROTC.
1975	*Schlesinger v. Ballard*, 419 U.S. 498 (1975), was a United States Supreme Court case that upheld a federal statute granting female naval officers four more years of commissioned service before mandatory discharge than male Naval officers.[205] A federal statute granted female Naval officers fourteen years of commissioned service while allowing only nine years of commissioned service for male Naval officers before mandatory discharge. The Supreme Court held that the law passed intermediate scrutiny equal protection analysis because women, excluded from combat duty, had fewer opportunities for advancement in the military. The Court found the statute to directly compensate for the past statutory barriers to advancement.[206]
1976	Fran McKee became the navy's first female unrestricted line flag officer.
1978	Navy Nurse Joan C. Bynum became the first black woman promoted to the rank of Captain.
1978	Judge John Sirica ruled the law banning navy women from ships to be unconstitutional in the case *Owens v. Brown*. That same year, Congress approved a change to Title 10 USC Section 6015 to permit the navy to assign women to fill sea duty billets on support and noncombatant ships.
1979	Lieutenant Lynn Spruill became the first female navy pilot qualified to land on aircraft carriers.
1979	The first woman in the navy to qualify as a surface warfare officer did so this year.
1980	The first women graduated from the Naval Academy. There were 81 women in the class of 1980 at the Naval Academy, and 55 of them graduated. Elizabeth Belzer was the first female graduate and Janie L. Mines was the first black female graduate.

1984	Kristine Holderied became the first female valedictorian of the Naval Academy.
1990	Rear Admiral Marsha J. Evans became the first woman to command a Naval Station.
1990	Lieutenant Commander Darlene Iskra became the first navy woman to command a ship, USS *Opportune* (ARS-41).
1991	The Tailhook scandal occurred, in which Navy (and Marine Corps) aviators were accused of sexually assaulting 83 women (and 7 men) at the Tailhook convention in Las Vegas.
1993	Before the "Don't Ask Don't Tell" policy was enacted in 1993, lesbians and bisexual women (and gay men and bisexual men) were banned from serving in the military. In 1993 the "Don't Ask Don't Tell" policy was enacted, which mandated that the military could not ask servicemembers about their sexual orientation.[207,208] However, until the "Don't Ask Don't Tell" policy was ended in 2011, service members (including but not limited to female service members) were still expelled from the military if they engaged in sexual conduct with a member of the same sex, stated that they were lesbian, gay, or bisexual, and/or married or attempted to marry someone of the same sex.[209]
1995	USS *Benfold* is the first destroyer to be built to accommodate females.
1996	Patricia Tracey became the first female three-star officer (vice admiral) in the navy.
1998	CDR Maureen A. Farren became the first woman to command a combatant ship in the navy.
1998	Lillian Fishburne became the first African-American woman promoted to flag rank in the navy.
2006	Carol M. Pottenger became the first woman to command an expeditionary strike group in the navy.
2010	Nora Tyson became the first woman to command a carrier strike group in the navy.
2011	The "Don't Ask Don't Tell" policy was ended in 2011, thus putting an end to service members (including but not limited to female service members) being expelled from the military if they engaged in sexual conduct with a member of the same sex, stated that they were lesbian, gay, or bisexual, and/or married or attempted to marry someone of the same sex.
2011	The first group of female submariners in the navy completed nuclear power school and officially reported on board two ballistic and two guided missile submarines in November 2011.
2012	Commander Monika Washington Stoker became the first African American woman to take command of a navy missile destroyer.
2012	Five "Tigertails" of Carrier Airborne Early Warning Squadron One Two Five (VAW-125), embarked aboard the Nimitz-class aircraft carrier USS *Carl Vinson* (CVN-70) as part of Carrier Air Wing Seventeen (CVW-17), flew an historic flight on 25 January when they participated in the navy's first all-female E-2C Hawkeye combat mission.
2012	On 22 June 2012, a sailor assigned to USS *Ohio* (SSGN-726) became the first female supply officer to qualify in submarines in the navy. Lt. Britta Christianson of Ohio's Gold Crew received her Submarine Supply Corps "dolphins" from the Gold Crew Commanding Officer Capt. Rodney Mills during a brief ceremony at Puget Sound Naval Shipyard and Intermediate Maintenance Facility (PSNS & IMF).

2012	On 5 December 2012, three sailors assigned to USS *Maine* (SSBN-741) and USS *Wyoming* (SSBN-742) became the first female unrestricted line officers to qualify in submarines in the navy. LTJG Marquette Leveque, a native of Fort Collins, Colorado, assigned to the Gold Crew of Wyoming, and LTJG Amber Cowan and LTJG Jennifer Noonan [ROTC Cornell University], a native of Scituate MA, both of Maine's Blue Crew received their submarine "dolphins" during separate ceremonies at Naval Submarine Base Kings Bay, Ga., and Naval Base Kitsap-Bangor, Wash.
2012	Robin Braun became the first female commander of the Navy Reserve, making her the first female three star aviator and the first woman to lead any Reserve component of the military.
2014	Michelle J. Howard became the first female four-star admiral in the navy.
2014	Jan E. Tighe became the first woman to command a numbered fleet when she assumed command of the navy's Tenth Fleet on April 2, 2014.
2014	In July 2014, Marine Corps Captain Katie Higgins became the first female pilot to join the Blue Angels, the navy's flight demonstration squadron. She piloted the team's KC-130 Hercules support aircraft, "Fat Albert."
2015	Nora Tyson was installed as the commander of the navy's Third Fleet, making her the first woman to lead a navy operational fleet.
2015	Cheryl Hansen became the first female commander of the Naval Construction Battalion Center in Gulfport, Mississippi.
2015	In December 2015, Defense Secretary Ash Carter stated that starting in 2016 all combat jobs would open to women.
2016	In March 2016, Defense Secretary Ash Carter approved final plans from military service branches and the U.S. Special Operations Command to open all combat jobs to women, and authorized the military to begin integrating female combat soldiers "right away."
2016	It was announced on June 30, 2016 that, beginning on that date, otherwise qualified United States service members could not any longer be discharged, denied reenlistment, involuntarily separated, or denied continuation of service because of being transgender (including but not limited to transgender women).
2016	In August 2016, Dominique Saavedra became the first enlisted female sailor to earn her submarine qualification.
2018	Beginning on January 1, 2018, openly transgender people (including but not limited to transgender women) were allowed to join the military.

Careers

In the navy, women are currently eligible to serve in all ratings. In 2013 Leon Panetta removed the U.S. military's ban on women serving in combat, overturning a 1994 rule prohibiting women from being assigned to smaller ground combat units. Panetta's decision gave the U.S. military services until January 2016 to seek special exceptions if they believed any positions must remain closed to women. The services had until May 2013 to draw up a plan for opening all units to women and until the end of 2015 to actually implement it. In December 2015, Defense Secretary Ash Carter stated that starting in 2016 all combat jobs would open to women.

The former policy set by Congress and the Secretary of Defense, effective 1 October 1994, excluded women from direct ground combat billets in the military, stating:

> "Service members who are eligible to be assigned to all positions for which they are qualified, except that women shall be excluded from assignment to units below the brigade level whose primary mission is to engage in direct combat on the ground as defined below. "Direct ground combat is engaging an enemy on the ground with individual or crew-served weapons, while being exposed to hostile fire and to a high probability of direct physical contact with the hostile force's personnel. Direct combat take place well forward on the battlefield while locating and closing with the enemy to defeat them by fire, maneuver, or shock effect." However, qualified and motivated women are encouraged to investigate the diver and explosive ordnance disposal (EOD) fields."

Careers in the navy

Dress

- A certified maternity uniform is mandatory for all pregnant servicewomen in the navy when the regular uniform no longer fits.

Grooming standards

- **Hair:** The navy deems that hairstyles shall not be "outrageously multi-colored" or "faddish," to include shaved portions of the scalp (other than the neckline), or have designs cut or braided into the hair. Hair coloring must look natural and complement the individual. Haircuts and styles shall present a balanced appearance. Lopsided and extremely asymmetrical styles are not authorized. Pigtails, widely spaced individual hanging locks, and braids that protrude from the head, are not authorized. Multiple braids are authorized. Braided hairstyles shall be conservative and conform to the guidelines listed herein. When a hairstyle of multiple braids is worn, braids shall be of uniform dimension, small in diameter (approx. 1/4 inch), and tightly interwoven to present a neat, professional, well-groomed appearance. Foreign material (i.e., beads, decorative items) shall not be braided into the hair. Short hair may be braided in symmetrical fore and aft rows (cornrowing) that minimize scalp exposure. Cornrow ends shall not protrude from the head, and shall be secured only with inconspicuous rubber bands that match the color of the hair. Appropriateness of a hairstyle shall also be judged by its appearance when headgear is worn. All headgear shall fit snugly and comfortably around the largest part of the head without distortion or excessive gaps. Hair shall not show from under the front of the brim of the combination hat, garrison, or command ball caps. Hairstyles which do not allow headgear to be worn in this manner, or which interfere with the proper wear of protective masks or equipment are prohibited. When in uniform, the hair may touch, but not fall below a horizontal line level with the lower edge of the back of the collar. On July 11, 2018 Navy women became allowed to wear their hair

in ponytails, locks, wider buns and at times below their collars, although subject to strict guidelines on the matter.
- **Cosmetics:** The navy prefers that cosmetics be applied in good taste so that colors blend with natural skin tone and enhance natural features. Exaggerated or faddish cosmetic styles are not authorized and shall not be worn. Care should be taken to avoid artificial appearance. Lipstick colors shall be conservative and complement the individual. Long false eyelashes shall not be worn when in uniform.
- **Tattoos:** Navy policy stipulates that any tattoo/body art/brand that is obscene, sexually explicit or advocates discrimination of any sort is prohibited. No tattoos/body art/brands on the head, face, neck, or scalp and individual tattoos/body art/brands exposed by wearing a short sleeve uniform shirt shall be no larger in size than the wearer's hand with fingers extended and joined with the thumb touching the base of the index finger.
- **Jewelry:** Conservative jewelry is authorized for all personnel and shall be in good taste while in uniform. Eccentricities or faddishness are not permitted. Jewelry shall not present a safety or FOD (Foreign object damage) hazard. Jewelry shall be worn within the following guidelines
    - **Earrings:** Earrings for women are an optional item, and are not required for wear. When worn the earring shall be a 4-6mm ball (gold for officers/CPOs, and silver for E-6 and below), plain with brushed, matte finish, screw-on or post type. Pearl earrings may be worn with Dinner Dress or Formal uniforms.
    - **Rings:** While in uniform, only one (1) ring per hand is authorized, plus a wedding/engagement ring set. Rings are not authorized for wear on thumbs.
    - **Necklaces:** While in uniform, only one (1) necklace may be worn and it shall not be visible.
    - **Bracelets:** While in uniform, only one (1) of each may be worn. Ankle bracelets are not authorized while in uniform.
- **Fingernails:** Fingernails for women shall not exceed 1/4 inch beyond the end of the finger. They shall be kept clean. Nail polish may be worn, but colors shall be conservative and complement the skin tone.

Health and fitness standards

The Physical Fitness Assessment (PFA) is conducted twice a year for all sailors, which includes:
- Body Composition Assessment (BCA). Body composition is assessed by:
    - An initial weight and height screening

- A Navy-approved circumference technique to estimate body fat percentage

Physical Readiness Test (PRT) include different standards for male and female sailors. PRT is a series of physical activities designed to evaluate factors that enable members to perform physically. Factors evaluated are:

- Muscular strength and endurance via:
    1. Curl-ups
    2. Push-ups
- Aerobic capacity via:
    1. 1.5-mile run/walk, or
    2. 500-yard or 450-meter swim

PT Fitness Standards (NSW/NSO programs only):
- The PST consists of five (5) events:
1. 500-yard swim (using sidestroke or breaststroke)
2. Push-Ups (as many as possible in 2-minutes)
3. Sit-Ups (as many as possible in 2-minutes)
4. Pull-Ups (as many as possible, no time limit)
5. 1 ½ mile run

Navy family life

Benefits

Frontiero v. Richardson, 411 U.S. 677[199] (1973), was a landmark Supreme Court case which decided that benefits given by the military to the family of service members cannot be given out differently because of sex.

Marriage

Spouse co-location assignments are fully supported by the Chief of Naval Personnel and when requested become the highest priority and main duty preference consistent with the needs of the navy. While not always possible, every effort, within reason, will be made for military couples and family members to move & serve together. Co-op assignments are not guaranteed.

The service member requesting transfer to join with his/her spouse or family member must have a minimum of one year on board his/her present command at the time of transfer.

Military couples may not be permanently assigned to the same ship or the same shipboard deployable command. For shore assignments, the couple will not assign to the same reporting senior without the gaining CO's approval. Unusual circumstances may require a couple being temporarily assigned to the same afloat activity, which is allowable at the CO's discretion.

Pregnancy and parenting resources

- Pregnant servicewomen may remain on board up to their 20th week of pregnancy.
- An extension of up to one year may be granted in order to receive maternity benefits, provided the member's performance has been satisfactory and first-term sailors have PTS approval.
- No later than 6 months after being returned to full duty by a HCP, the servicewoman is required to take the PFA and conform to acceptable height/weight standards.
- No servicewomen may be assigned overseas or travel overseas after the completion of the 28th week of pregnancy.
- The New Parent Support Home Visitation Program (NPSHVP) is a team of professionals providing supportive and caring services to military families with new babies. Navy families and other military families expecting a child or with children up to three years of age are assessed to determine if they need help managing the demands of a new baby. In the program, new Moms and Dads can be referred to community new baby programs and are eligible to participate in a voluntary home visitation program, free of charge. The New Parent Support Home Visitation Program was developed to assist military families in ways that friends and family would do if you were back home. This program offers expectant parents and parents of newborn and young children the opportunity to learn new skills as parents and to improve existing parenting skills, in the privacy of their own home.

Controversies

Gender identity

Beginning on January 1, 2018, openly transgender people (including but not limited to transgender women) were allowed to join the military.

Pregnancy

In her 1995 book *Tailspin: Women at War in the Wake of Tailhook*, Jean Zimmerman reported that there was a perception in the navy that women sailors use pregnancy to escape or avoid deployed ship duty. In an example cited by Zimmerman, in 1993 as the USS *Cape Cod* prepared to depart on a deployment cruise, 25 female sailors, out of a crew of 1,500, reported being pregnant shortly before the scheduled departure and were reassigned to shore duty. Although Zimmerman felt that the number of pregnancies was small and should not be regarded as significant, the senior enlisted sailor on the ship, Command

Master Chief Alice Smith rejoined, "Just about every division has been decimated by the number of pregnancies. Now tell me that's not going to hurt a ship."[210] A 1997 study by the Navy Personnel Research and Development Center found that female sailors assigned to ships experienced higher pregnancy and abortion rates than shore-based female sailors.[211]

A Navy policy change in June 2007 extended post-partum tours of duty ashore from 4 months to 12 months. A Virginia Pilot article in October 2007 reported on the navy's policy decision as a means to improve long term retention of trained personnel. The chief of women's policy for the chief of personnel noted that far more men than women fail to deploy or are sent back from deployment, "because of sports injuries, discipline issues or testing positive for drugs."[212]

In 2009, Andrew Tilghman reported in the Military Times on a Naval Inspector General (IG) report noting that, in the wake of this change, Navy shore commands based in Norfolk reported that 34% of their assigned members were pregnant sailors reassigned from ship duty. Since shore-based assignments for pregnant sailors were extended in 2007, the number of navy women leaving deploying units to have children rose from 1,770 in June 2006 to 3,125 as of 1 August 2009. Tilghman further reports that Navy Personnel Command is reviewing the report.[213]

Sexual orientation

Before the "Don't Ask Don't Tell" policy was enacted in 1993, lesbians and bisexual women (and gay men and bisexual men) were banned from serving in the military. In 1993 the "Don't Ask Don't Tell" policy was enacted, which mandated that the military could not ask servicemembers about their sexual orientation. However, until the policy was ended in 2011 service members were still expelled from the military if they engaged in sexual conduct with a member of the same sex, stated that they were lesbian, gay, or bisexual, and/or married or attempted to marry someone of the same sex.

Women on submarines

In July 1994, policy changes were made expanding the number of assignments available to women in the navy. At this time, repeal of the combat exclusion law gave women the opportunity to serve on surface combatant ships but still excluded assignments for women to serve on board submarines. Previously there had been concern about bringing women onto submarines because living quarters offered little privacy and weren't considered suitable for mixed-gender habitation.

In October 2009, the Secretary of the Navy announced that he and the Chief of Naval Operations were moving aggressively to change the policy. Reasons included the fact that larger SSGN and SSBN submarines now in the Fleet had more available space and could accommodate female Officers with little or no modification. Also, the availability of qualified female candidates with the desire to serve in this capacity was cited. It was noted that women now represented 15% of the Active Duty Navy and that women today earn about half of all science and engineering bachelor's degrees. A policy change was deemed to serve the aspirations of women, the mission of the navy and the strength of its submarine force.

In February 2010, the Secretary of Defense approved the proposed policy and signed letters formally notifying Congress of the intended change. After receiving no objection, the Department of the Navy officially announced on 29 April 2010, that it had authorized women to serve on board submarines moving forward.

The first group of U.S. female submariners completed nuclear power school and officially reported on board two ballistic and two guided missile submarines in November 2011.

Admirals

Alene Duerk became the first female admiral in the navy in 1972. Michelle J. Howard became the first female four-star admiral in the navy in 2014.

	Name	Com-mission	Position	Com-munity	RDML	RADM	VADM	ADM	Re-tired	Notes
1	Michelle J. Howard	1982 (USNA)	Vice Chief of Naval Operations	Surface Warfare	2006	2010	2012	2014	2017	Retired.
2	Patricia A. Tracey	1970	Director, Navy Staff, N09B, Office of the Chief of Naval Operations	URL	?	?	1996		2004	First woman to earn third star in the US Navy.
3	Ann E. Rondeau	1974 (OCS)	President, National Defense University	Fleet Support	1999	2002	2005		2012	Retired.
4	Nancy Elizabeth Brown	1974 (OCS)	Director for C4 Systems (J6)	URL	2000	2003	2006		2009	Retired.
5	Carol M. Pottenger	1977 (ROTC)	Deputy Chief of Staff for Capability and Development, Supreme Allied Commander Transformation	Surface Warfare	2003	2007	2010		2013	Retired.
6	Nanette M. DeRenzi	1984 (OIS)	Judge Advocate General of the Navy	JAG	2009[214]	2009	2012		2015	Retired.
7	Robin Braun	1980	Chief of Navy Reserve/Commander, Navy Reserve Force	Reserve, Naval Aviator	2007	2011	2012		2016	Retired.
8	Nora W. Tyson	1979 (OCS)	Commander, US Third Fleet	Naval Flight Officer	2007	2011	2013		2017	First woman to command a carrier strike group.
9	Jan Tighe[[Category:Articles with hCards[215]]]	1984 (USNA)	Commander, U.S. Fleet Cyber Command, Commander U. S. 10th Fleet	IDW/-Crypto	2010	2013	2014			First female IDW flag officer. First woman to command a numbered fleet.

					2011	2014	2015		Currently on active duty.
78	Raquel C. Bono[[Category:Articles with hCards[216]]]	1979	Director, Defense Health Agency	Medical Corps					Currently on active duty.
11	Fran McKee	1950	Assistant Chief of Naval Personnel for Human Resource Management	URL	1976	1978		1981	First woman line officer promoted to flag rank in the United States Navy. Second woman promoted to flag rank in the United States Navy
12	Roberta L. Hazard	1960	Assistant Chief of Naval Personnel, Personnel Readiness and Community Support 1989–1992	URL	1984	1989		1992	First woman to command a navy training command (NTC San Diego 1982).
13	Marsha J. Evans	1967	Superintendent of the Naval Postgraduate School 1995–1998	Fleet Support	1992	1996		1998	Retired.
14	Joan Marie Engel	1969	18th Director, Navy Nurse Corps 1994–1998	SHCE (Nurse Corps)	1994	1997		2000	18th Director, Navy Nurse Corps.
15	Barbara E. McGann	1970 (OCS)	Provost, Naval War College 2000–2002	URL	1994	1998		2002	Notes.
16	Ronne Froman	1970	Director, Ashore Readiness, Chief of Naval Operations, Washington, D.C. 2000 – 2001	Fleet Support	1995	1999		2001	First woman commander of Navy Region Southwest (aka "Navy Mayor of San Diego"), 1997–2000.
17	Bonnie Burnham Potter	1975 (OIS)	Fleet Surgeon, U.S. Atlantic Fleet 1999–	Medical Corps	1997	2000		2003	First female physician to become a flag officer in the military.

#	Name		Position				Notes
18	Kathleen Paige	1971	Program Director, Aegis Ballistic Missile Defense 2003–2005	Engineering Duty Officer	1996	2001	2005 Retired.
19	Karen A. Harmeyer	1975	Chief of Staff, Chief of Naval Operations, N093R, Washington, D.C.	SHCE (Nurse Corps)	1997	2001	2002 Retired. 1st female two-star in the Reserves.
20	Kathleen L. Martin	1973 (OIS)	Deputy Surgeon General of the Navy/ Vice Chief, Bureau of Medicine and Surgery 2002–2005	SHCE (Nurse Corps)	1998	2001	2005 19th Director of the Navy Nurse Corps from August 1998 to August 2001. First Nurse Corps officer to be assigned to the position of Deputy Surgeon General of the Navy.
21	Annette E. Brown	1974 (OCS)	Commander, Navy Region Southeast (2002)	Fleet Support	1999	2002	2005 Retired.
22	Linda J. Bird	1974 (OCS)	Director, Supply, Ordnance and Logistics Operations Division, N41 2003–2005	Supply Corps	1999	2002?	2005 Retired.
23	Elizabeth M. Morris[[Category:Articles with hCards[217]]]	1973 (OIS)	Deputy Chief for Reserve Affairs at the Bureau of Medicine and Surgery 2005–2006?	SHCE (Nurse Corps)	2001	2004	2006 Retired.
24	Nancy J. Lescavage	1972 (OIS)	Senior Health Care Executive Regional Director, TRICARE Regional Office – West	SHCE (Nurse Corps)	2003	2004	Retired. 20th Director of the Navy Nurse Corps.
25	Donna L. Crisp[[Category:Articles with hCards[218]]]	1974 (OCS)	Commander, Joint POW/-MIA Accounting Command	URL	2001	2005	Retired.

	Name	Year (Source)	Position	Branch	Year	Year	Year	Notes
26	Ann D. Gilbride[[Category:Articles with hCards[219]]]	1978 (OCS)	Director, National Maritime Intelligence Center	Reserve	2003	2006		? Retired.
27	Sharon H. Redpath[[Category:Articles with hCards[220]]]	1976 (ROTC)	Vice Commander, Navy Expeditionary Combat Command, Commander, Navy Expeditionary Logistics Support Group	Reserve	2003	2006		2009 Retired
28	Elizabeth A. Hight	1977 (OCS)	Vice Director, Defense Information Systems Agency	URL	2003	2006		? Retired. First woman to Command the JTF-GNO, after serving as its Deputy Commander. First woman Vice Director at DISA.
29	Christine Bruzek-Kohler	1974	Commander, Navy Medicine West, Naval Medical Center San Diego	Nurse Corps	2004	2009		2010 Retired. 21st Director of the Navy Nurse Corps.
30	Christine S. Hunter[[Category:Articles with hCards[221]]]	1980	deputy director, TRICARE Management Activity	Medical	2004	2009		Retired.
31	Wendi B. Carpenter	1977 (AOCS)	Commander, Navy Warfare Development Command, Norfolk	Reserve	2004	2008		2011 Retired. First female naval aviator promoted to Flag rank.
32	Karen Flaherty	1973 (OIS)	Deputy Surgeon General of Navy Medicine	Nurse Corps	2003	2008		Retired. 22nd Director of the Navy Nurse Corps.
33	Moira N. Flanders[[Category:Articles with hCards[222]]]	1978 (OCS)	Director, Inter-American Defense College	URL	2005	2007		Retired.

#	Name	Commission	Position	Designator	Year	Year	Notes
34	Kathleen M. Dussault[[Category:Articles with hCards[223]]]	1979 (OCS)	Director, Supply, Ordnance and Logistics Operations Division (OPNAV N41)	Supply Corps	2006	2009	Retired.
35	Janice M. Hamby[[Category:Articles with hCards[224]]]	1980 (ROTC)	Vice Director for C4 Systems (J6)	URL, then Information Professional	2006	2009	2012 Retired.
36	Elizabeth S. Niemyer[[Category:Articles with hCards[225]]]	1981	Director, Navy Nurse Corps	Nurse Corps	2008	2010	Retired. 23rd Director of the Navy Nurse Corps
37	Patricia E. Wolfe[[Category:Articles with hCards[226]]]	1981 (ROTC)	Commander, Navy Expeditionary Logistics Support Group (NAVELSG)	Reserve, Supply Corps	2007	2010	Retired.
38	Cynthia A. Covell[[Category:Articles with hCards[227]]]	1980 (OCS)	Director, Total Force Requirements Division (OPNAV N12)	Navy Human Resources Officer	2008	2011	Retired.
39	Margaret D. Klein	1981 (USNA)	Senior Advisor to the Secretary of Defense for Military Professionalism	Naval Flight Officer	2008	2011	2017 82nd Commandant of Midshipmen, USNA – first woman.
40	Sandy Daniels	1980 (USNA)	Senior Advisor for Space to the Deputy Chief of Naval Operations for Information Dominance (OPNAV N2/N6)	Reserve	2007	2012	Retired.

	Name	Year	Position	Corps			Notes
41	Katherine L. Gregory	1982 (USNA)	Commander, Naval Facilities Engineering Command, Chief of Civil Engineers	CEC	2010	2012	First female CEC admiral.
42	Elizabeth L. Train[[Category:Articles with hCards228]]	1983 (OCS)	Director, National Maritime Intelligence-Integration Office, Commander, Office of Naval Intelligence	Intelligence	2009	2012	Currently on active duty.
43	Paula C. Brown[[Category:Articles with hCards229]]	1982	Deputy Commander, Naval Facilities Engineering Command, Deputy Chief of Civil Engineers	CEC	2010	2013	Currently on active duty.
44	Elaine C. Wagner[[Category:Articles with hCards230]]	1984	Deputy Chief, Bureau of Medicine and Surgery, Wounded, Ill and Injured	Dental Corps	2010	2013	2017 Retired. Chief of the Naval Dental Corps, 2010 – 2017.
45	Althea H. Coetzee[[Category:Articles with hCards231]]	1985 (USNA)	Deputy Director, Contingency Contracting, Defense Procurement and Acquisition Policy (DPAP), OSD (Acquisition Technology & Logistics)	Supply Corps	2011	2014	Currently on active duty.
46	Janet R. Donovan[[Category:Articles with hCards232]]	1983	Deputy Judge Advocate General (Reserve Affairs & OPS)	JAG	2012	2014	Currently serving.
47	Martha E. G. Herb[[Category:Articles with hCards233]]	1979 (OCS)	Director Inter-American Defense College	Reserve	2010	2014	Currently on active duty.

48 Valerie K. Huegel[[Category:Articles with hCards[234]]]	1980 (OCS)	Commander, Navy Expeditionary Logistics Support Group	Supply Corps	2011	2014		Currently on active duty.
49 Rebecca J. McCormick-Boyle[[Category:Articles with hCards[235]]]	1981	Chief of Staff, Bureau of Medicine and Surgery	Nurse Corps	2011	2014		Currently on active duty.
50 Margaret G. Kibben	1986 (OIS)	Chaplain of the United States Marine Corps, deputy chief of Navy Chaplains	Chaplain Corps	2010	2014		18th Chaplain of the USMC, first female chaplain at USNA.
51 Alene B. Duerk	1943	Director Navy Nurse Corps 1970–1975	Nurse Corps	1972		1975	First female admiral in the United States Navy. Director Navy Nurse Corps 1970–1975.
52 Maxine Conder	1951	Director, Navy Nurse Corps 1975–1979	Nurse Corps	1975		1979?	Director, Navy Nurse Corps.
53 Frances Shea-Buckley	1951	14th Director, Navy Nurse Corps 1979–1983	Nurse Corps	1979		1983	14th Director, Navy Nurse Corps.
54 Pauline Hartington	1953	Commander, Naval Training Center Orlando	URL	1981		1983?	Second woman line officer selected for flag rank.
55 Grace Hopper	1944	Head, Training and Technology Directorate/Special Advisor to the Commander, Naval Data Automation Command	URL?	1983		1986	Co-inventor of COBOL. *Arleigh Burke*-class guided missile destroyer USS *Hopper* (DDG-70) named for RADM Hopper.
56 Mary Joan Nielubowicz	1951	15th Director, Navy Nurse Corps 1983–1987	Nurse Corps	1983		1987	Retired. 15th Director, Navy Nurse Corps.

#	Name	Year	Position	Corps	Year		Year	Notes
57	Mary F. Hall	1959	16th Director, Navy Nurse Corps 1987–1991	Nurse Corps	1987		1991	Retired. Director, Navy Nurse Corps.
58	Louise C. Wilmot	1964	Commander, Naval Base Philadelphia –1994	URL	1988		1994	Retired. First woman to command a naval base.
59	Mariann Stratton	1966	17th Director, Navy Nurse Corps 1991–1994	Nurse Corps	1991		1994	Retired. 17th Director, Navy Nurse Corps.
60	Maryanne T. Gallagher Ibach	1964		Reserve Nurse Corps	1990		1995	Retired. First Reserve flag officer for Navy Nurse Corps.
61	Katharine L. Laughton	1963	Commander, Naval Space Command, Dahlgren, VA 1995–1997	Fleet Support	1993		1997	Retired.
62	Nancy A. Fackler	1962	Deputy Director of the Navy Nurse Corps for Reserve Affairs	Reserve Nurse Corps	1994		1997	retired.
63	Jacqueline O. (Allison) Barnes	????	Director, On-Site Inspection Directorate 1998-2000	Fleet Support	1996		2000	Retired.
64	Lillian E. Fishburne	1973 (OCS)	Director, Information Transfer Division for the Space, Information Warfare, Command and Control Directorate ?-2001	URL	1998		2001	Retired. First African-American woman to achieve flag rank.
65	Marianne B. Drew	1967	Deputy Commander, Navy Personnel Command	Reserve, Fleet Support	1998		2002	Retired.
66	Eleanor Mariano	1977	White House Physician	Medical Corps	2000		2001	Retired. First Filipino-American flag officer.

#	Name	Year	Position	Category	Date	Notes
67	Rosanne M. Levitre[[Category:Articles with hCards[236]]]	1973 (OCS)	Director of Intelligence, J2, U.S. Joint Forces Command	Intelligence	2000	2005 Retired. First Director, Navy Intelligence, Surveillance, and Reconnaissance (ISR), FORCEnet. First female Intel officer selected for flag rank in the United States Navy.
68	Carol I. Turner	1977	Senior Health Care Executive, U.S. Navy Commander, Navy Medicine Support Command	Dental Corps	2003	2008? Retired. First female Chief of the Naval Dental Corps, 2003–2007.
69	Deborah Loewer	1976 (OCS)	Commander, Mine Warfare Command 2005–2006	Surface Warfare	2003	2007 Retired. First warfare-qualified woman selected for flag rank in the United States Navy.
70	Cynthia A. Dullea[[Category:Articles with hCards[237]]]	1980 (OIS)	Deputy Commander, Navy Medicine National Capital Area	Reserve	2007	Retired.
71	Maude Elizabeth Young[[Category:Articles with hCards[238]]]	1984 (USNA)	Director, Systems Engineering National Reconnaissance Office; Commander, SPAWAR Space Field Activity (SSFA), PEO for Space Systems, USN	URL	2008	Retired.
72	Eleanor V. Valentin	1982	Director, Medical Service Corps, Commander, Navy Medicine Support Command, Jacksonville, Florida	MSC	2009	Retired. 16th director of the Medical Service Corps (first female director)

Women in the United States Navy

73	Robin L. Graf[[Category:Articles with hCards[239]]]	1981 (OCS)	Deputy Commander, Navy Recruiting Command	URL	2009	Retired.
74	Diane E. H. Webber[[Category:Articles with hCards[240]]]	?	Commander, Navy Cyber Forces	URL	2009	Currently on active duty.
75	Ann Claire Phillips[[Category:Articles with hCards[241]]]	1983 (ROTC)	Commander, Expeditionary Strike Group Two	Surface Warfare	2010	Retired.
76	Gretchen S. Herbert	1984 (ROTC)	Assistant Chief of Naval Operations, Next Generation Enterprise Network (NGEN)	URL	2010	Retired.
77	Margaret A. Rykowski	1987	Fleet Surgeon, Third Fleet	NNC	2010	Retired.
78	Sandra E. Adams[[Category:Articles with hCards[242]]]	1981 (OCS)	Deputy Commander, Naval Expeditionary Combat Command	URL (SWO)	2011	Currently on active duty.
79	Amie B. Andrews[[Category:Articles with hCards[243]]]	?? (ROTC)	Commander, Navy Recruiting Command	Navy Human Resources Officer	2011	Currently on active duty.
80	Cindy L. Jaynes[[Category:Articles with hCards[244]]]	1983 (OCS)	Program Executive Officer for Air ASW, Assault & Special Mission Programs, PEO(A)	AMDO	2011	Currently on active duty.

81	Christina M. Alvarado[[Category:Articles with hCards[245]]]	1988	Deputy Commander, Navy Medicine East	Nurse Corps	2013		Currently on active duty.
82	Babette Bolivar[[Category:Articles with hCards[246]]]		Commander, Navy Region Northwest	EOD	2013		Currently on active duty.
83	Priscilla B. Coe[[Category:Articles with hCards[247]]]		Deputy Chief of Staff, Bureau of Medicine and Surgery, Deputy Chief, Navy Reserve Dental Corps	Dental Corps	2013		Currently on active duty.
84	Lisa Franchetti[[Category:Articles with hCards[248]]]	1985 (NROTC)	Commander, U.S. Naval Forces Korea, Commander, U.S. Navy Region Korea	SWO	2013		Currently on active duty.
85	Alma M. Grocki[[Category:Articles with hCards[249]]]	1981 (USNA)	Deputy Chief of Staff for Fleet Maintenance, Commander, U.S. Pacific Fleet	Reserve EDO	2013		Currently serving.
86	Deborah P. Haven[[Category:Articles with hCards[250]]]		Commander, Defense Contract Management Agency International	Reserve Supply Corps	2013	2016	Currently serving.
87	Nancy A. Norton[[Category:Articles with hCards[251]]]	1987 (OCS)	Commander, Joint Forces Headquarters - Department of Defense Information Network (JFHQ-DODIN); Director of the Defense Information Agency (DISA)[252]	URL	2013	2018	Currently on active duty.

88	Barbara Sweredoski[[Category:Articles with hCards253]]	1985 (NROTC)	Reserve Deputy, Military Personnel Plans & Policy N13R	HR	2013	Currently serving.
89	Cynthia Thebaud[[Category:Articles with hCards250]]	1985 (USNA)	Commander, Logistics Group Western Pacific, Commander, Task Force 73, Singapore Area Coordinator	SWO	2013	Currently on active duty.
90	Dawn E. Cutler[[Category:Articles with hCards254]]	1989 (NROTC)	Chief of Information (CHINFO)	PAO	2016	Retired August 2017.
91	Danelle Barrett	1989 (NROTC)	Cyber Security Division Director/Deputy Department of the Navy Chief Information Officer	IDWO	2017	Currently on active duty.
92	Roseanne Roberts	1962	Helicopter captain, HC-3, Naval Air Force Pacific,	HC-3		Retired
93	Kelly Aeschbach[[Category:Articles with hCards255]]	19?? (NROTC)	Deputy Director of Intelligence, U.S. Forces Afghanistan/Assistant Deputy Chief of Staff for Intelligence, North Atlantic Treaty Organization Headquarters Resolute Support256			Currently on active duty.

References

 Wikimedia Commons has media related to *Women in the United States Navy*.

Further reading

- Godson, Susan H. (2001). *Serving Proudly: A History of Women in the U.S. Navy*. Annapolis, MD: Naval Institute Press. ISBN 1-55750-317-6.
- Ebbert, Jean and Marie-Beth Hall (1999). *Crossed Currents: Navy Women in a Century of Change [Third Edition, Revised and Updated]*. Washington, D.C.: Brassey's. ISBN 978-1-57488-193-6.
- Ebbert, Jean and Marie-Beth Hall (2002). *The First, the Few, the Forgotten: Navy and Marine Corps Women in World War I*. Annapolis, MD: The Naval Institute Press. ISBN 1-55750-203-X.
- Sterner, Doris M. (1997). *In and Out of Harm's Way: A history of the U.S. Navy Nurse Corps*. Seattle, WA: Peanut Butter Publishing. ISBN 0-89716-706-6.
- Hancock, Joy Bright Captain, U.S. Navy (Retired) (1972). *Lady in the Navy: A Personal Reminiscence*. Annapolis, MD: Naval Institute Press. ISBN 0-87021-336-9.
- Collins, Winifred Quick Captain, U.S. Navy (Retired); Levine, Herbert (1997). *More Than A Uniform: A Navy Woman in a Navy Man's World*. Denton, TX: University of North Texas Press. ISBN 1-57441-022-9.
- Holm, Jeanne Maj Gen, USAF (Ret) (1972). *Women in the Military: An Unfinished Revolution [Revised Edition]*. Novato, CA: Presidio Press. ISBN 0891414509.
- Zimmerman, Jean (1995). *Tailspin: Women at War in the Wake of Tailhook*. New York: Doubleday. ISBN 0-385-47789-9.

Bibliographies

- Women in the Navy[257], a bibliography compiled in 1998 by Diana Simpson, Bibliographer, Air University Library, Maxwell AFB.
- Women in the U.S. Navy: Bibliography and Sources[258] from the Naval Historical Center.
- 30 Years of Women at USNA[259], selected bibliography of resources available in the Naval Academy's Nimitz Library.
- Bibliography[260] on women in the military from the Women in Military Service for America (WIMSA) Memorial

External links

- Office of Women's Policy (N134W)[261] Bureau of Naval Personnel
- Sea Services Leadership Association[262] supporting motivated Sea Service officers since 1978. (Formerly Women Officers Professional Association.)
- Women Redefined[263] - a Facebook Page for Women in the Navy
- Women in the Navy Flickr Images[264]
- Navy For Moms Community[265]

Women in the United States Air Force

There have been **women in the United States Air Force** since 1948, and women continue to serve in it today.[266]

History

1940s

The National Security Act of 1947 made the Air Force a separate military service. That year, some Women's Army Corps (WACs) members continued serving in the Army but performed Air Force duties. In 1948 they were able to transfer to Women in the Air Force (called WAF), and some did. WAF was created in 1948 with the Women's Armed Services Integration Act, which gave women permanent status in the Regular and Reserve forces of the Air Force. Esther McGowin Blake was the first woman in the Air Force, having enlisted in the WAF the first minute of the first hour of the first day regular Air Force duty was authorized for women on July 8, 1948. The first commissioner of the WAF was Geraldine Pratt May, who was also the first Air Force woman to become a colonel.

Korean War

During the Korean War, medical air evacuation nurses were the only women in the Air Force allowed to serve in the Korean battle zone. Other women carried out support roles at rear-echelon bases in Japan, as air traffic controllers, weather observers, radar operators, and photo interpreters. By the end of the Korean War, 12,800 WAF officers and enlisted women were serving worldwide.

Figure 53: *Janet Wolfenbarger was the first female four-star general in the Air Force.*

Vietnam War

600 to 800 WAFs served in Southeast Asia during the Vietnam War. In addition to serving as nurses and medical evacuation personnel, WAFs also served in a variety of support staff assignments in hospitals, with MASH Units, in service clubs, in headquarters offices, and in intelligence, as well as in a variety of personnel positions. In 1967 Public Law 90-130 was signed into law; it removed legal ceilings on women's promotions that had kept them out of the general and flag ranks, and dropped the two percent ceiling on officer and enlisted strengths for women in the armed forces. In 1969 women were allowed to join the Air Force Reserve Officers Training Corps. In 1971 Jeanne M. Holm became the first female airman promoted to brigadier general.

Women in the Air Force since 1972

Frontiero v. Richardson, 411 U.S. 677[267] (1973), was a landmark Supreme Court case[268] which decided that benefits given by the military to the family of service members cannot be given out differently because of sex. Air Force Lieutenant Sharron Frontiero and her husband Joseph, a veteran and full-time student, were the plaintiffs.

Figure 54: *Esther McGowin Blake was the first woman in the Air Force, having enlisted in the WAF the first minute of the first hour of the first day regular Air Force duty was authorized for women on July 8, 1948.*

In 1976 the WAF was ended and women were allowed into the Air Force as equal members.

Also in 1976, the Air Force Academy first admitted women; in 1986, the Air Force Academy's top graduate was a woman for the first time (Terrie Ann McLaughlin).

Also in 1986, six Air Force women served as pilots, copilots, and boom operators on the KC-135 and KC-10 tankers that refueled FB-111s during the raid on Libya.

Women in the Air Force served in Operation Desert Shield (1990-1991) and Operation Desert Storm (1991).

Before the "Don't Ask Don't Tell" policy was enacted in 1993, lesbians and bisexual women (and gay men and bisexual men) were banned from serving in the military. In 1993 the "Don't Ask Don't Tell" policy was enacted, which mandated that the military could not ask servicemembers about their sexual orientation.[269,270] However, until the policy was ended in 2011 service members were still expelled from the military if they engaged in sexual conduct with a member of the same sex, stated that they were lesbian, gay, or bisexual, and/or married or attempted to marry someone of the same sex.[271]

Figure 55: *Captain Kim Campbell inspecting damage to her A-10 Thunderbolt II during the Iraq War in 2003*

On April 28, 1993, combat exclusion was lifted from aviation positions by Les Aspin, permitting women to serve in almost any aviation capacity.

Also in 1993, Sheila Widnall became the first female Secretary of the Air Force, making her the first woman to lead a U.S. military branch in the Department of Defense.

In 1994, the Pentagon declared:

> *Service members are eligible to be assigned to all positions for which they are qualified, except that women shall be excluded from assignment to units below the brigade level whose primary mission is to engage in direct combat on the ground.*

That policy also excluded women being assigned to certain organizations based upon proximity to direct combat or "collocation" as the policy specifically referred to it. According to the Army, collocation occurs when, "the position or unit routinely physically locates and remains with a military unit assigned a doctrinal mission to routinely engage in direct combat."

Kelly Flinn, sometimes referred to as Kelly Flynn, was the first female B-52 pilot in the Air Force, but was discharged from the Air Force in 1997 after an adulterous affair with the husband of an enlisted subordinate, for military offenses including disobeying a direct order from her commanding officer to break off the affair, and for lying to him about having done so. Flinn's trouble with the Air Force received widespread media attention at the time and was discussed in a Senate hearing on May 22, 1997.

Women in the Air Force served in the Afghanistan War from 2001 until 2014, and in the Iraq War from 2003 until 2011.

The Air Force Academy sexual assault scandal in 2003 involved allegations of sexual assault at the Air Force Academy, as well as allegations that the alleged incidents had been ignored by the Academy's leadership.

The United States Air Force Basic Training scandal involved 43 female trainees who alleged being victimized by their Military Training Instructors during and after basic military training starting from 2009. Seventeen male instructors were accused of offenses ranging from seeking improper relationships to rape and 35 instructors were removed from their posts pending investigations. Nine of the accused instructors belonged to the 331st Training Squadron. The commander of the 331st Training Squadron, Lt. Col. Mike Paquette, was removed from command in June 2012 because of the problems in his unit. In August 2012 the commander of the 737th training group, Col. Glenn Palmer, was also relieved from his position due to the scandal.

In 2012 Janet Wolfenbarger became the Air Force's first female four-star general.

In 2013 Defense Secretary Leon Panetta removed the military's ban on women serving in combat, overturning the 1994 rule. Panetta's decision gave the military services until January 2016 to seek special exceptions if they believed any positions must remain closed to women. The services had until May 2013 to draw up a plan for opening all units to women and until the end of 2015 to actually implement it.

In December 2015, Defense Secretary Ash Carter stated that starting in 2016 all combat jobs would open to women.

In March 2016, Ash Carter approved final plans from military service branches and the U.S. Special Operations Command to open all combat jobs to women, and authorized the military to begin integrating female combat soldiers "right away."

It was announced on June 30, 2016 that, beginning on that date, otherwise qualified United States service members could not any longer be discharged, denied reenlistment, involuntarily separated, or denied continuation of service because of being transgender (including but not limited to transgender women). Beginning on January 1, 2018, openly transgender people (including but not limited to transgender women) were allowed to join the military.

References

 Wikimedia Commons has media related to *Women in the United States Air Force*.

Women in the United States Coast Guard

There have been **women in the United States Coast Guard** since 1918, and women continue to serve in it today.[272]

History

World War I

In 1918, twin sisters Genevieve and Lucille Baker of the Naval Coastal Defense Reserve became the first uniformed women to serve in the Coast Guard.

World War II

On November 23, 1942, the Coast Guard Women's Reserve, nicknamed SPARS or SPARs, was created with the signing of Public Law 773 by President Franklin Delano Roosevelt.[273] Dorothy Stratton transferred from the Navy WAVES to serve as the Reserve's director. Dorothy Tuttle was the first woman to enlist in the Coast Guard Women's Reserve, and in all 11,868 enlisted women and 978 female officers served in it during World War II. After the war, the Coast Guard Women's Reserve was ended in 1947 but recreated in a smaller form in 1949.

Korean War era

Approximately 200 women who had been in the Coast Guard Women's Reserve reenlisted and served during the Korean War. They mostly served at the Coast Guard Headquarters in Washington, D.C.

Vietnam War

The Vietnam War gave the Coast Guard a surplus of qualified male applicants, and the Coast Guard did not make a systematic effort to attract women during that time.[274]

Women in the Coast Guard since 1972

Frontiero v. Richardson, 411 U.S. 677[275] (1973), was a landmark Supreme Court case which decided that benefits given by the military to the family of service members cannot be given out differently because of sex.[276]

In 1974 the Coast Guard Women's Reserve was ended and women became part of the regular Coast Guard.

In 1976 the Coast Guard Academy first admitted women; in 1985 the Coast Guard Academy's top graduate was a woman for the first time.

In 1977 the first Coast Guard women were assigned to sea duty as crew members aboard *Morgenthau* and *Gallatin*.

In 1978 the Coast Guard opened all assignments to women.

In 1979 LTJG Beverly G. Kelley became the first female commanding officer afloat in U.S. history when she took command of USCGC *Cape Newagen*.

Women in the Coast Guard served in Operation Desert Shield (1990-1991) and Operation Desert Storm (1991).

In 1993 Patricia A. Stolle became the first woman in the Coast Guard to advance to Master Chief Petty Officer.[277]

Women in the Coast Guard also served in the Afghanistan War from 2001 until 2014, and in the Iraq War from 2003 until 2011.

In 2011 Sandra Stosz was chosen by the Commandant of the United States Coast Guard, ADM Robert J. Papp to become the superintendent of the Coast Guard Academy. As such, she was the first woman to lead a United States military service academy.

Notes

Footnotes

Citations

 Wikimedia Commons has media related to *Women in the United States Coast Guard*.

References used

<templatestyles src="Template:Refbegin/styles.css" />

- "Women's History Chronology"[278]. *Women & the U. S. Coast Guard*. U.S. Coast Guard Historian's Office. Retrieved 16 August 2015.

Five Star Rank

Five-star rank

A **five-star rank** is a very senior military rank, first established in the United States in 1944, with a five-star general insignia,[279] and corresponding ranks in other countries. The rank is that of the most senior operational military commanders, and within NATO's "standard rank scale" it is designated by the code OF-10.

Not all armed forces have such a rank, and in those that do the actual insignia of the "five-star ranks" may not contain five stars. For example: the insignia for the French OF-10 rank *maréchal de France* contains 7 stars; the insignia for the Portuguese *marechal* contains four gold stars; and many of the insignia of the ranks in Commonwealth of Nations contain no stars at all.

Typically, five-star officers hold the rank of general of the army, admiral of the fleet, field marshal, marshal or general of the air force, and several other similarly named ranks. Five-star ranks are extremely senior—usually the highest ranks. As an active rank, the position exists only in a minority of countries and is usually held by only a very few officers during wartime. In times of peace, it is usually held only as an honorary rank. Traditionally, five-star ranks are granted to distinguished military commanders for notable wartime victories and/or in recognition of a record of achievement during the officer's career, whether in peace or in war. Alternatively, a five-star rank (or even higher ranks) may be assumed by heads of state in their capacities as commanders-in-chief of their nation's armed forces.

Despite the rarity and seniority of five-star officers, even more senior ranks have been adopted in the United States, namely, admiral of the navy and general of the armies. Other names for highly senior ranks from the twentieth century include *généralissime* (France), *generalisimo* (Spain) and *generalissimus* (USSR).

Figure 56: *The insignia used by US generals and admirals of OF-10 rank.*

Australian five-star ranks

- Admiral of the fleet[280]
- Field marshal
- Marshal of the Royal Australian Air Force

Only one Australian born officer (Sir Thomas Blamey) has held a substantive Australian five-star rank (field marshal).[281] HM King George VI and HRH Prince Philip, Duke of Edinburgh have held all three Australian five-star ranks in an honorary capacity, and have been the only holders of the Australian ranks of admiral of the fleet and marshal of the RAAF.

Figure 57: *Australian Army Field Marshal shoulder board*

Figure 58: *RAN Admiral of the Fleet shoulder board*

Figure 59: *Marshal of the RAAF sleeve/shoulder insignia*

Brazilian five-star ranks

Five-star ranks in Brazil are only used in wartime.

- Marshal (Brazil) (*Marechal*)
- Grand Admiral (*Almirante*)
- Marshal of the Air (*Marechal-do-Ar*)

Figure 60: *Almirante*

Figure 61: *Marechal*

Figure 62: *Marechal-do-Ar*

Croatian five-star ranks

- *Stožerni general* (lit. "staff general", usually translated as general of the army) awarded to six men, none of whom are in active duty.
- *Admiral flote* (admiral of the fleet). The rank was called *stožerni admiral* (lit. "staff admiral") until 1999; only Sveto Letica was awarded this rank – in March 1996, three months before his retirement.

Figure 63: *Croatian Armed Forces (stožerni general) insignia*

Figure 65: *Flag used on the official car of Marshal of the Air Force in India. It has five stars on it.*

Figure 64: *Croatian Navy (admiral flote) insignia*

Indian five-star ranks

- Admiral of the fleet, never been held
- Field marshal, held by K. M. Cariappa and Sam Manekshaw

- Marshal of the Air Force, held by Arjan Singh

Figure 66: *Field marshal epaulette*

Figure 67: *Marshal of the Indian Air Force shoulder insignia*

Figure 68: *Marshal of the Indian Air Force sleeve insignia*

Around 1998, the Indian Air Force introduced gorget patches (or collar tabs) for its air officers. For marshals of the Indian Air Force, the patches display five stars.[282]

Indonesian five-star ranks

The Indonesian five star ranks are:

- *Jenderal besar* (grand general) - only held by three people: Jenderal Besar Soedirman, Jenderal Besar Abdul Haris Nasution, Jenderal Besar Soeharto (2nd President of Indonesia)
- *Laksamana besar* (grand admiral) - never awarded
- *Marsekal besar* (grand marshal) - never awarded

Figure 69: *Jenderal besar rank insignia*

Figure 70: *Laksamana besar rank insignia*

Figure 71: *Marsekal besar rank insignia*

Italian five-star ranks

Figure 72: *General of the Italian Army - shoulder board*

Five-star rank

Figure 73: *Admiral of the Italian Navy - sleeve*

Figure 74: *General of the Italian Air Force - sleeve*

Pakistani five-star ranks

- Field marshal (Pakistan Army five-star rank), Ayub Khan

The following ranks have never been awarded:

- Admiral of the fleet
- Marshal of the Pakistan Air Force

Polish five-star ranks

Marshal of Poland (*Marszałek Polski*) is a Polish Army five-star rank. There are today no living marshals of Poland, since this rank is bestowed only on military commanders who have achieved victory in war.

Figure 75: *Marshal of Poland cap insignia*

Figure 76: *Marshal of Poland shoulder-strap insignia*

Spanish five-star ranks

- Captain general (Army)
- Captain general of the Navy
- Air captain general (Air Force)

These ranks have been reserved for the reigning monarch.

Figure 77: *Capitán general ("Captain general") shoulder board*

Figure 78: *Capitán general de la Armada ("Captain general of the Navy") shoulder board and sleeve*

Figure 79: *Capitán general del Aire ("Air captain general") shoulder board and sleeve*

Thai five-star ranks

- Chom Phon (Thai: จอมพล), Royal Thai Army
- Chom Phon Ruea (Thai: จอมพลเรือ), Royal Thai Navy
- Chom Phon Akat (Thai: จอมพลอากาศ), Royal Thai Air Force

Figure 80: *Chom Phon (Field Marshal)*

Figure 81: *Chom Phon Ruea (Admiral of the Fleet)*

Figure 82: *Chom Phon Akat (Marshal of the Royal Thai Air Force)*

The monarch of Thailand is appointed to the three ranks automatically upon accession as he is the constitutional Head of the Royal Thai Armed Forces. Since 1973 the three ranks have been reserved for members of the royal family.

UK five-star ranks

The worn insignia of British five-star commanders do not contain stars; the vehicle star plate, mounted on the front of a staff car, does display five stars.[283]

- Admiral of the fleet (awarded to 121 men to date)
- Field Marshal (awarded to 140 men to date)
- Marshal of the Royal Air Force (awarded to 27 men to date)

- Captain General of the Royal Marines (awarded to five members of the English Royal Family, currently held by Prince Harry, Duke of Sussex)

Figure 83: *Royal Navy Admiral of the Fleet shoulder board*

Figure 84: *Royal Navy Admiral of the Fleet sleeve lace*

Figure 85: *Field Marshal Army epaulette*

Figure 86: *Captain General of the Royal Marines epaulette*

Figure 87: *Marshal of the RAF shoulder board*

Figure 88: *Marshal of the RAF sleeve insignia*

Promotion to the ranks of Admiral of the Fleet and Marshal of the Royal Air Force is now generally held in abeyance in peacetime with exceptions for special circumstances. Promotion to the rank of Field Marshal was generally stopped in 1995 as a cost-cutting measure but is still made in some cases. The most recent appointments to five-star ranks are the promotions in 2012 of The Prince of Wales to honourary five-star rank in all three services, and of former Chief of the Defence Staff Lord Guthrie of Craigiebank to the honorary rank of Field Marshal. In 2014 the former Chief of the Defence Staff Lord Stirrup was promoted to the honourary rank of Marshal of the Royal Air Force.

During World War II and after, serving NATO, a small number of British five-star commanders have held the additional title Supreme Allied Commander, given operational control over all air, land, and sea units led by the four-star commanders of multi-national forces.

U.S. five-star ranks

- Fleet Admiral (held by four officers)
- General of the Army (held by five officers)
- General of the Air Force (held by one officer)

Before the five-star ranks were established in 1944, two officers had previously been promoted from their four-star ranks to the superior and unique ranks of Admiral of the Navy and General of the Armies: Admiral George Dewey (appointment 1903 retroactive to 1899, died 1917) and General John J. Pershing (appointed 1919, died 1948). In 1944 the Navy and Army specified that these officers were considered senior to any officers promoted to the five-star ranks within their services (but it was not clear if they were senior by rank or by seniority due to an earlier date of rank).

Five-star ranks were created in the US military during World War II because of the awkward situation created when some American senior commanders were placed in positions commanding allied officers of higher rank. US officers holding five-star rank never retire; they draw full active duty pay for life. The five-star ranks were retired in 1981 on the death of General of the Army Omar Bradley.

Nine Americans have been promoted to five-star rank, one of them, Henry H. Arnold, in two services (US Army then later in the US Air Force). As part of the bicentennial celebration, George Washington was, 177 years after his death, permanently made senior to all other US generals and admirals with the title *General of the Armies* effective on 4 July 1976. The appointment stated he was to have "rank and precedence over all other grades of the Army, past or present".[284]

During World War II and (later) serving NATO, a small number of American five-star commanders have also held the additional title of Supreme Allied Commander, given operational control over all air, land, and sea units led by the four-star commanders of multi-national forces.

Figure 89: *Fleet admiral collar device, sleeve stripes and shoulder board*

Figure 90: *General of the Army shoulder strap*

Figure 91: *General of the Air Force shoulder epaulet*

Unified Combatant Commands

Unified combatant command

A **unified combatant command** (**UCC**) is a United States Department of Defense command that is composed of forces from at least two Military Departments and has a broad and continuing mission.[285] These commands are established to provide effective command and control of U.S. military forces, regardless of branch of service, in peace and war.[286] They are organized either on a geographical basis (known as "area of responsibility", AOR) or on a functional basis, such as special operations, power projection, or transport. UCCs are "joint" commands with specific badges denoting their affiliation.

The creation and organization of the unified combatant commands is legally mandated in Title 10, U.S. Code Sections 161–168.

The **Unified Command Plan** (**UCP**) establishes the missions, command responsibilities, and geographic areas of responsibility of the unified combatant commands.[287] As of May 2018, there are ten unified combatant commands. Six have regional responsibilities, and four have functional responsibilities. Each time the Unified Command Plan is updated, the organization of the combatant commands is reviewed for military efficiency and efficacy, as well as alignment with national policy.

Each unified command is led by a **combatant commander** (**CCDR**),[288] who is a four-star general or admiral. CCDRs exercise combatant command (COCOM),[289] a specific type of nontransferable command authority over assigned forces, regardless of branch of service, that is vested only in the CCDRs by federal law in 10 U.S.C. § 164[290].[291] The chain of command for operational purposes (per the Goldwater–Nichols Act) goes from the President through the Secretary of Defense to the combatant commanders.

Figure 92: *President George W. Bush and Secretary of Defense Robert Gates meeting with the joint chiefs and combatant commanders*

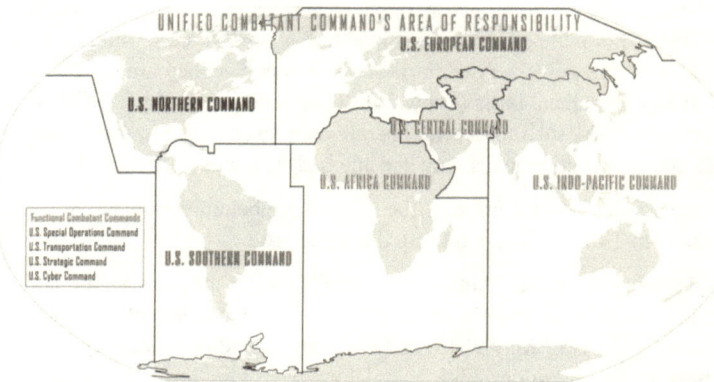

Figure 93: *Geographic Combatant Command Areas of Responsibility*

Geographic combatant commands

† Three geographic combatant commands have their headquarters located outside their geographic area of responsibility.

Emblem	Command	Acronym	Established	Headquarters

Emblem	Command	Acronym	Established	Headquarters
	United States Africa Command	USAFRICOM	October 1, 2007	Kelley Barracks, Stuttgart, Germany †
	United States Central Command	USCENTCOM	January 1, 1983	MacDill Air Force Base, Florida †
	United States European Command	USEUCOM	August 1, 1952	Patch Barracks, Stuttgart, Germany
	United States Indo-Pacific Command	USINDOPACOM	January 1, 1947	Camp H. M. Smith, Hawaii
	United States Northern Command	USNORTHCOM	October 1, 2002	Peterson Air Force Base, Colorado
	United States Southern Command	USSOUTHCOM	June 6, 1963	Doral, Florida †

Functional combatant commands

Emblem	Command	Acronym	Established	Headquarters
	United States Cyber Command	USCYBERCOM	May 4, 2018	Fort George G. Meade, Maryland
	United States Special Operations Command	USSOCOM	April 16, 1987	MacDill Air Force Base, Florida
	United States Strategic Command	USSTRATCOM	June 1, 1992	Offutt Air Force Base, Nebraska
	United States Transportation Command	USTRANSCOM	July 1, 1987	Scott Air Force Base, Illinois

History

The current system of unified commands in the US military emerged during World War II with the establishment of geographic theaters of operation composed of forces from multiple service branches that reported to a single commander who was supported by a joint staff.[292] A unified command structure also existed to coordinate British and American military forces operating under the Combined Chiefs of Staff, which was composed of the British Chiefs of Staff Committee and the American Joint Chiefs of Staff.[293] In the European Theater, Allied military forces fell under the command of the Supreme Headquarters Allied Expeditionary Force (SHAEF). After SHAEF was dissolved at the end of the war, the American forces were unified under a single command, the US Forces, European Theater (USFET), commanded by General of the Army Dwight D. Eisenhower. Unified commands in the Pacific Theater proved more difficult to organize as neither General of the Army Douglas MacArthur nor Fleet Admiral Chester W. Nimitz was willing to become subordinate to the other.

The Joint Chiefs of Staff continued to advocate in favor of establishing permanent unified commands, and President Harry S. Truman approved the first plan on 14 December 1946.[294] Known as the "Outline Command Plan," it would become the first in a series of Unified Command Plans.Wikipedia:Citation needed The original "Outline Command Plan" of 1946 established seven unified commands: Far East Command, Pacific Command, Alaskan Command, Northeast Command, the U.S. Atlantic Fleet, Caribbean Command, and European Command. However, on 5 August 1947, the CNO recommended instead that CINCLANTFLT be established as a fully unified commander under the broader title of Commander in Chief, Atlantic (CINCLANT). The Army and Air Force objected, and CINCLANTFLT was activated as a unified command on 1 November 1947. A few days later, the CNO renewed his suggestion for the establishment of a unified Atlantic Command. This time his colleagues withdrew their objections, and on 1 December 1947, the U.S. Atlantic Command (LANTCOM) was created under the Commander in Chief, Atlantic (CINCLANT).[295]

Under the original plan, each of the unified commands operated with one of the service chiefs (the Chief of Staff of the Army or Air Force, or the Chief of Naval Operations) serving as an executive agent representing the Joint Chiefs of Staff.[296] This arrangement was formalized on 21 April 1948 as part of a policy paper titled the "Function of the Armed Forces and the Joint Chiefs of Staff" (informally known as the "Key West Agreement").[297] The responsibilities of the unified commands were further expanded on 7 September 1948 when the commanders' authority was extended to include the coordination of the administrative and logistical functions in addition to their combat responsibilities.[298]

Far East Command and U.S. Northeast Command were disestablished under the Unified Command Plan of 1956–57.

A 1958 "reorganization in National Command Authority relations with the joint commands" with a "direct channel" to unified commands such as Continental Air Defense Command (CONAD) was effected after President Dwight Eisenhower expressed concernWikipedia:Citing sources about nuclear command and control. CONAD itself was disestablished in 1975.

Although not part of the original plan, the Joint Chiefs of Staff also created specified commands that had broad and continuing missions but were composed of forces from only one service.[299] Examples include the U.S. Naval Forces, Eastern Atlantic and Mediterranean and the U.S. Air Force's Strategic Air Command. Like the unified commands, the specified commands reported directly to the JCS instead of their respective service chiefs.[300] These commands have not existed since the Strategic Air Command was disestablished in 1992. The relevant section of federal law, however, remains unchanged, and the President retains the power to establish a new specified command.[301]

The Goldwater–Nichols Defense Reorganization Act of 1986 clarified and codified responsibilities that commanders-in-chief (CINCs) undertook, and which were first given legal status in 1947. After that act, CINCs reported directly to the United States Secretary of Defense, and through him to the President of the United States.

The U.S. Atlantic Command became the Joint Forces Command in the 1990s after the Soviet threat to the North Atlantic had disappeared and the need rose for an integrating and experimentation command for forces in the continental United States. The Joint Forces Command was disbanded on 3 August 2011 and its components placed under the Joint Staff and other combatant commands.

On 24 October 2002, Secretary of Defense Donald H. Rumsfeld announced that in accordance with Title 10 of the US Code (USC), the title of "Commander-in-Chief" would thereafter be reserved for the President, consistent with the terms of Article II of the United States Constitution. Thereafter, the military CINCs would be known as "combatant commanders", as heads of the unified combatant commands.

A sixth geographical unified command, United States Africa Command (US-AFRICOM), was approved and established in 2007 for Africa. It operated under U.S. European Command during its first year, and transitioned to independent Unified Command Status in October 2008. In 2009, it focused on synchronizing hundreds of activities inherited from three regional commands that previously coordinated U.S. military relations in Africa.[302]

President Donald Trump announced on 18 August 2017 that the United States Cyber Command (USCYBERCOM) would be elevated to the status of a unified combatant command from a sub-unified command. It was also announced that the separation of the command from the NSA would be considered. USCYBERCOM was elevated on 4 May 2018.

Sub-unified combatant commands

A sub-unified command, or, subordinate unified command, may be established by combatant commanders when authorized to do so by the Secretary of Defense or the president.[303] They are created to conduct a portion of the mission or tasking of their parent geographic or functional command. Sub-unified commands may be either functional or geographic, and the commanders of sub-unified commands exercise authority similar to that of combatant commanders.

Examples of current and former sub-unified commands are the Alaskan Command (ALCOM) under USNORTHCOM, the United States Forces Korea (USFK) under USINDOPACOM, and United States Forces – Afghanistan (USFOR-A) under USCENTCOM.

Combatant commanders

Each CCMD is headed by a four-star general or admiral recommended by the Secretary of Defense, nominated for appointment by the President of the United States, confirmed by the Senate and commissioned, at the President's order, by the Secretary of Defense. The Goldwater–Nichols Act and its subsequent implementation legislation also resulted in specific Joint Professional Military Education (JPME) requirements for officers before they could attain flag or general officer rank thereby preparing them for duty in Joint assignments such as UCC staff or Joint Chiefs of Staff assignments, which are strictly controlled tour length rotations of duty. However, in the decades following enactment of Goldwater–Nichols, these JPME requirements have yet to come to overall fruition. This is particularly true in the case of senior naval officers, where sea duty/shore duty rotations and the culture of the naval service has often discounted PME and JPME as a measure of professional development for success. Although slowly changing, the JPME requirement still continues to be frequently waived in the case of senior admirals nominated for these positions.[304]

The operational chain of command runs from the President to the Secretary of Defense to the combatant commanders of the combatant commands. The Chairman of the Joint Chiefs of Staff may transmit communications to the Commanders of the combatant commands from the President and Secretary of Defense and advises both on potential courses of action, but the Chairman does not exercise military command over any combatant forces. Under Goldwater–Nichols, the service chiefs (also four stars in rank) are charged with the responsibility of the "strategic direction, unified operation of combatant commands, and the integration of all land, naval, and air forces in an efficient "unified combatant command" force. Furthermore, the Secretaries of the Military Departments (i.e. Secretary of the Army, Secretary of the Navy, and the Secretary of the Air Force) are legally responsible to "organize, train and equip" combatant forces and, as directed by the Secretary of Defense, assign their forces for use by the combatant commands. The Secretaries of the Military Departments also do not exercise any operational control over their forces.Wikipedia:Citation needed

Each combatant command can be led by a general or flag officer from any of the military services. Most commands have traditional service affiliations, USTRANSCOM, which has always been commanded by an Air Force general, being the prime example. In recent years, though, non-traditional appointments have become more common. EUCOM was traditionally an Army command with USAF generals on occasion, but was held by a Marine from 2003 through 2006. CENTCOM was traditionally an Army and Marine command but William J. Fallon, commander from 2007 through 2008, was a Navy admiral. PACOM (now INDOPACOM) has always been commanded by a Navy admiral due to the wide expanse of ocean, although Air Force generals have been nominated for the post. U.S. Atlantic Command (USACOM) was also a traditional Navy assignment until it was successively commanded by Marine, Army, and Air Force generals, thereby becoming the first to have had commanders from all four services (USACOM was redesignated as JFCOM in 1999).[305] CENTCOM and SOUTHCOM were traditionally Army general positions until the Marines received their first CCDR assignments. This led the way for General Pace to become the first Marine Vice Chairman of the Joint Chiefs of Staff and ultimately Chairman of the Joint Chiefs of Staff. CCDRs are strong candidates for either position.Wikipedia:Citation needed The two newest commands, AFRICOM and NORTHCOM, have had the fewest number of commanders, with all of AFRICOM's being Army until 2016, when General Thomas D. Waldhauser took command, and NORTHCOM's alternating between the Air Force and Navy, until its first Army commander, General Charles H. Jacoby Jr., took command in August 2011.

UCC area coverage by country

Command	Country name	Country code[306]
USCENTCOM	Afghanistan	AF
USEUCOM	Albania	AL
USAFRICOM	Algeria	DZ
USEUCOM	Andorra	AD
USAFRICOM	Angola	AO
USINDOPACOM	Antarctica	AQ
USSOUTHCOM	Antigua and Barbuda	AG
USSOUTHCOM	Argentina	AR
USEUCOM	Armenia	AM
USSOUTHCOM	Aruba	AW
USINDOPACOM	Australia	AU
USEUCOM	Austria	AT
USEUCOM	Azerbaijan	AZ
USNORTHCOM	Bahamas	BS
USCENTCOM	Bahrain	BH
USINDOPACOM	Bangladesh	BD
USSOUTHCOM	Barbados	BB
USEUCOM	Belarus	BY
USEUCOM	Belgium	BE
USSOUTHCOM	Belize	BZ
USAFRICOM	Benin	BJ
USNORTHCOM	Bermuda	BM
USINDOPACOM	Bhutan	BT
USSOUTHCOM	Bolivia	BO
USAFRICOM	Botswana	BW
USEUCOM	Bosnia and Herzegovina	BA
USSOUTHCOM	Brazil	BR
USNORTHCOM	British Virgin Islands	VG
USINDOPACOM	Brunei	BN
USEUCOM	Bulgaria	BG
USAFRICOM	Burkina Faso	BF
USINDOPACOM	Burma	BU
USAFRICOM	Burundi	BI
USINDOPACOM	Cambodia	KH

USAFRICOM	Cameroon	CM
USNORTHCOM	Canada	CA
USAFRICOM	Cape Verde	CV
USSOUTHCOM	Cayman Islands	KY
USAFRICOM	Central African Republic	CF
USAFRICOM	Chad	TD
USSOUTHCOM	Chile	CL
USINDOPACOM	China	CN
USSOUTHCOM	Colombia	CO
USAFRICOM	Comoros	KM
USSOUTHCOM	Costa Rica	CR
USEUCOM	Croatia	HR
USSOUTHCOM	Cuba	CU
USSOUTHCOM	Curacao	CW
USEUCOM	Cyprus	CY
USEUCOM	Czech Republic	CZ
USAFRICOM	Democratic Republic of the Congo	CD
USEUCOM	Denmark	DK
USAFRICOM	Djibouti	DJ
USSOUTHCOM	Dominica	DM
USSOUTHCOM	Dominican Republic	DO
USSOUTHCOM	Ecuador	EC
USCENTCOM	Egypt	EG
USSOUTHCOM	El Salvador	SV
USAFRICOM	Equatorial Guinea	GQ
USAFRICOM	Eritrea	ER
USEUCOM	Estonia	EE
USAFRICOM	Ethiopia	ET
USINDOPACOM	Fiji	FJ
USEUCOM	Finland	FI
USEUCOM	France	FR
USAFRICOM	Gabon	GA
USAFRICOM	Gambia	GM
USEUCOM	Georgia	GE
USEUCOM	Germany	DE
USAFRICOM	Ghana	GH
USEUCOM	Greece	GR

USSOUTHCOM	Grenada	GD
USSOUTHCOM	Guatemala	GT
USAFRICOM	Guinea	GN
USAFRICOM	Guinea-Bissau	GW
USSOUTHCOM	Guyana	GY
USSOUTHCOM	Haiti	HT
USEUCOM	Holy See (The Vatican)	VA
USSOUTHCOM	Honduras	HN
USEUCOM	Hungary	HU
USEUCOM	Iceland	IS
USINDOPACOM	India	IN
USINDOPACOM	Indonesia	ID
USCENTCOM	Iran	IR
USCENTCOM	Iraq	IQ
USEUCOM	Ireland	IE
USEUCOM	Israel	IL
USEUCOM	Italy	IT
USAFRICOM	Ivory Coast	CI
USSOUTHCOM	Jamaica	JM
USINDOPACOM	Japan	JP
USCENTCOM	Jordan	JO
USCENTCOM	Kazakhstan	KZ
USAFRICOM	Kenya	KE
USINDOPACOM	Kiribati	KI
USEUCOM	Kosovo	XK
USCENTCOM	Kuwait	KW
USCENTCOM	Kyrgyzstan	KG
USINDOPACOM	Laos	LA
USEUCOM	Latvia	LV
USCENTCOM	Lebanon	LB
USAFRICOM	Lesotho	LS
USAFRICOM	Liberia	LR
USAFRICOM	Libya	LY
USEUCOM	Liechtenstein	LI
USEUCOM	Lithuania	LT
USEUCOM	Luxembourg	LU
USEUCOM	Macedonia	MK

USAFRICOM	Madagascar	MG
USAFRICOM	Malawi	MW
USINDOPACOM	Malaysia	MY
USINDOPACOM	Maldives	MV
USAFRICOM	Mali	ML
USEUCOM	Malta	MT
USINDOPACOM	Marshall Islands	MH
USAFRICOM	Mauritania	MR
USAFRICOM	Mauritius	MU
USAFRICOM	Mayotte	YT
USNORTHCOM	Mexico	MX
USINDOPACOM	Micronesia	FM
USEUCOM	Moldova	MD
USEUCOM	Monaco	MC
USINDOPACOM	Mongolia	MN
USEUCOM	Montenegro	ME
USAFRICOM	Morocco	MA
USAFRICOM	Mozambique	MZ
USINDOPACOM	Myanmar	MM
USAFRICOM	Namibia	NA
USINDOPACOM	Nauru	NR
USINDOPACOM	Nepal	NP
USEUCOM	Netherlands	NL
USINDOPACOM	New Zealand	NZ
USSOUTHCOM	Nicaragua	NI
USAFRICOM	Niger	NE
USAFRICOM	Nigeria	NG
USINDOPACOM	North Korea	KP
USEUCOM	Norway	NO
USCENTCOM	Oman	OM
USCENTCOM	Pakistan	PK
USINDOPACOM	Palau	PW
USSOUTHCOM	Panama	PA
USINDOPACOM	Papua New Guinea	PG
USSOUTHCOM	Paraguay	PY
USSOUTHCOM	Peru	PE
USINDOPACOM	Philippines	PH

USEUCOM	Poland	PL
USEUCOM	Portugal	PT
USCENTCOM	Qatar	QA
USAFRICOM	Republic of the Congo	CG
USAFRICOM	Réunion	RE
USEUCOM	Romania	RO
USEUCOM	Russia	RU
USAFRICOM	Rwanda	RW
USAFRICOM	Saint Helena, Ascension and Tristan da Cunha	SH
USSOUTHCOM	Saint Kitts and Nevis	KN
USSOUTHCOM	Saint Lucia	LC
USNORTHCOM	Saint Pierre and Miquelon	PM
USSOUTHCOM	Saint Vincent and the Grenadines	VC
USINDOPACOM	Samoa	WS
USEUCOM	San Marino	SM
USAFRICOM	Sao Tome and Principe	ST
USCENTCOM	Saudi Arabia	SA
USAFRICOM	Senegal	SN
USEUCOM	Serbia	RS
USAFRICOM	Seychelles	SC
USAFRICOM	Sierra Leone	SL
USINDOPACOM	Singapore	SG
USEUCOM	Slovakia	SK
USEUCOM	Slovenia	SI
USINDOPACOM	Solomon Islands	SB
USAFRICOM	Somalia	SO
USAFRICOM	South Africa	ZA
USINDOPACOM	South Korea	KR
USAFRICOM	South Sudan	SS
USEUCOM	Spain	ES
USINDOPACOM	Sri Lanka	LK
USAFRICOM	Sudan	SD
USSOUTHCOM	Suriname	SR
USAFRICOM	Swaziland	SZ
USEUCOM	Sweden	SE
USEUCOM	Switzerland	CH
USCENTCOM	Syria	SY

USINDOPACOM	Taiwan	TW
USCENTCOM	Tajikistan	TJ
USAFRICOM	Tanzania	TZ
USINDOPACOM	Thailand	TH
USINDOPACOM	Timor-Leste	TL
USAFRICOM	Togo	TG
USINDOPACOM	Tonga	TO
USSOUTHCOM	Trinidad and Tobago	TT
USAFRICOM	Tunisia	TN
USEUCOM	Turkey	TR
USCENTCOM	Turkmenistan	TM
USNORTHCOM	Turks & Caicos Islands	TC
USINDOPACOM	Tuvalu	TV
USAFRICOM	Uganda	UG
USEUCOM	Ukraine	UA
USCENTCOM	United Arab Emirates	AE
USEUCOM	United Kingdom	GB
USNORTHCOM	United States	US
USSOUTHCOM	Uruguay	UY
USCENTCOM	Uzbekistan	UZ
USINDOPACOM	Vanuatu	VU
USSOUTHCOM	Venezuela	VE
USINDOPACOM	Vietnam	VN
USAFRICOM	Western Sahara	EH
USCENTCOM	Yemen	YE
USAFRICOM	Zambia	ZM
USAFRICOM	Zimbabwe	ZW

References

- 10 U.S.C. § 161.[307]
- "AFRICOM FAQs"[308]. United States Africa Command. Archived from the original[309] on 21 April 2010. Retrieved 27 August 2010.
- "DefenseLINK - Unified Command Plan"[310]. United States Department of Defense. Retrieved 15 January 2009.
- Holder, Leonard; Murray, Williamson (Spring 1998), "Prospects for Military Education"[311], *Joint Force Quarterly*, **18**

- Joint Chiefs of Staff (20 December 1977). "History of the Unified Command Plan, 1946-1977"[312] (PDF). Archived from the original[313] (PDF) on 28 May 2010. Retrieved 21 August 2010.
- Joint Chiefs of Staff (July 1985). "History of the Unified Command Plan, 1977-1983"[314] (PDF). Archived from the original[315] (PDF) on 28 May 2010. Retrieved 21 August 2010.
- "Joint Publication 1, Doctrine for the Armed Forces of the United States"[316] (PDF). Joint Chiefs of Staff. 20 March 2009. Archived from the original[317] (PDF) on 27 October 2011. Retrieved 22 August 2009.
- "Joint Publication 1-02, Department of Defense Dictionary of Military and Associated Terms"[318] (PDF). Joint Chiefs of Staff. 31 January 2011. Retrieved 24 March 2011.
- "Joint Warfighting Center History"[319]. United States Joint Forces Command. Archived from the original[320] on 8 December 2006. Retrieved 6 February 2007.
- "Specified Command"[321]. *Naval Advancement*. Retrieved 21 August 2016.
- Story, William C. (21 June 1999). "Military Changes to the Unified Command Plan: Background and Issues for Congress"[322] (PDF). Congressional Research Service. Retrieved 22 August 2010.
- "US Creating New Africa Command To Coordinate Military Efforts"[323]. United States Department of State. Archived from the original[324] on 21 October 2012. Retrieved 12 August 2013.
- "U.S. Central Command Area of Responsibility Countries"[325]. USCENTCOM. Archived from the original[326] on 8 August 2013. Retrieved 12 August 2013.
- "The Region EUCOM, Stronger Together"[327]. USEUCOM. Archived from the original[328] on 23 August 2013. Retrieved 12 August 2013.
- "USNORTHCOM 101"[329]. NRT. Archived from the original[330] on 13 May 2014. Retrieved 12 August 2013.
- "ADM Keating's Letter"[331] (PDF). USPACOM. Retrieved 12 August 2013.
- "Area of Responsibility (USSOUTHCOM)"[332]. USSOUTHCOM. Archived from the original[333] on 13 August 2013. Retrieved 12 August 2013.

External links

 Wikimedia Commons has media related to *Unified Combatant Command*.

- Interactive Map - US Africa Command (USAFRICOM) area of operation[334] from the United States Army Africa
- Unified Command Plan[335] Department of Defense
- Unified Command Plan[336] GlobalSecurity.org

United States Africa Command

United States Africa Command	
	 Emblem of United States Africa Command
Active	Established: 1 October 2007 Activated: 1 October 2008[337]
Country	United States of America
Type	Unified combatant command
Size	2,000 (1,500 stationed at HQ in Germany)
Part of	Department of Defense
Headquarters	Kelley Barracks, Stuttgart, Germany
Nickname(s)	U.S. AFRICOM, USAFRICOM
Engagements	2011 military intervention in Libya Tongo Tongo ambush
Website	www.africom.mil[338]
Commanders	
Commander	General Thomas D. Waldhauser, USMC

Deputy for Military Operations	Lieutenant General James C. Vechery, USAF
Deputy for Civil-Military Engagement	Ambassador Alexander M. Laskaris, U.S. Department of State

The **United States Africa Command (USAFRICOM, U.S. AFRICOM,** and **AFRICOM)**, is one of ten unified combatant commands of the United States Armed Forces, headquartered at Kelley Barracks, Stuttgart, Germany. It is responsible for U.S. military operations, including fighting regional conflicts and maintaining military relations with 53 African nations. Its area of responsibility covers all of Africa except Egypt, which is within the area of responsibility of the United States Central Command. U.S. AFRICOM headquarters operating budget was $276 million in fiscal year 2012.

The Commander of U.S. AFRICOM reports to the Secretary of Defense. In individual countries, U.S. Ambassadors continue to be the primary diplomatic representative for relations with host nations.

Function

In 2007, the White House announced, "[AFRICOM] will strengthen our security cooperation with Africa and create new opportunities to bolster the capabilities of our partners in Africa. Africa Command will enhance our efforts to bring peace and security to the people of Africa and promote our common goals of development, health, education, democracy, and economic growth in Africa."

General Carter F. Ham said in a 2012 address at Brown University that U.S. strategy for Sub-Saharan Africa is to strengthen democratic institutions and boost broad-based economic growth.

The U.S. Africa Command is currently operating along five lines of effort:

1. Neutralize al-Shabaab and transition the security responsibilities of the African Union Mission in Somalia (AMISOM) to the Federal Government of Somalia (FGS)
2. Degrade violent extremist organizations in the Sahel Maghreb and contain instability in Libya
3. Contain and degrade Boko Haram
4. Interdict illicit activity in the Gulf of Guinea and Central Africa with willing and capable African partners
5. Build peacekeeping, humanitarian assistance and disaster response capacity of African partners

History (2000–2006)

Prior to the creation of AFRICOM, responsibility for U.S. military operations in Africa was divided across three unified commands: United States European Command (EUCOM) for West Africa, United States Central Command (CENTCOM) for East Africa, and United States Pacific Command (PACOM) for Indian Ocean waters and islands off the east coast of Africa.

A U.S. military officer wrote the first public article calling for the formation of a separate African command in November 2000. Following a 2004 global posture review, the United States Department of Defense began establishing a number of Cooperative Security Locations (CSLs) and Forward Operating Sites (FOSs) across the African continent, through the auspices of EUCOM which had nominal command of West Africa at that time. These locations, along with Camp Lemonnier in Djibouti, would form the basis of AFRICOM facilities on the continent. Areas of military interest to the United States in Africa include the Sahara/Sahel region, over which Joint Task Force Aztec Silence is conducting anti-terrorist operations (Operation Enduring Freedom - Trans Sahara), Djibouti in the Horn of Africa, where Combined Joint Task Force – Horn of Africa is located (overseeing Operation Enduring Freedom - Horn of Africa), and the Gulf of Guinea.

The website **Magharebia.com** was launched by USEUCOM in 2004 to provide news about North Africa in English, French and Arabic. When AFRICOM was created, it took over operation of the website. Information operations of the United States Department of Defense was criticized by the Senate Armed Forces Committee and defunded by Congress in 2011. The site was closed down in February 2015.

In 2007, the United States Congress approved $500 million for the Trans-Saharan Counterterrorism Initiative (TSCTI) over six years to support countries involved in counterterrorism against threats of Al Qaeda operating in African countries, primarily Algeria, Chad, Mali, Mauritania, Niger, Senegal, Nigeria, and Morocco. This program builds upon the former Pan Sahel Initiative (PSI), which concluded in December 2004 and focused on weapon and drug trafficking, as well as counterterrorism. Previous U.S. military activities in Sub-Saharan Africa have included Special Forces associated Joint Combined Exchange Training. Letitia Lawson, writing in 2007 for a Center for Contemporary Conflict journal at the Naval Postgraduate School, noted that U.S. policy towards Africa, at least in the medium-term, looks to be largely defined by international terrorism, the increasing importance of African oil to American energy needs, and the dramatic expansion and improvement of Sino-African relations since 2000.

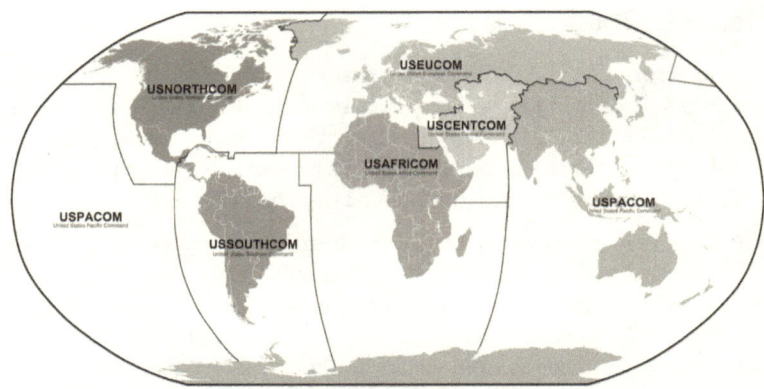

Figure 94: *In this map, U.S. AFRICOM Area of Responsibility is shown in green*

Creation of AFRICOM (2006–2008)

In mid-2006, Defense Secretary Donald Rumsfeld formed a planning team to advise on requirements for establishing a new Unified Command for the African continent. In early December, he made his recommendations to President George W. Bush.

On 6 February 2007, Defense Secretary Robert Gates announced to the Senate Armed Services Committee that President George W. Bush had given authority to create the new African Command. U.S. Navy Rear Admiral Robert Moeller, the director of the AFRICOM transition team, arrived in Stuttgart, Germany to begin creating the logistical framework for the command. On 28 September the U.S. Senate confirmed General William E. "Kip" Ward as AFRICOM's first commander and AFRICOM officially became operational as a sub-unified command of EUCOM with a separate headquarters. On 1 October 2008, the command separated from USEUCOM and began operating on its own as a full-fledged combatant command.

Geographic scope

The territory of the command consists of all of the African continent except for Egypt, which remains under the direct responsibility of USCENTCOM, as it closely relates to the Middle East. USAFRICOM also covers island countries commonly associated with Africa:

- Cape Verde
- São Tomé and Príncipe
- Comoros

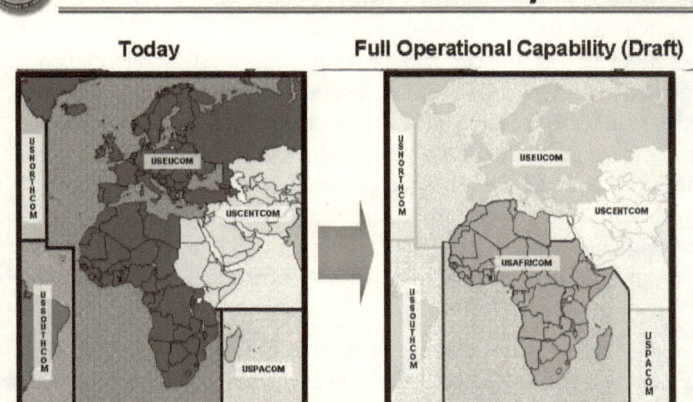

Figure 95: *February 2007 Draft Map of U.S. AFRICOM showing its creation from parts of USEUCOM, USCENTCOM and USPACOM.*

- Madagascar
- Mauritius
- Seychelles

The U.S. military areas of responsibility involved were transferred from three separate U.S. unified combatant commands. Most of Africa was transferred from the United States European Command with the Horn of Africa and Sudan transferred from the United States Central Command. Responsibility for U.S. military operations in the islands of Madagascar, the Comoros, the Seychelles and Mauritius was transferred from the United States Pacific Command.

Headquarters and facilities

The AFRICOM headquarters is located at Kelley Barracks, a small urban facility near Stuttgart, Germany, and is staffed by 1,500 personnel. In addition, the command has military and civilian personnel assigned at Camp Lemonnier, Djibouti; RAF Molesworth, United Kingdom; MacDill Air Force Base, Florida; and in Offices of Security Cooperation and Defense Attaché Offices in about 38 African countries.

Selection of the headquarters

It was reported in June 2007 that African countries were competing to host the headquarters because it would bring money for the recipient country.[339] However, of all the African nations, only Liberia has publicly expressed a willingness to host AFRICOM's headquarters. The U.S. declared in February 2008 that AFRICOM would be headquartered in Stuttgart for the "foreseeable future". In August 2007, Dr. Wafula Okumu, a research fellow at the Institute for Security Studies in South Africa, testified before the United States Congress about the growing resistance and hostility on the African continent. Nigeria announced it will not allow its country to host a base and opposed the creation of a base on the continent. South Africa and Libya also expressed reservations of the establishment of a headquarters in Africa.

The *Sudan Tribune* considered it likely that Ethiopia, a strong U.S. ally in the region, will house USAFRICOM's headquarters due to the collocation of AFRICOM with the African Union's developing peace and security apparatus. Prime Minister Meles Zenawi stated in early November that Ethiopia would be willing to work together closely with USAFRICOM. This was further reinforced when a U.S. Air Force official said on 5 December 2007, that Addis Ababa was likely to be the headquarters.[340]

On 18 February 2008 General Ward told an audience at the Royal United Services Institute in London that some portion of that staff headquarters being on the continent at some point in time would be "a positive factor in helping us better deliver programs."[341] General Ward also told the BBC the same day in an interview that there are no definite plans to take the headquarters or a portion of it to any particular location on the continent.[342]

President Bush denied that the United States was contemplating the construction of new bases on the African continent.[343] U.S. plans include no large installations such as Camp Bondsteel in Kosovo, but rather a network of "cooperative security locations" at which temporary activities will be conducted. There is one U.S. base on the continent, Camp Lemonnier in Djibouti, with approximately 2,300 troops stationed there having been inherited from USCENTCOM upon standup of the command.

In general, U.S. Unified Combatant Commands have an HQ of their own in one location, subordinate service component HQs, sometimes one or two collocated with the main HQ or sometimes spread widely, and a wide range of operating locations, main bases, forward detachments, etc. USAFRICOM initially appears to be considering something slightly different; spreading the actually COCOM HQ over several locations, rather than having the COCOM HQ in one place and the putative "U.S. Army Forces, Africa", its air component, and "U.S. Naval Forces, Africa" in one to four separate locations.

AFRICOM will not have the traditional J-type staff divisions, Wikipedia:Please clarify instead having outreach, plans and programs, knowledge development, operations and logistics, and resources branches.[344] AFRICOM went back to a traditional J-Staff in early 2011 after General Carter Ham took command. Wikipedia:Citation needed

Personnel

U.S. Africa Command completed fiscal year 2010 with approximately 2,000 assigned personnel, which includes military, civilian, contractor, and host nation employees. About 1,500 work at the command's main headquarters in Stuttgart. Others are assigned to the command's units in England and Florida, along with security cooperation officers posted at U.S. embassies and diplomatic missions in Africa to coordinate Defense Department programs within the host nation.

As of December 2010, the command has five Senior Foreign Service officers in key positions as well as more than 30 personnel from 13 U.S. Government Departments and Agencies serving in leadership, management, and staff positions. Some of the agencies represented are the United States Department's of State, Treasury, and Commerce, United States Agency for International Development, and the United States Coast Guard.

U.S. Africa Command has limited assigned forces and relies on the Department of Defense for resources necessary to support its missions.

Components

On 1 October 2008, the Seventeenth Air Force was established at Ramstein Air Base, Germany as the United States Air Force component of the Africa Command. Brig. Gen. Tracey Garrett was named as commander of the new USMC component, U.S. Marine Corps Forces Africa (MARFORAF), in November 2008. MARFORAF is a dual-mission arrangement for United States Marine Corps Forces, Europe.

On 3 December 2008 the U.S. announced that Army and Navy headquarters units of AFRICOM would be hosted in Italy. The AFRICOM section of the Army's Southern European Task Force would be located in Vicenza and Naval Forces Europe in Naples would expand to include the Navy's AFRICOM component.[345] Special Operations Command, Africa (SOCAFRICA) is also established, gaining control over Joint Special Operations Task Force-Trans Sahara (JSOTF-TS) and Special Operations Command and Control Element – Horn of Africa (SOCCE-HOA).[346]

The U.S. Army has allocated a brigade to the Africa Command.[347]

U.S. Army Africa (USARAF)

Headquartered on Caserma Ederle in Vicenza, Italy, U.S. Army Africa, in concert with national and international partners, conducts sustained security engagement with African land forces to promote peace, stability, and security in Africa. As directed, it can deploy as a contingency headquarters in support of crisis response.

The 2nd Brigade Combat Team, 1st Infantry Division, the "Dagger Brigade", is being aligned with AFRICOM.

U.S. Naval Forces, Africa (NAVAF)

U.S. Naval Forces Europe - Naval Forces Africa (NAVEUR-NAVAF) area of responsibility (AOR) covers approximately half of the Atlantic Ocean, from the North Pole to Antarctica; as well as the Adriatic, Baltic, Barents, Black, Caspian, Mediterranean and North Seas. NAVEUR-NAVAF covers all of Russia, Europe and nearly the entire continent of Africa. It encompasses 105 countries with a combined population of more than one billion people and includes a landmass extending more than 14 million square miles.

The area of responsibility covers more than 20 million square nautical miles of ocean, touches three continents and encompasses more than 67 percent of the Earth's coastline, 30 percent of its landmass, and nearly 40 percent of the world's population.

Task Force 60 will normally be the commander of Naval Task Force Europe and Africa.Wikipedia:Citation needed Any naval unit within the USEUCOM or USAFRICOM AOR may be assigned to Task Force 60 as required upon by the Commander of the Sixth Fleet.

U.S. Air Forces Africa (AFAFRICA)

Air Forces Africa (AFAFRICA) is located at Ramstein Air Base, Germany, and serves as the air and space component to U.S. Africa Command (AFRICOM) located at Stuttgart, Germany. Air Forces Africa shares a headquarters and units with United States Air Forces in Europe, and its component Air Force, 3AF (AFAFRICA) conducts sustained security engagement and operations as directed to promote air safety, security and development on the African continent. Through its Theater Security Cooperation (TSC) events, Air Forces Africa carries out AFRICOM's policy of seeking long-term partnership with the African Union and regional organizations as well as individual nations on the continent.

Air Forces Africa works with other U.S. Government agencies, to include the State Department and the U.S. Agency for International Development (USAID), to assist African partners in developing national and regional security institution capabilities that promote security and stability and facilitate development.

3AF succeeds the Seventeenth Air Force by assuming the AFAFRICA mission upon the 17AF's deactivation on 20 April 2012.

U.S. Marine Corps Forces, Africa (MARFORAF)

U.S. Marine Corps Forces, Africa conducts operations, exercises, training, and security cooperation activities throughout the AOR. In 2009, MARFORAF participated in 15 ACOTA missions aimed at improving partners' capabilities to provide logistical support, employ military police, and exercise command and control over deployed forces.

MARFORAF conducted military to military events in 2009 designed to familiarize African partners with nearly every facet of military operations and procedures, including use of unmanned aerial vehicles, tactics, and medical skills. MARFORAF, as the lead component, continues to conduct Exercise AFRICAN LION in Morocco—the largest annual Combined Joint Chiefs of Staff (CJCS) exercise on the African continent—as well as Exercise SHARED ACCORD 10, which was the first CJCS exercise conducted in Mozambique.

In 2013, the Special Purpose Marine Air-Ground Task Force - Crisis Response - Africa was formed to provide quick response to American interests in North Africa by flying marines in Bell Boeing V-22 Osprey aircraft from bases in Europe.

Subordinate Commands

U.S. Special Operations Command, Africa

Special Operations Command Africa was activated on 1 October 2008 and became fully operationally capable on 1 October 2009. SOCAFRICA is a Subordinate-Unified Command of United States Special Operations Command, operationally controlled by U.S. Africa Command, collocated with US-AFRICOM at Kelley Barracks, Stuttgart-Möhringen, Germany. Also on 1 October 2008, SOCAFRICA assumed responsibility for the Special Operations Command and Control Element – Horn of Africa, and on 15 May 2009, SOCAFRICA assumed responsibility for Joint Special Operations Task Force Trans – Sahara (JSOTF-TS) – the SOF component of Operation Enduring Freedom – Trans Sahara.

SOCAFRICA's objectives are to build operational capacity, strengthen regional security and capacity initiatives, implement effective communication strategies in support of strategic objectives, and eradicate violent extremist organizations and their supporting networks. SOCAFRICA forces work closely with both U.S. Embassy country teams and African partners, maintaining a small but sustained presence throughout Africa, predominantly in the OEF-TS and CJTF-HOA regions. SOCAFRICA's persistent SOF presence provides an invaluable resource that furthers USG efforts to combat violent extremist groups and builds partner nation CT capacity.

On 8 April 2011, Naval Special Warfare Unit 10, operationally assigned and specifically dedicated for SOCAFRICA missions, was commissioned at Panzer Kaserne, near Stuttgart, Germany. It is administratively assigned to Naval Special Warfare Group 2 on the U.S. East Coast.

Organizations included in SOCAFRICA include:[348]

- Special Operations Command Forward—East (Special Operations Command and Control Element—Horn of Africa)
- Special Operations Command Forward—Central (AFRICOM Counter—Lord's Resistance Army Control Element)
- Special Operations Command Forward—West (Joint Special Operations Task Force—Trans Sahara)
- Naval Special Warfare Unit 10, Joint Special Operations Air Component Africa, and SOCAFRICA Signal Detachment
- Commander SOCAFRICA serves as the Special Operations Adviser to Commander, USAFRICOM.

Combined Joint Task Force – Horn of Africa

Combined Joint Task Force – Horn of Africa (CJTF-HOA) conducts operations in the East Africa region to build partner nation capacity in order to promote regional security and stability, prevent conflict, and protect U.S. and

coalition interests. CJTF-HOA's efforts, as part of a comprehensive whole-of-government approach, are aimed at increasing African partner nations' capacity to maintain a stable environment, with an effective government that provides a degree of economic and social advancement for its citizens.

Programs and operations

Programs

- African Contingency Operations Training and Assistance
- Africa Partnership Station is the U.S. Africa Command's primary maritime security engagement program which strengthens maritime security through maritime training with various nations.
- Combating Terrorism Fellowship Program
- Pandemic Response Program
- State Partnership Program connects a U.S. state's National Guard to an African nation for military training and relationship-building.

Operations

- Operation Enduring Freedom - Horn of Africa
- Operation Enduring Freedom - Trans Sahara
- Operation Ocean Shield - Indian Ocean
- Operation Odyssey Dawn - Libya, was the first major combat deployment directed by Africa Command.[349]
- Operation Onward Liberty - Liberia
- Operation Unified Protector - Libya
- Operation Odyssey Lightning - Libya

List of commanders

No.	Image	Name	Service	Start	End	Time in office
1.		General William E. Ward	U.S. Army	1 October 2007	8 March 2011	1,254 days
2.		General Carter F. Ham	U.S. Army	8 March 2011	5 April 2013	759 days
3.		General David M. Rodriguez	U.S. Army	5 April 2013	18 July 2016	1,200 days
4.		General Thomas D. Waldhauser	U.S. Marine Corps	18 July 2016	Incumbent	744 days

Further reading

- "AFRICOM Arrives", *Jane's Defence Weekly*, 1 October 2008
- McFate, Sean (January 2008). "US Africa Command: next step or next stumble?". *African Affairs*. **107** (426): 111–120. doi: 10.1093/afraf/adm084[350].

External links

Wikimedia Commons has media related to *United States Africa Command*.

- Official website[351] and March 2010 posture statement[352] Wikipedia:Link rot
- United States Army Africa official website[353]
- Africa Interactive Map[354] from the United States Army Africa
- APCN (Africa Partner Country Network)[355]
- "Advanced Questions for General William E. "Kip" Ward, U.S. Army Nominee for Commander, U.S. Africa Command"[356] (PDF). (165 KB), U.S. Senate Committee on Armed Services testimony.
- "*U.S. Africa Command: A New Strategic Paradigm?*"[357] (PDF). Archived from the original[358] (PDF) on 28 February 2008. (1.03 MB) by Sean McFate in *Military Review*[359], January–February 2008
- *Africa's Security Challenges and Rising Strategic Significance*[360], *Strategic Insights*, January 2007
- "AFRICOM public brief"[361] (PDF). (652 KiB), United States Department of Defense, 2 February 2007
- "Blood Oil"[362] by Sebastian Junger in *Vanity Fair*, February 2007. Retrieved 28 January 2007
- "Africa Command: 'Follow the oil'"[363] in *World War 4 Report*, 16 February 2007
- The Americans Have Landed[364], *Esquire*, 27 June 2007. Retrieved 2007-08-10.
- Does Africa need Africom?[365]
- ResistAFRICOM website[366]
- Criticism of AFRICOM[367]
- Secret US Military Documents Reveal a Constellation of American Military Bases Across Africa[368]

United States Central Command

United States Central Command	
	Emblem of the United States Central Command
Founded	1983
Country	United States of America
Type	Unified Combatant Command
Part of	Department of Defense
Headquarters	MacDill Air Force Base Tampa, Florida, U.S.
Nickname(s)	CENTCOM
Engagements	Persian Gulf War Iraq War War in Afghanistan
Commanders	
Combatant Commander	General Joseph Votel, USA
Deputy Commander	Lieutenant General Charles Brown, USAF
Notable commanders	General David Petraeus Admiral William Fallon General John Abizaid General Tommy Franks General Anthony Zinni General James Mattis General Norman Schwarzkopf
Insignia	

Combat service identification badge (U.S. Army only)	

The **United States Central Command** (**USCENTCOM** or **CENTCOM**) is a theater-level Unified Combatant Command of the U.S. Department of Defense. It was established in 1983, taking over the 1980 Rapid Deployment Joint Task Force (RDJTF) responsibilities.

The CENTCOM Area of Responsibility (AOR) includes countries in the Middle East, parts of northern Africa, and Central Asia, most notably Afghanistan and Iraq. CENTCOM has been the main American presence in many military operations, including the Persian Gulf War (Operation Desert Storm, 1991), the War in Afghanistan (Operation Enduring Freedom, 2001–2014), and the Iraq War (Operation Iraqi Freedom, 2003–2011). As of 2015[369], CENTCOM forces are deployed primarily in Afghanistan (Operation Resolute Support, 2015–present), Iraq and Syria (Operation Inherent Resolve, 2014–present) in supporting and advise-and-assist roles.

As of 1 September 2016[369], CENTCOM's commander was General Joseph Votel, U.S. Army.

Of all six American regional unified combatant commands, CENTCOM is among the three with headquarters outside its area of operations (the other two being USAFRICOM and USSOUTHCOM). CENTCOM's main headquarters is located at MacDill Air Force Base, in Tampa, Florida. A forward headquarters was established in 2002 at Camp As Sayliyah in Doha, Qatar, which in 2009 transitioned to a forward headquarters at Al Udeid Air Base in Qatar.

History

United States Central Command (CENTCOM) was established on January 1, 1983.[370] As its name implies, CENTCOM covers the "central" area of the globe located between the European and Pacific Commands. When the hostage crisis in Iran and the Soviet invasion of Afghanistan underlined the need to strengthen U.S. interests in the region, President Jimmy Carter established the Rapid Deployment Joint Task Force (RDJTF) in March 1980. Steps were taken to transform the RDJTF into a permanent unified command over a two-year period. The first step was to make the RDJTF independent of

U.S. Readiness Command, followed by the activation of CENTCOM in January 1983. Overcoming skeptical perceptions that the command was still an RDJTF in all but name, designed to support a Cold War strategy, took time.

The Iran–Iraq War clearly underlined the growing tensions in the region, and developments such as Iranian mining operations in the Persian Gulf led to CENTCOM's first combat operations. On 17 May 1987, the USS *Stark* (FFG-31), conducting operations in the Persian Gulf during the Iran-Iraq War, was struck by Exocet missiles fired by an Iraqi aircraft, resulting in 37 casualties. Soon afterward, as part of what became known as the "Tanker War", the Federal government of the United States reflagged and renamed 11 Kuwaiti oil tankers. In Operation Earnest Will, these tankers were escorted by USCENTCOM's Middle East Force through the Persian Gulf to Kuwait and back through the Strait of Hormuz.

By late 1988, the regional strategy still largely focused on the potential threat of a massive Soviet invasion of Iran. Exercise Internal Look has been one of CENTCOM's primary planning events. It had frequently been used to train CENTCOM to be ready to defend the Zagros Mountains from a Soviet attack and was held annually.[371] In autumn 1989, the main CENTCOM contingency plan, OPLAN 1002-88, assumed a Soviet attack through Iran to the Persian Gulf. The plan called for five-and-two-thirds US divisions to deploy, mostly light and heavy forces at something less than full strength (apportioned to it by the Joint Strategic Capability Plan [JSCAP]). The original plan called for these five-and-two-thirds divisions to march from the Persian Gulf to the Zagros Mountains and prevent the Soviet Ground Forces (army) from seizing the Iranian oil fields.

After 1990, General Norman Schwarzkopf reoriented CENTCOM's planning to fend off a threat from Iraq, and Internal Look moved to a biennial schedule. There was a notable similarity between the 1990 Internal Look exercise scripts and the real-world movement of Iraqi forces which culminated in Iraq's invasion of Kuwait during the final days of the exercise. U.S. President George Bush responded quickly. A timely deployment of forces and the formation of a coalition deterred Iraq from invading Saudi Arabia, and the command began to focus on the liberation of Kuwait. The buildup of forces continued, reinforced by United Nations Security Council Resolution 678, which called for Iraqi forces to leave Kuwait. On January 17, 1991, U.S. and coalition forces launched Operation Desert Storm with a massive air interdiction campaign, which prepared the theater for a coalition ground assault. The primary coalition objective, the liberation of Kuwait, was achieved on February 27, and the next morning a ceasefire was declared, just one hundred hours after the commencement of the ground campaign.

The end of formal hostilities did not bring the end of difficulties with Iraq. Operation Provide Comfort, implemented to provide humanitarian assistance to the Kurds and enforce a "no-fly" zone in Iraq, north of the 36th parallel, began in April 1991. In August 1992, Operation Southern Watch began in response to Saddam's noncompliance with U.N. Security Council Resolution 688 condemning his brutal repression of Iraqi civilians in southeastern Iraq. Under the command and control of Joint Task Force Southwest Asia, coalition forces in this operation enforced a no-fly zone south of the 32nd parallel. In January 1997, Operation Northern Watch replaced Provide Comfort, with a focus on enforcing the northern no-fly zone. Throughout the decade, CENTCOM carried out a string of operations—Vigilant Warrior, Vigilant Sentinel, Desert Strike, Desert Thunder (I and II), and Desert Fox—to try to coerce Saddam into greater compliance with U.S. wishes.

The 1990s also brought significant challenges in Somalia as well as from the growing threat of regional terrorism. To prevent widespread starvation in the face of clan warfare, the command responded in 1992 with Operation Provide Relief to supply humanitarian assistance to Somalia and northeastern Kenya. CENTCOM's Operation Restore Hope supported UNSCR 794 and a multinational Unified Task Force, which provided security until the U.N. created UNOSOM II in May 1993. In spite of some UNOSOM II success in the countryside, the situation in Mogadishu worsened, and the significant casulties of the Battle of Mogadishu ultimately led President Bill Clinton to order the withdrawal of all U.S. troops from Somalia. Throughout the decade following the Gulf War, terrorist attacks had a major impact on CENTCOM forces in the region. Faced with attacks such as the 1996 bombing of the Khobar Towers, which killed 19 American airmen, the command launched Operation Desert Focus, designed to relocate U.S. installations to more defensible locations (such as Prince Sultan Air Base), reduce the U.S. forward "footprint" by eliminating nonessential billets, and return dependents to the United States. In 1998 terrorists attacked the U.S. embassies in Kenya and Tanzania, killing 250 persons, including 12 Americans. The October 2000 attack on the USS *Cole*, resulting in the deaths of 17 U.S. sailors, was linked to Osama bin Laden's Al Qaida organization.

From April to July 1999, CENTCOM conducted Exercise Desert Crossing 1999, centered on the scenario of Saddam Hussein being ousted as Iraq's dictator. It was held in the offices of Booz Allen Hamilton in McLean, Virginia.:[6-7] The exercise concluded that unless measures were taken, "fragmentation and chaos" would ensue after Saddam Hussein's overthrow.

The September 11 terrorist attacks on New York and Washington DC led President George W. Bush to declare a war against international terrorism. CENTCOM soon launched Operation Enduring Freedom to expel the Taliban gov-

Figure 96: *U.S. armored vehicle in Al-Hasakah, Democratic Federation of Northern Syria, May 2017*

ernment in Afghanistan, which was harboring Al Qaida terrorists and hosting terrorist training camps.

Exercise Internal Look has been employed for explicit war planning on at least two occasions: Internal Look '90, which dealt with a threat from Iraq, and Internal Look '03, which was used to plan what became Operation Iraqi Freedom. Iraqi Freedom, the 2003 United States invasion of Iraq, began on 19 March 2003.

Following the defeat of both the Taliban regime in Afghanistan (9 November 2001) and Saddam Hussein's government in Iraq (8 April 2003), CENTCOM has continued to provide security to the new freely-elected governments in those countries, conducting counterinsurgency operations and assisting host nation security forces to provide for their own defense.

Beginning in October 2002, CENTCOM conducted operations in the Horn of Africa to combat terrorism, establish a secure environment, and foster regional stability. These operations involved a series of Special Operations Forces raids, humanitarian assistance, consequence management, and a variety of civic action programs.

The command has also remained poised to provide disaster relief throughout the region; its most recent significant relief operations have been a response to the October 2005 earthquake in Pakistan, and the large-scale evacuation of American citizens from Lebanon in 2006.

On 1 October 2008, the Department of Defense transferred responsibility for Sudan, Eritrea, Ethiopia, Djibouti, Kenya, and Somalia to the newly established Africa Command. Egypt, home to Exercise Bright Star, the Department of Defense's largest reoccurring military exercise, remained in the CENTCOM Area of Responsibility.

In January 2015, CENTCOM's Twitter feed was reported to have been hacked on 11 January by ISIS sympathizers. This situation lasted for less than one hour; no classified information was posted and "none of the information posted came from CENTCOM's server or social media sites"; however, some of the slides came from the federally funded Lincoln Laboratory at the Massachusetts Institute of Technology.

In August 2015, intelligence analysts working for CENTCOM complained to the media, alleging that CENTCOM's senior leadership was altering or distorting intelligence reports on the Islamic State of Iraq and the Levant. In February 2017, the Inspector General of the United States Department of Defense completed its investigation and cleared the senior leadership of CENTCOM, concluding that "allegations of intelligence being intentionally altered, delayed or suppressed by top CENTCOM officials from mid-2014 to mid-2015 were largely unsubstantiated."

In January 2018, Turkey urged the United States to remove its troops from Syrian city of Manbij, saying that otherwise they might come under attack from Turkish troops; however, CENTCOM commander Joseph Votel confirmed an American commitment to keeping troops in Manbij.

Structure

CENTCOM's main headquarters is located at MacDill Air Force Base, in Tampa, Florida. CENTCOM headquarters staff directorates include personnel, intelligence, operations, logistics, plans & policy, information systems, training & exercises, and resources, and other functions. The intelligence section is known as Joint Intelligence Center, Central Command, or JICCENT, which serves as a Joint Intelligence Center for the co-ordination of intelligence. Under the intelligence directorate, there are several divisions including the Afghanistan-Pakistan Center of Excellence.

CENTCOM directs four "service component commands" and one subordinate unified command and no fighting units directly subordinate to it:

The United States Army Central (USARCENT), and the United States Air Forces Central Command (USAFCENT), both headquartered at Shaw Air Force Base in South Carolina, the United States Marine Forces Central Command (USMARCENT), headquartered at MacDill Air Force Base, Florida and

Figure 97: *Al Udeid Air Base in Qatar*

the United States Naval Forces Central Command (USNAVCENT), headquartered at Naval Support Activity Bahrain in the Kingdom of Bahrain. MacDill Air Force Base also hosts a Sub-unified command called the Special Operations Command Central (USSOCCENT).Wikipedia:Citation needed

Two major subordinate multi-service commands reporting to Central Command were responsible for Afghanistan: Combined Joint Task Force 180 and Combined Forces Command Afghanistan (CFC-A). CFC-A was disestablished in February 2007. From that point onward, the International Security Assistance Force directed most U.S. forces in Afghanistan, and a U.S. general, General Dan K. McNeill, assumed command of ISAF that same month.[372]

Temporary task forces include the Central Command Forward - Jordan (CF-J), which was announced in April 2013. CF-J's stated purpose was to work with the Jordanian armed forces to improve the latter's capabilities. There was speculation, however, that another reason for its establishment was to serve as a base from which raids into Syria could be launched to seize Syrian WMD if necessary, and as a launch pad for looming American military action in Syria.

On 1 October 2008 Combined Joint Task Force - Horn of Africa at Camp Lemonnier in Djibouti was transferred to United States Africa Command (US-AFRICOM). The United States Forces – Iraq or USF-I, was a major subordinate multi-service command during the Iraq War order of battle until it was disestablished in 2011.Wikipedia:Citation needed

Elements of other Unified Combatant Commands, especially United States Special Operations Command (USSOCOM), operate in the CENTCOM area.

It appears that SOCCENT does *not* direct the secretive Task Force 88, the ad-hoc grouping of Joint Special Operations Command 'black' units such as Delta Force and Army Rangers, which is tasked to pursue the most sensitive high-value targets such as Al Qaeda and the Taliban leadership since 11 September 2001. Rather TF 77, which started out as Task Force 11 and has gone through a number of name/number changes, reports directly to Joint Special Operations Command, part of USSOCOM.Wikipedia:Citation needed

As of 2015[369] CENTCOM forces are deployed primarily in Iraq and Afghanistan in combat roles and have support roles at bases in Kuwait, Bahrain, Qatar, the United Arab Emirates, Oman, Pakistan, and central Asia. CENTCOM forces have also been deployed in Jordan and Saudi Arabia.

War planning

The following code names are known to have been associated with war planning per William Arkin:[:46]

- CENTCOM OPORDER 01-97, Force Protection
- SOCEUR SUPPLAN 1001-90, 9 May 1989
- CENTCOM CONPLAN 1010, July 2003
- CENTCOM CONPLAN 1015-98, possible support to OPLAN 5027 for Korea, 15 March 1991
- CENTCOM 1017, 1999
- CONPLAN 1020
- CONPLAN 1067, for possible Biological Warfare response
- CENTCOM CONPLAN 1100-95, 31 March 1992

Globalsecurity.org also lists OPLAN 1002 (Defense of the Arabian Peninsula).WP:NOTRS

Geographic scope

With the 1983 establishment of CENTCOM Egypt, Sudan, Kenya, Ethiopia, Somalia and Djibouti came within the area of responsibility (AOR). Thus CENTCOM directed the 'Natural Bond' exercises with Sudan, the 'Eastern Wind' exercises with Somalia, and the 'Jade Tiger' exercises with Oman, Somalia, and Sudan. Exercise Jade Tiger involved the 31st Marine Expeditionary Unit with Oman from 29 November 1982 – 8 Dec 1982.[:404]

Israel is surrounded by CENTCOM countries but remains in United States European Command (EUCOM). General Norman Schwarzkopf expressed the position over Israel frankly in his 1992 autobiography: 'European Command also kept Israel, which from my viewpoint was a help: I'd have had difficulty

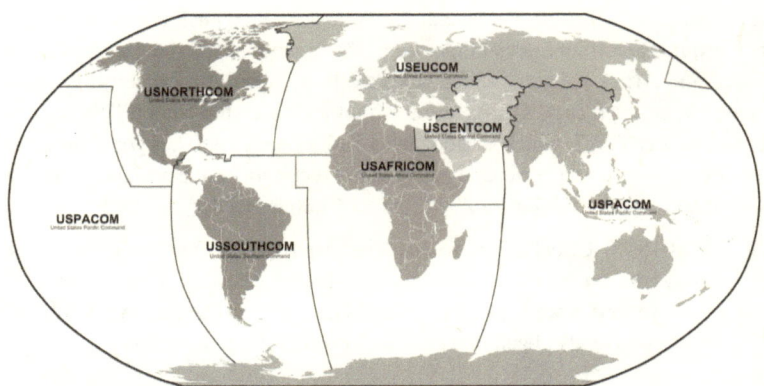

Figure 98: *In this map, CENTCOM Area Of Responsibility is shown in yellow*

impressing the Arabs with Central Command's grasp of geopolitical nuance if one of the stops on my itinerary had been Tel Aviv.':318

On 7 February 2007, plans were announced for the creation of a United States Africa Command which transferred strategic interest responsibility for all of Africa to the new USAFRICOM, except for Egypt. On 1 October 2008, the Africa Command became operational and Combined Joint Task Force – Horn of Africa, the primary CENTCOM force on the continent, started reporting to AFRICOM at Stuttgart instead of CENTCOM in Tampa.

The U.S. armed forces use a variable number of base locations depending on its level of operations. With ongoing warfare in Iraq and Afghanistan in 2003, the United States Air Force used 35 bases, while in 2006 it used 14, including four in Iraq. The United States Navy maintains one major base and one smaller installation, with extensive deployments afloat and ashore by U.S. Navy, U.S. Marine Corps and U.S. Coast Guard ships, aviation units and ground units.

Commanders

As of March 2016[369], GEN Joseph Votel is commander. He took command from General Lloyd Austin, United States, who took command from Mattis, who took command from Lieutenant General John R. Allen, USMC, the deputy commander since July 2008, who took temporary command when the previous commander, General David Petraeus, USA, left to take command of the International Security Assistance Force (ISAF) in Afghanistan on 23 June 2010.

United States Central Command

No.	Image	Name	Service	Start	End	Time in office
1.		GEN Robert Kingston	United States Army	1 January 1983	27 November 1985	1,061 days
2.		Gen George B. Crist	United States Marine Corps	27 November 1985	23 November 1988	1,092 days
3.		GEN H. Norman Schwarzkopf	United States Army	23 November 1988	9 August 1991	989 days
4.		Gen Joseph P. Hoar	United States Marine Corps	9 August 1991	5 August 1994	1,092 days
5.		GEN J. H. Binford Peay III	United States Army	5 August 1994	13 August 1997	1,104 days
6.		Gen Anthony Zinni	United States Marine Corps	13 August 1997	6 July 2000	1,058 days
7.		GEN Tommy Franks	United States Army	6 July 2000	7 July 2003	1,096 days
8.		GEN John Abizaid	United States Army	7 July 2003	16 March 2007	1,348 days
9.		ADM William J. Fallon	United States Navy	16 March 2007	28 March 2008	378 days
(Acting)		LTG Martin Dempsey	United States Army	28 March 2008	31 October 2008	217 days
10.		GEN David Petraeus	United States Army	31 October 2008	30 June 2010	607 days
(Acting)		LtGen John R. Allen	United States Marine Corps	30 June 2010	11 August 2010	42 days

11.		Gen James Mattis	United States Marine Corps	11 August 2010	22 March 2013		954 days
12.		GEN Lloyd Austin	United States Army	22 March 2013	30 March 2016		1,104 days
13.		GEN Joseph Votel	United States Army	30 March 2016		*Incumbent*	854 days

Unit decorations

The unit awards depicted below are for Headquarters, US Central Command at MacDill AFB. Award for unit decorations do not apply to any subordinate organization such as the service component commands or any other activities unless the orders specifically address them.

Award streamer	Award	Dates	Notes
	Joint Meritorious Unit Award	2 August 1990 – 21 April 1991	Department of the Army General Order (DAGO) 1991-22 & 1992-34[373]
	Joint Meritorious Unit Award	1 August 1992 – 4 May 1993	DAGO 1994-12 & 1996-01
	Joint Meritorious Unit Award	8 October 1994 – 16 March 1995	DAGO 2001–25
	Joint Meritorious Unit Award	1 September 1996 – 6 January 1997	Joint Staff Permanent Order (JSPO) J-ISO-0012-97
	Joint Meritorious Unit Award	1 October 1997 – 15 July 1998	JSPO J-ISO-0241-98
	Joint Meritorious Unit Award	16 July 1998 – 1 November 1999	JSPO J-ISO-0330-99 / DAGO 2001–25
	Joint Meritorious Unit Award	2 November 1999 – 15 March 2001	
	Joint Meritorious Unit Award	11 September 2001 – 1 May 2003	DAGO 2005–09
	Joint Meritorious Unit Award	2 May 2003 – 31 December 2005	
	Joint Meritorious Unit Award	1 January 2006 – 1 March 2008	JSPO J-ISO-0061-08
	Joint Meritorious Unit Award	2 March 2008 – 1 July 2010	
	Joint Meritorious Unit Award	2 July 2010 – 31 July 2012	

References

- Anthony Cordesman, USCENTCOM Mission and History[374], Center for Strategic and International Studies, August 1998

External links

- U.S. Central Command official website[375]
- Multi-National Force – Iraq.com mnf-iraq.com[376] (in English)
- Multi-National Force – Iraq[377] shurakaal-iraq.com (in Arabic)
- Spiegel, Peter (5 January 2007). "Naming New Generals A Key Step In Shift On Iraq"[378]. *Los Angeles Times*.
- Foreign Policy, Pentagon Ups the Ante in Syria Fight[379]
- http://www.armytimes.com/story/military/pentagon/2014/12/30/iraq-1st-infantry-funk/21062071/ - Combined Joint Forces Land Component Command - Iraq

United States European Command

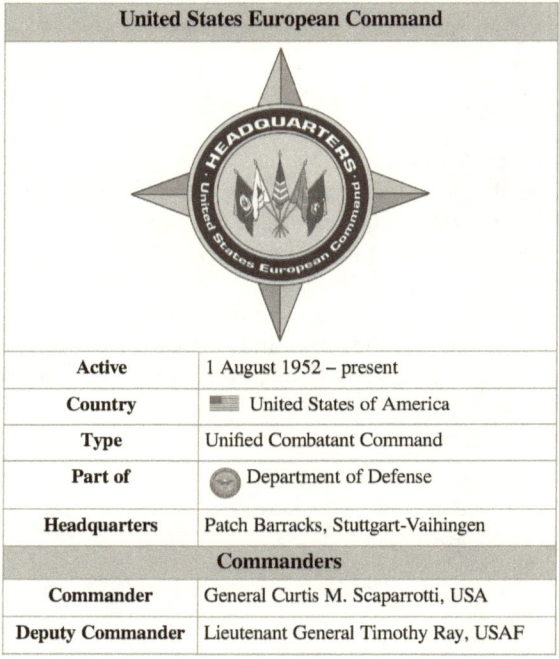

United States European Command	
Active	1 August 1952 – present
Country	United States of America
Type	Unified Combatant Command
Part of	Department of Defense
Headquarters	Patch Barracks, Stuttgart-Vaihingen
Commanders	
Commander	General Curtis M. Scaparrotti, USA
Deputy Commander	Lieutenant General Timothy Ray, USAF

The **United States European Command (EUCOM)** is one of ten Unified Combatant Commands of the United States military, headquartered in Stuttgart, Germany. Its area of focus covers 21,000,000 square miles (54,000,000 km^2) and 51 countries and territories, including Europe, Russia, Greenland, and Israel. The Commander of the United States EUCOM simultaneously serves as the Supreme Allied Commander, Europe (SACEUR) within NATO—an intergovernmental military alliance. During the Gulf War and Operation Northern Watch, EUCOM controlled the forces flying from Incirlik Air Base.

History and significant operations

Prior to 1952, the title "European Command (EUCOM)" referred to a single-service, United States Army command. The senior U.S. Army administrative command in the European region had previously been designated European Theater of Operations United States Army (ETOUSA) from 8 June 1942 – 1 July 1945; USFET from 1 July 1945 – 15 March 1947; and then EUCOM 15 March 1947 – 1 August 1952.

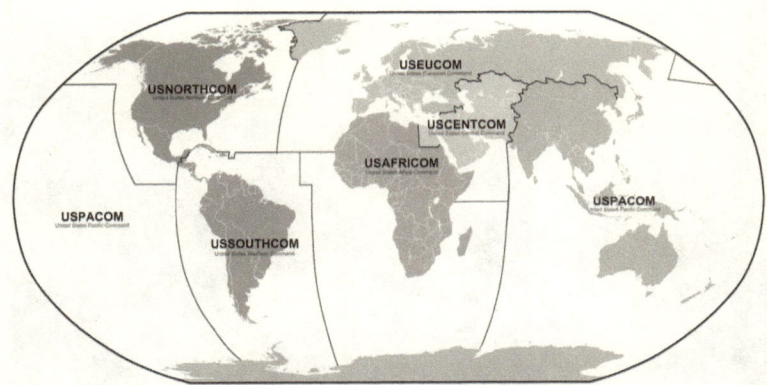

Figure 99: *EUCOM Area of responsibility in orange*

The first unified command in the European area was established by the Joint Chiefs of Staff on 1 August 1952. Designated the U.S. European Command (USEUCOM), it was established to provide "unified command and authority" over all U.S. forces in Europe. Prior to 1 August 1952, the U.S. Air Force, U.S. Navy, and U.S. Army presence in Europe maintained separate commands that reported directly to the Joint Chiefs of Staff. The respective titles of the service commands were: Commander-in-Chief, U.S. Air Forces in Europe (USAFE); Commander-in-Chief, U.S. Naval Forces, Eastern Atlantic and Mediterranean; and Commander-in-Chief, U.S. European Command. In line with the creation of the joint-service European Command, the Army command in Europe was redesignated U.S. Army Europe on 1 August 1952.

The unified command structure was born of the need to address changes wrought not only by America's rapid post-war demobilization but the end of the occupation of Germany in 1949. Questions arose over the U.S. commitment to the defense of Western Europe against the Soviet Union (USSR). Providing for the common defense was a great concern, especially after the Berlin Crisis of 1948–49 when the Soviet Union blocked access to the divided city and the U.S. and United Kingdom responded with an unprecedented airlift. In 1949 the allies established the North Atlantic Treaty Organization (NATO).

In 1952 the area of responsibility included continental Europe, the United Kingdom, North Africa and Turkey. The AOR was subsequently expanded to include Southwest Asia as far east as Iran and as far south as Saudi Arabia.

After the Korean War began, the perceived threat to Europe grew. In early 1951, NATO established Allied Command Europe. General Dwight D. Eisenhower was called from retirement to become the first Supreme Allied Commander Europe. The United States sent massive reinforcements to Europe to

Figure 100: *EUCOM headquarters in the IG Farben Building, Frankfurt, 1952*

deter the Soviet Union. From 1950 to 1953 United States military personnel in Europe grew from 120,000 to over 400,000. United States Air Forces in Europe grew from three groups with 35,000 personnel to eleven wings with 136,000 personnel. Sixth Fleet in the Mediterranean doubled to more than 40 warships. United States Army, Europe, grew from one infantry division and three constabulary regiments to two corps with five divisions (including two mobilized National Guard divisions) and in November 1950 activated a new field army, Seventh Army, at Patch Barracks, Stuttgart. The Army activated the 10th Special Forces Group at Fort Bragg in 1952 and deployed it to Bad Tölz in November 1953 for unconventional warfare missions in the Soviet Bloc countries. To provide for national command within NATO and to help control this build-up of forces, Gen. Eisenhower proposed a separate command for all United States forces in Europe. Because the senior United States commander would continue as Supreme Allied Commander Europe, Eisenhower recommended giving "a maximum of delegated authority" to a four-star deputy.

Eisenhower returned to the United States just as the new command was established. The first United States Commander-in-Chief Europe (USCINCEUR) was General Matthew Ridgway, former commander of Eighth Army and the Far East Command during the Korean War. His deputy was General Thomas T. Handy, commander of United States Army, Europe.

Headquarters EUCOM initially shared the I.G. Farben Building in Frankfurt, Germany, with Headquarters United States Army, Europe. By 1953 over 400,000 U.S. troops were stationed in Europe. In 1954, the headquarters moved to Camp des Loges, a French Army base west of Paris and a short distance from SHAPE. There, EUCOM prepared plans for the defense of Western Europe within the NATO framework against the Soviet Union and Warsaw Pact. EUCOM used the Military Assistance Program to help its NATO partners build their military capabilities, including after 1955 the German Bundeswehr. In 1955, EUCOM established a Support Operations Command Europe, soon renamed Support Operations Task Force Europe (later became Special Operations, Europe) for special operations missions. In 1961, EUCOM began operating an airborne command post, Operation Silk Purse.

During the 1961 Berlin Crisis, on 25 August 1961, the Department of Defense announced 148,000 reserve personnel would be called on 1 October for twelve months of active duty service. 27,000 of these would be from Air Force Reserve and Air National Guard flying squadrons and support units to augment the Air Force, and 112,000 were U.S. Army Reserve. Many Army Reservists were sent to Europe to bring ground combat units up to full strength.

Civil war broke out in Lebanon in 1958 due to mounting religious and political conflicts (see "1958 Lebanon crisis"). EUCOM conducted a major contingency operation, Operation Blue Bat, in response to Lebanon's request to restore stability within the government.

In 1966, following disagreements by the French with certain NATO military policies, President Charles de Gaulle stated that all forces within France's borders would have to come under French control by April 1969. Soon afterward, France announced that SHAPE and its subordinate headquarters must leave French territory by April 1967. The following year, SHAPE moved to Mons, Belgium, while Headquarters EUCOM moved to Patch Barracks in Stuttgart, Germany. Headquarters Seventh Army moved to Heidelberg, where it merged with Headquarters United States Army, Europe. At Patch Barracks, EUCOM renovated the buildings, built a new operations center, and modernized communications infrastructure.

EUCOM continued to prepare for the defense of Europe and began a series of annual REFORGER (Return of Forces to Germany) exercises in 1967. Cold War crises continued, including the 1968 Warsaw Pact invasion of Czechoslovakia. But, because of the Vietnam War, the number of the American forces in Europe slowly declined. Troop strength in Europe fell to 265,000 by 1970.

During the 1970s, force protection concerns in Europe increased as terrorist groups, such as the Red Army Faction and the Red Brigades, targeted American facilities and personnel with bombings, kidnapping and assassinations. Palestinian terrorist organizations conducted terror operations in Europe, such as the kidnapping of Israeli athletes during the 1972 Summer Olympics in Munich.

Figure 101: *US Army units in West Germany, 1987*

EUCOM and its components continued to provide military assistance throughout Europe, as well as humanitarian assistance, disaster relief, noncombatant evacuation, support to peacekeeping operations, and other non-traditional missions in Europe, Africa and the Middle East. For example, after the Congo became independent in 1960, EUCOM joined in several multinational operations in that country, including peacekeeping, humanitarian assistance, and noncombatant evacuation in 1960, November 1964 (Operation Dragon Rouge), the 1967 second Stanleyville mutiny and again in 1978 (during Shaba II). In the Middle East, EUCOM provided military assistance to Israel and noncombatant evacuation of American citizens in 1967, 1973, and 1982–1984.

In the late 1970s, the Soviet Union deployed SS-20 intermediate-range ballistic missiles into Eastern Europe and in 1979 invaded Afghanistan. NATO responded with a "two-track" decision to step up negotiations while deploying American intermediate-range Pershing II missiles and Ground Launched Cruise Missiles (GLCM) to counter Soviet actions.

During the 1980s, American forces in Europe increased to over 350,000. EUCOM established Fleet Marine Force Europe (later MARFOREUR) in 1980.

The 1983 Unified Command Plan transferred responsibility for the Middle East from EUCOM to a new combatant command, U.S. Central Command (CENTCOM), but EUCOM retained responsibility for Israel, Lebanon and

Syria. At the same time, EUCOM was formally assigned responsibility for Africa south of the Sahara. Thus the area of responsibility became Europe (including the United Kingdom and Ireland), the Mediterranean Sea (including the islands), and the Mediterranean littoral (excluding Egypt, Sudan, Kenya, Ethiopia, Somalia and Djibouti).

The Goldwater-Nichols Act of 1986, together with Chairman of the Joint Chiefs of Staff, Gen. Colin L. Powell, who served from 1989 to 1993, further strengthened the role of combatant commanders. Goldwater-Nichols also established United States Special Operations Command, which led to the activation of a new sub-unified command, Special Operations Command, Europe.

During the 1980s, negotiations continued with the Soviet Union on strategic and theater-level arms limitation. In 1987, the Intermediate-Range Nuclear Forces Treaty (INF Treaty) called an end to the deployment of SS-20s, Pershing IIs and GLCMs. In 1990, NATO and Warsaw Pact members signed a treaty on conventional armed forces in Europe (CFE).

In 1989, the Soviet Union and other Soviet Bloc countries in Eastern Europe collapsed and the Cold War came to an end. The citizens from both East and West Berlin began tearing down the Berlin Wall on 9 November 1989. As a sign of reduced tensions, in 1991 EUCOM took its airborne command post off alert. Meanwhile, in 1991, EUCOM and its components provided forces -primarily VII Corps- to CENTCOM for Operation Desert Storm.

EUCOM supports programs in former Soviet Bloc countries such as the Joint Contract Team Program, NATO Partnership for Peace and the National Guard Bureau State Partnership Program. It was also active in operations in the Balkans, including Bosnia, Macedonia and Kosovo. During this time, EUCOM's assigned forces were lowered below 120,000.

Since 1990, EUCOM has hosted or co-hosted the annual International Military Chiefs of Chaplains Conference, the only one of its kind in the world, working to foster cooperation among religious leaders and understanding of religion as both a force for war and a force for peace.

In 1999, changes to the command's area of responsibility were announced, after amendments to the Unified Command Plan. The United States Atlantic Command areas that had included the waters off Europe and the west coast of Africa were to be transferred to European Command. U.S. European Command already had responsibility for all U.S. land and air military planning in Europe and most of Africa. The change gave EUCOM the responsibility for maritime planning in the same general area of operations. The changes were made effective on Oct. 1, 2000. The Atlantic Command areas that presently include the waters off Europe and the west coast of Africa were also transferred to European Command.

Immediately after the terrorist attacks against New York and Washington, D.C., on 11 September 2001, NATO invoked Article V of the treaty and deployed NATO early warning aircraft to help monitor the skies over North America. EUCOM provided major forces for subsequent operations in Afghanistan and stepped up its efforts to protect United States interests in Europe and Africa. Subsequent terrorist attacks in the EUCOM theater in Casablanca, Madrid, London and Algiers prompted EUCOM to launch Operation Enduring Freedom Trans-Sahara in 2007 while continuing to provide rotational forces to Afghanistan and Iraq.

The 2002 Unified Command Plan transferred responsibility for Lebanon and Syria to CENTCOM, but EUCOM retained responsibility for Israel, and assumed responsibility for Russia (formerly held by the Joint Staff) and for an increased portion of the North Atlantic, to include Iceland and the Portuguese Azores (formerly held by the U.S. Joint Forces Command).

Joint Task Force East provided from forces rotating from continental United States though bases in Bulgaria and Romania, was initially intended to be provided by a rotating US-based brigade. Two bases at Constanţa, Romania were developed, apparently with the main facility at Mihail Kogălniceanu Airfield. Initially however, Joint Task Force East was to have been provided by a rotational 2nd Cavalry Regiment Stryker squadron. The Task Force was originally planned to be called the Eastern Europe Task Force. However, since the stresses of the Iraq and Afghan deployments, the army provision of Joint Task Force East has been replaced by a Marine force known as the Black Sea Rotational Force.

In 2003, the headquarters reorganized to establish the EUCOM Plans and Operations Center (EPOC). From 2006 to 2008, EUCOM helped stand-up a new geographic unified combatant command, United States Africa Command (AFRICOM), which moved to nearby Kelley Barracks and took over responsibility for Department of Defense activities in Africa on 1 October 2008.

Timeline

1967: U.S. European Command headquarters moves to Patch Barracks, Stuttgart, Germany.
1970: 265,000 US troops stationed in Europe.
1980: 350,000 US troops stationed in Europe.
1983: U.S. Central Command is established and takes over responsibility for DoD activities in the Middle East from EUCOM.
1990: VII Corps (US Army) and other USAREUR units are deployed from EUCOM to Saudi Arabia for the Gulf War.
1992: VII Corps (US Army) after redeploying from Saudi Arabia and Kuwait

is withdrawn from EUCOM and inactivated.
1999: US troops stationed in Europe fall below 120,000.
2002: V Corps (US Army) is deployed from EUCOM to Kuwait for the Iraq War invasion.
2003: General James L. Jones becomes the first US Marine to be EUCOM Commander.
2006: V Corps (US Army) is deployed from EUCOM to Iraq as the command and control element for Multi-National Corps–Iraq.
2008: U.S. Africa Command is established and takes over responsibility for DoD activities in Africa from EUCOM.
2009: Navy Admiral James G. Stavridis becomes EUCOM's 15th Commander and the first Navy Admiral to lead the HQ.
2012: V Corps (US Army) is deployed from EUCOM to Afghanistan, providing command and control of all United States ground forces engaged in the theater.
2013: V Corps (US Army) is inactivated after redeploying from Afghanistan, leaving EUCOM without a Corps HQ for the first time since 1951.

Operations

The following list details all operations in which EUCOM has been involved since its inception.

1950s

- Lebanon Crisis 1958 – USEUCOM transported 2,000 troops and more than 4.5 million tons of equipment to Lebanon.

1960s

- Congo Crisis 1960 – USEUCOM transported UN troops and cargo to the Congo.
- Cyprus Crisis 1964 – USEUCOM positioned ships near the island to conduct evacuation of non military personnel and deterrent operations if needed.
- Congo Crisis 1964 – USEUCOM transported Belgian paratroopers in a rescue operation in the Congo.
- Cyprus Crisis 1965 – Airlifted UN peacekeepers and equipment to Cyprus.
- Congo Crisis 1967 – Provided airlift support for supplies, Congolese troops, and refugees.

1970s

- Jordan Hostage Crisis 1970
- Operation Nickel Grass 1973 – Support of Israel in the Yom Kippur War.
- Operation Night Reach 1973 – Transported UN peacekeepers to Middle East at end of Yom Kippur War.
- Cyprus Crisis 1974
- Operation Nimrod Spar 1974/1975 – Cleared the Suez Canal.
- Airlift 1978 – Airlifted multinational forces to Zaire to counter invasion by Angola.

1980s

- Iranian Hostage Crisis 1981 – Release of 52 hostages held for 444 days.
- Hostage Crisis 1982 – Italy – Release of Brigadier General James L. Dozier.
- Operation Arid Farmer 1983 – Supported in the Crisis in Chad.
- Beirut Bombing 1983 – USEUCOM coordinated evacuation and treatment of wounded Marines and identified and returned to CONUS the remains of 241 Marines killed.
- Beirut Air Bridge 1984–1998 – Provided administrative and logistical support the US Embassy in Beirut.
- Operation Eldorado Canyon 1986 – USAF and USN air strikes on Libya in retaliation for terrorist bombing of La Belle Disco in West Berlin.

1990s

- Operation Steel Box/Golden Python 1990 – Supported withdrawal of chemical munitions from Germany and coordination of delivery/transport to Johnson Atoll.
- Hostage Situation 1990–1992 – Hostage release support for Americans kidnapped and held in the Middle East.
- Desert Storm and Proven Force 1991 – War to remove Iraq from Kuwait.
- Provide Comfort II 1991 – Kurdish security zone in northern Iraq.
- Operation Restore Hope 1992–1994 – Assisted in US Somalian security efforts.
- Operation Deny Flight 1993–1995 – Support to UN/NATO enforcement of no-fly zone over Bosnia-Herzegovina.
- Operation Sharp Guard 1993–1996
- Operation Able Sentry/Sabre 1993–1999 – Task force attached to UN Preventive Deployment Force in Macedonia to monitor border activity.
- Operation Vigilant Warrior 1994 – Response to Iraqi buildup along Kuwait border.
- Operation United Shield 1995 – Support of US withdrawal from Somalia.

- Operation Quick Lift 1995 – Support of NATO Rapid Reaction Force and Croatia forces deployment to Bosnia-Herzegovina.
- Operation Nomad Vigil 1995 – deployment to Albania in support of Predator Unmanned Aerial Vehicle.
- Operation Deliberate Force 1995 – NATO air strikes on Bosnian Serb military forces.
- Operation Desert Strike 1996 – Missile Strikes on Iraq.
- Operation Northern Watch 1997–present – Enforcement of No Fly Zone over northern Iraq.
- Operation Assured Lift 1997 – In support of Liberian cease-fire monitoring.
- Operation High Flight 1997 – Search and Rescue effort at Windhoek, Namibia.
- Operations Phoenix Scorpion I & II 1997–1998 – support to UN weapons inspectors in Iraq.
- Operation Auburn Endeavor 1998 – relocation of uranium fuel from Tbilisi, Georgia.
- Operation Determined Falcon 1998 – Show of Force over Albania near Kosovo.
- Operation Calm Support 1998–1999 – Support to Kosovo Diplomatic Observer Mission mission to Kosovo.
- Operation Resolute Response 1998 – Support to US embassy bombings in Kenya and Tanzania.
- Operation Flexible Anvil/Sky Anvil 1998 – Planning for Balkan/Kosovo operations.
- Operation Eagle Eye 1998–1999 – Monitoring compliance with United Nations Security Council Resolution 1199 in Kosovo.
- Operation Desert Fox 1998 – Air Strikes on Iraq.
- Operation Allied Force JTF Noble Anvil 1999 – Air war over Serbia to withdraw forces from Kosovo.

2000s

- Operation Essential Harvest 2001 – Successful NATO program to disarm NLA in Macedonia.
- Operation Enduring Freedom 2001–present – USEUCOM theater planning and execution of the Global War on Terrorism.
- Operation Avid Recovery 2002 – Explosive Ordance Disposal support to Nigeria.

Structure

The main service component commands of EUCOM are the United States Army Europe, United States Naval Forces Europe/U.S. Sixth Fleet, United States Air Forces in Europe and United States Marine Corps Forces, Europe

The United States Army Europe (formerly Seventh Army) is based in Germany. It controls two brigades, one aviation brigade, and several supporting units while also providing support to other Army units in Europe. Previously it had two divisions, although for almost all of the Cold War it controlled two corps of two divisions each. V Corps was deactivated in 2013 upon its return from Afghanistan. VII Corps was deactivated in 1992 after returning to Germany after the Gulf War.

The Sixth Fleet provides ships to NATO Joint Force Command Naples' Operation Active Endeavour, deterring threats to shipping in the Straits of Gibraltar and the remainder of the Mediterranean. Joint Task Force Aztec Silence, a special operations force established under the command of Commander, Sixth Fleet, has been involved in fighting Operation Enduring Freedom - Trans Sahara. It also has a growing role around the shores of West and East Africa, under the direction of United States Africa Command. It previously had a significant Mediterranean presence function against the Soviet Navy's 5th Operational Squadron (Mediterranean Squadron, effectively fleet sized), and for most of the Cold War was the most powerful maritime striking force along NATO's southern flank.

The United States Air Forces in Europe, the Wing-support command, and Third Air Force, USAFE's Warfighting Headquarters are both based at Ramstein Air Base in Germany. They are now much reduced from their high Cold War strength and provide a pool of airpower closer to many trouble spots than aircraft flying from the United States.

The United States Marine Corps Forces, Europe is headquartered in Panzer Kaserne in Böblingen (Stuttgart), Germany, and serves as the Marine Corps component of EUCOM. MARFOREUR is integral in the planning and execution of Black Sea Rotational Force.

A subordinate unified command of EUCOM is SOCEUR (Special Operations Command Europe), headquartered at Patch Barracks in Stuttgart-Vaihingen, Germany. Special forces units within the AOR include the 352nd Special Operations Group of the USAF, based at RAF Mildenhall in the UK, a U.S. Navy SEALs unit, and Naval Special Warfare Unit 2 and 1st BN, 10th Special Forces Group located at Panzer Kaserne, Germany.

EUCOM is also headquartered at Patch Barracks in Stuttgart-Vaihingen, Germany. The Iceland Defense Force also formed part of EUCOM from 2002, when it was transferred from Joint Forces Command in the October 2002 Unified Command Plan change, until 2006 when it was disestablished.

The Kaiserslautern Military Community is the largest U.S. community outside of the U.S., while the Landstuhl Regional Medical Center is the largest U.S. military hospital overseas, treating wounded Soldiers from Iraq and Afghanistan.

Service components

- United States Army Europe (USAREUR) (Lucius D. Clay Kaserne, Wiesbaden, Germany):
  - 2nd Stryker Cavalry Regiment: Rose Barracks, Vilseck, Germany
  - 173rd Airborne Brigade Combat Team: Vicenza, Italy
  - 12th Combat Aviation Brigade: Katterbach Kaserne, Ansbach, Germany
  - 7th Army Joint Multinational Training Command: Grafenwoehr, Germany
  - US Army NATO Brigade: Heuberg Kaserne, Sembach, Germany
  - 19th Battlefield Coordination Detachment: Kaiserslautern, Germany
  - 10th Army Air & Missile Defense Command: Kaiserslautern, Germany
  - 21st Theater Sustainment Command: Panzer Kaserne, Kaiserslautern, Germany
    - 16th Sustainment Brigade: Smith Barracks, Baumholder, Germany
    - 18th Military Police Brigade: Grafenwoehr, Germany
    - 30th Medical Brigade: Sembach, Germany
    - 7th Mission Support Command: Kaiserslautern, Germany
    - 1st Human Resources Sustainment Center
    - 405th Army Field Support Brigade: Daenner Kaserne, Kaiserslautern, Germany
    - 409th Contracting Support Brigade: Kaiserslautern, Germany
    - 266th Financial Management Support Center
- United States Naval Forces Europe (NAVEUR) (Naples, Italy):
  - United States Sixth Fleet (Naples, Italy)
  - Navy Region Europe (Naples, Italy)
- United States Air Forces in Europe (USAFE) (Ramstein Air Base, Germany):
  - Third Air Force (Ramstein Air Base, Germany)
- United States Marine Corps Forces, Europe (MARFOREUR) (Panzer Kaserne, Böblingen, Germany)

U.S. European Command administers the low-profile U.S. military storage installations in Israel. William Arkin in his book *Code Names* revealed the locations of some of the American bases in Israel.[380] Arkin writes that the sites do not appear on maps, and their exact locations are classified. According to the book, some of the sites are located at Ben Gurion Airport, Nevatim, Ovda air base, and in Herzliya Pituah. The sites are numbered as "site 51," "site 53," "site 54," "site 55" and "site 56." Some of the depots are underground, others were built as open hangars. According to Arkin, site 51 holds ammunition and equipment in underground depots. Site 53 is munitions storage and war reserve vehicles at Israeli Air Force bases, site 54 is an emergency military hospital near Tel Aviv with 500 beds, and Sites 55 and 56 are ammunition depots.

Subordinate unified commands

- Special Operations Command, Europe (SOCEUR) – (Panzer Kaserne, Böblingen, Germany)

Additional supporting units

- George C. Marshall European Center for Security Studies (Garmisch, Germany)
- NATO School (Oberammergau, Germany)
- Joint Intelligence Operations Center Europe Analytic Center (RAF Molesworth, Huntingdonshire, UK)

Commanders-in-chief / commanders

Previously, this position held the title "Commander-in-Chief (CINC), United States European Command". However, following an order dated 24 October 2002 by Secretary of Defense Donald Rumsfeld, all CINCs in the United States military were retitled "Commanders" and the use of "CINC" as an acronym was forbidden.

	Name	Photo	Branch	Term began	Term ended	Time in office
1.	General Matthew Ridgway		U.S. Army	30 May 1952	11 July 1953	407 days
2.	General Alfred Gruenther		U.S. Army	1 July 1953	20 November 1956	1,238 days
3.	General Lauris Norstad		U.S. Air Force	20 November 1956	1 January 1963	2,233 days

4.	General Lyman Lemnitzer		U.S. Army	1 January 1963	1 July 1969	2,373 days
5.	General Andrew Goodpaster		U.S. Army	1 July 1969	15 December 1974	1,993 days
6.	General Alexander M. Haig, Jr.		U.S. Army	15 December 1974	1 July 1979	1,659 days
7.	General Bernard W. Rogers		U.S. Army	1 July 1979	26 June 1987	2,917 days
8.	General John Galvin		U.S. Army	26 June 1987	23 June 1992	1,824 days
9.	General John Shalikashvili		U.S. Army	23 June 1992	22 October 1993	486 days
10.	General George Joulwan		U.S. Army	22 October 1993	11 July 1997	1,358 days
11.	General Wesley Clark		U.S. Army	11 July 1997	3 May 2000	1,027 days
12.	General Joseph Ralston		U.S. Air Force	3 May 2000	17 January 2003	989 days
13.	General James L. Jones		U.S. Marine Corps	17 January 2003	7 December 2006	1,420 days
14.	General Bantz J. Craddock		U.S. Army	7 December 2006	30 June 2009	936 days
15.	Admiral James G. Stavridis		U.S. Navy	30 June 2009	10 May 2013	1,410 days
16.	General Philip M. Breedlove		U.S. Air Force	10 May 2013	3 May 2016	1,089 days

| 17. | General Curtis M. Scaparrotti | | U.S. Army | 3 May 2016 | Incumbent | 820 days |

References

- Duke, Simon; *U.S. Military Forces and Installations in Europe*[381], Oxford University Press for SIPRI, 1989

External links

> Wikimedia Commons has media related to *United States European Command*.

- Official website[382]

United States Indo-Pacific Command

United States Indo-Pacific Command	
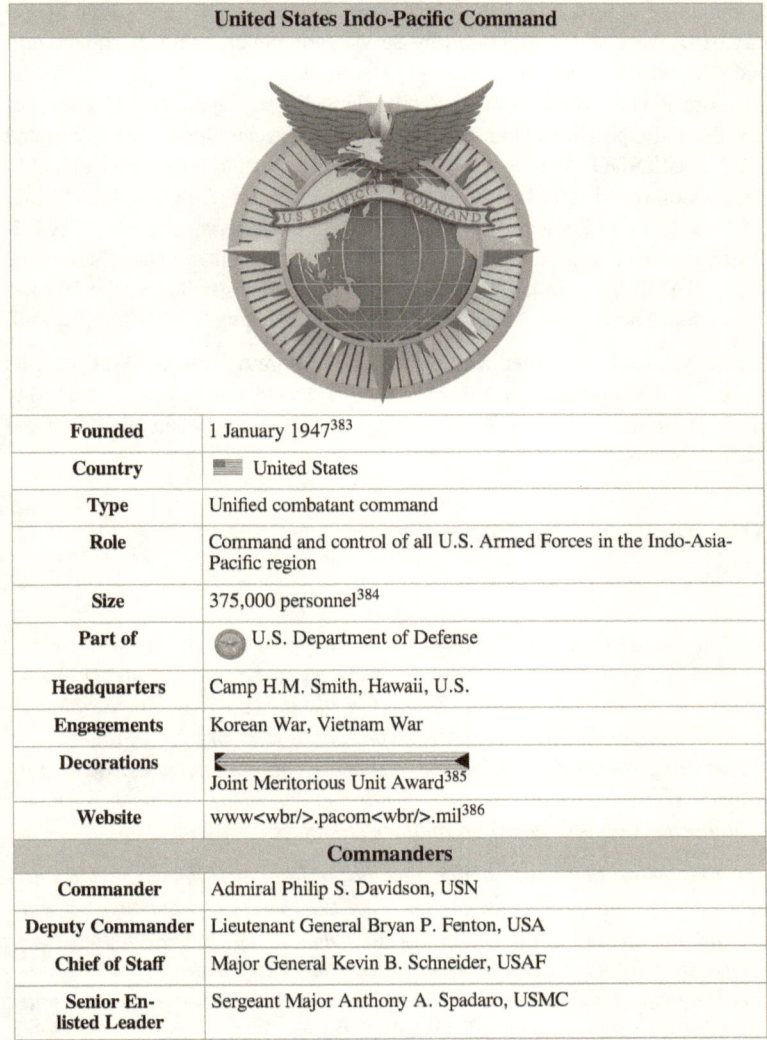	
Founded	1 January 1947[383]
Country	United States
Type	Unified combatant command
Role	Command and control of all U.S. Armed Forces in the Indo-Asia-Pacific region
Size	375,000 personnel[384]
Part of	U.S. Department of Defense
Headquarters	Camp H.M. Smith, Hawaii, U.S.
Engagements	Korean War, Vietnam War
Decorations	Joint Meritorious Unit Award[385]
Website	www<wbr/>.pacom<wbr/>.mil[386]
Commanders	
Commander	Admiral Philip S. Davidson, USN
Deputy Commander	Lieutenant General Bryan P. Fenton, USA
Chief of Staff	Major General Kevin B. Schneider, USAF
Senior Enlisted Leader	Sergeant Major Anthony A. Spadaro, USMC

United States Indo-Pacific Command (USINDOPACOM) is a unified combatant command of the United States Armed Forces responsible for the Indo-Asia-Pacific region. It is the oldest and largest of the unified combatant commands. Its commander, the senior U.S. military officer in the Pacific, is responsible for military operations in an area which encompasses more than 100 million square miles (260,000,000 km^2), or roughly 52 percent of the

Earth's surface, stretching from the waters off the west coast of the United States to the west coast of India, and from the Arctic to the Antarctic. The Commander reports to the President of the United States through the Secretary of Defense and is supported by Service component and subordinate unified commands, including U.S. Army Pacific, U.S. Pacific Fleet, U.S. Pacific Air Forces, U.S. Marine Forces Pacific, U.S. Forces Japan, U.S. Forces Korea, Special Operations Command Korea, and Special Operations Command Pacific. USINDOPACOM also has two direct reporting units (DRUs) - U.S. Pacific Command Joint Intelligence Operations Center (JIOC) and the Center for Excellence in Disaster Management and Humanitarian Assistance (CFE-DMHA) as well as a Standing Joint Task Force, Joint Interagency Task Force West (JIATF-W). The USINDOPACOM headquarters building, the Nimitz-MacArthur Pacific Command Center, is located on Camp H.M. Smith, Hawaii.

Formerly known as **United States Pacific Command (USPACOM)** since its inception, the command was renamed to U.S. Indo-Pacific Command on May 30, 2018, in recognition of the increasing connectivity between the Indian and Pacific Oceans.[387]

Mission

United States Indo-Pacific Command protects and defends, in concert with other U.S. Government agencies, the territory of the United States, its people, and its interests. With allies and partners, we will enhance stability in the Indo-Asia-Pacific region by promoting security cooperation, encouraging peaceful development, responding to contingencies, deterring aggression and, when necessary, fighting to win. This approach is based on partnership, presence and military readiness.

We recognize the global significance of the Indo-Asia-Pacific region and understand that challenges are best met together. Consequently, we will remain an engaged and trusted partner committed to preserving the security, stability, and freedom upon which enduring prosperity in the Indo-Asia-Pacific region depends. We will collaborate with the Services and other Combatant Commands to defend America's interests.

Geographic scope

USINDOPACOM's Area of Responsibility (AOR) encompasses the Pacific Ocean from Antarctica at 92°W, north to 8°N, west to 112°W, northwest to 50°N/142°W, west to 170°E, north to 53°N, northeast to 62°30'N/175°W, north to 64°45'N/175°W, south along the Russian territorial waters to the People's Republic of China, Mongolia, the Democratic People's Republic of Korea, the Republic or Korea, and Japan; the countries of Southeast Asia and the southern Asian landmass to the western border of India; the Indian Ocean east and south of the line from the India/Pakistan coastal border west to 68°E, south along 68°E to Antarctica; Australia; New Zealand; Antarctica, and Hawaii.

- 36 nations
- More than half the world's population
- 3,200 different languages
- 5 of 7 U.S. collective defense treaties[388]

Force structure

Component Commands

Emblem	Command	Acronym	Commander	Established	Headquarters	Subordinate Commands
	United States Army Pacific	US-ARPAC	General Robert B. Brown	October 1, 2000	Fort Shafter, Hawaii	• Eighth Army • 7th Infantry Division • 25th Infantry Division • United States Army Alaska • United States Army Japan • 8th Theater Sustainment Command • 311th Signal Command (Theater) • 94th Army Air & Missile Defense Command • 9th Mission Support Command • 196th Infantry Brigade • 500th Military Intelligence Brigade • 18th Medical Command • 5th Battlefield Coordination Detachment
	United States Pacific Fleet	US-PACFLT	Admiral John C. Aquilino	July 22, 1907	Naval Station Pearl Harbor, Hawaii	• United States Third Fleet • United States Seventh Fleet • Naval Air Force Pacific • Naval Surface Force Pacific • U.S. Naval Forces Japan • U.S. Naval Forces Korea • Joint Region Marianas • Logistics Group Western Pacific • Navy Region Hawaii

Emblem	Command	Acronym	Commander	Established	Headquarters	Subordinate Commands
	United States Pacific Air Forces	PACAF	Lt Gen Jerry P. Martinez (Acting)	August 3, 1944	Joint Base Pearl Harbor-Hickam, Hawaii	• Fifth Air Force • Seventh Air Force • Eleventh Air Force
	United States Marine Corps Forces Pacific	MARFORPAC	Lieutenant General David H. Berger	July 27, 1992	Camp H.M. Smith, Hawaii	• I Marine Expeditionary Force • III Marine Expeditionary Force • Marine Corps Activity Guam • Marine Rotational Force – Darwin

Subordinate Unified Commands

Emblem	Command	Acronym	Commander	Established	Headquarters	Subordinate Commands
	United States Forces Japan	USFJ	Lieutenant General Jerry P. Martinez	July 1, 1957	Yokota Air Base, Tokyo, Japan	
	United States Forces Korea	USFK	General Vincent K. Brooks	January 1, 1983	Yongsan Garrison, Seoul, South Korea	• Eighth United States Army • Seventh Air Force • U.S. Naval Forces Korea • U.S. Marine Forces Korea
	Special Operations Command Pacific	SOCPAC	Major General Bryan P. Fenton	November 1, 1965	Camp H.M. Smith, Hawaii	• Special Operations Command Korea

Direct Reporting Units

Emblem	Command	Acronym	Commander	Established	Headquarters	Subordinate Commands
	Joint Intelligence Operations Center Pacific	JIOC	Colonel Matthew G. Rau	January 1, 1983	Joint Base Pearl Harbor-Hickam, Hawaii	
	Center for Excellence in Disaster Management and Humanitarian Assistance	CFE-DM	Joseph D. Martin	1994	Joint Base Pearl Harbor-Hickam, Hawaii	

Standing Joint Task Force

Emblem	Command	Acronym	Commander	Established	Headquarters	Subordinate Commands
	Joint Interagency Task Force West	JIATF West	Rear Admiral Keith M. Smith, USCG	February 10, 1989	Camp H.M. Smith, Hawaii	

Ballistic Missile Defense for the United States outside of NORAD: Hawaii, Guam, & the Pacific region

In the Pacific Region, instead of NORAD, the United States Pacific Command must make the decision that an incoming ballistic missile is a threat to the United States. Hawaii is the only state in the United States with a pre-programmed Wireless Emergency Alert that can be sent quickly to wireless devices if a ballistic missile is heading toward Hawaii. If the missile is fired from North Korea, the missile would take approximately 20 minutes to reach Hawaii. The United States Indo-Pacific Command would take less than 5 minutes to make a determination that the missile could impact Hawaii and would then notify the Hawaii Emergency Management Agency (HI-EMA). HI-EMA would issue the Civil Defense Warning (CDW) that an inbound missile could impact Hawaii and that people should Shelter-in-Place: *Get Inside, Stay Inside, and Stay Tuned*. People in Hawaii would have 12 to 15 minutes before impact. Federal Emergency Management Agency (FEMA) is not required to be notified for approval to cancel an alert. Signal carriers allow people to block alerts from state and law enforcement agencies, but not those issued by the President. FEMA can send alerts to targeted audiences but has not implemented this as of January 2018. Other states can take as long as 30 minutes to create, enter and distribute a missile alert. As of January 2018, the nationwide system for Wireless Emergency Alerts to mobile devices has never been tested.

History

Establishment of Unified Commands in the Pacific

USINDOPACOM has evolved through the gradual consolidation of various commands in the Pacific and Far East. Its origins can be traced to the command structure established early in World War II to wage the war in the Pacific.

In April 1942, U.S. military forces in the Pacific Theatre were divided into two commands: the Southwest Pacific Area (SWPA) under Army General Douglas MacArthur; and the Pacific Ocean Areas (POA) under Navy Admiral Chester W. Nimitz. Each had command of all U.S. military forces assigned to his area. The authority of the POA Commander-in-Chief (CINCPOA) was technically separate from that of the Commander in Chief, Pacific Fleet (CINCPAC), but Admiral Nimitz was assigned to both positions and bore the title CINCPAC/CINCPOA.

Efforts to establish a unified command for the entire Pacific AOR proved impossible during the war. The divergent interests of the Army and the Navy precluded the subordination of either of the two principal commanders in the Pacific Theatre. When the war ended in September 1945, the command arrangement carried forward with Fleet Admiral Nimitz as CINCPAC/CINCPOA and General of the Army MacArthur as Commander in Chief, U.S. Army Forces Pacific (CINCAFPAC).

Command arrangements after World War II were defined by the "Outline Command Plan" – in a sense, the first Unified Command Plan (UCP) – approved by President Harry S. Truman on 14 December 1946 and authorized by the National Security Act of 1947. The plan called for the establishment of seven unified combatant commands as "an interim measure for the immediate postwar period."[389]

The first three unified commands were established in the Pacific. The Joint Chiefs of Staff implementing directive of 16 December 1946 established the Far East Command (FECOM), Pacific Command (PACOM), and Alaskan Command (ALCOM) effective 1 January 1947. The commands, their areas of responsibility, and their missions were as follows:

- **Far East Command**: U.S. forces in Japan, Korea, the Ryukyus, the Philippines, and the Mariana and Bonin Islands. The Commander-in-Chief, Far East (CINCFE) would carry out occupation duties, maintain the security of the command, plan and prepare for a general emergency in the area, support the Commander-in-Chief, Pacific (CINCPAC), and command U.S. forces in China in an emergency.

- **Pacific Command**: U.S. forces allocated by the Joint Chiefs of Staff within the Pacific Area. CINCPAC would defend the United States against attack through the Pacific, conduct operations in the Pacific, maintain security of U.S. island positions and of sea and air communications, support U.S. military commitments in China, plan and prepare for a general emergency, and support CINCFE and Commander-in-Chief, Alaskan Command (CINCAL).
- **Alaskan Command**: U.S. forces in Alaska, including the Aleutian Islands. CINCAL would protect Alaska and its sea and air communications, defend the United States from attack through Alaska and the Arctic, plan and prepare for a general emergency, and support CINCFE, CINCPAC, and the Commanding General of the Strategic Air Command (CG SAC).

General of the Army Douglas MacArthur was appointed CINCFE; Army Major General Howard A. Craig was assigned as CINCAL. U.S. Navy Admiral John Henry Towers was designated CINCPAC. At the time of appointment, he was serving as Admiral Nimitz' direct successor as CINCPAC/CINCPOA. Admiral Towers retained his position as Commander-in-Chief, U.S. Pacific Fleet; his title was abbreviated CINCPACFLT to avoid confusion with the newly established Pacific Command. Headquarters for both CINCPAC and CINCPACFLT were located at Makalapa, Pearl Harbor, in the Territory of Hawai'i.

Then-PACOM's original AOR ranged from Burma and the eastern Indian Ocean to the west coast of the Americas. Following a 1949 review of missions and deployments of U.S. forces, the Joint Chiefs of Staff revised the Unified Command Plan on 16 February 1950. The Volcano Islands were transferred to FECOM's AOR; likewise, responsibility for South Korea was transferred from FECOM to PACOM. The duty of protecting the Panama Canal remained assigned to Commander in Chief, Atlantic Command (CINCLANT); one year later, however, the Western approaches to the Canal would be reassigned to CINCPAC.

The Korean War

The outbreak of the Korean War and subsequent developments in the Far East tested the U.S. unified command structure in the Pacific. Although General MacArthur, as CINCFE, had been relieved of responsibility for South Korea, early U.S. reaction to North Korea's invasion of the South on 25 June 1950 came through his command. On 10 July, at the request of the United Nations, President Truman directed General MacArthur to establish the United Nations Command (UNC) for the purpose of directing operations against North Korean forces. U.S. forces assigned to FECOM were assigned to UNC with General MacArthur designated Commander-in-Chief, UNC (CINCUNC). The primary responsibility of CINCFE, however, remained the defense of Japan. During the war, CINCPAC was ordered to support CINCUNC/CINCFE.

With CINCFE focused on combat operations during the Korean War, the Joint Chiefs of Staff, over strong objection from FECOM, transferred the Mariana, Bonin and Volcano Islands to PACOM. In late 1951, PACOM was also assigned responsibility for the Philippines, the Pescadores, and Formosa (Taiwan).

Reorganization of 1956

The new Unified Command Plan approved by Secretary of Defense Charles Wilson on 21 June 1956 produced significant changes to the command structure in the Pacific. ALCOM would remain as a unified command because of its strategic location, retaining its mission for the ground defense of the Alaskan region. Its other responsibilities, however, were reduced: the duty for protection of sea communications in Alaskan waters was assumed by PACOM. The responsibilities of the Continental Air Defense Command (CONAD) would be likewise expanded to include the air defense of Alaska and the Northeast.

UCP 1956 also disestablished FECOM as a separate unified command. U.S. military deployments to Japan and Korea were decreasing after the end of Japanese reconstruction and the Korean War. The JCS, therefore, believed that the divided command structure in the Pacific should be abolished and FECOM's responsibility reassigned to PACOM. A subsequent outline plan to disestablish FECOM and transfer its responsibilities was approved by SECDEF and the JCS effective 1 July 1957. Under the plan, two subordinate unified commands under CINCPAC were established: Commander, U.S. Forces Japan (COMUSJAPAN) and Commander, U.S. Forces Korea (COMUSKOREA). The latter was dual-hatted as CINCUNC.

The UCP further specified that no unified commander would exercise direct command of any of its Service components or subordinate commands. As such, Admiral Felix Stump gave up direct command of the Pacific Fleet, delegating the responsibility of CINCPACFLT to his Deputy, Admiral Maurice E. Curts. CINCPAC's staff was thereafter separated from CINCPACFLT's staff, and moved from Pearl Harbor to a new headquarters building (the former Aiea Naval Hospital) at Camp H.M. Smith. Service components for the Army and Air Force – U.S. Army Pacific (USARPAC) and U.S. Pacific Air Forces (PACAF) – were also assigned to PACOM.

The Vietnam War

Command over U.S. forces engaged in the Vietnam War was designated by CINCPAC to three subordinate commands. U.S. Military Assistance Command, Vietnam (USMACV), activated 8 February 1962 to direct U.S. support to South Vietnam's military forces, largely controlled all U.S. forces and operations within South Vietnam. Naval gunfire support and air strikes on targets in Vietnam, however, were delegated to PACFLT and the U.S. 7th Fleet. PACAF and PACFLT were responsible for conducting air and naval operations against North Vietnam and Laos. Control of B-52s employed to conduct air strikes against targets in South Vietnam remained under the Strategic Air Command.

Command adjustments, 1971–1979

A new Unified Command Plan was approved in 1971. Effective 1 January 1972, the Pacific Command assumed responsibility for the Indian Ocean and the countries of southern Asia extending westward to the eastern border of Iran (which then fell under EUCOM's responsibility). The Alaskan Command transferred responsibility for the Aleutian Islands and parts of the Arctic Ocean to PACOM, as well. ALCOM would remain a distinct unified command until it was disestablished by another Unified Command Plan on 1 July 1975. An amendment to this plan on 1 May 1976 adjusted PACOM's boundaries yet again. The amendment gave CINCPAC responsibility for the entire Indian Ocean to the east coast of Africa, including the Gulfs of Aden and Oman and all of the Indian Ocean Islands excepting the Malagasy Republic. This decision expanded PACOM's AOR across more than 50% of the Earth's surface an area of over 100 million square miles.

U.S. Army Pacific (USARPAC) was disestablished 31 December 1974 as part of a bid by the Army to reduce its headquarters. The much smaller U.S. Army CINCPAC Support Group (CSG) took over USARPAC's duty to assist and coordinate with CINCPAC Headquarters and PACOM service components on Army matters. In 1979, U.S. Army Western Command (WESTCOM) was activated as the new Army component for PACOM. WESTCOM was redesignated USARPAC effective 30 August 1990.

Unified Command Plan of 1983

The establishment of U.S. Central Command (USCENTCOM) for the Middle East on 1 January 1983 resulted in reassignment of responsibilities from PACOM to the new command. CENTCOM took responsibility for Afghanistan and Pakistan from PACOM; the India-Pakistan border became the boundary between CENTCOM and PACOM.

Despite the adjustment, UCP 1983 actually increased the size of PACOM's AOR. The Joint Chiefs of Staff assigned responsibility over China to PACOM, presuming that increased political-military contacts between China and the United States could best be handled at the unified command level. A similar decision was made to assign North Korea to PACOM, reasoning that unifying responsibility for the Korean Peninsula under CINCPAC would greatly enhance his ability to make the transition from peace to war should he be called upon to do so. Madagascar was assigned to PACOM because the island impinged directly upon CINCPAC's mission of protecting U.S. sea lines of communication in the Indian Ocean. Responsibility for Mongolia and Alaska also fell to CINCPAC under the new plan.

At the request of then-CINCPAC Admiral William Crowe, his title and that of his command were changed to USCINCPAC and USPACOM, respectively.

Boundary adjustment and Alaskan Command, 1989

On 26 June 1989, Secretary of Defense Dick Cheney endorsed the recommendation from the Joint Chiefs of Staff to reassign the Gulfs of Aden and Oman from USPACOM to USCENTCOM's AOR. Though a modest shift, the change meant that the new boundary between the commands would no longer cut through the Strait of Hormuz. At the same time, the Alaskan Command (ALCOM) was reestablished as a subordinate command to PACOM.

Transfers of responsibility, 2002–2006

Under UCP 2002, effective 21 January, Secretary of Defense Donald Rumsfeld assigned Antarctica to USPACOM. Secretary Rumsfeld also approved assignment of responsibility for Russia to EUCOM with USPACOM in a supporting role for the Russian Far East. Later reassignments under the 2004 and 2006 plans placed the entire Seychelles Archipelago in the USCENTCOM's AOR and extended U.S. Northern Command (USNORTHCOM)'s boundary westward to encompass all of the Aleutian islands, respectively.

On 24 October 2002, the Secretary issued a memorandum declaring that the title "Commander in Chief" should only refer to the President of the United States. Effective that date, all combatant commanders deleted "in Chief" from their titles. USCINCPAC was redesignated Commander, U.S. Pacific Command (CDRUSPACOM).

Transfer of Alaskan Command, 2014

In a move to streamline command and control of forces in Alaska and integrate forces in defense of North America, Secretary of Defense Chuck Hagel approved the transfer of ALCOM to USNORTHCOM.

Renaming of Pacific Command, 2018

On 30 May 2018, at the change-of-command ceremony between Admirals Harry B. Harris Jr. and Philip S. Davidson, Defense Secretary Jim Mattis announced that Pacific Command has been renamed Indo-Pacific Command "in recognition of the increasing connectivity of the Indian and Pacific Oceans." U.S. officials stated that the change was instituted to "better reflect the command's areas of responsibility, which includes 36 nations as well as both the Pacific and Indian Oceans."[390]

Commanders

U.S. Pacific Command

No.	Image	Commander	Tenure
1.		Admiral John H. Towers, USN	1 January 1947 – 28 February 1947
2.		Admiral Louis E. Denfeld, USN	28 February 1947 – 3 December 1947
3.		Admiral DeWitt C. Ramsey, USN	12 January 1948 – 30 April 1949
4.		Admiral Arthur W. Radford, USN	30 April 1949 – 10 July 1953
5.		Admiral Felix B. Stump, USN	10 July 1953 – 31 July 1958

6.		Admiral Harry D. Felt, USN	31 July 1958 – 30 June 1964
7.		Admiral Ulysses S. Grant Sharp, Jr., USN	30 June 1964 – 31 July 1968
8.		Admiral John S. McCain, Jr., USN	31 July 1968 – 1 September 1972
9.		Admiral Noel A.M. Gayler, USN	1 September 1972 – 30 August 1976
10.		Admiral Maurice F. Weisner, USN	30 August 1976 – 31 October 1979
11.		Admiral Robert L.J. Long, USN	31 October 1979 – 1 July 1983
12.		Admiral William J. Crowe, Jr., USN	1 July 1983 – 18 September 1985
13.		Admiral Ronald J. Hays, USN	18 September 1985 – 30 September 1988
14.		Admiral Huntington Hardisty, USN	30 September 1988 – 1 March 1991
15.		Admiral Charles R. Larson, USN	1 March 1991 – 11 July 1994

16.		Admiral Richard C. Macke, USN	19 July 1994 – 31 January 1996
17.		Admiral Joseph W. Prueher, USN	31 January 1996 – 20 February 1999
18.		Admiral Dennis C. Blair, USN	20 February 1999 – 2 May 2002
19.		Admiral Thomas B. Fargo, USN	2 May 2002 – 26 February 2005
20.		Admiral William J. Fallon, USN	26 February 2005 – 12 March 2007
21.		Admiral Timothy J. Keating, USN	26 March 2007 – 19 October 2009
22.		Admiral Robert F. Willard, USN	19 October 2009 – 9 March 2012
23.		Admiral Samuel J. Locklear III, USN	9 March 2012 – 27 May 2015
24.		Admiral Harry B. Harris, Jr., USN	27 May 2015 – 30 May 2018

U.S. Indo-Pacific Command

No.	Image	Commander	Tenure
25.		Admiral Philip S. Davidson, USN	30 May 2018 – present

External links

Wikimedia Commons has media related to *United States Indo-Pacific Command*.

- Official website[391]

United States Northern Command

United States Northern Command	
	Emblem of United States Northern Command
Founded	1 October 2002 (15 years, 10 months)[392]
Country	United States of America
Type	Unified Combatant Command
Role	"USNORTHCOM partners to conduct Homeland Defense and Civil Support operations within the assigned area of responsibility to defend, protect, and secure the United States and its interests."[393]
Part of	Department of Defense
Headquarters	Peterson AFB, Colorado Springs, Colorado, U.S.
Motto(s)	"We have the watch"[394]
Decorations	Joint Meritorious Unit Award
Commanders	
Commander	General Terrence J. O'Shaughnessy, USAF[395]
Deputy Commander	Lieutenant General Reynold N. Hoover, USA
Command Senior Enlisted Leader	SgtMaj Paul McKenna, USMC

United States Northern Command (**USNORTHCOM**)[396] is a Unified Combatant Command of the U.S. military tasked with providing military support for civil authorities in the U.S., and protecting the territory and national interests of the United States within the contiguous United States, Alaska (not Hawaii), Puerto Rico, Canada, Mexico, The Bahamas, and the air, land and

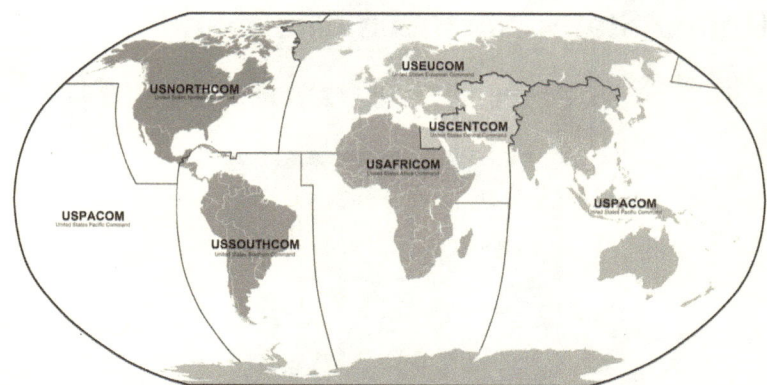

Figure 102: *NORTHCOM Area Of Responsibility (in purple)*

sea approaches to these areas. It is the U.S. military command which, if applicable, would be the primary defender against a mainland invasion of the United States.

USNORTHCOM was created on 25 April 2002 when President George W. Bush approved a new Unified Command Plan, following the September 11 attacks. USNORTHCOM went operational on 1 October 2002.

The support that USNORTHCOM provides to civil authorities is legally limited by the Posse Comitatus Act, which sets some limits on the role of the U.S. military in civilian law enforcement. However, in case of national emergency, natural or man-made, its Air Forces Northern National Security Emergency Preparedness Directorate will take charge of the situation or event.[397]

Creation

USNORTHCOM was established on 25 April 2002 when President George W. Bush approved a new Unified Command Plan, and attained initial operating capability on 1 October 2002.

Mission

According to the UCP, Northern Command's mission is to:

- Conduct operations to deter, prevent, and defeat threats and aggression aimed at the United States, its territories, and interests within the assigned area of responsibility and,

- As directed by the President or Secretary of Defense provide military assistance to civil authorities including consequence management operations

Area of responsibility

USNORTHCOM's Area of Responsibility (AOR) includes air, land and sea approaches and encompasses the contiguous United States, Alaska, Canada, Mexico and the surrounding water out to approximately 500 nautical miles (930 km). It also includes the Gulf of Mexico, the Straits of Florida, portions of the Caribbean region to include The Bahamas, Puerto Rico, the U.S. Virgin Islands, the British Virgin Islands, Bermuda, and the Turks and Caicos Islands. The commander of USNORTHCOM is responsible for theater security cooperation with Canada, Mexico, and The Bahamas. In May 2011, NORTHCOM was mobilized in the wake of the BP oil spill in the Gulf of Mexico to provide air, ground, and logistical support. In October 2014, NORTHCOM took administrative control of Alaskan Command.

Organizational structure

Headquarters

Commander, U.S. Northern Command is concurrently Commander of the U.S.-Canadian North American Aerospace Defense Command (NORAD). The two are co-located at Peterson Air Force Base in Colorado Springs, Colorado. General Ralph Eberhart was the first CDRUSNORTHCOM.

USNORTHCOM headquarters has approximately 1,200 uniformed and civilian members, and few permanent forces. Forces from all branches of the U.S. military may be assigned to the Command as needed to complete its mission.

Subordinate Commands

USNORTHCOM exercises command and control of two subordinate unified commands, four service component commands, and several standing Joint Task Forces (JTFs). The subordinate unified commands are Special Operations Command-North, which was activated on 31 December 2012, and Alaskan Command, which was transferred from US Pacific Command (USPACOM) control to USNORTHCOM control on 1 October 2014. USNORTHCOM service components include U.S. Fifth Army/ARNORTH, First Air Force/AFNORTH, USFF/NAVNORTH, and U.S. Marine Corps Forces Reserve/MARFORNORTH. USNORTHCOM's Joint Task Forces include Joint

Force Headquarters National Capital Region, Joint Task Force-Civil Support, and Joint Task Force North.

Between 1 October 2002 and 2007, Northern Command deactivated Joint Force Headquarters Homeland Security and activated Joint Force Headquarters National Capital Region and Standing Joint Task Force North.[398] On 31 December 2012, Special Operations Command-North was activated, and will be led by a general instead of a colonel.

List of commanders

Note: The National Defense Authorization Act of 2008 stipulates that at least one deputy commander of USNORTHCOM be a National Guard general officer unless the commander is already such an officer.[399,400]

	Image	Name	Branch	Term began	Term ended
1.		General Ralph E. Eberhart	USAF	22 October 2002	5 November 2004
2.		Admiral Timothy J. Keating	USN	5 November 2004	23 March 2007
3.		General Victor E. Renuart Jr.	USAF	23 March 2007	19 May 2010
4.		Admiral James A. Winnefeld, Jr.	USN	19 May 2010	3 August 2011
5.		General Charles H. Jacoby Jr.	USA	3 August 2011	5 December 2014
6.		Admiral William E. Gortney	USN	5 December 2014	13 May 2016

7.		General Lori J. Robinson	USAF	13 May 2016	24 May 2018
8.		General Terrence J. O'Shaughnessy	USAF	24 May 2018	Incumbent

Planning and strategy

Northern Command has created several classified "concept plans" (e.g. "Defense Support of Civil Authorities") that are intended to address the 15 National Planning Scenarios that NORTHCOM must be prepared to respond to.

However the GAO found that the national strategy to defend the United States is several years out of date.[401]

Domestic operations and training

NORTHCOM operates extensive domestic intelligence operations which both share and receive information from local, state and federal law enforcement agencies. Employees of the Federal Bureau of Investigation, Central Intelligence Agency, National Security Agency, Defense Intelligence Agency, National Geospatial-Intelligence Agency, and other agencies maintain offices at NORTHCOM and receive daily intelligence briefings.

Northern Command has completed several joint training exercises with local, state and federal law enforcement agencies, the Department of Homeland Security, and the Federal Emergency Management Agency (FEMA).

In Exercise Vigilant Shield 2008, Northern Command, Pacific Command, the Department of Homeland Security, and numerous law enforcement agencies across the U.S. conducted exercises to test their "response abilities against a variety of potential threats".

Related legislation

The Military Commissions Act of 2006 lifted many restrictions placed on the military to support civilian administration by the Posse Comitatus Act, however the US Supreme Court ruled in June 2008 that significant portions of the MCA were unconstitutional. The "John Warner Defense Authorization Act of 2007" H.R. 5122 (2006) effectively nullified the limits of the Insurrection Act when it was passed; however, the bill was amended in 2008.

On 1 October 2008, the 3rd Infantry Division's 1st Brigade Combat Team was assigned to U.S. Northern Command, marking the first time an active unit had been given a dedicated assignment to Northern Command. The force will be known for the first year as a CBRNE Consequence Management Response Force, and will serve as an on-call federal response force for terrorist attacks and other natural or manmade emergencies and disasters.

Further reading

- Colonel Cronen; R. Barry (December 2009). "U.S. Northern Command & Defense Support of Civil Authorities"[402]. *Center for Army Lessons Learned (CALL) Newsletter*. **9** (10).

External links

- United States Northern Command[403]

United States Southern Command

United States Southern Command	
Emblem of the United States Southern Command.	
Active	1963 – present
Country	United States of America
Type	Unified Combatant Command
Part of	Department of Defense
Headquarters	Doral, Florida
Nickname(s)	USSOUTHCOM
Engagements	Operation Unified Response Operation Continuing Promise Operation New Horizons Invasion of Panama
Commanders	
Combatant Commander	Admiral Kurt W. Tidd, USN
Military Deputy Commander	Lieutenant General Joseph P. DiSalvo, USA

The **United States Southern Command** (**USSOUTHCOM**), located in Doral, Florida in Greater Miami, is one of ten Unified Combatant Commands (CCMDs) in the United States Department of Defense. It is responsible for providing contingency planning, operations, and security cooperation for Central and South America, the Caribbean (except US commonwealths, territories, and possessions), their territorial waters, and for the force protection of US military resources at these locations. USSOUTHCOM is also responsible for ensuring the defense of the Panama Canal and the canal area. As explained below, USSOUTHCOM has been under scrutiny due to several human rights and rule of law controversies in which it has been embroiled for nearly a decade.

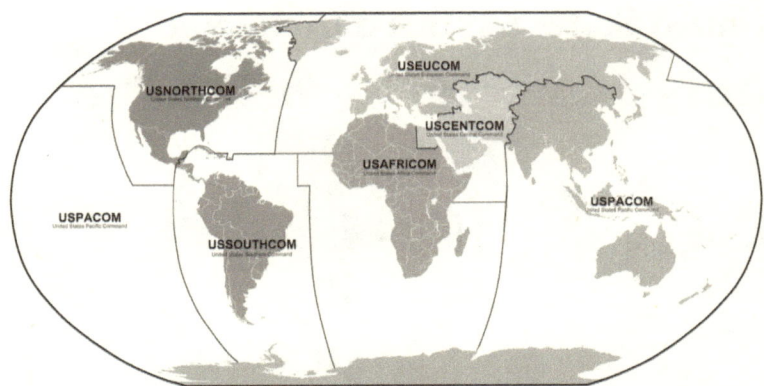

Figure 103: *In this map, SOUTHCOM Area Of Responsibility is shown in dark red*

Under the leadership of a four-star Commander, USSOUTHCOM is organized into a headquarters with six main directorates, component commands and military groups that represent SOUTHCOM in the region. The current commander is Admiral Kurt W. Tidd, USN.

USSOUTHCOM is a joint command[404] of more than 1,201 military and civilian personnel representing the United States Army, Navy, Air Force, Marine Corps, Coast Guard, and several other federal agencies. Civilians working at USSOUTHCOM are, for the most part, civilian employees of the Army, as the Army is USSOUTHCOM's Combatant Command Support Agent. The Services provide USSOUTHCOM with component commands which, along with their Joint Special Operations component, two Joint Task Forces, one Joint Interagency Task Force, and Security Cooperation Offices, perform USSOUTHCOM missions and security cooperation activities. USSOUTHCOM exercises its authority through the commanders of its components, Joint Task Forces/Joint Interagency Task Force, and Security Cooperation Organizations.

Area of interest

The USSOUTHCOM Area of Responsibility (AOR) encompasses 32 nations (19 in Central and South America and 13 in the Caribbean), of which 31 are democracies, and 14 U.S. and European territories. As of October 2002, the area of focus covered 14.5 million square miles (23.2 million square kilometers.)

The United States Southern Command area of interest includes:

- The land mass of Latin America south of Mexico

Figure 104: *SOUTHCOM Area Of Focus*

- The waters adjacent to Central and South America
- The Caribbean Sea, its 12 island nations and European territories
- A portion of the Atlantic Ocean

Components

USSOUTHCOM accomplishes much of its mission through its service components, four representing each service, one specializing in Special Operations missions, and one specializing in educating and sharpening future leaders of the Western Hemisphere via effort of Joint Forces and Diplomacy much like the North Atlantic Treaty Organization's Defense College:

U.S. Army South (Sixth Army)

United States Army South (ARSOUTH) forces include aviation, intelligence, communication, and logistics units. Located at Fort Sam Houston, Texas, it supports regional disaster relief and counterdrug efforts. ARSOUTH also exercises oversight, planning, and logistical support for humanitarian and civic assistance projects throughout the region in support of the USSOUTHCOM Theater Security Cooperation Strategy. ARSOUTH provides Title 10 and Executive Agent responsibilities throughout the Latin American and Caribbean region. In 2013, around four thousand troops were deployed in Latin America.

Air Forces Southern

Located at Davis-Monthan Air Force Base, Arizona, AFSOUTH consists of a staff; a Falconer Combined Air and Space Operations Center for command and control of air activity in the USSOUTHCOM area and an Air Force operations group responsible for Air Force forces in the area. AFSOUTH serves as the executive agent for forward operating locations; provides joint/combined radar surveillance architecture oversight; provides intra-theater airlift; and supports USSOUTHCOM's Theater Security Cooperation Strategy through regional disaster relief exercises and counter-drug operations. AFSOUTH also provides oversight, planning, execution, and logistical support for humanitarians and civic assistance projects and hosts a number of Airmen-to-Airmen conferences. Twelfth Air Force is also leading the way in bringing the Chief of Staff of the Air Force's Warfighting Headquarters (WFHQ) concept to life. The WFHQ is composed of a command and control element, an Air Force forces staff and an Air Operations Center. Operating as a WFHQ since June 2004, Twelfth Air Force has served as the Air Force model for the future of Combined Air and Space Operations Centers and WFHQ Air Force forces.

U.S. Naval Forces Southern Command & U.S. Fourth Fleet

Located at Naval Station Mayport, Florida, USNAVSO exercises command and control over all U.S. naval operations in the USSOUTHCOM area including naval exercises, maritime operations, and port visits. USNAVSO is also the executive agent for the operation of the cooperative security location at Comalapa, El Salvador, which provides basing in support of aerial counter narco-terrorism operations.

On 24 April 2008, Admiral Gary Roughead, the Chief of Naval Operations, announced that the United States Fourth Fleet would be re-established, effective 1 July, responsible for U.S. Navy ships, aircraft and submarines operating in the Caribbean Sea, as well as Central and South America. Rear Admiral Joseph D. Kernan was named as the fleet commander and Commander, U.S. Naval Forces Southern Command. Up to four ships are deployed in the waters in and around Latin American, at any given time.

U.S. Marine Corps Forces, South

Located in Doral, Florida, USMARFORSOUTH commands all United States Marine Corps Forces (MARFORs) assigned to USSOUTHCOM; advises US-SOUTHCOM on the proper employment and support of MARFORs; conducts deployment/redeployment planning and execution of assigned/attached MARFORs; and accomplishes other operational missions as assigned.

Special Operations Command South

Located at Homestead Air Reserve Base near Miami, Florida, Special Operations Command South (USSOCSOUTH) provides the primary theater contingency response force and plans, prepares for, and conducts special operations in support of USSOUTHCOM. USSOCSOUTH controls all Special Operations Forces in the region and also establishes and operates a Joint Special Operations Task Force when required. As a Theater Special Operations Command (TSOC), USSOCSOUTH is a sub-unified command of USSOUTHCOM.

SOCSOUTH has five assigned or attached subordinate commands including "Charlie" Company, 3rd Battalion, 7th Special Forces Group (Airborne) (7th

Figure 105: *BG Mulholland, SOCSOUTH Commander in 2014, honors 7th SFG(A) soldiers in Honduras*

SFG(A)); "Charlie" Company, 3rd Battalion, 160th Special Operations Aviation Regiment (Airborne); Naval Special Warfare Unit FOUR; 112th Signal Detachment SOCSOUTH; and Joint Special Operations Air Component-South.

There are also three task forces with specific missions in the region that report to U.S. Southern Command:

Joint Task Force Bravo

Located at Soto Cano Air Base, Honduras, JTF-Bravo operates a forward, all-weather day/night C-5-capable airbase. JTF – Bravo organizes multilateral exercises and supports, in cooperation with partner nations, humanitarian and civic assistance, counterdrug, contingency and disaster relief operations in Central America.

Joint Task Force Guantanamo

Located at U.S. Naval Station Guantanamo Bay, Cuba, JTF – Guantanamo conducts detention and interrogation operations in support of the War on Terrorism, coordinates and implements detainee screening operations, and supports law enforcement and war crimes investigations as well as Military Commissions for Detained Enemy Combatants. JTF – Guantanamo is also prepared to support mass migration operations at Naval Station GTMO.

Joint Interagency Task Force South

Located in Key West, Florida, JIATF South is an interagency task force that serves as the catalyst for integrated and synchronized interagency counter-drug operations and is responsible for the detection and monitoring of suspect air and maritime drug activity in the Caribbean Sea, Gulf of Mexico, and the eastern Pacific. JIATF- South also collects, processes, and disseminates counter-drug information for interagency operations. Manta Air Base was one of JIATF-South's bases, in Ecuador until September 19, 2009.

Human Rights Controversies

Beginning in late 2014 in response to a request by then Senate Armed Services Committee Chair Carl Levin, USSOUTHCOM's William J. Perry Center for Hemispheric Defense Studies (CHDS), located at the National Defense University in Washington, D.C., was also under investigation by the Department of Defense Office of Inspector General. Insider national security whistleblower complaints included that the Center knowingly protected a CHDS professor from Chile who belonged to the DINA state terrorist organization (whose attack against a former Chilean foreign minister in 1976 in Washington, D.C. resulted in two deaths, including that of an American); the clandestine participation of Center officials in the 2009 Honduran coup, as well as gross mismanagement, corruption, homophobia, racism, and sexism. In 2015 the Center for Public Integrity quoted an internal Southern Command document that reported that CHDS "staff had exchanged 'racially charged emails' — including one directed at President Barack Obama; used offensive language such as 'faggot,' 'buttboy' and 'homo'; and that 'women employees feel that they are treated inappropriately.' Even senior leaders used 'inappropriate hand gestures,' it said, and mentioned simulations of masturbation." However, unlike the 2012 SouthCom prostitution scandal, there is no public information that suggests any wrongdoers were punished in any way, while those complaining about such malfeasance were harassed by senior officials. "Reports that NDU hired foreign military officers with histories of involvement in human rights abuses, including torture and extra-judicial killings of civilians, are stunning, and they are repulsive," said Senator Patrick Leahy, D-Vermont, the author of the "Leahy Law" prohibiting U.S. assistance to military units and members of foreign security forces that violate human rights.[405,406]

On March 10, 2017, Daniel P. Meyer, executive director for Intelligence Community Whistleblowing & Source Protection (ICW&SP), Office of the Inspector General of the Intelligence Community (IC IG), announced that classified Congressional Disclosure #1703 relating to the CHDS scandal had been sent "to both the House Permanent Subcommittee on Intelligence and the Senate Select Committee on Intelligence via a classified network, protecting the lawful disclosure of classified information." Four days later, Department of Defense Inspector General Glenn Fine wrote an email to a senior member of Congress announcing that "Given the seriousness and scope of [the] allegations, OIG staff is conducting a careful analysis of each allegation. While this has taken longer than we would have preferred, we want to ensure that appropriate consideration is given."

In February 2017, the controversial role played by the Perry Center in Latin America was underscored after the Miami Herald published an article on former CHDS Dean Craig Deare, who had been appointed by General Michael

Flynn to be the Western Hemisphere chief for the U.S. National Security Council. Citing Deare's former CHDS colleagues, the story noted that Deare, in addition to security concerns and lax personal conduct, had "a checkered record of support for and involvement with some of the Western Hemisphere's most notorious human rights abusers." It pointed out that he was also "a central figure" in then SASC Chair Levin's request for a DoD OIG investigation that included questions about what role the William Perry Center may have played in the illegal Honduras military coup.[407] It added that the probe of CHDS included the question of whether the Center "still bore vestiges of the old School of the Americas, the U.S. program that trained Latin America military officers, many of whom then went on to be brutal dictators in their home countries." A day after its publication in the Herald, Deare offered a controversial analysis of Trump Administration policies and the role of key First Family figures during a supposedly "off-the-record" talk before a score of Beltway "insider" invitees at the Woodrow Wilson Center. Following media coverage of Deare's reported criticism of the Trump policies, allegedly 'awkward' comments about Ivanka Trump's good looks, and the Miami Herald article, Deare was unceremoniously shown the door at the NSC the day after his appearance at the Wilson Center.

Humanitarian assistance and disaster relief

USSOUTHCOM's overseas humanitarian assistance and disaster relief programs build the capacity of host nations to respond to disasters and build their self-sufficiency while also empowering regional organizations.

These programs provide valuable training to U.S. military units in responding effectively to assist the victims of storms, earthquakes, and other natural disasters through the provision of medical, surgical, dental, and veterinary services, as well as civil construction projects.

The Humanitarian Assistance Program funds projects that enhance the capacity of host nations to respond when disasters strike and better prepare them to mitigate acts of terrorism. Humanitarian Assistance Program projects such as technical aid and the construction of disaster relief warehouses, emergency operation centers, shelters, and schools promote peace and stability, support the development of the civilian infrastructure necessary for economic and social reforms, and improve the living conditions of impoverished regions in the AOR.

Humanitarian assistance exercises such as Exercise Nuevos Horizontes (New Horizons) involve construction of schools, clinics, and water wells in countries throughout the region. At the same time, medical readiness exercises involving teams consisting of doctors, nurses and dentists also provide general and specialized health services to host nation citizens requiring care. These humanitarian assistance exercises, which last several months each, provide much needed services and infrastructure, while providing critical training for deployed U.S. military forces. These exercises generally take place in rural, underprivileged areas. USSOUTHCOM attempts to combine these efforts with those of host-nation doctors, either military or civilian, to make them even more beneficial.

In 2006, USSOUTHCOM sponsored 69 Medical Readiness Training Exercises in 15 nations, providing medical services to more than 270,000 citizens from the region. During 2007, USSOUTHCOM is scheduled to conduct 61 additional medical exercises in 14 partner nations.

USSOUTHCOM sponsors disaster preparedness exercises, seminars and conferences to improve the collective ability of the U.S. and its partner nations to respond effectively and expeditiously to disasters. USSOUTHCOM has also supported the construction or improvement of three Emergency Operations Centers, 13 Disaster Relief Warehouses and prepositioned relief supplies across the region. Construction of eight additional Emergency Operation Centers and seven additional warehouses is ongoing.

This type of multinational disaster preparedness has proven to increase the ability of USSOUTHCOM to work with America's partner nations. For example, following the 2005 Hurricane Stan in Guatemala, USSOUTHCOM deployed 11 military helicopters and 125 personnel to assist with relief efforts. In conjunction with their Guatemalan counterparts, they evacuated 48 victims and delivered nearly 200 tons of food, medical supplies and communications equipment. Following Tropical Storm Gamma in Honduras, JTF-Bravo deployed nine helicopters and more than 40 personnel to assist with relief efforts. They airlifted more than 100,000 pounds of emergency food, water and medical supplies. USSOUTHCOM was deployed to Haiti following the 2010 Haiti earthquake to lead the humanitarian effort.

USSOUTHCOM also conducts counternarcotics and counternarcoterrorism programs.

History

The United States Southern Command (USSOUTHCOM) traces its origins to 1903 when the first U.S. Marines arrived in Panama to ensure US control of the Panama Railroad connecting the Atlantic and Pacific Oceans across the narrow waist of the Panamanian Isthmus.

The Marines protected the Panamanian civilian uprising led by former Panama Canal Company general manager Philippe-Jean Bunau-Varilla guaranteeing his creation of the Panamanian state. Following the signing of the Hay–Bunau-Varilla Treaty granting control of the Panama Canal Zone to the United States, the Marines remained to provide security during the early construction days of the Panama Canal.

In 1904, Army Colonel William C. Gorgas was sent to the Canal Zone (as it was then called) as Chief Sanitary Officer to fight yellow fever and malaria. In two years, yellow fever was eliminated from the Canal Zone. Soon after, malaria was also brought under control. With the appointment of Army Lieutenant Colonel George W. Goethals to the post of chief engineer of the Isthmian Canal Commission by then President Theodore Roosevelt in 1907, the construction changed from a civilian to a military project.

In 1911, the first troops of the U.S. Army's 10th Infantry Regiment arrived at Camp E. S. Otis, on the Pacific side of the Isthmus. They assumed primary responsibility for Canal defense. In 1914, the Marine Battalion left the Isthmus to participate in operations against Pancho Villa in Mexico . On 14 August 1914, seven years after Goethals' arrival, the Panama Canal opened to world commerce.

The first company of coast artillery troops arrived in 1914 and later established fortifications at each end (Atlantic and Pacific) of the Canal as the Harbor Defenses (HD) of Cristobal and HD Balboa, respectively, with mobile forces of infantry and light artillery centrally located to support either end. By 1915, a consolidated command was designated as Headquarters, U.S. Troops, Panama Canal Zone. The command reported directly to the Army's Eastern Department headquartered at Fort Jay, Governors Island, New York. The headquarters of this newly created command was first located in the Isthmian Canal Commission building in the town of Ancon, adjacent to Panama City. It relocated in 1916 to the nearby newly designated military post of Quarry Heights, which had begun construction in 1911.

On 1 July 1917, the Panama Canal Department was activated as a geographic command of the U.S. Army. It remained as the senior Army headquarters in the region until activation of the **Caribbean Defense Command** (CDC) on 10 February 1941. The CDC, co-located at Quarry Heights, was commanded by Lieutenant General Daniel Van Voorhis, who continued to command the Panama Canal Department.

The new command eventually assumed operational responsibility over air and naval forces assigned in its area of operations, which included all US forces and bases in the Caribbean basin outside the continental United States. By early 1942, a Joint Operations Center had been established at Quarry Heights. Meanwhile, 960 jungle-trained officers and enlisted men from the CDC deployed to New Caledonia in the southwest Pacific to help form the 5307th

Composite Unit (Provisional), codenamed 'Galahad' and later nicknamed Merrill's Marauders for its famous exploits in Burma.[408] In the meantime, military strength in the area was gradually rising and reached its peak in January 1943, when 68,000 personnel were defending the Panama Canal. Military strength was sharply reduced with the termination of World War II. Between 1946 and 1974, total military strength in Panama fluctuated between 6,600 and 20,300 (with the lowest force strength in 1959).

In December 1946, President Harry S. Truman approved recommendations of the Joint Chiefs of Staff for a comprehensive system of military commands to put responsibility for conducting military operations of all military forces in various geographical areas, in the hands of a single commander. Although the Caribbean Command was designated by the Defense Department on 1 November 1947, it did not become fully operational until 10 March 1948, when the old Caribbean Defense Command was inactivated.

On 6 June 1963, reflecting the fact that the command had a responsibility for U.S. military operations primarily in Central and South America, rather than in the Caribbean, it was formally redesignated as the United States Southern Command. From 1975 until late 1994 total military strength in Panama remained at about 10,000 personnel.

In January 1996 and June 1997, two phases of changes to the Department of Defense Unified Command Plan (UCP) were completed. Each phase of the UCP change added territory to SOUTHCOM's area of responsibility. The impact of the changes is significant. The new AOR includes the Caribbean, its 13 island nations and several U.S. and European territories, the Gulf of Mexico, as well as significant portions of the Atlantic and Pacific Oceans . The 1999 update to the UCP also transferred responsibility of an additional portion of the Atlantic Ocean to SOUTHCOM. On 1 October 2000, Southern Command assumed responsibility of the adjacent waters in the upper quadrant above Brazil, which was presently under the responsibility of U.S. Joint Forces Command.

The new AOR encompasses 32 nations (19 in Central and South America and 13 in the Caribbean), of which 31 are democracies, and 14 U.S. and European territories covering more than 15,600,000 square miles (40,000,000 km^2).

With the creation of the United States Department of Homeland Security, US-SOUTHCOM Area of Responsibility (October 2002) experienced minor upper boundary redistribution or changes decreasing its total boundary by 1.1 square miles. (14.5 million square miles (23.2 million square kilometers.)

With the implementation of the Panama Canal Treaties (the Panama Canal Treaty of 1977 and the Treaty concerning the Permanent Neutrality and Operations of the Panama Canal), the U.S. Southern Command was relocated in Miami, Florida on 26 September 1997.

A new headquarters building was constructed and opened in 2010 adjacent to the old rented building in the Doral area of Miami-Dade County. The complex features state-of-the-art planning and conference facilities. This capability is showcased in the 45,000-square-foot Conference Center of the Americas, which can support meetings of differing classification levels and multiple translations, information sources and video conferencing.

In 2012, as many as a dozen SouthCom service members, together with a number of Secret Service officers, were disciplined after they were found to have brought prostitutes to their rooms shortly before President Obama arrived for a summit in Cartagena, Colombia. According to the Associated Press seven Army soldiers and two Marines received administrative punishments for what an official report cited by the wire service said was misconduct consisting "almost exclusively of patronizing prostitutes and adultery." Hiring prostitutes, the report added, "is a violation of the U.S. military code of justice." In 2014, SouthCom commander Kelly testified that while border security was an 'Existential' threat to the country, due to Budget sequestration in 2013 his forces were unable to respond to 75% of illicit trafficking events.

USSOUTHCOM's *2017-2027 Theater Strategy* states that potential challenges in the future include transregional and transnational threat networks (T3Ns) which include traditional criminal organizations, as well as the expanding potential of extremist organizations such as ISIL and Hezbollah operating in the region by taking advantage of weak Caribbean and Latin American institutions. USSOUTHCOM also notes that the region is "extremely vulnerable to natural disasters and the outbreak of infectious diseases" due to issues with governance and inequality. Finally, the report recognizes the growing presence of China, Iran and Russia in the region, and that the intentions of these nations bring "a challenge to every nation that values nonaggression, rule of law, and respect for human rights". These challenges have been used to promote relationships between the United States and other governments in the region.

State Partnership Program

US SOUTHCOM currently has 22 state partnerships under the state partnership program (SPP). SPP creates a partnership between a state of the US and a foreign nation by linking the host nation military or security forces with the National Guard. SOUTHCOM is equaled only by EUCOM in its number of partnerships.

Commanders

The US Southern Command was activated in 1963 and emerged from the 1947 set up US Caribbean Command. Last commander of the US Caribbean Command from January 1961 to June 1963 and first commander of the US Southern Command since June 1963 was Lieutenant General–later General–Andrew P. O'Meara.

No.	Image	Name	Branch	Term began	Term ended
1.		General Andrew P. O'Meara	USA	June 1963	February 1965
2.		General Robert W. Porter Jr.	USA	February 1965	February 1969
3.		General George R. Mather	USA	February 1969	September 1971
4.		General George V. Underwood Jr.	USA	September 1971	January 1973
5.		General William B. Rosson	USA	January 1973	July 1975
6.		LTG Dennis P. McAuliffe	USA	August 1975	September 1979
7.		LTG Wallace H. Nutting	USA	October 1979	May 1983
8.		General Paul F. Gorman	USA	May 1983	March 1985

9.		General John R. Galvin	USA	March 1985	June 1987
10.		General Frederick F. Woerner Jr.	USA	June 1987	July 1989
11.		General Maxwell R. Thurman	USA	September 1989	November 1990
12.		General George A. Joulwan	USA	November 1990	November 1993
(Acting)		MG W. A. Worthington	USA	December 1993	January 1994
13.		General Barry McCaffrey	USA	February 1994	February 1996
(Acting)		Rear Admiral James Perkins	USN	March 1996	June 1996
14.		General Wesley Clark	USA	July 1996	July 1997
15.		General Charles E. Wilhelm	USMC	25 September 1997	8 September 2000
16.		General Peter Pace	USMC	8 September 2000	30 September 2001

(Acting)		MG Gary D. Speer	USA	30 September 2001	18 August 2002
17.		General James T. Hill	USA	18 August 2002	9 November 2004
18.		General Bantz J. Craddock	USA	9 November 2004	19 October 2006
19.		Admiral James G. Stavridis	USN	19 October 2006	25 June 2009
20.		General Douglas M. Fraser	USAF	25 June 2009	19 November 2012
21.		General John F. Kelly	USMC	19 November 2012	14 January 2016
22.		Admiral Kurt W. Tidd	USN	14 January 2016	Incumbent

- On April 25, 2018, SOUTHCOM was awarded with the medal of the Order of San Carlos.

Further reading

- Conn, Stetson; Engelman, Rose C.; Fairchild, Byron (2000) [1964], *Guarding the United States and its Outposts*[409], United States Army in World War II, Washington, D.C.: Center of Military History, United States Army
- Vasquez, Cesar A. "A History of the United States Caribbean Defense Command (1941-1947)." Florida International University, doctoral thesis (2016).

External links

- Official website[410]
- Latin, Caribbean allies hail new U.S. Southern Command chief[411] by John Yearwood, *Miami Herald*, 26 June 2009

United States Cyber Command

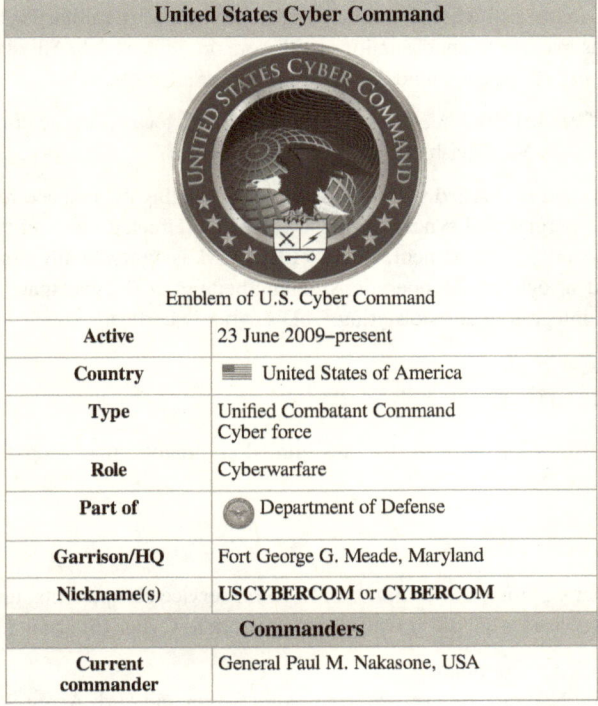

United States Cyber Command	
Emblem of U.S. Cyber Command	
Active	23 June 2009–present
Country	United States of America
Type	Unified Combatant Command Cyber force
Role	Cyberwarfare
Part of	Department of Defense
Garrison/HQ	Fort George G. Meade, Maryland
Nickname(s)	**USCYBERCOM** or **CYBERCOM**
Commanders	
Current commander	General Paul M. Nakasone, USA

United States Cyber Command (**USCYBERCOM**) is one of ten unified commands of the United States Department of Defense. It unifies the direction of cyberspace operations, strengthens DoD cyberspace capabilities, and integrates and bolsters DoD's cyber expertise.

USCYBERCOM was created in 2009 at the National Security Agency (NSA) headquarters in Fort George G. Meade, Maryland. It cooperates with NSA networks and has been concurrently headed by the Director of the National Security Agency since its inception. While originally created with a defensive mission in mind, it has increasingly been viewed as an offensive force. On 18

August 2017, it was announced that USCYBERCOM would be elevated to the status of a full and independent Unified Combatant Command, This elevation occurred on 4 May 2018.

Mission statement

According to the US Department of Defense (DoD), USCYBERCOM "plans, coordinates, integrates, synchronizes and conducts activities to: direct the operations and defense of specified Department of Defense information networks and; prepare to, and when directed, conduct full spectrum military cyberspace operations in order to enable actions in all domains, ensure US/Allied freedom of action in cyberspace and deny the same to our adversaries."

The text "9ec4c12949a4f31474f299058ce2b22a", located in the command's emblem, is the MD5 hash of their mission statement.

The command is charged with pulling together existing cyberspace resources, creating synergies and synchronizing war-fighting effects to defend the information security environment. USCYBERCOM is tasked with centralizing command of cyberspace operations, strengthening DoD cyberspace capabilities, and integrating and bolstering DoD's cyber expertise.[412]

Organization

USCYBERCOM is an armed forces unified command under Department of Defense (DoD).

Service components

U.S. Cyber Command is composed of several service components, units from military services who will provide Joint services to Cyber Command.
- Army Cyber Command (Army)
  - Army Network Enterprise Technology Command / 9th Army Signal Command (NETCOM/9thSC(A))
    - Cyber Protection Brigade
  - United States Army Intelligence and Security Command will be under the operational control of ARCYBER for cyber-related actions.
    - 1st Information Operations Command (Land)
    - 780th Military Intelligence Brigade (Cyber)
- Fleet Cyber Command/Tenth Fleet (Navy)[413]
  - Naval Network Warfare Command
  - Navy Cyber Defense Operations Command
  - Naval Information Operation Commands

- Combined Task Forces
- Air Forces Cyber/Twenty-Fourth Air Force (Air Force)[414,415]
  - 67th Cyberspace Wing
  - 688th Cyberspace Wing
  - 624th Operations Center
  - 5th Combat Communications Group
- Marine Corps Cyberspace Command (Marine Corps)

Military specialties

These are the known military specialties directly involved with cyber. Service members enlisted under these specialties may be assigned to their respective Cybercommand Service Component Command.

- US Army - 17A Cyber Warfare Officer,[416] 170A Cyber Operations Technician, 17C enlisted Cyber Warfare Specialists (up-coming),
- US Navy - CTN Cryptologic Technician Networks
- US Air Force - 1B4X1 (Enlisted) - Cyberspace Warfare Operations - (Not open to first term airmen) & 17S (Officer)[417]
- US Marine Corps - 0651 Marine Cyber Network Operator and 2611 Cryptologic Digital Network Operator/Analyst[418]

Cyber teams

In 2015 the U.S. Cyber Command added 133 new cyber teams. The breakdown was:

- Thirteen National Mission Teams to defend against broad cyberattacks
- Sixty-eight Cyber Protection Teams to defend priority DoD networks and systems against priority threats
- Twenty-seven Combat Mission Teams to provide integrated cyberspace attacks in support of operational plans and contingency operations
- Twenty-five Support Teams to provide analytic and planning support

Background

An intention by the U.S. Air Force to create a 'cyber command' was announced in October 2006. An Air Force Cyber Command was created in a provisional status in November 2006. However, in October 2008, it was announced the command would not be brought into permanent activation.

On 23 June 2009, the Secretary of Defense directed the Commander of U.S. Strategic Command (USSTRATCOM) to establish USCYBERCOM. In May 2010, General Keith Alexander outlined his views in a report for the United States House Committee on Armed Services subcommittee:

> *My own view is that the only way to counteract both criminal and espionage activity online is to be proactive. If the U.S. is taking a formal approach to this, then that has to be a good thing. The Chinese are viewed as the source of a great many attacks on western infrastructure and just recently, the U.S. electrical grid. If that is determined to be an organized attack, I would want to go and take down the source of those attacks. The only problem is that the Internet, by its very nature, has no borders and if the U.S. takes on the mantle of the world's police; that might not go down so well.*

Initial operational capability was attained on 21 May 2010. General Alexander was promoted to four-star rank, becoming one of 38 US Generals, and took charge of U.S. Cyber Command in a ceremony at Fort Meade that was attended by Commander of U.S. Central Command GEN David Petraeus, and Secretary of Defense Robert M. Gates.[419] USCYBERCOM reached full operational capability on 31 October 2010.[420]

The command assumed responsibility for several existing organizations. The Joint Task Force for Global Network Operations (JTF-GNO) and the Joint Functional Component Command for Network Warfare (JFCC-NW) were absorbed by the command. The Defense Information Systems Agency, where JTF-GNO operated, provides technical assistance for network and information assurance to USCYBERCOM, and is moving its headquarters to Ft. Meade.

President Obama signed into law, on 23 December 2016, the National Defense Authorization Act (NDAA) for fiscal year (FY) 2017, which elevated USCYBERCOM to a unified combatant command. The FY 2017 NDAA also specified that the dual-hatted arrangement of the commander of USCYBERCOM will not be terminated until the Secretary of Defense and Chairman of the Joint Chiefs of Staff jointly certify that ending this arrangement will not pose risks to the military effectiveness of CYBERCOM that are unacceptable to the national security interests of the United States.

Concerns

There are concerns that the Pentagon and NSA will overshadow any civilian cyber defense efforts. There are also concerns on whether the command will assist in civilian cyber defense efforts. According to Deputy Secretary of Defense William J. Lynn, the command "will lead day-to-day defense and protection of all DoD networks. It will be responsible for DoD's networks – the dot-mil world. Responsibility for federal civilian networks – dot-gov – stays with the Department of Homeland Security, and that's exactly how it should be." Alexander notes, however, that if faced with cyber hostilities an executive order could expand Cyber Command's spectrum of operations to include, for instance, assisting the Department of Homeland Security in defense of their networks.

Some military leaders claim that the existing cultures of the Army, Navy, and Air Force are fundamentally incompatible with that of cyber warfare. Major Robert Costa (USAF) even suggested a sixth branch of the military, an Information (Cyber) Service with Title 10 responsibilities analogous to its sister services in 2002 noting,

> While no one [Instrument of National Power] operates in a vacuum..., Information increasingly underpins the other three [Diplomatic, Economic and Military], yet has proven to be the most vulnerable, even as US society becomes more dependent on it in peace, conflict, and war. To attack these centers of gravity, an adversary will use the weakest decisive point, ...the Information IOP. In addition, the other IOPs benefit from Unity of Effort–Constitutional balances of power ensure the Diplomatic and Military IOPs exercised by the President in concert with Congress are focused, while the Economic IOP achieves Unity of Action through international market controls and an international body of law. [In 2002], [t]he Information IOP however, [was] rudderless, lacking both Unity of Action and Unity of Command.

Others have also discussed the creation of a cyber-warfare branch. Lieutenant Colonel Gregory Conti[421] and Colonel John "Buck" Surdu (chief of staff of the United States Army Research, Development and Engineering Command) stated that the three major services are *properly positioned to fight kinetic wars, and they value skills such as marksmanship, physical strength, the ability to leap out of airplanes and lead combat units under enemy fire.*

Conti and Surdu reasoned, "Adding an efficient and effective cyber branch alongside the Army, Navy and Air Force would provide our nation with the capability to defend our technological infrastructure and conduct offensive operations. Perhaps more important, the existence of this capability would serve as a strong deterrent for our nation's enemies."

In response to concerns about the military's right to respond to cyber attacks, General Alexander stated "The U.S. must fire back against cyber attacks swiftly and strongly and should act to counter or disable a threat even when the identity of the attacker is unknown" prior to his confirmation hearings before the United States Congress. This came in response to incidents such as a 2008 operation to take down a government-run extremist honeypot in Saudi Arabia. "Elite U.S. military computer specialists, over the objections of the CIA, mounted a cyberattack that dismantled the online forum".

"The new U.S. Cyber Command needs to strike a balance between protecting military assets and personal privacy." stated Alexander, in a Defense Department release. If confirmed, Alexander said, his main focus will be on building capacity and capability to secure the networks and educating the public on the command's intent.

"This command is not about an effort to militarize cyber space," he said. "Rather, it's about safeguarding our military assets."

In July 2011, Deputy Defense Secretary William Lynn announced in a conference that "We have, within Cyber Command, a full spectrum of capabilities, but the thrust of the strategy is defensive." "The strategy rests on five pillars, he said: treat cyber as a domain; employ more active defenses; support the Department of Homeland Security in protecting critical infrastructure networks; practice collective defense with allies and international partners; and reduce the advantages attackers have on the Internet."

In 2013, USCYBERCOM held a classified exercise in which reserve officers (with extensive experience in their civilian cyber-security work) easily defeated active duty cybermen. In 2015 Eric Rosenbach, the principal cyber adviser to Defense Secretary Ash Carter, said DoD was looking at alternatives to staffing with just active-duty military. Beginning that year, USCYBERCOM added 133 teams (staffing out at 6,000 people), with the intent that at least 15% of the personnel would be reserve cyber operations airmen. These new teams had achieved "initial operating capability" (IOC) as of 21 October 2016. Officials noted that IOC is not the same as combat readiness, but is the first step in that direction.

President Barack Obama's Commission on Enhancing National Cybersecurity is expected to release its substantial report prior to 20 January 2017. The report will make recommendations regarding the intertwining roles of the military, government administration and the private sector in providing cyber security. Incoming President Trump has indicated that he wants a full review of Cyber Command.

International effects and reactions

The creation of U.S. Cyber Command appears to have motivated other countries in this arena. In December 2009, South Korea announced the creation of a cyber warfare command. Reportedly, this is in response to North Korea's creation of a cyber warfare unit. In addition, the British GCHQ has begun preparing a cyber force. Furthermore, a shift in military interest in cyber warfare has motivated the creation of the first U.S. Cyber Warfare Intelligence Center. In 2010, China introduced a department dedicated to defensive cyber war and information security in response to the creation of USCYBERCOM.

Leadership

List of Cyber Command commanders

No.	Image	Rank	Name	Service	Start of Term	End of Term
1.		GEN	Keith B. Alexander	USA	21 May 2010	28 March 2014
(Acting)		LtGen	Jon M. Davis	USMC	29 March 2014	2 April 2014
2.		ADM	Michael S. Rogers	USN	3 April 2014	4 May 2018
3.		GEN	Paul M. Nakasone	USA	4 May 2018	*Incumbent*

The current Deputy Commander is Lieutenant General Vincent R. Stewart, USMC.

External links

 Wikimedia Commons has media related to *United States Cyber Command*.

- U.S. Cyber Command website[422]
- "NSA Chief may lose US Cyber Command role"[423]. Retrieved 2013-11-04.
- "But NSA & Cyber Command are to stay under one chief"[424]. Retrieved 2013-12-14.
- US Cyber Command Fact Sheet[425]
- US Cyber Command Fact Sheet PowerPoint[426]
- The official facebook page of the United States Cyber Command[427]

United States Special Operations Command

United States Special Operations Command	
(USSOCOM)	

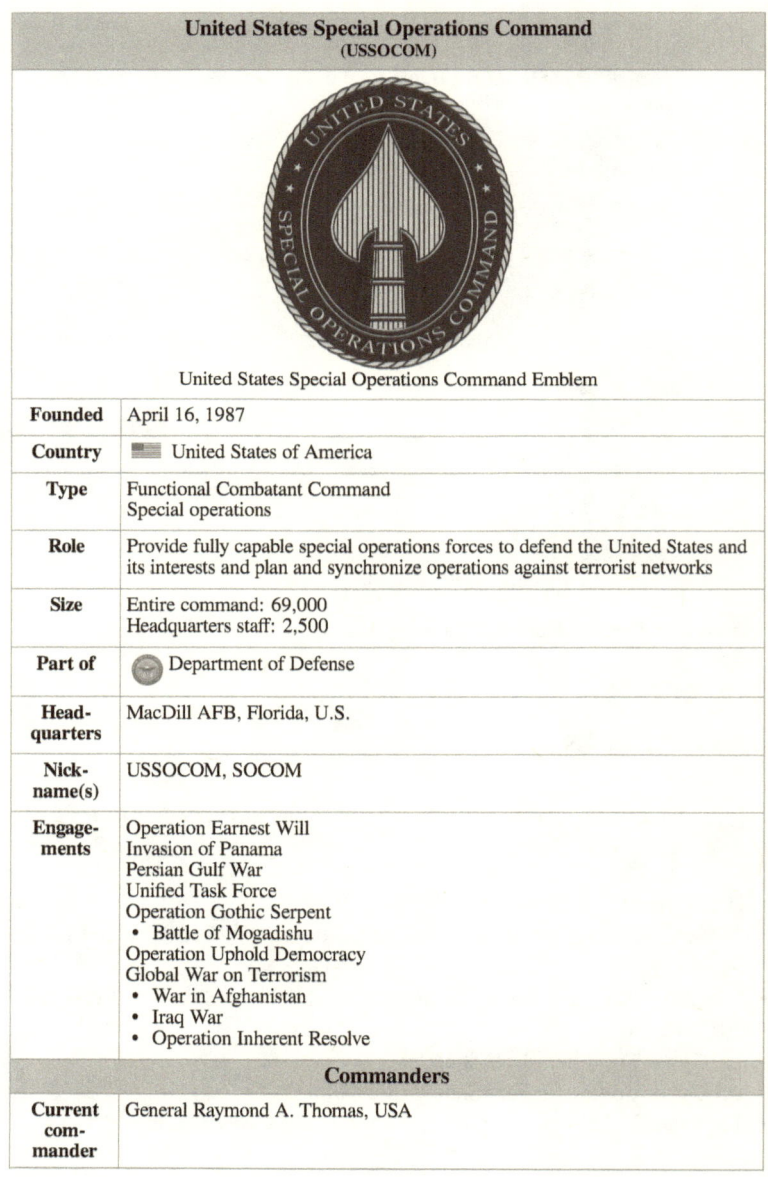

United States Special Operations Command Emblem

Founded	April 16, 1987
Country	United States of America
Type	Functional Combatant Command Special operations
Role	Provide fully capable special operations forces to defend the United States and its interests and plan and synchronize operations against terrorist networks
Size	Entire command: 69,000 Headquarters staff: 2,500
Part of	Department of Defense
Headquarters	MacDill AFB, Florida, U.S.
Nickname(s)	USSOCOM, SOCOM
Engagements	Operation Earnest Will Invasion of Panama Persian Gulf War Unified Task Force Operation Gothic Serpent • Battle of Mogadishu Operation Uphold Democracy Global War on Terrorism • War in Afghanistan • Iraq War • Operation Inherent Resolve
Commanders	
Current commander	General Raymond A. Thomas, USA

The **United States Special Operations Command** (**USSOCOM** or **SOCOM**) is the Unified Combatant Command charged with overseeing the various Special Operations Component Commands of the Army, Marine Corps, Navy, and Air Force of the United States Armed Forces. The command is part of the Department of Defense and is the only Unified Combatant Command legislated into being by the U.S. Congress. USSOCOM is headquartered at MacDill Air Force Base in Tampa, Florida.

The idea of an American unified special operations command had its origins in the aftermath of Operation Eagle Claw, the disastrous attempted rescue of hostages at the American embassy in Iran in 1980. The ensuing investigation, chaired by Admiral James L. Holloway III, the retired Chief of Naval Operations, cited lack of command and control and inter-service coordination as significant factors in the failure of the mission. Since its activation on 16 April 1987, U.S. Special Operations Command has participated in many operations, from the 1989 invasion of Panama to the ongoing Global War on Terrorism.

USSOCOM conducts several covert and clandestine missions, such as direct action, special reconnaissance, counter-terrorism, foreign internal defense, unconventional warfare, psychological warfare, civil affairs, and counter-narcotics operations. Each branch has a Special Operations Command that is unique and capable of running its own operations, but when the different special operations forces need to work together for an operation, USSOCOM becomes the joint component command of the operation, instead of a SOC of a specific branch.

History

The unworkable command and control structure of separate U.S. military special operations forces (SOF), which led to the failure of Operation Eagle Claw in 1980, highlighted the need within the Department of Defense for reform and reorganization. Since the incident, the Army Chief of Staff, General Edward C. "Shy" Meyer, called for a further restructuring of special operations capabilities, eventually helping to create the U.S. Delta Force. Although unsuccessful at the joint level, Meyer nevertheless went on to consolidate Army SOF units under the new 1st Special Operations Command in 1982, a significant step to improve the U.S. Army's SOF.

By 1983, there was a small but growing sense in the Congress for the need for military reforms. In June, the Senate Armed Services Committee (SASC) began a two-year-long study of the Defense Department, which included an examination of SOF spearheaded by Senator Barry Goldwater (R-AZ). With concern mounting on Capitol Hill, the Department of Defense created the

Figure 106: *Senator Barry Goldwater, Former Chairman of the Senate Armed Services Committee*

Joint Special Operations Agency on 1 January 1984; this agency, however, had neither operational nor command authority over any SOF. The Joint Special Operations Agency thus did little to improve SOF readiness, capabilities, or policies, and therefore was insufficient. Within the Defense Department, there were a few staunch SOF supporters. Noel Koch, Principal Deputy Assistant Secretary of Defense for International Security Affairs, and his deputy, Lynn Rylander, both advocated SOF reforms.

At the same time, a few on Capitol Hill were determined to overhaul United States Special Operations Forces. They included Senators Sam Nunn (D-GA) and William Cohen (R-ME), both members of the Armed Services Committee, and Representative Dan Daniel (D-VA), the chairman of the United States House Armed Services Subcommittee on Readiness. Congressman Daniel had become convinced that the U.S. military establishment was not interested in special operations, that the country's capability in this area was second rate, and that SOF operational command and control was an endemic problem. Senators Nunn and Cohen also felt strongly that the Department of Defense was not preparing adequately for future threats. Senator Cohen agreed that the U.S. needed a clearer organizational focus and chain of command for special operations to deal with low-intensity conflicts.

In October 1985, the Senate Armed Services Committee published the results of its two-year review of the U.S. military structure, entitled "Defense Organization: The Need For Change." Mr. James R. Locher III, the principal author of this study, also examined past special operations and speculated on the most likely future threats. This influential document led to the Goldwater-Nichols Defense Reorganization Act of 1986. By spring 1986, SOF advocates had introduced reform bills in both houses of Congress. On 15 May, Senator Cohen introduced the Senate bill, co-sponsored by Senator Nunn and others, which called for a joint military organization for SOF and the establishment of an office in the Defense Department to ensure adequate funding and policy emphasis for low-intensity conflict and special operations. Representative Daniel's proposal went even further—he wanted a national special operations agency headed by a civilian who would bypass the Joint Chiefs and report directly to the Secretary of Defense; this would keep Joint Chiefs and the Services out of the SOF budget process.

Congress held hearings on the two bills in the summer of 1986. Admiral William J. Crowe Jr., Chairman of the Joint Chiefs of Staff, led the Pentagon's opposition to the bills. He proposed, as an alternative, a new Special Operations Forces command led by a three-star general. This proposal was not well received on Capitol Hill—Congress wanted a four-star general in charge to give SOF more clout. A number of retired military officers and others testified in favor of the need for reform. By most accounts, retired Army Major General Richard Scholtes gave the most compelling reasons for change. Scholtes, who commanded the joint special operations task force in Grenada, explained how conventional force leaders misused SOF during the operation, not allowing them to use their unique capabilities, which resulted in high SOF casualties. After his formal testimony, Scholtes met privately with a small number of Senators to elaborate on the problems that he had encountered in Grenada.

Both the House and Senate passed SOF reform bills, and these went to a conference committee for reconciliation. Senate and House conferees forged a compromise. The bill called for a unified combatant command headed by a four-star general for all SOF, an Assistant Secretary of Defense for Special Operations and Low-Intensity Conflict, a coordinating board for low-intensity conflict within the National Security Council, and a new Major Force Program (MFP-11) for SOF (the so-called "SOF checkbook"). The final bill, attached as a rider to the 1987 Defense Authorization Act, amended the Goldwater-Nichols Act and was signed into law in October 1986. Congress clearly intended to force DOD and the Administration to face up to the realities of past failures and emerging threats. DOD and the Administration were responsible for implementing the law, and Congress subsequently had to pass two additional bills to ensure proper implementation. The legislation promised to

Figure 107: *General James Lindsay the first Commander in Chief, Special Operations Command*

improve SOF in several respects. Once implemented, MFP-11 provided SOF with control over its own resources, better enabling it to modernize the force. Additionally, the law fostered interservice cooperation: a single commander for all SOF promoted interoperability among the forces assigned to the same command. The establishment of a four-star Commander in Chief and an Assistant Secretary of Defense for Special Operations and Low Intensity Conflict eventually gave SOF a voice in the highest councils of the Defense Department.

Implementing the provisions and mandates of the Nunn-Cohen Amendment to the National Defense Authorization Act for Fiscal Year 1987, however, was neither rapid nor smooth. One of the first issues to surface was appointing an ASD (SO/LIC), whose principal duties included monitorship of special operations activities and low-intensity conflict activities of the Department of Defense. The Congress even increased the number of assistant secretaries of defense from 11 to 12, but the Department of Defense still did not fill this new billet. In December 1987, the Congress directed Secretary of the Army John O. Marsh to carry out the ASD (SO/LIC) duties until a suitable replacement was approved by the Senate. Not until 18 months after the legislation passed did Ambassador Charles Whitehouse assume the duties of ASD (SO/LIC).

Meanwhile, the establishment of USSOCOM provided its own measure of excitement. A quick solution to manning and basing a brand new unified com-

Figure 108: *MH-60 landing on Hercules*

mand was to abolish an existing command. United States Readiness Command (USREDCOM), with an often misunderstood mission, did not appear to have a viable mission in the post Goldwater-Nichols era, and its Commander in Chief, General James Lindsay, had had some special operations experience. On 23 January 1987, the Joint Chiefs of Staff recommended to the Secretary of Defense that USREDCOM be disestablished to provide billets and facilities for USSOCOM. President Ronald Reagan approved the establishment of the new command on 13 April 1987. The Department of Defense activated USSOCOM on 16 April 1987 and nominated General Lindsay to be the first Commander in Chief Special Operations Command (USCINCSOC). The Senate accepted him without debate.

Operation Earnest Will

USSOCOM's first tactical operation involved 160th Special Operations Aviation Regiment (Airborne) ("Night Stalkers") aviators, SEALs, and Special Boat Teams (SBT) working together during Operation Earnest Will in September 1987. During Operation Earnest Will, the United States ensured that neutral oil tankers and other merchant ships could safely transit the Persian Gulf during the Iran–Iraq War. Iranian attacks on tankers prompted Kuwait to ask the United States in December 1986 to register 11 Kuwaiti tankers as American ships so that they could be escorted by the U.S. Navy. President Reagan agreed to the Kuwaiti request on 10 March 1987, hoping it would deter Iranian

Figure 109: *One of two Iranian oil platforms set ablaze after shelling by American destroyers.*

attacks. The protection offered by U.S. naval vessels, however, did not stop Iran, which used mines and small boats to harass the convoys steaming to and from Kuwait. In late July 1987, Rear Admiral Harold J. Bernsen, commander of the Middle East Force, requested NSW assets. Special Boat Teams deployed with six Mark III Patrol Boats and two SEAL platoons in August. The Middle East Force decided to convert two oil servicing barges, Hercules and Wimbrown VII, into mobile sea bases. The mobile sea bases allowed SOF in the northern Persian Gulf to thwart clandestine Iranian mining and small boat attacks.

On 21 September, Nightstalkers flying MH-60 and Little Birds took off from the frigate USS *Jarrett* to track an Iranian ship, *Iran Ajr*. The Nightstalkers observed *Iran Ajr* turn off her lights and begin laying mines. After receiving permission to attack, the helicopters fired guns and rockets, stopping the ship. As *Iran Ajr*'s crew began to push mines over the side, the helicopters resumed firing until the crew abandoned ship. Special Boat Teams provided security while a SEAL team boarded the vessel at first light and discovered nine mines on the vessel's deck, as well as a logbook revealing areas where previous mines had been laid. The logbook implicated Iran in mining international waters.

Within a few days, the Special Operations forces had determined the Iranian pattern of activity; the Iranians hid during the day near oil and gas platforms in Iranian waters and at night they headed toward the Middle Shoals Buoy, a navigation aid for tankers. With this knowledge, SOF launched three Little Bird helicopters and two patrol craft to the buoy. The Little Bird helicopters arrived first and were fired upon by three Iranian boats anchored near the buoy. After a short but intense firefight, the helicopters sank all three boats. Three days later, in mid-October, an Iranian Silkworm missile hit the tanker *Sea Isle City* near the oil terminal outside Kuwait City. Seventeen crewmen and the American captain were injured in the missile attack. During Operation Nimble Archer, four destroyers shelled two oil platforms in the Rostam oil field. After the shelling, a SEAL platoon and a demolition unit planted explosives on one of the platforms to destroy it. The SEALs next boarded and searched a third platform 2 miles (3 km) away. Documents and radios were taken for intelligence purposes.

On 14 April 1988, 65 miles (100 km) east of Bahrain, the frigate USS *Samuel B. Roberts* hit a mine, blowing an immense hole in its hull. Ten sailors were injured. During Operation Praying Mantis the U.S. retaliated fiercely, attacking the Iranian frigate *Sahand* and oil platforms in the Sirri and Sassan oil fields. After U.S. warships bombarded the Sirri platform and set it ablaze, a UH-60 with a SEAL platoon flew toward the platform but was unable to get close enough because of the roaring fire. Secondary explosions soon wrecked the platform. Thereafter, Iranian attacks on neutral ships dropped drastically. On 18 July, Iran accepted the United Nations cease fire; on 20 August 1988, the Iran–Iraq War ended. The remaining SEALs, patrol boats, and helicopters then returned to the United States. Special operations forces provided critical skills necessary to help CENTCOM gain control of the northern Persian Gulf and balk Iran's small boats and minelayers. The ability to work at night proved vital, because Iranian units used darkness to conceal their actions. Additionally, because of Earnest Will operational requirements, USSOCOM would acquire new weapons systems—the patrol coastal ships and the Mark V Special Operations Craft.

Somalia

Special Operations Command first became involved in Somalia in 1992 as part of Operation Provide Relief. C-130s circled over Somali airstrips during delivery of relief supplies. Special Forces medics accompanied many relief flights into the airstrips throughout southern Somalia to assess the area. They were the first U.S. soldiers in Somalia, arriving before U.S. forces who supported the expanded relief operations of Restore Hope. The first teams into Somalia were CIA Special Activities Division paramilitary officers with elements of JSOC. They conducted very high risk advanced force operations prior to the entry of the follow on forces. The first casualty of the conflict came from this team and was a Paramilitary officer and former Delta Force operator name Larry Freedman. Freedman was awarded the Intelligence Star for *"extraordinary heroism"* for his actions.

The earliest missions during Operation Restore Hope were conducted by Navy SEALs. The SEALs performed several hydro-graphic reconnaissance missions to find suitable landing sites for Marines. On 7 December, the SEALs swam into Mogadishu Harbor, where they found suitable landing sites, assessed the area for threats, and concluded that the port could support offloading ships. This was a tough mission because the SEALs swam against a strong current which left many of them overheated and exhausted. Furthermore, they swam through raw sewage in the harbor, which made them sick. When the first SEALs hit the shore the following night, they were surprised to meet members of the news media. The first Marines came ashore soon thereafter, and the press redirected their attention to them. Later, the SEALs provided personal security for President George Bush during a visit to Somalia. In December 1992, Special Forces assets in Kenya moved to Somalia and joined Operation Restore Hope. January 1993, a Special Forces command element deployed to Mogadishu as the Joint Special Operations Forces-Somalia (JSOFOR) that would command and control all special operations for Restore Hope. JSOFOR's mission was to make initial contact with indigenous factions and leaders; provide information for force protection; and provide reports on the area for future relief and security operations. Before redeploying in April, JSOFOR elements drove over 26,000 miles (42,000 km), captured 277 weapons, and destroyed over 45,320 pounds (20,560 kg) of explosives.

In August 1993, Secretary of Defense Les Aspin directed the deployment of a Joint Special Operations Task Force (JSOTF) to Somalia in response to attacks made by General Mohamed Farrah Aidid's supporters upon U.S. and UN forces. The JSOTF, named Task Force (TF) Ranger, was charged with a mission named Operation Gothic Serpent to capture Aidid. This was an especially arduous mission, for Aidid had gone underground, after several Lockheed AC-130 air raids and UN assaults on his strongholds.

While Marines from the 24th MEU provided an interim QRF (Force Recon Det and helicopters from HMM-263), the task force arrived in the country, and began training exercises. The Marines were asked to take on the Aidid snatch mission, but having the advantage of being in the area for more than two months, decided after mission analysis that the mission was a "no-go" due to several factors, centered around the inability to rescue the crew of a downed helicopter (re: the indigenous forces technique of using RPGs against helicopters and blocking the narrow streets in order to restrict the movement of a ground rescue force). This knowledge was not passed on to the Rangers, due to the Marines operating from the USS Wasp and the Rangers remaining

Figure 110: *Bravo Company, 3rd Battalion of the 75th Ranger Regiment in Somalia, 1993.*

on land. TF Ranger was made up of operators from Delta Force, 75th Ranger Regiment, 160th SOAR, SEALs from the Naval Special Warfare Development Group, and Air Force special tactics units. During August and September 1993, the task force conducted six missions into Mogadishu, all of which were successes. Although Aidid remained free, the effect of these missions seriously limited his movements.

On 3 October, TF Ranger launched its seventh mission, this time into Aidid's stronghold the Bakara Market to capture two of his key lieutenants. The mission was expected to take only one or two hours. Helicopters carried an assault and a ground convoy of security teams launched in the late afternoon from the TF Ranger compound at Mogadishu airport. The TF came under increasingly heavy fire, more intense than during previous missions. The assault team captured 24 Somalis including Aidid's lieutenants and were loading them onto the convoy trucks when a MH-60 Blackhawk was hit by a rocket-propelled grenade (RPG). A small element from the security force, as well as an MH-6 assault helicopter and an MH-60 carrying a fifteen-man combat search and rescue (CSAR) team, rushed to the crash site. The battle became increasingly worse. An RPG struck another MH-60, crashing less than 1 mile (1.6 km) to the south of the first downed helicopter. The task force faced overwhelming Somali mobs that overran the crash sites, causing a dire situation. A Somali mob overran the second site and, despite a heroic defense, killed everyone except the pilot, whom they took prisoner. Two defenders of

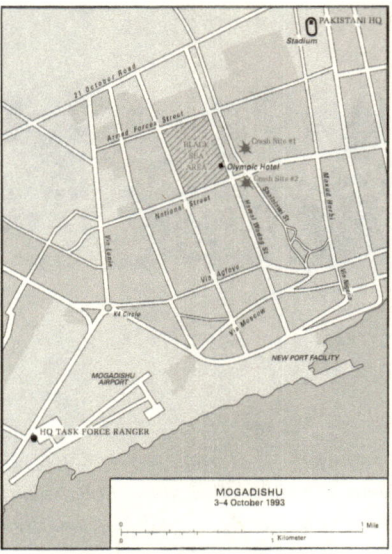

Figure 111: *Map of the main battle sites during the Battle of Mogadishu.*

this crash site, Master Sergeant Gary Gordon and Sergeant First Class Randall Shughart, were posthumously awarded the Medal of Honor. About this time, the mission's quick reaction force (QRF) also tried to reach the second crash site. This force too was pinned by Somali fire and required the fire support of two AH-6 helicopters before it could break contact and make its way back to the base.

The assault and security elements moved on foot towards the first crash area, passing through heavy fire, and occupied buildings south and southwest of the downed helicopter. They fought to establish defensive positions so as not to be pinned down by very heavy enemy fire, while treating their wounded, and worked to free the pilot's body from the downed helicopter. With the detainees loaded on trucks, the ground convoy force attempted to reach the first crash site. Unable to find it amongst the narrow, winding alleyways, the convoy came under devastating small arms and RPG fire. The convoy had to return to base after suffering numerous casualties, and sustaining substantial damage to their vehicles.

Reinforcements, consisting of elements from the QRF, 10th Mountain Division soldiers, Rangers, SEALs, Pakistan Army tanks and Malaysian armored personnel carriers, finally arrived at 1:55 am on 4 October. The combined force worked until dawn to free the pilot's body, receiving RPG and small arms fire throughout the night. All the casualties were loaded onto the armored personnel carriers, and the remainder of the force was left behind and had no choice but to move out on foot. AH-6 gunships raked the streets with fire to support the movement. The main force of the convoy arrived at the Pakistani Stadium-compound for the QRF-at 6:30 am, thus concluding one of the bloodiest and fiercest urban firefights since the Vietnam War. Task Force Ranger experienced a total of 17 killed in action and 106 wounded. Various estimates placed Somali casualties above 1,000. Although Task Force Ranger's few missions were successes, the overall outcome of Operation Gothic Serpent was deemed a failure because of the Task Force's failure to complete their stated mission, capturing Mohamed Farrah Aidid. Most U.S. forces pulled out of Somalia by March 1994. The withdrawal from Somalia, was completed on March 1995. Even though Operation Gothic Serpent failed, USSOCOM still made significant contributions to operations in Somalia. SOF performed reconnaissance and surveillance missions, assisted with humanitarian relief, protected American forces and conducted riverine patrols. Additionally, they ensured the safe landing of the Marines and safeguarded the arrival of merchant ships carrying food.

Iraq

USSOCOM's 10th Special Forces Group, elements of JSOC and CIA/SAD Paramilitary Officers linked up again and were the first to enter Iraq prior to the invasion. Their efforts organized the Kurdish Peshmerga to defeat Ansar Al Islam in Northern Iraq before the invasion. This battle was for control of a territory in Northeastern Iraq that was completely occupied by Ansar Al Islam, an ally of Al Qaeda. This was a very significant battle and led to the death of a substantial number of terrorists and the uncovering of a chemical weapons facility at Sargat. These terrorists would have been in the subsequent insurgency had they not been eliminated during this battle. Sargat was the only facility of its type discovered in the Iraq war. This battle may have been the Tora Bora of Iraq, but it was a sound defeat for Al Qaeda and their ally Ansar Al Islam.Wikipedia:Citation needed This combined team then led the Peshmerga against Saddam's northern Army. This effort kept Saddam's forces in the north and denied the ability to redeploy to contest the invasion force coming from the south. This effort may have saved the lives of hundreds if not thousands of coalition service men and women.

At the launch of the Iraq War dozens of 12-member Special Forces teams infiltrated southern and western Iraq to hunt for Scud missiles and pinpoint bombing targets. Scores of Navy SEALs seized oil terminals and pumping stations on the southern coast. Air Force combat controllers flew combat missions in MC-130H Combat Talon IIs and established austere desert airstrips to begin the flow of soldiers and supplies deep into Iraq. It was a far cry from the Persian Gulf war of 1991, where Special Operations forces were kept largely on the sidelines. But it would not be a replay of Afghanistan, where Army Special Forces and Navy SEALs led the fighting. After their star turn in Afghanistan, many special operators were disappointed to play a supporting role in Iraq. Many special operators felt restricted by cautious commanders. From that point, USSOCOM has since killed or captured hundreds of insurgents and Al-Qaeda terrorists. It has conducted several foreign internal defense missions successfully training the Iraqi security forces.

Current role

United States Special Operations Command played a pivotal role in fighting the former Taliban government in Afghanistan in 2001 and toppling it thereafter, as well as combating the insurgency and capturing Saddam Hussein in Iraq. USSOCOM in 2004 was developing plans to have an expanded and more complex role in the global campaign against terrorism, and that role continued to emerge before and after the killing of Osama bin Laden in Pakistan in 2011. In 2010, "of about 13,000 Special Operations forces deployed overseas, about 9,000 [were] evenly divided between Iraq and Afghanistan."

War in Afghanistan

In the initial stages of the War in Afghanistan, USSOCOM forces linked up with CIA Paramilitary Officers from Special Activities Division to defeat the Taliban without the need for large-scale conventional forces. This was one of the biggest successes of the global War on Terrorism. These units linked up several times during this war and engaged in several furious battles with the enemy. One such battle happened during Operation Anaconda, the mission to squeeze life out of a Taliban and Al-Qaeda stronghold dug deep into the Shah-i-Kot mountains of eastern Afghanistan. The operation was seen as one of the heaviest and bloodiest fights in the War in Afghanistan. The battle on an Afghan mountaintop called Takur Ghar featured special operations forces from all 4 services and the CIA. Navy SEALs, Army Rangers, Air Force Combat Controllers, and Pararescuemen fought against entrenched Al-Qaeda fighters atop a 10,000-foot (3,000 m) mountain. Subsequently, the entrenched Taliban became targets of every asset in the sky. According to an executive summary, the battle of Takur Ghar was the most intense firefight American special operators have been involved in since 18 U.S. Army Rangers were killed in Mogadishu, Somalia, in 1993. During Operation Red Wings on 28 June 2005, four Navy SEALs, pinned down in a firefight, radioed for help. A Chinook helicopter, carrying 16 service members, responded but was shot down. All

Figure 112: *A 7th SFG Special Forces medic in Kandahar Province, Afghanistan, in September 2008.*

members of the rescue team and three of four SEALs on the ground died. It was the worst loss of life in Afghanistan since the invasion in 2001. The Navy SEAL Marcus Luttrell alone survived. Team leader Michael P. Murphy was awarded the Medal of Honor for his actions in the battle.

Global presence

SOC chief Olson said in 2011 that SOCOM "is a microcosm of the Department of Defense, with ground, air, and maritime components, a global presence, and authorities and responsibilities that mirror the Military Departments, Military Services, and Defense Agencies." In 2010, special operations forces were deployed in 75 countries, compared with about 60 at the beginning of 2009. In 2011, SOC spokesman Colonel Tim Nye (Army) was reported to have said that the number of countries with SOC presence will likely reach 120 and that joint training exercises will have been carried out in most or all of those countries during the year. One study identified joint-training exercises in Belize, Brazil, Bulgaria, Burkina Faso, Germany, Indonesia, Mali, Norway, Panama, and Poland in 2010 and also, through mid-year 2011, in the Dominican Republic, Jordan, Romania, Senegal, South Korea, and Thailand, among other nations. In addition, SOC forces executed the high-profile killing of Osama bin Laden in Pakistan in 2011.

Figure 113: *U.S. Air Force Special Tactics Commandos training in Jordan*

In November 2009 *The Nation* reported on a covert JSOC/Blackwater antiterrorist operation in Pakistan.[428]

In 2010, White House counterterrorism director John O. Brennan said that the United States "will not merely respond after the fact" of a terrorist attack but will "take the fight to al-Qaeda and its extremist affiliates whether they plot and train in Afghanistan, Pakistan, Yemen, Somalia and beyond." Olson said, "In some places, in deference to host-country sensitivities, we are lower in profile. In every place, Special Operations forces activities are coordinated with the U.S. ambassador and are under the operational control of the four-star regional commander."

The conduct of actions by SOC forces outside of Iraq and Afghan war zones has been the subject of internal U.S. debate, including between representatives of the Bush administration such as John B. Bellinger III, on one hand, and the Obama administration on another. The United Nations in 2010 also "questioned the administration's authority under international law to conduct such raids, particularly when they kill innocent civilians. One possible legal justification – the permission of the country in question – is complicated in places such as Pakistan and Yemen, where the governments privately agree but do not publicly acknowledge approving the attacks," as one report put it.

Figure 114: *The Joint Special Operations Command insignia*

Subordinate Commands

Joint Special Operations Command

Joint Special Operations Command (JSOC) is a component command of the USSOCOM and is charged to study special operations requirements and techniques to ensure interoperability and equipment standardization, plan and conduct special operations exercises and training, and develop Joint Special Operations Tactics. It was established in 1980 on recommendation of Col. Charlie Beckwith, in the aftermath of the failure of Operation Eagle Claw.[429]

Units

- The U.S. Army's 1st Special Forces Operational Detachment-Delta, popularly known as Delta Force, is the first of the two counter-terrorism, special mission units that fall under the Joint Special Operations Command. Modeled after the British Special Air Service, Delta Force is regarded as one of the premier special operations forces in the world. Delta also includes a stringent training and selection process. Delta recruits primarily from the most proficient and highly skilled soldiers of the U.S. Army Special Operations Command, although it encompasses the capability of recruiting throughout the U.S. Armed Forces. Recruits must pass a rigid selection course before beginning training, known as the Operators'

Training Course (OTC). Delta has received training from numerous U.S. government agencies and other tier one SOF and has created a curriculum based on this training and techniques that it has developed. Delta conducts clandestine and covert special operations all over the world. It has the capability to conduct myriad special operations missions but specializes in counter-terrorism and hostage rescue operations.
- The Intelligence Support Activity (ISA, The Activity) is the support branch of JSOC and USSOCOM. Its primary missions are to provide Human Intelligence (HUMINT) and Signal Intelligence (SIGINT) mainly for Delta and DEVGRU's operations. Before the establishing of the Strategic Support Branch in 2001, the ISA required the permission of the CIA to conduct covert operations, which considerably lessened its effectiveness in its support of JSOC operations as a whole.
- The U.S. Army's 75th Ranger Regiment: Regimental Reconnaissance Company (formerly known as Regimental Reconnaissance Detachment/RRD) is a unit that is rumored to be the newest operational member of the Joint Special Operations Command. The unit is believed to have been formally invited to join JSOC in 2007 due to its extensive training and unique capabilities to conduct special reconnaissance and close target reconnaissance (CTR) operations.
- The U.S. Navy's Naval Special Warfare Development Group (DEVGRU, SEAL Team Six) is the second of the two counter-terrorism, special mission units that fall under the Joint Special Operations Command. DEVGRU is the U.S. Navy's counterpart to Delta, specializing in maritime counter-terrorism. DEVGRU recruits the most proficient operators from Naval Special Warfare, specifically the U.S. Navy SEALs. Like Delta, DEVGRU can conduct a variety of special operations missions, but trains primarily for maritime counter-terrorism and hostage rescue operations. DEVGRU has gained prolific notoriety in recent years, due to high-profile hostage rescue operations and their role in the killing of Osama Bin Laden.
- The Air Force 24th Special Tactics Squadron (24th STS) is the AFSOC component of JSOC. The 24th STS consists of specially selected AFSOC personnel, including Pararescuemen, Combat Controllers, and TACPs. These special operators usually serve with Delta Force and DEVGRU, because of the convenience of the 24th STS's ability to synchronize and control the different elements of air power and enhance air operations deep in enemy territory; As well as providing needed medical assistance in the case of Pararescuemen.
- The Joint Communications Unit (JCU) is a technical unit of the United States Special Operations Command charged to standardize and ensure interoperability of communication procedures and equipment of the Joint

Special Operations Command and its subordinate units. The JCU was activated at Ft. Bragg, NC in 1980, after the failure of Operation Eagle Claw. The JCU has earned the reputation of "DoD's Finest Communicators".[430]

Portions of JSOC units have made up the constantly changing special operations task force, operating in the U.S. Central Command area of operations. The Task Force 11, Task Force 121, Task Force 6-26 and Task Force 145 are creations of the Pentagon's post-11 September campaign against terrorism, and it quickly became the model for how the military would gain intelligence and battle insurgents in the future. Originally known as Task Force 121, it was formed in the summer of 2003, when the military merged two existing Special Operations units, one hunting Osama bin Laden in and around Afghanistan, and the other tracking Sadaam Hussein in Iraq.

Special Operations Command – Joint Capabilities

Special Operations Command – Joint Capabilities (SOC-JC) was transferred to USSOCOM from the soon to be disestablished United States Joint Forces Command in 2011. Its primary mission was to train conventional and SOF commanders and their staffs, supports USSOCOM international engagement training requirements, and supports implementation of capability solutions in order to improve strategic and operational Warfighting readiness and joint interoperability. SOC-JC must also be prepared to support deployed Special Operations Joint Task Force (SOJTF) Headquarters (HQ).

The Government Accountability Office wrote that SOC-JC was disestablished in 2013, and positions were to be zeroed out in 2014.

Army

On 1 December 1989 the United States Army Special Operations Command (USASOC) activated as the 16th major Army command. These special operations forces have been America's spearhead for unconventional warfare for more than 40 years. USASOC commands such units as the well known Special Forces (SF, or the "Green Berets"), the Rangers, and such relatively unknown units as Psychological Operations Groups (PSYOP) and a Civil Affairs Brigade (CA). These are one of the USSOCOM's main weapons for waging unconventional warfare and counter-insurgency. The significance of these units is emphasized as conventional conflicts are becoming less prevalent as insurgent and guerrilla warfare increases.

United States Army Special Operations Command (Airborne):[431]

Name

Figure 115: *USASOC Shoulder sleeve insignia*

1st Special Forces Command (Airborne)

1st Special Forces Operational Detachment-Delta

75th Ranger Regiment

Army Special Operations Aviation Command

John F. Kennedy Special Warfare Center and School

Headquarters Fort Bragg, North CarolinaFt. Bragg, North Carolina Fort Benning, GeorgiaFt. Bragg, North Carolina Ft. Bragg, North Carolina Structure and purpose The ▇ 1st SFC(A) manages seven special forces groups (the ▢ 1st SFG(A), ▇ 3rd SFG(A), ▇ 5th SFG(A), ▇ 7th SFG(A), ▇ 10th SFG(A), ▇ 19th SFG(A) (ARNG) and ▇ 20th SFG(A) (ARNG)) that are trained for unconventional warfare, foreign internal defense, special reconnaissance, direct action and counter-terrorism missions. The command also manages two military information support groups (the 4th POG(A) and 8th POG(A)) that are trained to conduct psychological operations; the 95th Civil Affairs Brigade (Airborne) that enables military commanders and U.S. ambassadors to improve relationships with various stakeholders via five operational battalions (91st CA BN, 92nd CA BN, 96th CA BN, 97th CA BN and 98th CA BN); and the 528th Sustainment Brigade (Airborne) that provides combat service support and combat health support units via a Special Troops Battalion; the 112th Special Operations Signal Battalion (Airborne), an ARSOF Support Operations Cell, six ARSOF Liaison Elements; and two Medical Role II teams. The command also has an organic Military Intelligence Battalion providing multi-source intelligence information and analysis. Elite special operations and counter-terrorism unit under the control of Joint Special Operations Command. Three maneuver battalions (the 1st Ranger BN, 2nd Ranger BN, and 3rd Ranger BN) and a Special Troops Battalion of elite airborne infantry specializing in direct action raids and airfield seizures. Organizes, mans, trains, resources and equips Army special operations aviation units to provide responsive, special operations aviation support to Special Operations Forces (SOF) consisting of five units: USASOC Flight Company (UFC), Special Operations Training Battalion (SOATB), Technology Applications Program Office (TAPO), Systems Integration Management Office (SIMO) and the 160th Special Operations Aviation Regiment (160th SOAR)The SWCS selects and trains Army Special Forces, Civil Affairs and Military Information Support Operations Soldiers consisting of five distinct units and the Directorate of Training and Doctrine: 1st Special Warfare Training Group (Airborne), Special Warfare Education Group (Airborne), Special Warfare Medical Group (Airborne), Special Forces Warrant Officer Institute, and David K. Thuma Noncommissioned Officers Academy.

Units:

- United States Army Special Forces (SF) aka Green Berets perform several doctrinal missions: unconventional warfare, foreign internal defense, special reconnaissance, direct action and counter-terrorism. These missions make Special Forces unique in the U.S. military, because they are employed throughout the three stages of the operational continuum: peacetime, conflict and war. Foreign internal defense operations, SF's main peacetime mission, are designed to help friendly developing nations by working with their military and police forces to improve their technical skills, understanding of human rights issues, and to help with humanitarian and civic action projects. Special Forces unconventional warfare capabilities provide a viable military option for a variety of operational taskings that are inappropriate or infeasible for conventional forces. Special Forces are the U.S. military's premier unconventional warfare force.

Foreign internal defense and unconventional warfare missions are the bread and butter of Special Forces soldiers. For this reason SF candidates are trained extensively in weapons, engineering, communications and medicine. SF soldiers are taught to be warriors first and teachers second because they must be able to train their team and be able to train their allies during a FID or UW mission. Often SF units are required to perform additional, or collateral, activities outside their primary missions. These collateral activities are coalition warfare/support, combat search and rescue, security assistance, peacekeeping, humanitarian assistance, humanitarian de-mining and counter-drug operations.

- The 1st Special Forces Operational Detachment-Delta (1st SFOD-D), commonly referred to as Delta Force, Combat Applications Group/"CAG", "The Unit", Army Compartmented Element, or within JSOC as Task Force Green, is an elite Special Mission Unit of the United States Army, under the organization of the USASOC but is controlled by the Joint Special Operations Command (JSOC). It is used for hostage rescue and counterterrorism, as well as direct action and reconnaissance against high-value targets. 1st SFOD-D and its U.S. Navy counterpart, DEVGRU, "SEAL Team 6", perform many of the most highly complex and dangerous missions in the U.S. military. These units are also often referred to as "Tier One" and special mission units by the U.S. government.
- The 75th Ranger Regiment (U.S. Army Rangers) is the premier light-infantry unit of the United States Army and is headquartered at Fort Benning, Georgia. The 75th Ranger Regiment's mission is to plan and conduct special missions in support of U.S. policy and objectives. The Rangers are a flexible and rapid-deployable force. Each battalion can deploy anywhere in the world within 18 hours notice. The Army places much importance on the 75th Ranger Regiment and its training; it possesses the capabilities to conduct conventional and most special operations missions. Rangers are capable of infiltrating by land, sea, or air and direct action operations such as conducting raids or assaulting buildings or airfields.

- The 160th Special Operations Aviation Regiment (Night Stalkers) headquartered at Fort Campbell, Kentucky provides aviation support to units within USSOCOM. The Regiment consists of MH-6 and AH-6 light helicopters, MH-60 helicopters and MH-47 heavy assault helicopters. The capabilities of the 160th SOAR (A) have been evolving since the early 1980s. Its focus on night operations resulted in the nickname, the "Night Stalkers." The primary mission of the Night Stalkers is to conduct overt or covert infiltration, exfiltration, and resupply of special operations forces across a wide range of environmental conditions.

Figure 116: *Special Forces on a patrol in Afghanistan.*

- 4th Psychological Operations Group (Airborne) and 8th Psychological Operations Group (Airborne) Soldiers use persuasion to influence perceptions and encourage desired behavior. PSYOP soldiers supports national objectives at the tactical, operational and strategic levels of operations. Strategic psychological operations advance broad or long-term objectives; global in nature, they may be directed toward large audiences or at key communicators. Operational psychological operations are conducted on a smaller scale. 4th POG(A) is employed by theater commanders to target groups within the theater of operations. 4th POG(A) purpose can range from gaining support for U.S. operations to preparing the battlefield for combat. Tactical psychological operations are more limited, used by commanders to secure immediate and near-term goals. In this environment, these force-enhancing activities serve as a means to lower the morale and efficiency of enemy forces.
- 95th Civil Affairs Brigade (Airborne) specialists identify critical requirements needed by local citizens in war or disaster situations. They also locate civilian resources to support military operations, help minimize civilian interference with operations, support national assistance activities, plan and execute noncombatant evacuation, support counter-drug operations and establish and maintain liaison with civilian aid agencies and other nongovernmental organizations. In support of special operations, these culturally oriented, linguistically capable Soldiers may also be tasked to provide functional expertise for foreign internal defense operations,

Figure 117: *United States Marine Corps Forces Special Operations Command emblem*

unconventional warfare operations and direct action missions.
- 528th Sustainment Brigade –Special Operations– (Airborne) (SBSO(A)) has a difficult mission supporting USASOC. In their respective fields, signal and support soldiers provide supplies, maintenance, equipment and expertise allowing Special Operation Forces to "shoot, move and communicate" on a continuous basis. Because USASOC often uses Special Operations Forces-unique items, soldiers assigned to these units are taught to operate and maintain a vast array of specialized equipment not normally used by their conventional counterparts. SBSO(A) also provides the USASOC with centralized and integrated material management of property, equipment maintenance, logistical automation and repair parts and supplies.
- John F. Kennedy Special Warfare Center (USAJFKSWCS) trains USSOCOM and Army Special Operations Forces through development and evaluation of special operations concepts, doctrines and trainings.

Marine Corps

In October 2005, the Secretary of Defense directed the formation of United States Marine Corps Forces Special Operations Command, the Marine component of United States Special Operations Command. It was determined that the

Figure 118: *DA/SR Operators from 1st SOB (Special Operations Battalion) respond to enemy fire in Afghanistan*

Marine Corps would initially form a unit of approximately 2500 to serve with USSOCOM. On February 24, 2006 MARSOC activated at Camp Lejeune, North Carolina. MARSOC initially consisted of a small staff and the Foreign Military Training Unit (FMTU), which had been formed to conduct foreign internal defense. FMTU is now designated as the Marine Special Operations Advisor Group (MSOAG).

As a service component of USSOCOM, MARSOC is tasked by the Commander USSOCOM to train, organize, equip, and deploy responsive U.S. Marine Corps special operations forces worldwide, in support of combatant commanders and other agencies. MARSOC has been directed to conduct foreign internal defense, direct action and special reconnaissance. MARSOC has also been directed to develop a capability in unconventional warfare, counter-terrorism, and information operations. MARSOC deployed its first units in August 2006, six months after the group's initial activation. MARSOC reached full operational capability in October 2008.

Units

- Marine Raider Regiment (Marine Raiders) consists of a Headquarters Company and three Marine Raider Battalions, the 1st, 2nd and 3rd. The Regiment provides tailored military combat-skills training and advisor

support for identified foreign forces in order to enhance their tactical capabilities and to prepare the environment as directed by USSOCOM as well as the capability to form the nucleus of a Joint Special Operations Task Force. Marines and Sailors of the MRR train, advise and assist friendly host nation forces – including naval and maritime military and paramilitary forces – to enable them to support their governments' internal security and stability, to counter subversion and to reduce the risk of violence from internal and external threats. MRR deployments are coordinated by MARSOC, through USSOCOM, in accordance with engagement priorities for Overseas Contingency Operations.
- Marine Intelligence Battalion (MIB) trains, sustains, maintains combat readiness, and provides intelligence support at all operational levels in order to support MARSOF training and operations worldwide with mission-specific intelligence capability.
- Marine Special Operations Support Group (MSOSG) trains, equips, structures, and provides specially qualified Marine forces, including, operational logistics, intelligence, Military Working Dogs, Firepower Control Teams, and communications support in order to sustain worldwide special operations missions as directed by Commander, U.S. Marine Corps Forces Special Operations Command (COMMARFORSOC).
- The Marine Special Operations School (MSOS) performs the screening, recruiting, training, assessment and doctrinal development functions for MARSOC. It includes two subordinate Special Missions Training Branches (SMTBs), one on each coast.
  - The Special Mission Training Branch—East provide special operations training in tactics, techniques and procedures, and evaluation and certification of MARSOC forces to specified conditions and standards for SOF. The Marines of MSOS are operators with the training, experience and mature judgment to plan, coordinate, instruct and supervise development of SOF special reconnaissance and direct action skills.

Navy

The United States Naval Special Warfare Command (NAVSPECWARCOM, NAVSOC, or NSWC) was commissioned April 16, 1987, at Naval Amphibious Base Coronado in San Diego as the Naval component to the United States Special Operations Command. Naval Special Warfare Command provides vision, leadership, doctrinal guidance, resources and oversight to ensure component special operations forces are ready to meet the operational requirements of combatant commanders. Today, SEAL Teams and Special Boat Teams comprise the elite combat units of Naval Special Warfare. These teams are organized, trained, and equipped to conduct a variety of missions to include

Figure 119: *United States Naval Special Warfare Command emblem.*

Figure 120: *SEALs emerge from the water during a demonstration.*

direct action, special reconnaissance, counter-terrorism, foreign internal defense, unconventional warfare and support psychological and civil affairs operations. Their highly trained operators are deployed worldwide in support of National Command Authority objectives, conducting operations with other conventional and special operations forces.

Units

- United States Navy SEALs have distinguished themselves as an individually reliable, collectively disciplined and highly skilled special operations force. The most important trait that distinguishes Navy SEALs from all

Figure 121: *A special warfare combatant-craft crewmen from Special Boat Team 22 fires a GAU-17 from a Special Operations Craft – Riverine (SOC-R)*

other military forces is that SEALs are maritime special operations, as they strike from and return to the sea. SEALs (SEa, Air, Land) take their name from the elements in and from which they operate. SEALs are experts in direct action and special reconnaissance missions. Their stealth and clandestine methods of operation allow them to conduct multiple missions against targets that larger forces cannot approach undetected. Because of the dangers inherent in their missions, prospective SEALs go through what is considered by many military experts to be the toughest training regime in the world.

- Naval Special Warfare Development Group (DEVGRU), referred to as SEAL Team Six, the name of its predecessor which was officially disbanded in 1987.
- SEAL Delivery Vehicle Teams are SEAL teams with an added underwater delivery capability who use the SDV MK VIII and the Advanced SEAL Delivery System (ASDS), submersibles that provides NSW with an unprecedented capability that combines the attributes of clandestine underwater mobility and the combat swimmer.
- Special Warfare Combatant-craft Crewmen (SWCC) operate and maintain state-of-the-art surface craft to conduct coastal patrol and interdiction and support special operations missions. Focusing on infiltration and

Figure 122: *Air Force Special Operations Command emblem.*

exfiltration of SEALs and other SOF, SWCCs provide dedicated rapid mobility in shallow water areas where larger ships cannot operate. They also bring to the table a unique SOF capability: Maritime Combatant Craft Aerial Delivery System—the ability to deliver combat craft via parachute drop. Like SEALs, SWCCs must have excellent physical fitness, highly motivated, combat-focused and responsive in high stress situations.

Air Force

Air Force Special Operations Command was established May 22, 1990, with headquarters at Hurlburt Field, Florida. AFSOC is one of the 10 Air Force Major Commands or MAJCOMs, and the Air Force component of United States Special Operations Command. It holds operational and administrative oversight of subordinate special operations wings and groups in the regular Air Force, Air Force Reserve Command and the Air National Guard.

AFSOC provides Air Force special operations forces for worldwide deployment and assignment to regional unified commands. The command's SOF are composed of highly trained, rapidly deployable airmen, conducting global special operations missions ranging from precision application of firepower via airstrikes or close air support, to infiltration, exfiltration, resupply and refueling of SOF operational elements. AFSOC's unique capabilities include

Figure 123: *An AC-130U Spooky from the 4th Special Operations Squadron*

Figure 124: *Combat Controllers from the 21st Special Tactics Squadron conducting close air support training with A-10 pilots in Nevada*

airborne radio and television broadcast for psychological operations, as well as aviation foreign internal defense instructors to provide other governments military expertise for their internal development.

The command's core missions include battlefield air operations; agile combat support; aviation foreign internal defense; information operations; precision aerospace fires; psychological operations; specialized air mobility; specialized refueling; and intelligence, surveillance and reconnaissance.

Units

- Combat Controllers (CCT) are ground combat forces specialized in a traditional pathfinder role while having a heavy emphasis on simultaneous air traffic control, fire support (via airstrikes, close air support and command, control, and communications in covert or austere environments.
- Pararescuemen (PJ) are the only Department of Defense specialty specifically trained and equipped to conduct conventional and unconventional personnel recovery operations. A PJ's primary function is as a personnel recovery specialist with emergency trauma medical capabilities in humanitarian and combat environments.
- Special Operations Weather Technicians (SOWT) gather, assess, and interpret weather and environmental intelligence from forward deployed locations, working alongside special operations forces.

Organization

- The 1st Special Operations Wing (1 SOW) is located at Hurlburt Field, Florida. Its mission focus is unconventional warfare: counter-terrorism, combat search and rescue, personnel recovery, psychological operations, aviation assistance to developing nations, "deep battlefield" resupply, interdiction and close air support. The wing's core missions include aerospace surface interface, agile combat support, combat aviation advisory operations, information operations, personnel recovery/recovery operations, precision aerospace fires, psychological operations dissemination, specialized aerospace mobility and specialized aerial refueling. Among its aircraft is the MC-130 Combat Talon II, a low-level terrain following special missions transport that can evade radar detection and slip into enemy territory at a 200-foot (61 m) altitude for infiltration/exfiltration missions, even in zero visibility, dropping off or recovering men or supplies with pinpoint accuracy. It also operates the AC-130 Spooky and Spectre gunships that provide highly accurate airborne gunfire for close air support of conventional and special operations forces on the ground.

- The 24th Special Operations Wing (24 SOW) is located at Hurlburt Field, Florida. It is composed of the 720th Special Tactics Group, 724th Special Tactics Group, Special Tactics Training Squadron and 16 recruiting locations across the United States. The Special Tactics Squadrons, under the 720th STG and 724th STG, are made up of Special Tactics Officers, Combat Controllers, Combat Rescue Officers, Pararescuemen, Special Operations Weather Officers and Airmen, Air Liaison Officers, Tactical Air Control Party operators, and a number of combat support airmen which comprise 58 Air Force specialties.
- The 27th Special Operations Wing (27 SOW) is located at Cannon AFB, New Mexico. Its primary mission includes infiltration, exfiltration and re-supply of special operations forces; air refueling of special operations rotary wing and tiltrotor aircraft; and precision fire support. These capabilities support a variety of special operations missions including direct action, unconventional warfare, special reconnaissance, counter-terrorism, personnel recovery, psychological operations and information operations.
- The 193d Special Operations Wing (193 SOW) is an Air National Guard (ANG) unit, operationally gained by AFSOC, and located at Harrisburg International Airport/Air National Guard Station (former Olmsted Air Force Base), Pennsylvania. Under Title 32 USC, the 193 SOW performs state missions for the Governor of Pennsylvania as part of the Pennsylvania Air National Guard. Under Title 10 USC, the 193 SOW is part of the Air Reserve Component (ARC) of the United States Air Force. Its primary wartime and contingency operations mission as an AFSOC-gained unit is psychological operations (PSYOP). The 193 SOW is unique in that it is the only unit in the U.S. Air Force to fly and maintain the Lockheed EC-130J Commando Solo aircraft.
- The 919th Special Operations Wing (919 SOW) is an Air Force Reserve Command (AFRC) unit, operationally gained by AFSOC, and located at Eglin AFB Auxiliary Field #3/Duke Field, Florida. The 919 SOW flies and maintains the MC-130E Combat Talon I and MC-130P Combat Shadow special operations aircraft designed for covert operations.
- The 352d Special Operations Wing (352 SOW) at RAF Mildenhall, United Kingdom serves as the core to United States European Command's standing Joint Special Operations Air Component headquarters. The squadron provides support for three flying squadrons, one special tactics squadron and one maintenance squadron for exercise, logistics, and war planning; aircrew training; communications; aerial delivery; medical; intelligence; security and force protection; weather; information technologies and transformation support and current operations.
- The 353d Special Operations Group (353 SOG) is the focal point for all U.S. Air Force special operations activities throughout the United

States Pacific Command (USPACOM) theater. Headquartered at Kadena AB, Okinawa, Japan the group is prepared to conduct a variety of high-priority, low-visibility missions. Its mission is air support of joint and allied special operations forces in the Pacific. It maintains a worldwide mobility commitment, participates in Pacific theater exercises as directed and supports humanitarian and relief operations.

- The United States Air Force Special Operations School (USAFSOS) at Hurlburt Field, Florida is a primary support unit of the Air Force Special Operations Command. The USAFSOS prepares special operations Airmen to successfully plan, organize, and execute global special operations by providing indoctrination and education for AFSOC, other USSOCOM components, and joint/interagency/ coalition partners.

List of USSOCOM Combatant Commanders

№	Combatant Commanders	Took office	Left office	Time in office	Defence branch
1	General **James J. Lindsay** (born 1932)	16 April 1987	27 June 1990	3 years, 72 days	USA
2	General **Carl W. Stiner** (born 1936)	27 June 1990	20 May 1993	2 years, 327 days	USA
3	General **Wayne A. Downing** (1940–2007)	20 May 1993	29 February 1996	2 years, 285 days	USA
4	General **Henry H. Shelton** (born 1942)	29 February 1996	25 September 1997	1 year, 209 days	USA
-	Rear admiral **Raymond C. Smith, Jr.** *Acting*	25 September 1997	5 November 1997	41 days	USN
5	General **Peter J. Schoomaker** (born 1946)	5 November 1997	27 October 2000	2 years, 357 days	USA
6	General **Charles R. Holland** (born 1946)	27 October 2000	2 September 2003	2 years, 310 days	USAF
7	General **Bryan D. Brown** (born 1946)	2 September 2003	9 July 2007	3 years, 310 days	USA

8		Admiral **Eric T. Olson** (born 1952)	9 July 2007	8 August 2011	4 years, 30 days	USN
9		Admiral **William H. McRaven** (born 1955)	8 August 2011	28 August 2014	3 years, 20 days	USN
10		General **Joseph L. Votel** (born 1958)	28 August 2014	30 March 2016	1 year, 215 days	USA
11		General **Raymond A. Thomas** (born 1958)	30 March 2016	*Incumbent*	2 years, 124 days	USA

USSOCOM medal

The United States Special Operations Command Medal was introduced in 1994 to recognize individuals for outstanding contributions to, and in support of, special operations.Wikipedia:Citation needed Since it was created, there have been more than 50 recipients, four of whom are not American, namely;

- Lieutenant General Samuel V. Wilson
- Colonel Ralph Puckett
- SCPO Kristin Beck
- Kaptein Gunnar Sønsteby of Norway (2008),[432]
- Generał broni Włodzimierz Potasiński (2010, posthumously),[433]
- Generał brygady Jerzy Gut (June 2014) and
- Generał dywizji Piotr Patalong (October 2014)., all from Poland.

References

Citations

Bibliography

<templatestyles src="Template:Refbegin/styles.css" />

- Briscoe, Charles (2001). *Weapon of Choice: ARSOF in Afghanistan*. Combat Studies Institute Press.
- Couch, Dick (March 2007). *Chosen Soldier: The Making of a Special Forces Warrior*. Three Rivers Press. ISBN 0-307-33939-4.
- Couch, Dick (2006). *Down Range: Navy SEALs in the War on Terrorism*. New York, New York: Three Rivers Press. ISBN 1-4000-8101-7.

Figure 125: *USSOCOM Medal Ribbon Bar*

- Kelley, Stephen Andrew (June 2007). "Better Lucky Than Good: Operation Earnest Will as Gunboat Diplomacy"[434] (PDF). Naval Postgraduate School. Archived from the original[435] (PDF) on 18 March 2009. Retrieved 12 May 2008.
- Luttrell, Marcus; Patrick Robinson (June 2007). *Lone Survivor: The Eyewitness Account of Operation Redwing and the Lost Heroes of SEAL Team 10*. Little, Brown and Company. ISBN 0-316-06759-8.
- Pirnie, Bruce R. (August 1998). *Assessing Requirements for Peacekeeping, Humanitarian Assistance and Disaster Relief*. RAND Corporation. ISBN 0-8330-2594-5.
- Pushies, Fred (2007). *U.S. Air Force Special Ops*. Osceola, Wisconsin: MBI Publishing Company. ISBN 0-7603-0733-4.
- Smith, Michael (2007). *Killer Elite: The Inside Story of America's Most Secret Special Operations Team*. New York, New York: St. Martin's Press. ISBN 0-312-36272-2.
- Sweetman, Jack (March 1999). *Great American Naval Battles*. Naval Institute Press. ISBN 1-55750-794-5.
- David Tucker, Christopher J. Lamb (2007). *United States Special Operations Forces*. Columbia University Press. ISBN 0-231-13190-9.
- Wise, Harold Lee (May 2007). *Inside the Danger Zone: The U.S. Military in the Persian Gulf, 1987–1988*. US Naval Institute Press. ISBN 1-59114-970-3.

Web

- USDOD. U.S. DOD Dictionary of Military Terms[436]. United States of America: *U.S. Department of Defense*. 5 June 2003.
- USDOD. U.S. DOD Dictionary of Military Terms: Joint Acronyms and Abbreviations[436]. United States of America: *U.S. Department of Defense*. 5 June 2003.
- Talmadge, Eric (27 February 2008). "New US Submarines Trade Nukes for SEALs"[437]. Fox News. Associated Press. Archived from the original[438] on 8 March 2008.

- Eric Schmitt, Michael R. Gordon (4 February 2008). "Leak on Cross-Border Chases From Iraq"[439]. *New York Times*.
- von Zielbauer, Paul (27 April 2007). "Criminal Charges Are Expected Against Marines, Official Says"[440]. *New York Times*.
- Graham, Bradley (2 November 2005). "Elite Marine Unit to Help Fight Terrorism"[441]. *Washington Post*. Retrieved 27 May 2010. Check date values in: |year= / |date= mismatch (help)

External links

 Wikimedia Commons has media related to *United States Special Operations Command*.

- U.S. Special Operations Command[442]
- U.S. Army Special Operations Command[443]
- U.S. Marine Corps Forces Special Operations Command[444]
- U.S. Naval Special Warfare Command[445]
- Air Force Special Operations Command[446]
- Department of Defense[447]
- Joint Special Operations University[448]

<indicator name="good-star"> ⊕ </indicator>

United States Strategic Command

United States Strategic Command	
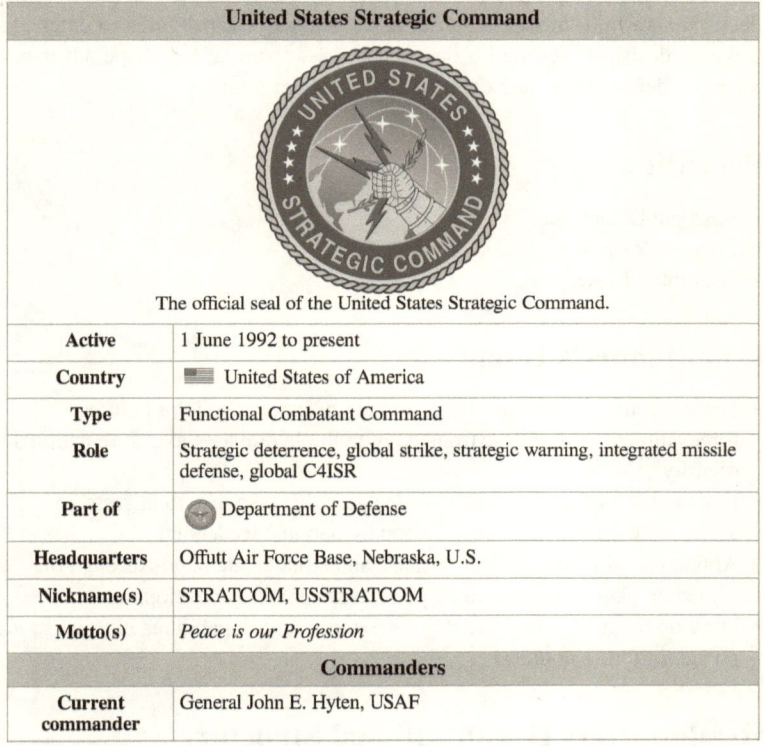 The official seal of the United States Strategic Command.	
Active	1 June 1992 to present
Country	United States of America
Type	Functional Combatant Command
Role	Strategic deterrence, global strike, strategic warning, integrated missile defense, global C4ISR
Part of	Department of Defense
Headquarters	Offutt Air Force Base, Nebraska, U.S.
Nickname(s)	STRATCOM, USSTRATCOM
Motto(s)	*Peace is our Profession*
Commanders	
Current commander	General John E. Hyten, USAF

United States Strategic Command (USSTRATCOM), is one of ten unified commands in the United States Department of Defense. Headquartered at Offutt Air Force Base, Nebraska, USSTRATCOM is responsible for strategic deterrence, global strike, and operating the Defense Department's Global Information Grid. It also provides a host of capabilities to support the other combatant commands, including strategic warning; integrated missile defense; and global command, control, communications, computers, intelligence, surveillance, and reconnaissance (C4ISR). This dynamic command gives national leadership a unified resource for greater understanding of specific threats around the world and the means to respond to those threats rapidly.

Mission statement

USSTRATCOM employs tailored nuclear, cyber, space, global strike, joint electronic warfare, missile defense, and intelligence capabilities to deter aggression, decisively respond if deterrence fails, assure allies, shape adversary behavior, defeat terror, and define the force of the future.

Priorities

- Strategic Deterrence
- Decisive Response
- A Combat-Ready Force

Commander's Intent

- Embrace strategic deterrence, consisting of innovative joint fighting forces integrated and synchronized in multiple domains to ensure national security.
- Ensure that we can and will provide a decisive response to aggression, against any threat, when called upon by national leadership.
- Anticipate and meet tactical, theater, and strategic demands through our campaign plan, our operational plans, and capability development.
- Develop the next generation of professionals and capabilities in order to prevail in future conflicts.

Headquarters Organizational Structure

- J1 - Manpower & Personnel: Develops and administers command manpower and personnel policies, human resources, and personnel assignment programs.

- J2 - Intelligence: Responsible for delivering all-source intelligence while enabling the execution of assigned strategic deterrence, space and cyberspace operations. Directs all intelligence-related support for the Commander and ensures unity of intelligence effort across the Command.

- J3 - Global Operations: Coordinates the planning, employment and operation of DoD strategic assets and combines all current operations, intelligence, and global command and control operations. Subdivisions within J3 include Combat and Information Operations, Current Operations, Logistics, and Joint Electromagnetic Spectrum Operations (JEMSO).

Figure 126: *A Minuteman III ICBM in its missile silo*

Figure 127: *USS West Virginia, Ohio Class SSBN*

Figure 128: *B-52 and B-2 flying in formation*

- J4 - Logistics: The Logistics Directorate plans, coordinates and executes joint logistics functions, and provides capability-based readiness assessments and facilities management in support of U.S. Strategic Command's global mission.
- J5 - Plans and Policy: Responsible for coordinating the development and implementation of national security policy as it applies to the command and the execution of its mission. Develops future plans, policy and strategy across all mission areas as outlined in the Unified Command Plan.
- J6 - C4 Systems: Coordinates, facilitates, monitors and assesses systems, networks and communications requirements.
- J7 - Joint Exercises, Training and Assessments: Manages the USSTRATCOM Commander's Joint Exercises, Training, and Assessments programs in order to ensure readiness to perform the Command missions. Provides modeling and simulation support for exercises and training events to the Joint Chiefs of Staff (JCS), Combatant Commands, and other Major Commands (MAJCOM). Manages the Joint Lessons Learned Program. Augments the battle staff during a crisis.
- J8 - Capability and Resource Integration: Conducts force management and analysis to include integrating, coordinating, prioritizing, and advocating USSTRATCOM future concepts, mission capability needs, weapons system development, support for emerging technologies, and command and control architecture across the mission areas. Responsible for all command requirement processes, and ensures appropriate decision

support tools and assessment processes are in place to enhance operational capabilities.
- J10 - Joint Reserve Directorate: The Joint Reserve Directorate advises CDRUSSTRATCOM and staff on matters related to the Army, Air Force, Navy, and Marine Corps Reserve personnel assigned to USSTRATCOM. The J10 coordinates Reserve funding requests with the applicable service.

Component Structure

U.S. Strategic Command's day-to-day planning and execution for the primary mission areas is done by the following USSTRATCOM components:

- JFCC - Global Strike (JFCC-GS), Offutt AFB, NE – Conducts kinetic (nuclear and conventional) and non-kinetic effects planning. GS manages global force activities to assure allies and to deter and dissuade actions detrimental to the United States and its global interests; should deterrence fail, employs global strike forces in support of combatant commander.
- JFCC - Space (JFCC Space), Vandenberg AFB, CA – Continuously co-ordinates, plans, integrates, commands and controls space operations to provide tailored, responsive, local and global effects, and on order, denies the enemy the same, in support of national, USSTRATCOM, and combatant commander objectives.
- JFCC - Integrated Missile Defense (JFCC-IMD) Schriever AFB, CO – Synchronizes operational-level global missile defense planning, operations support, and the development of missile defense effects for DoD. When directed, also provides alternate missile defense execution support.
- JFCC - Intelligence, Surveillance and Reconnaissance (JFCC-ISR) Bolling AFB, Washington, D.C. – Identifies and recommends appropriate re-sources to meet high priority intelligence requirements. Essentially, ISR helps ensure the best use of resources to provide decision makers and troops with crucial information when and where they need.
- Joint Warfare Analysis Center (JWAC) Dahlgren, VA – The Joint Warfare Analysis Center (JWAC) provides combatant commands, Joint Staff, and other customers with precise technical solutions in order to carry out the national security and military strategies of the United States. JWAC maintains and enhances its ability to conduct comprehensive technical analysis.

Service components

Army

- Army Space and Missile Defense Command/Army Forces Strategic Command (SMDC/ARSTRAT)

Marines

- Marine Corps Forces Strategic Command (MARFORSTRAT) Helps to coordinate USMC and StratCom in areas such as "space, cyberspace, electronic warfare, and combating weapons of mass destruction".

Navy

- Fleet Forces Command (USFF)

Air Force

- Air Force Global Strike Command (AFGSC)
- Air Force Space Command (AFSPC)

Command Posts

Global Operations Center

The Global Operations Center, or GOC, is the nerve center for USSTRATCOM. The GOC is responsible for the global situational awareness of the Commander, USSTRATCOM, and is the mechanism by which he exercises operational command and control of the Nation's global strategic forces.

Airborne Command Post

U.S. Strategic Command's Airborne Command Post (ABNCP), also called "Looking Glass", allows USSTRATCOM the ability to command, control, and communicate with its nuclear forces should ground-based command centers become inoperable.

Figure 129: *Gen. Curtis E. LeMay Building, U.S. Strategic Command Headquarters*

Figure 130: *E-6B Mercury, USSTRATCOM ABNCP*

Figure 131: *USSTRATCOM Airborne Command Post crew members responding to their aircraft during an alert response exercise*

History

USSTRATCOM was originally formed in 1992, as a successor to Strategic Air Command in response to the end of the Cold War and a new vision of nuclear warfare in U.S. defense policy. Department of Defense changes in command structure due to the "Goldwater-Nichols Act" of 1986, led to a single command responsible for all strategic nuclear weapons. As a result, USSTRATCOM's principal mission was to deter military attack, and if deterrence failed, to counter with nuclear weapons.

Throughout its history, it has drawn from important contributions from many different organizations stretching back to World War II. Providing national leadership with a single command responsible for all strategic nuclear forces, General George Butler, in establishing the new command, borrowed from the work of General Curtis LeMay, an early commander of Strategic Air Command. LeMay was a very vocal advocate for a strong national defense, particularly as regards nuclear weapons.

Being a Unified Command, another major concern for Gen. Butler was inter-service rivalry, having soldiers, sailors, airmen and marines in one command. There had been decades of rivalry between the branches of the U.S. military regarding control of nuclear weapons. Even though a compromise had established the **Joint Strategic Target Planning Staff**, there were systemic and institutional problems that could not be overcome.

USSTRATCOM was re-structured October 1, 2002 by Secretary of Defense, Donald Rumsfeld. It was now to merge with the United States Space Command and assume all duties for full-spectrum global strike, operational space support, integrated missile defense, and global Command, Control, Communications, Computers, Intelligence, Surveillance and Reconnaissance (C^4ISR) and specialized planning. Its duties now include intelligence and cyber support as well as monitoring orbiting satellites and space debris.

In February 2008, USSTRATCOM succeeded in destroying a satellite, USA193, about to re-enter the earth's atmosphere.

USSTRATCOM also supported United States Africa Command's 2011 military intervention in Libya in a variety of ways, including long-range conventional strikes and intelligence, surveillance and reconnaissance (ISR).

An intention by the U.S. Air Force to create a 'cyber command' was announced in October 2006. On May 21, 2010, part of USSTRATCOM's responsibility regarding cyber-warfare operations was spun off into a 10th Unified Command, the United States Cyber Command. As a result, USSTRATCOM's Joint Task Force-Global Network Operations (JTF-GNO) and Joint Functional Component Command – Network Warfare (JFCC-NW) were disestablished.

List of Combatant Commanders

	Photo	Name	Term Began	Term Ended
1.		General George L. Butler, USAF	June 1992	February 14, 1994
2.		Admiral Henry G. Chiles, Jr., USN	February 14, 1994	February 21, 1996
3.		General Eugene E. Habiger, USAF	February 21, 1996	August 1, 1998
4.		Admiral Richard W. Mies, USN	August 1, 1998	2002
5.		Admiral James O. Ellis, Jr., USN	2002	July 9, 2004

6.		General James E. Cartwright, USMC	July 9, 2004 (acting) September 1, 2004	August 10, 2007
Acting		Lt. Gen C. Robert Kehler, USAF	August 10, 2007	October 3, 2007
7.		General Kevin P. Chilton, USAF	October 3, 2007	January 28, 2011
8.		General C. Robert Kehler, USAF	January 28, 2011	November 15, 2013
9.		Admiral Cecil D. Haney, USN	November 15, 2013	November 3, 2016
10.		General John E. Hyten, USAF	November 3, 2016	*Present*

External links

 Wikimedia Commons has media related to *United States Strategic Command*.

- United States Strategic Command Official Website[449]
- US Strategic Command Airborne Command Post Fact Sheet[450]
- Air Force Magazine[451], Journal of the Air Force Assoc., August 2008.
- FAS: United States Space Command (USSPACECOM)[452]
- GAO Report: Additional Actions Needed by U.S. Strategic Command to Strengthen Implementation of Its Many Missions and New Organization[453]

United States Transportation Command

United States Transportation Command	
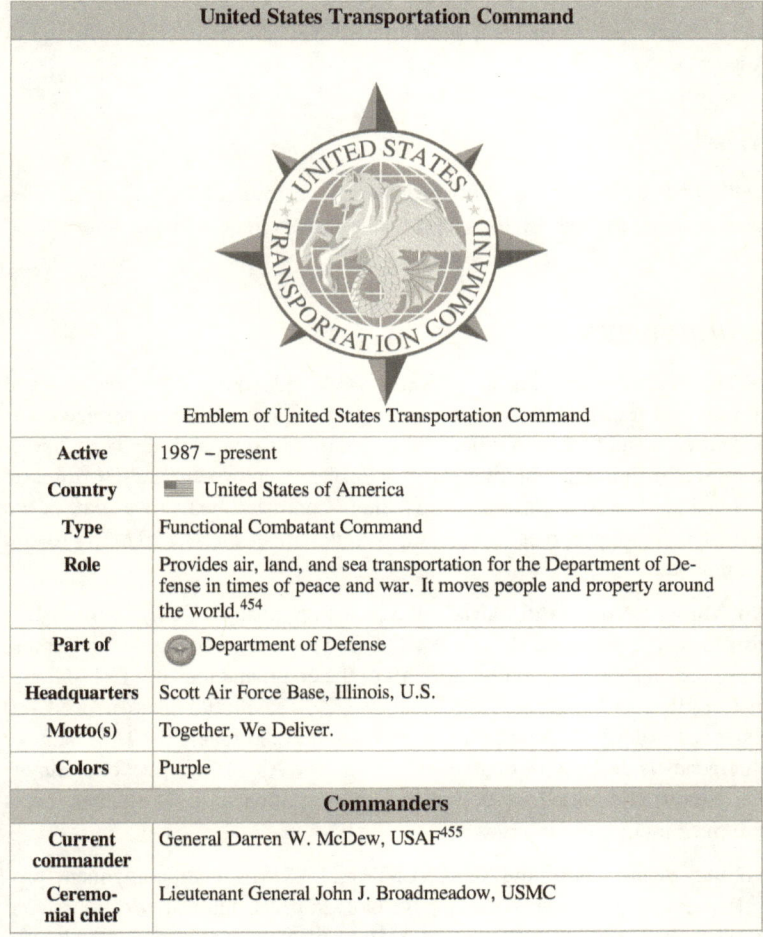 Emblem of United States Transportation Command	
Active	1987 – present
Country	United States of America
Type	Functional Combatant Command
Role	Provides air, land, and sea transportation for the Department of Defense in times of peace and war. It moves people and property around the world.[454]
Part of	Department of Defense
Headquarters	Scott Air Force Base, Illinois, U.S.
Motto(s)	Together, We Deliver.
Colors	Purple
Commanders	
Current commander	General Darren W. McDew, USAF[455]
Ceremonial chief	Lieutenant General John J. Broadmeadow, USMC

The **United States Transportation Command** (**USTRANSCOM**) is one of ten unified commands of the United States Department of Defense. The command is located at Scott Air Force Base, Illinois, and was established in 1987.

This command is the single manager of the United States' global defense transportation system. USTRANSCOM is tasked with the coordination of people and transportation assets to allow the US to project and sustain forces, whenever, wherever, and for as long as they are needed. The commander of USTRANSCOM is General Darren W. McDew, formerly head of the Air Mobility Command, the air component of TRANSCOM, who was confirmed in August 2015.

Mission

USTRANSCOM provides full-spectrum global mobility solutions and related enabling capabilities for supported customers' requirements in peace and war.[456]

Components

USTRANSCOM coordinates missions worldwide using both military and commercial transportation resources. It is composed of three service component commands: The Air Force's Air Mobility Command, the Navy's Military Sealift Command and the Army's Surface Deployment and Distribution Command. The Joint Enabling Capabilities Command, which was part of the former U.S. Joint Forces Command, is now part of the U.S. Transportation Command.

Air Mobility Command (AMC), the air component of USTRANSCOM, is also located at Scott AFB. The AMC fleet provides refueling and cargo and personnel transport capability. Aircraft of the command include: C-17 Globemaster III, C-5 Galaxy, C-130 Hercules, KC-135 Stratotanker, and KC-10 Extender. Additional long-range airlift aircraft are available if a U.S. national emergency is declared through the Civil Reserve Air Fleet, a fleet of commercial aircraft committed to support the transportation of U.S. military forces and material in times of crisis.

Military Sealift Command (MSC) USTRANSCOM's sealift component, provides sea transportation worldwide for DoD in peace and war. Headquartered in Norfolk, Virginia. MSC uses a mixture of government-owned and commercial ships for three primary functions: Surge sealift, principally used to move unit equipment from the United States to theaters of operations all over the world; prepositioned sealift, comes under USTRANSCOM's command once the ships have been released into the common-user fleet; and sustainment sealift, the life line to keep deployed forces continuously supplied. MSC assets include Fast Sealift and Ready Reserve Force ships. In addition, MSC charters and books space on commercial ships.

Military Surface Deployment and Distribution Command (SDDC), located at Scott Air Force Base, Illinois, is the commercial surface lift component and

Figure 132: *The Military Sealift Command large, medium-speed roll-on/roll-off ship USNS Red Cloud (T-AKR 313) participates in Combined Joint Logistics Over-the-Shore (CJLOTS) 2015 at Anmyeon Beach, Republic of Korea.*

primary surface distribution manager for USTRANSCOM. SDDC's provides global surface deployment command and control and distribution operations. SDDC has a presence in 24 water ports worldwide. In an average year, SDDC manages and directs the movement of 3.7 million measurement tons (4.2 million m³) of ocean cargo, 500,000 personal-property moves, 600,000 domestic freight shipments, 72,000 privately owned vehicles and 518,000 passengers. SDDC assets include 10,000 containers and 1,350 railroad cars. Within the United States, the SDDC works with the Federal Highway Administration to designate the Strategic Highway Network.

Joint Operational Support Airlift Center (JOSAC) specializes in the airlift of senior defense officials within the continental United States. JOSAC is located at Scott Air Force Base, Illinois.

Joint Enabling Capabilities Command (JECC) provides mission-tailored, ready joint capability packages to combatant commanders. JECC is located at Naval Station Norfolk, Virginia and is divided into three subordinate joint commands that provide capabilities across seven unique functional areas. It aims to bring tailored, mission-specific forces to a joint force commander within hours of notification. The JECC subordinate joint commands are:

- Joint Planning Support Element (JPSE) – Provides rapidly deployable, tailored, ready, joint planners, operators, logisticians, knowledge managers

Figure 133: *Berliners watch a Douglas C-54 Skymaster land at Tempelhof Airport, during the Berlin Airlift in 1948.*

and intelligence specialists in order to accelerate the formation and increase the effectiveness of newly formed joint force headquarters. JPSE is co-located with the JECC headquarters at Naval Station Norfolk, Virginia.
- Joint Communications Support Element (JCSE) – Provides rapidly deployable, en route, early entry and scalable command, control, communications, computer, intelligence, surveillance and reconnaissance (C4ISR) capabilities across the full spectrum of operations in order to facilitate rapid establishment of joint force headquarters and bridge joint C4ISR requirements. JCSE is located at MacDill Air Force Base, Florida.
- Joint Public Affairs Support Element (JPASE) - Provides ready, rapidly deployable, joint public affairs capabilities to combatant commanders in order to facilitate rapid establishment of joint force headquarters, bridge joint public affairs requirements and conduct public affairs training to meet theater information challenges. JPASE is located in Suffolk, Virginia.

History

World War II, the Berlin blockade, the Korean War, and the Vietnam War all demonstrated that the United States needed to maintain a capable and ready transportation system for national security. In 1978, however, command post exercise Exercise Nifty Nugget exposed great gaps in understanding between military and civilian participants: mobilization and deployment plans fell apart, and as a result, the United States and its NATO allies "lost the war". Two major recommendations came out of Nifty Nugget. First, the Transportation Operating Agencies (later called the Transportation Component Commands) should have a direct reporting chain to the Joint Chiefs of Staff (JCS). Second, the JCS should establish a single manager for deployment and execution. As a result, the JCS formed the **Joint Deployment Agency** (JDA) at MacDill Air Force Base in Florida in 1979.

Despite its many successes, the JDA could not handle the job. Although the JDA had responsibility for integrating deployment procedures, it did not have authority to direct the Transportation Operating Agencies or Unified and Specified Commanders in Chief to take corrective actions, keep databases current, or adhere to milestones. According to several independent studies on transportation, the Department of Defense (DOD) needed to consolidate transportation. Consequently, President Ronald Reagan on 18 April 1987 ordered the Secretary of Defense to establish a **Unified Transportation Command** (UTC), a directive made possible in part by the Goldwater-Nichols Department of Defense Reorganization Act of 1986, which revoked the law prohibiting consolidation of military transportation functions.

The UTC Implementation Plan (IP) outlined the new unified command's responsibilities, functions, and organization. Christened United States Transportation Command (USTRANSCOM), its mission was to "provide global air, sea and land transportation to meet national security needs". It had three transportation component commands—the Air Force's Military Airlift Command (replaced by Air Mobility Command in 1992), the Navy's Military Sealift Command, and the Army's Military Traffic Management Command, (renamed Military Surface Deployment and Distribution Command in 2004). The JDA's missions and functions transferred to USTRANSCOM on 18 April 1987, when the agency became the command's Directorate of Deployment. Additionally, the IP located the command at Scott AFB, to take advantage of Military Airlift Command's expertise in command and control. On 22 June 1987, the President nominated Air Force Gen. Duane H. Cassidy as the first Commander, USTRANSCOM, and on 1 July the Senate confirmed the recommendation, thus activating the command at Scott. The commander of USTRANSCOM received operational direction from the National Command Authority (NCA) through the Chairman of the Joint Chiefs of Staff.

USTRANSCOM appeared, at first glance, to be the long sought after remedy for DOD's fragmented and often criticized transportation system. Its establishment gave the United States, for the first time, a four-star, unified combatant

Figure 134: *Military Surface Deployment and Distribution Command, 597th Transportation Brigade, 842nd Trans. Battalion, orchestrates simultaneous terminal operations for the loading of unit equipment headed overseas and the offloading of cargo returning from Afghanistan at the Port of Beaumont and at Port of Port Arthur, Texas, Dec. 8-20, 2013. (Photo by Sarah Garner, SDDC, Headquarters)*

commander to serve as single-point-of-contact for **Defense Transportation System** (DTS) customers and to act as advocate for the DTS in DOD and before Congress. But it soon became apparent that, in reality, the nation's newest unified command was created half-baked. The IP allowed the Services to retain their single-manager charters for their respective transportation modes. Even more restrictive, the document limited USTRANSCOM's authorities primarily to wartime.

As a result, during peacetime, USTRANSCOM's component commands continued to operate day-to-day much as they did in the past. They controlled their industrial funds and maintained responsibility for service-unique missions, service-oriented procurement and maintenance scheduling, and DOD charters during peacetime single-manager transportation operations. They also continued to have operational control of forces. It took a wartime test by fire, Desert Shield/Desert Storm, to bring to maturity a fully operational, peacetime and wartime, USTRANSCOM.

The strategic deployment for Desert Shield/Desert Storm ranks among the largest in history. USTRANSCOM, in concert with its components, moved to the United States Central Command area of responsibility nearly 504,000 passengers, 3.7 million measurement tons (4.2 million m³) of dry cargo, and 6,100,000 short tons (5,500,000 t) of petroleum products in approximately seven months. This equated roughly to the deployment and sustainment of two Army corps, two Marine Corps expeditionary forces, and 28 Air Force tactical fighter squadrons.

The DOD learned much from the deployment to the Persian Gulf, and foremost among those lessons was that USTRANSCOM and its component commands needed to operate in peacetime as they would in wartime. Consequently, on 14 February 1992, the Secretary of Defense gave USTRANSCOM a new charter. Stating the command's mission to be "to provide air, land and sea transportation for the Department of Defense, both in time of peace and time of war," the charter greatly expanded the authorities of the USTRANSCOM commander. Under it, the **Service Secretaries** assigned the components to the USTRANSCOM commander in peace and war. In addition, the military departments assigned to him, under his combatant command, all transportation assets except those that were service-unique or theater-assigned. The charter also made the USTRANSCOM commander DOD's single-manager for transportation, other than service-unique and theater-assigned assets.

Because USTRANSCOM must respond quickly in support of United States interests worldwide, the command must focus its attention across a full spectrum of support from humanitarian operations to contingencies. In 1995, USTRANSCOM supported 76 humanitarian missions and 94 Joint Chiefs of Staff exercises, visiting approximately 80 percent of the 192 countries.

Since Desert Shield/Desert Storm, the Command has continued to provide transport support in contingencies—such as Desert Thunder (enforcement of UN resolutions in Iraq) and Operation Allied Force (NATO operations against Serbia)–and peacekeeping endeavors—for example, Operation Restore Hope (Somalia), Support Hope (Rwanda), Uphold Democracy (Haiti), Operation Joint Endeavor (Bosnia-Herzegovina), and Joint Guardian (Kosovo). It has also supported numerous humanitarian relief operations transporting relief supplies to victims of natural disasters at home and abroad. After the 11 September 2001 attacks, it became a vital partner in the United States' Global War On Terrorism supporting U.S. forces in Operation Enduring Freedom (Afghanistan) and the 2003 invasion of Iraq. From October 2001 to the present, USTRANSCOM, its components, and its national partners have transported over 2.2 million passengers and nearly 6,100,000 short tons (5,500,000 t) of cargo in support of the war on terrorism.

On 16 September 2003 Secretary of Defense Donald H. Rumsfeld designated the Commander, USTRANSCOM as the Distribution Process Owner (DPO) to serve "as the single entity to direct and supervise execution of the Strategic

Figure 135: *A West Virginia Air National Guard C-130 Hercules prepares to offload cargo at Camp Shelby Joint Forces Training Center, Miss., during Exercise Turbo Distribution, Oct. 28, 2015. TD is a joint-funded series of U.S. Transportation Command Field Training Exercises to train Joint Task Force - Port Opening Aerial Port Debarkation and Seaport of Debarkation capabilities. (U.S. Air Force photo by Staff Sgt. Kenneth W. Norman/Released)*

Distribution system" in order to "improve the overall efficiency and interoperability of distribution related activities—deployment, sustainment and redeployment support during peace and war." With the most capable and ready air, land, and sea strategic mobility forces in the world, and with the authorities as the DPO, USTRANSCOM will continue to support the United States and its allies, in peace and war.

Current Activities

As future conflicts become increasingly dynamic, U.S. forces require the agility to respond quickly, across traditional regional boundaries with a variety of strategic capabilities. Emerging contested environments, to include cyber, pose a significant challenge to the transportation and distribution networks in the mid- to long-term range, and require careful consideration of how to protect those networks. Sea-lanes, which have not been contested for U.S. forces since World War II, will likely be contested in the next major contingency. The assumption that United States forces will have uncontested access to international airspace and sea-lanes in the future is likely no longer valid.

USTRANSCOM is working with the military services and geographic combatant commanders to determine ways to protect those crucial strategic lanes.

Cyber threats remain a major concern for USTRANSCOM. Because of its extensive use of commercial capabilities, nearly 90 percent of USTRANSCOM missions are executed over unclassified and commercial networks. USTRANSCOM's Joint Cyber Center (JCC) uses a process knows as the Cyber Staff Estimate to assess risk, adjust defensive posture, and adopt operational or technical mitigations in performance of key missions. USTRANSCOM integrates cyber security language into a majority of its commercial contracts and co-chairs the National Defense Transportation Association Cybersecurity Committee.

Ensuring the United States' ability to fight at the time and place of its choosing requires enhanced readiness and improved future capabilities. The ability to project rapid power anywhere on the globe at any time sets the U.S. apart from the world, and to maintain this strategic advantage, USTRANSCOM ensures the US have the appropriate personnel, platforms, systems and training to maintain the strategic advantage.

Airlift and Aerial Refueling

Airlift forces move critical cargo and people to the point of need, while air refueling capabilities enable projection of forces across great distances to any location at any time. The Air Force's primary · airlift workhorse, the Boeing C-17 Globemaster III, remains the backbone of the United States' strategic airlift capability. To continue the C-17's airworthiness, and meet Federal Aviation Administration (FAA) 2020 mandates, the Air Force has planned a series of modifications for the early 2020s and is pursuing a mitigation plan to restore 16 of their C-17 aircraft from Backup Aircraft Inventory to Primary Mission Aircraft Inventory.

The Lockheed C-5 Galaxy fleet is currently undergoing a Reliability Enhancement and Re-engining Program modification through April 2018, which has delivered increased mission capable rates and will extend service life past 2040.

The Boeing KC-46 Pegasus will be critical to the entire joint and coalition force's ability to project combat power worldwide and give the United States and its allies an unparalleled rapid response capability for combat and disaster relief operations alike.

USTRANSCOM is implementing initiatives through the Civil Reserve Air Fleet (CRAF) contract to ensure wartime readiness capability while simultaneously offering best-value services for steady-state peacetime commercial augmentation.

Additionally, USTRANSCOM is building partnership capacity with other nations possessing air refueling competencies. Greater interoperability among nations will strengthen coalition partnerships and provide additional capability to the combatant commands.

Surface

Civil sector transportation infrastructure enables the movement of military forces. The Defense Personal Property Program (DP3), administered by SDDC, enables the movement and storage of service member, DoD employee, and U.S. Coast Guard (USCG) employee personal property and privately owned vehicles, by leveraging best-value transportation decisions and traffic management expertise in accordance with the Defense Transportation Regulation. DP3, in collaboration with Transportation Service Providers (TSP), manages over 550,000 personal property shipments for DoD and USCG customers at an annual cost of $2 billion.

The Defense Personal Property System (DPS) and its associated Program Management Office provide a centralized, web-based, single-point interface system for worldwide shipment of personal property. The DPS is a self-service system, offering real-time access for government, industry and customer users to input and retrieve data supporting the entire movement process – from pickup to delivery of household goods.

Sealift

Sealift moves roughly 90 percent of all DoD cargo and maintaining the readiness of the entire strategic sealift portfolio, both commercial and organic, is a top priority for USTRANSCOM.

Per the National Sealift Policy, USTRANSCOM relies upon the U.S.-flag commercial shipping industry, to the extent it is available, to provide sealift in peace, crisis and war, and the government-owned organic fleets to provide unique national defense capabilities not resident or available in sufficient numbers in commercial industry. USTRANSCOM's relationships with its U.S.-flag commercial sealift partners are formalized through agreements such as the Voluntary Intermodal Sealift Agreement (VISA), the Maritime Security Program (MSP) and the Voluntary Tanker Agreement (VTA).

USTRANSCOM has expressed concerns that the U.S.-flag commercial international trading sector is declining. In the past year, fourteen U.S.-flag internationally trading vessels within the VISA program were either reflagged to a foreign country or scrapped without replacement due, in large part, to the reduction in demand. This loss of U.S.-flag vessels represents a net decrease of over 327,000 square feet of roll-on/roll-off force projection capacity and over 600 U.S. merchant mariner jobs. The reduction of U.S.-flag vessels is forcing USTRANSCOM's commercial sealift partners to make adjustments to the

Figure 136: *USNS Shughart, a non-combatant RORO vessel, unloading Stryker armored vehicles*

services they provide by either removing liner capacity or expanding alliances with other carriers to take advantage of larger vessels.

Government-owned organic fleets are also facing challenges. Due to the age of vessels in the United States Maritime Administration's (MARAD) Ready Reserve Force, this fleet will begin to lose capacity in the mid to late-2020s, with significant losses in the 2030s.

Enabling Capabilities

USTRANSCOM provides direct enabling capabilities through its subordinate joint force command, the Joint Enabling Component Command (JECC). JECC bridges capability gaps by providing joint planning, public affairs, and communications capabilities in support of geographic combatant commands.

Global Distribution Network (GDN)

As the DoD Distribution Process Owner (DPO), USTRANSCOM is responsible for coordinating and overseeing the DoD distribution system with the goal of ensuring interoperability, synchronization, and alignment. The GDN enables joint force deployment, sustains it through all phases of operations, and brings it home. The GDN is a complex array of U.S. organic and commercial transportation capabilities directed by multiple commands and agencies.

Preparing for Tomorrow

USTRANSCOM is preparing for the fiscal year (FY) 2017 financial audit in accordance with the guidelines set forth in the National Defense Authorization Act for Fiscal Year 2010. In order to comply with Financial Improvement and Audit Readiness (FIAR), USTRANSCOM faces challenges to overcoming long-standing business processes that are not audit compliant, and legacy computer systems that cannot trace a transaction from inception to the financial statement.

USTRANSCOM continues to engage with the Army and Air Force Exchange Service and the Defense Commissary Agency to create greater efficiencies by increasing container utilization, combining loads on shared lanes with other DoD shippers, and using airlift only when appropriate and cost effective. USTRANSCOM's partnerships with the Defense Security Cooperation Agency (DSCA), the Defense Logistics Agency (DLA), the United Nations and foreign partners promote a whole-of-government approach, military-to-military cooperation, and service interoperability.

In coordination with the DSCA and DLA, USTRANSCOM is offering integrated transportation and distribution services for Foreign Military Sales (FMS) customers which provides customers with a single point of entry, pay-as-you-go capability that leverages the infrastructure and backbone of the DTS, as well as the secure storage and consolidation inherent in DLA's core mission.[457]

Awards

In April 2010, Defense Secretary Robert Gates presented the U.S. Transportation Command with the Joint Meritorious Unit Award.

Combatant Commanders

No.	Image	Name	Start of Term	End of Term
1.		General Duane H. Cassidy, USAF	1987	1989
2.		General Hansford T. Johnson, USAF	1989	1992

3.		General Ronald R. Fogleman, USAF	1992	1994
4.		General Robert L. Rutherford, USAF	1994	1996
5.		General Walter Kross, USAF	1996	1998
6.		General Charles T. Robertson Jr., USAF	1998	2001
7.		General John W. Handy, USAF	2001	2005
8.		General Norton A. Schwartz, USAF	2005	2008
9.		General Duncan J. McNabb, USAF	2008	2011
10.		General William M. Fraser III, USAF	2011	2014
11.		General Paul J. Selva, USAF	2014	2015

| 12. |  | General Darren W. McDew, USAF | 2015 | |

Sources

This article includes text from the public domain USTRANSCOM Official Homepage[458].

External links

 Wikimedia Commons has media related to *United States Transportation Command*.

- USTRANSCOM Official Website[459]
- Department of Defense Official Website[460]
- Military Sealift Command Official Website[461]
- Air Mobility Command Official Website[462]
- Joint Enabling Capabilities Command Official Website[463]
- Defense Logistics Agency Official Website[464]
- Defense Security Cooperation Agency Official Website[465]
- United States Maritime Administration Official Website[466]

Appendix

References

[1] With the establishment of the Continental Army.
[2] As stated on the official U.S. Navy website http://www.navy.mil/submit/view_styleguide.asp?sort=A, "armed forces" is capitalized when preceded by "United States" or "U.S.".
[3] **Note:** The other two services being the U.S. Public Health Service Commissioned Corps and the National Oceanic and Atmospheric Administration Commissioned Officer Corps.
[4] Title 10 of the United States Code §113 http//uscode.house.gov
[5] "World-Wide Military Command and Control System (WWMCCS), Department of Defense Directive 5100.30" http://www.dtic.mil/cgi-bin/GetTRDoc?AD=ADA272075&Location=U2&doc=GetTRDoc.pdf. Issued by Deputy Secretary of Defense David Packard on December 2, 1971.
[6] The United States Coast Guard has both military and law enforcement functions. Title 14 of the United States Code provides that "The Coast Guard as established 28 January 1915, shall be a military service and a branch of the armed forces of the United States at all times." Coast Guard units, or ships of its predecessor service, the Revenue Cutter Service, have seen combat in every war and armed conflict of the United States since 1790, including the Iraq War.
[7] https://www.law.cornell.edu/uscode/text/10/164
[8] For example, a lieutenant general in the Air Force is equivalent to a vice admiral in that Navy since they both carry a paygrade of O-9.
[9] Barber, Barrie. "Military looking for more tech-savvy recruits." http://www.springfieldnewssun.com/news/springfield-news/military-looking-for-more-tech-savvy-recruits--1341883.html *Springfield News-Sun.* 11 March 2012.
[10] (prior section 133b renumbered in 1986); DoD Directive 1005.8 dated 31 October 77 http://permanent.access.gpo.gov/websites/dodandmilitaryejournals/www.dtic.mil/whs/directives/corres/html2/d10058x.htm and AR 600-25 http://armypubs.army.mil/epubs/pdf/R600_25.pdf
[11] Naval History & Heritage Command. "Precedence of the U.S. Navy and the Marine Corps" http://www.history.navy.mil/browse-by-topic/heritage/origins-of-the-navy/precedence-of-the-navy-and-marines.html, U.S. Department of the Navy. 11 February 2016
[12] http://www.defense.gov/
[13] http://www.globalsecurity.org/military/ops/index.html
[14] http://biotech.law.lsu.edu/blaw/dodd/corres/html2/d10058x.htm
[15] http://www.usma.edu/Protocol/images/AR840-10.pdf
[16] http://www.drummajor.net/documents/USMC%20Drill%20and%20Ceremonies%20Manual.pdf
[17] https//web.archive.org
[18] http://afrotc.msu.edu/wp-content/uploads/2007/09/afman36-2203-dc-manual.pdf
[19] John Whiteclay Chambers, ed., *The Oxford Guide to American Military History* (1999)
[20] Jeremy Black, *America as a Military Power: From the American Revolution to the Civil War* (2002)
[21] Fred Anderson, ed. *The Oxford Companion to American Military History* (2000)
[22] Spencer C. Tucker, James Arnold, and Roberta Wiener eds. *The Encyclopedia of North American Colonial Conflicts to 1775: A Political, Social, and Military History* (2008) excerpt and text search https://www.amazon.com/dp/185109752X/
[23] James Titus, *The Old Dominion at War: Society, Politics and Warfare in Late Colonial Virginia* (1991)
[24] Fred Anderson, *The War That Made America: A Short History of the French and Indian War* (2006)
[25] Don Higginbotham, *The war of American independence: military attitudes, policies, and practice, 1763–1789* (1983)

[26] Lesson Plan on "What Made George Washington a Good Military Leader?" NEH EDSITEMENT http://edsitement.neh.gov/curriculum-unit/what-made-george-washington-good-military-leader

[27] Edward G. Lengel, *General George Washington: A Military Life* (2007)

[28] Richard H. Kohn, *Eagle and Sword: The Federalists and the Creation of the Military Establishment in America, 1783–1802* (1975)

[29] William B. Kessel and Robert Wooster, eds. *Encyclopedia of Native American wars and warfare* (2005) pp 50, 123, 186, 280

[30] Michael A. Palmer, *Stoddert's war: naval operations during the quasi-war with France* (1999)

[31] Frank Lambert, *The Barbary Wars: American Independence in the Atlantic World* (2007)

[32] J. C. A. Stagg, *The War of 1812: Conflict for a Continent* (2012)

[33] Walter R. Borneman, *1812: The War That Forged a Nation* (2005) is an American perspective; Mark Zuehlke, *For Honour's Sake: The War of 1812 and the Brokering of an Uneasy Peace* (2006) provides a Canadian perspective.

[34] Robert W. Merry, *A Country of Vast Designs: James K. Polk, the Mexican War and the Conquest of the American Continent* (2009) excerpt and text search https://www.amazon.com/dp/B003WUYRZO/

[35] K. Jack Bauer, *The Mexican War, 1846–1848* (1974); David S. Heidler, and Jeanne T. Heidler, *The Mexican War*. (2005)

[36] Louis P. Masur, *The Civil War: A Concise History* (2011)

[37] Benjamin Bacon, *Sinews of War: How Technology, Industry, and Transportation Won the Civil War* (1997)

[38] Utley, (1984)

[39] Jim Leeke, *Manila And Santiago: The New Steel Navy in the Spanish–American War* (2009)

[40] Graham A. Cosmas, *An Army for Empire: The United States Army in the Spanish–American War* (1998)

[41] Richard W. Stewart, "Emergence to World Power 1898–1902" Ch. 15 http://www.history.army.mil/books/AMH-V1/ch15.htm, in "American Military History, Volume I: The United States Army and the Forging of a Nation, 1775–1917" http://www.history.army.mil/books/AMH-V1/, (2004)

[42] William Braisted, *United States Navy in the Pacific, 1897–1909* (2008)

[43] Clodfelter p. 255

[44] Brian McAllister Linn, *The Philippine War 1899–1902* (University Press of Kansas, 2000).

[45] Henry J. Hendrix, *Theodore Roosevelt's Naval Diplomacy: The U.S. Navy and the Birth of the American Century* (2009)

[46] James E. Hewes, Jr. *From Root to McNamara: Army Organization and Administration, 1900–1963* (1975)

[47] Paolo Coletta, *Admiral Bradley A. Fiske and the American Navy* (1979)

[48] Lester D. Langley, *The Banana Wars: United States Intervention in the Caribbean, 1898–1934* (2001)

[49] Clodfelter p. 378

[50] Charles Byler, "Pacifying the Moros: American Military Government in the Southern Philippines, 1899–1913" *Military Review* (May–June 2005) pp 41–45. online http://www.au.af.mil/au/awc/awcgate/milreview/byler.pdf

[51] John S. D. Eisenhower, *Intervention!: The United States and the Mexican Revolution, 1913–1917* (1995)

[52] E. Bruce White and Francisco Villa, "The Muddied Waters of Columbus, New Mexico," *The Americas* 32#1 (July 1975), pp. 72–98 in JSTOR https://www.jstor.org/stable/980403

[53] Friedrich Katz, *The Secret War in Mexico: Europe, the United States, and the Mexican Revolution* (1984)

[54] James W. Hurst, *Pancho Villa and Black Jack Pershing: The Punitive Expedition in Mexico* (2007)

[55] Friedrich Katz, "Pancho Villa and the Attack on Columbus, New Mexico," *American Historical Review* 83#1 (1978), pp. 101–130 in JSTOR https://www.jstor.org/stable/1865904

[56] Kendrick A. Clements, "Woodrow Wilson and World War I," *Presidential Studies Quarterly* 34:1 (2004). pp 62+. online edition https://www.questia.com/PM.qst?a=o&d=5006516101

[57] Anne Venzon, ed., *The United States in the First World War: An Encyclopedia* (1995)
[58] Edward M. Coffman, *The War to End All Wars: The American Military Experience in World War I* (1998)
[59] Robert L. Willett, "Russian Sideshow" (Washington, D.C., Brassey's Inc., 2003), page 267
[60] Germany and the Soviet Union were not invited.
[61] Jeffery S. Underwood, *The Wings of Democracy: The Influence of Air Power on the Roosevelt Administration, 1933–1941* (1991) pp 34–35
[62] Safire 1997, pp. 297–8.
[63] Statistical and accounting branch office of the adjutant general p. 76
[64] Allan R. Millett, "A Reader's Guide To The Korean War," *Journal of Military History* (1997) Vol. 61 No. 3; p. 583+ online version http://www.dtic.mil/doctrine/jel/jfq_pubs/jfq2407.pdf
[65] James I. Matray, "Truman's Plan for Victory: National Self-Determination and the Thirty-Eighth Parallel Decision in Korea," *Journal of American History*, Sept. 1979, Vol. 66 Issue 2, pp 314–333, in JSTOR https://www.jstor.org/pss/1900879
[66] Stanley Sandler, ed., *The Korean War: An Encyclopedia* (Garland, 1995)
[67] John Prados, *Vietnam: The History of an Unwinnable War, 1945–1975* (2009)
[68] Mark Atwood Lawrence, *The Vietnam War: A Concise International History* (2010)
[69] Spencer Tucker, *Vietnam* (2000); for coverage of wach major operation see Stanley I. Kutler, ed., *Encyclopedia of the Vietnam War* (1996) and Spencer C. Tucker, ed. *Encyclopedia of the Vietnam War: A Political, Social, and Military History* (2001)
[70] Mark Clodfelter, *The Limits of Air Power: The American Bombing of North Vietnam* (2006)
[71] Lewis Sorley, *Westmoreland: The General Who Lost Vietnam* (2011)
[72] Robert D. Schulzinger, *Time for War: The United States and Vietnam, 1941–1975.* (1997) online edition https://www.questia.com/PM.qst?a=o&d=59258841&oplinknum=2
[73] Patrick Hagopian, *The Vietnam War in American Memory: Veterans, Memorials, and the Politics of Healing* (2009) excerpt and text search https://www.amazon.com/dp/1558496939
[74] George Q. Flynn, *The draft, 1940–1973* (1993)
[75] Bernard Rostker, *I want you!: the evolution of the All-Volunteer Force* (2006)
[76] Vijay Tiwathia, *The Grenada war: anatomy of a low-intensity conflict* (1987)
[77] Mark Adkin, *Urgent Fury: The Battle for Grenada: The Truth Behind the Largest U.S. Military Operation Since Vietnam* (1989)
[78] ch 8
[79] Thomas Donnelly, Margaret Roth and Caleb Baker, *Operation Just Cause: The Storming of Panama* (1991)
[80] Rick Atkinson, *Crusade: The Untold Story of the Persian Gulf War* (1994)
[81] Marc J. O'Reilly, *Unexceptional: America's Empire in the Persian Gulf, 1941–2007* (2008) p 173
[82] John L. Hirsch and Robert B. Oakley, *Somalia and Operation Restore Hope: Reflections on Peacemaking and Peacekeeping* (1995)
[83] John R. Ballard, *Upholding democracy: the United States military campaign in Haiti, 1994–1997* (1998)
[84] Richard C. Holbrooke, *To End a War* (1999) excerpt and text search https://www.amazon.com/dp/0375753605
[85] Christopher N. Koontz, *Enduring Voices: Oral Histories of the U.S. Army Experience in Afghanistan, 2003–2005* (2008) online http://www.history.army.mil/html/books/enduring_voices/index.html
[86] https://www.amazon.com/Beyond-Wild-Blue-History-1947-2007/dp/0312358113/
[87] https://books.google.com/books?id=E9zYgseL_AYC&pg=PP1
[88] https://books.google.com/books?id=ygqNt3ra-vYC
[89] https://books.google.com/books?id=_Rzy_yNMKbcC&pg=PP1
[90] https://www.amazon.com/Major-Problems-American-Military-History/dp/066933538X/
[91] https://books.google.com/books?id=EHI-RHlEv_wC&pg=PP1
[92] https://books.google.com/books?id=a3KLJN5kigQC&pg=PP1
[93] https://books.google.com/books?id=c_VtMBG6vw0C
[94] https://www.amazon.com/Air-Force-Illustrated-History-Century/dp/0760333084/
[95] https://books.google.com/books?id=rxVFCFnPKOEC&pg=PP1

[96] https://books.google.com/books?id=tE0pNg5aoPkC&pg=PP1
[97] https://books.google.com/books?id=hnJEcUb9oe0C&pg=PP1
[98] https://www.amazon.com/Semper-Fidelis-History-United-States/dp/0029215900/
[99] https://www.amazon.com/Common-Defense-Military-History-United/dp/1451623534/
[100] https://www.amazon.com/Presidents-Their-Generals-American-History-ebook/dp/B00OVWIWGW/
[101] http://www.miwsr.com/2014-105.aspx
[102] https://books.google.com/books?id=4-_WwWMkBRQC
[103] https://books.google.com/books?id=fZoaSDGQXLUC&pg=PP1
[104] https://books.google.com/books?id=747u1NJAtdYC&pg=PP1
[105] https://books.google.com/books?id=BIITnoCVy_YC&pg=PP1
[106] http://www.h-net.org/reviews/showpdf.php?id=42718
[107] http://www.routledge.com/cw/muehlbauer
[108] http://freepages.genealogy.rootsweb.com/~vanhornfamily/military.htm
[109] http://www.militaryhistorywiki.org
[110] http://library.uta.edu/usmexicowar/
[111] http://www.indianwars.org/
[112] https://web.archive.org/web/20100910042906/http://www.history.navy.mil/wars/foabroad.htm
[113] https://www.law.cornell.edu/uscode/text/10/113
[114] https://www.law.cornell.edu/uscode/text/10/162
[115] https://www.law.cornell.edu/uscode/text/10/3013
[116] https://www.law.cornell.edu/uscode/text/10/5013
[117] https://www.law.cornell.edu/uscode/text/10/8013
[118] 10 U.S.C. 113
[119] 10 U.S.C. §§ 3013, 5013 & 8013
[120] http://www.health.mil/aboutMHS.aspx
[121] tricare.mil http://www.tricare.mil/
[122] http://www.esd.whs.mil/Portals/54/Documents/DD/issuances/dodd/513410p.pdf
[123] http://www.esd.whs.mil/Portals/54/Documents/DD/issuances/dodd/510555p.pdf
[124] http://www.esd.whs.mil/Portals/54/Documents/DD/issuances/dodd/510536p.pdf
[125] http://www.esd.whs.mil/Portals/54/Documents/DD/issuances/dodd/510564p.pdf
[126] http://www.esd.whs.mil/Portals/54/Documents/DD/issuances/dodd/511805p.pdf
[127] http://www.esd.whs.mil/Portals/54/Documents/DD/issuances/dodd/510519p.pdf
[128] http://www.esd.whs.mil/Portals/54/Documents/DD/issuances/dodd/510521p.pdf
[129] http://www.esd.whs.mil/Portals/54/Documents/DD/issuances/dodd/514504p.pdf
[130] http://www.esd.whs.mil/Portals/54/Documents/DD/issuances/dodd/510522p.pdf
[131] http://www.esd.whs.mil/Portals/54/Documents/DD/issuances/dodd/510565p.pdf
[132] http://www.esd.whs.mil/Portals/54/Documents/DD/issuances/dodd/510542p.pdf
[133] http://www.esd.whs.mil/Portals/54/Documents/DD/issuances/dodd/510562p.pdf
[134] http://www.esd.whs.mil/Portals/54/Documents/DD/issuances/dodd/513409p.pdf
[135] http://www.esd.whs.mil/Portals/54/Documents/DD/issuances/dodd/510560p.pdf
[136] http://www.esd.whs.mil/Portals/54/Documents/DD/issuances/dodd/510523p.pdf
[137] http://www.esd.whs.mil/Portals/54/Documents/DD/issuances/dodd/510020p.pdf
[138] http://www.esd.whs.mil/Portals/54/Documents/DD/issuances/dodd/510568p.pdf
[139] http://www.esd.whs.mil/Portals/54/Documents/DD/issuances/dodd/510574p.pdf
[140] http://www.esd.whs.mil/Portals/54/Documents/DD/issuances/dodd/511010_dodd_2017.pdf
[141] http://www.esd.whs.mil/Portals/54/Documents/DD/issuances/dodd/510573p.pdf
[142] http://www.esd.whs.mil/Portals/54/Documents/DD/issuances/dodd/510572p.pdf
[143] http://www.esd.whs.mil/Portals/54/Documents/DD/issuances/dodd/134220p.pdf
[144] http://www.esd.whs.mil/Portals/54/Documents/DD/issuances/dodd/510087p.pdf
[145] http://www.esd.whs.mil/Portals/54/Documents/DD/issuances/dodd/510571p.pdf
[146] http://www.esd.whs.mil/Portals/54/Documents/DD/issuances/dodd/303001p.pdf
[147] http://www.esd.whs.mil/Portals/54/Documents/DD/issuances/dodd/511004p.pdf
[148] http://www.dtic.mil/whs/directives/corres/pdf/510601p.pdf
[149] http://www.dtic.mil/whs/directives/corres/pdf/510577p.pdf

[150] https://books.google.com/books?id=_Rzy_yNMKbcC&pg=PA165
[151] Updated Summary Tables, Budget of the United States Government Fiscal Year 2010 (Table S.12) http://www.whitehouse.gov/omb/budget/fy2010/assets/summary.pdf
[152] The New York Times, *Pentagon Expected to Request More War Funding* https://www.nytimes.com/2009/11/05/world/05military.html
[153] *Gates 'concerned' about delayed war supplemental* http://thehill.com/business-a-lobbying/103719-gates-concerned-about-delayed-war-supplemental-,
[154] David Isenberg, *Budgeting for Empire: The effect of Iraq and Afghanistan on Military Forces, Budgets and Plans* http://www.independent.org/pdf/policy_reports/2007-01-30-budgeting.pdf
[155] Center for Strategic and Budgetary Assessments-Cost of the Iraq & Afghanistan Wars Through 2008 http://www.csbaonline.org/4Publications/PubLibrary/R.20081215.Cost_of_the_Wars_i/R.20081215.Cost_of_the_Wars_i.pdf
[156] Defense Comptroller, *FY 2011 Program Acquisition Costs by Weapon System* http://comptroller.defense.gov/defbudget/fy2012/FY2012_Weapons.pdf
[157] https://www.whitehouse.gov/sites/default/files/omb/budget/fy2013/assets/hist.pdf
[158] http://clerk.house.gov/evs/2017/roll378.xml
[159] Liebelson, Dana. "NYT Misses Elephant in the Room: Defense Service Contractors." http://pogoblog.typepad.com/pogo/2012/01/nyt-misses-elephant-in-the-room-defense-service-contractors-.html *POGO*, 3 January 2012.
[160] Congressional Appropriations: An Updated Analysis http://www.house.gov/jec/fiscal/budget/restrain/update/update.htm
[161] The President's FY 2010 Budget http://www.whitehouse.gov/sites/default/files/omb/budget/fy2013/assets/budget.pdf
[162] Joint Chiefs Chairman Looks Beyond Current Wars https://www.nytimes.com/2007/10/22/washington/22mullen.html?_r=1
[163] **2015** data from:
[164] CRS Defense: FY2010 Authorization and Appropriations, pages 6–8 http://opencrs.com/getfile.php?rid=82228
[165] Bender, Bryan. "Pentagon accused of end run on budget cuts." http://articles.boston.com/2012-03-03/news/31119978_1_budget-cuts-war-budget-war-funding *Boston Globe*. 3 March 2012.
[166] Pellerin, Cheryl. "Carter: DOD Puts Strategy Before Budget for Future Force." http://www.globalsecurity.org/military/library/news/2012/05/mil-120530-afps04.htm *American Forces Press Service*, 30 May 2012.
[167] Pentagon Announces First-Ever Audit Of The Department Of Defense https://www.npr.org/sections/thetwo-way/2017/12/08/569394885/pentagon-announces-first-ever-audit-of-the-department-of-defense
[168] Drwiega, Andrew. " Missions Solutions Summit: Army Leaders Warn of Rough Ride Ahead http://www.aviationtoday.com/rw/services/finance-and-insurance/Missions-Solutions-Summit-Army-Leaders-Warn-of-Rough-Ride-Ahead_82218.html" *Rotor&Wing*, 4 June 2014. Accessed: 8 June 2014.
[169] http://www.usgovernmentspending.com/defense_spending
[170] https://web.archive.org/web/*/http://www.usgovernmentspending.com/defense_spending
[171] https://web.archive.org/web/20120913081050/http://www.acq.osd.mil/ie/download/bsr/BSR2012Baseline.pdf
[172] https://www.pbs.org/wgbh/pages/frontline/shows/pentagon/maps/9.html
[173] http://www.vetfriends.com/US-deployments-overseas/
[174] According to research by Dr. Elizabeth Norman, the nurses first referred to themselves as the "Battling Belles of Bataan" in 1942; the phrase "Angels of Bataan" appeared later, in 1945. E. Norman, We Band of Angels, pg. 53, pg 296 note 8.
[175] E. Norman, We Band of Angels, Appx. II; E. Monahan and R. Neidel-Greenlee, All This Hell, pg 193-195 (Appx. G).
[176] E. Monahan and R. Neidel-Greenlee, And If I Perish: Frontline U.S. Army Nurses in World War II, pg. 19 (First Anchor Books Ed, November 2004)(); E. Monahan and R. Neidel-Greenlee, All This Hell, pg 103.
[177] https://supreme.justia.com/cases/federal/us/411/677/

[178] Technically, the case was decided under the Fifth Amendment's Due Process Clause, not under the Equal Protection Clause of the Fourteenth Amendment, since the latter applies not to the federal government but to the states. However, because *Bolling v. Sharpe*, through the doctrine of reverse incorporation, made the standards of the Equal Protection Clause applicable to the federal government, it was for practical purposes an addition not to due process, but rather to equal protection jurisprudence.

[179] " Photo controversy highlights black women in Long Gray Line http://www.stripes.com/news/us/photo-controversy-highlights-black-women-in-long-gray-line-1.409585" by Errin Haines Whack, Associated Press, Stars and Stripes, May 14, 2016.

[180] Craig A. Rimmerman Gay rights, military wrongs: political perspectives on lesbians and gays in the military https://books.google.com/books?id=Go9XsJ47GswC&pg=PA249, Garland Pub., 1996 p. 249

[181] Thompson, Mark. (2008-01-28) 'Don't Ask, Don't Tell' Turns 15 http://www.time.com/time/nation/article/0,8599,1707545,00.html. TIME. Retrieved on 2010-11-30.

[182] Richard A. Gittins The Military Commander & the Law https://books.google.com/books?id=ENpnS9KApu8C&pg=PA215, DIANE Publishing, 1996 p. 215

[183] New York Times https://www.nytimes.com/2009/10/21/opinion/21iht-edbroadwell.html - October 11, 2009

[184] "Pentagon names 1st female commandant of West Point's cadets" *Army Times* December 15, 2015 http://www.armytimes.com/story/military/careers/army/2015/12/15/pentagon-names-1st-female-commandant-west-points-cadets/77359008/

[185] Trailblazer Becomes Army's First Female Infantry Officer - ABC News http://abcnews.go.com/US/trailblazer-armys-female-infantry-officer/story?id=38720413

[186] Medlicott Jr., Alexander (December 1966). "The Legend of Lucy Brewer: An Early American Novel". The New England Quarterly. 39 (4): 461–473. JSTOR 363418. doi:10.2307/363418.

[187] Medlicott Jr. 1966, p. 466.

[188] https://supreme.justia.com/cases/federal/us/411/677/

[189] Technically, the case was decided under the Fifth Amendment's Due Process Clause, not under the Equal Protection Clause of the Fourteenth Amendment, since the latter applies not to the federal government but to the states. However, because *Bolling v. Sharpe*, through the doctrine of reverse incorporation, made the standards of the Equal Protection Clause applicable to the federal government, it was for practical purposes an addition not to due process, but rather to equal protection jurisprudence.

[190] Craig A. Rimmerman Gay rights, military wrongs: political perspectives on lesbians and gays in the military https://books.google.com/books?id=Go9XsJ47GswC&pg=PA249, Garland Pub., 1996 p. 249

[191] Thompson, Mark. (2008-01-28) 'Don't Ask, Don't Tell' Turns 15 http://www.time.com/time/nation/article/0,8599,1707545,00.html. TIME. Retrieved on 2010-11-30.

[192] Richard A. Gittins The Military Commander & the Law https://books.google.com/books?id=ENpnS9KApu8C&pg=PA215, DIANE Publishing, 1996 p. 215

[193] New York Times https://www.nytimes.com/2009/10/21/opinion/21iht-edbroadwell.html - October 11, 2009

[194] Howard becomes Navy's first woman, first African American four-star admiral - St. Louis American: Local News http://www.stlamerican.com/news/local_news/article_766cbe98-0157-11e4-a01f-0019bb2963f4.html. Stlamerican.com (2014-07-01). Retrieved on 2014-07-25.

[195] Bureau of Medicine and Surgery, United States Navy. https://www.scribd.com/doc/63672595/White-Task-Force "White Task Force: the story of the Nurse Corps, United States Navy." (NAVMED 939 1945), pg. 7.

[196] MacGregor, Morris J. Jr., Integration of the Armed Forces 1940–1965 http://www.gutenberg.org/files/20587/20587-h/20587-h.htm *(c) 1980*

[197] Kathi Jackson, They Called Them Angels: American Military Nurses of World War II, pg 46 (2000)(First Nebraska paperback printing 2006).

[198]

[199] https://supreme.justia.com/cases/federal/us/411/677/

[200] Technically, the case was decided under the Fifth Amendment's Due Process Clause, not under the Equal Protection Clause of the Fourteenth Amendment, since the latter applies not to the

federal government but to the states. However, because *Bolling v. Sharpe*, through the doctrine of reverse incorporation, made the standards of the Equal Protection Clause applicable to the federal government, it was for practical purposes an addition not to due process, but rather to equal protection jurisprudence.

[201] Navy Office of Information, "Women on Submarines", Rhumblines, 5 October 2009.
[202] Milestones of Women in the US Navy http://www.history.navy.mil/special%20highlights/women/timeline1.htm. History.navy.mil. Retrieved on 2014-07-25.
[203] Ebbert, Jean; and Hall, Marie-Beth; Crossed Currents: Navy Women from WWI to Tailhook [Revised]: *Brassey's; 1999*.
[204] Milestones of Women in the US Navy http://www.history.navy.mil/special%20highlights/women/timeline2.htm. History.navy.mil. Retrieved on 2014-07-25.
[205] Varat, J.D. et al. *Constitutional Law Cases and Materials, Concise Thirteenth Edition*. Foundation Press, NY: 2009, p. 583
[206] Varat, p. 583
[207] Craig A. Rimmerman Gay rights, military wrongs: political perspectives on lesbians and gays in the military https://books.google.com/books?id=Go9XsJ47GswC&pg=PA249, Garland Pub., 1996 p. 249
[208] Thompson, Mark. (2008-01-28) 'Don't Ask, Don't Tell' Turns 15 http://www.time.com/time/nation/article/0,8599,1707545,00.html. TIME. Retrieved on 2010-11-30.
[209] Richard A. Gittins The Military Commander & the Law https://books.google.com/books?id=ENpnS9KApu8C&pg=PA215, DIANE Publishing, 1996 p. 215
[210] Zimmerman, pp. 170–171.
[211] Scarborough, Rowan, " Women in submarines face health issues http://www.washingtontimes.com/news/2010/apr/05/navy-faces-health-issues-for-women-in-submarines/", *Washington Times*, 5 April 2010, p. 1.
[212] Wiltrout, Kate, " Navy Strives to Retain Pregnant Sailors http://www.military.com/NewsContent/0,13319,152426,00.html/", *Virginia Pilot*, 11 October 2007.
[213] Tilghman, Andrew, " Report outlines pregnancy policy concerns http://militarytimes.com/news/2009/10/navy_pregnancy_101709w/", *Military Times*, 18 October 2009.
[214] DeRenzi never held the rank of rear admiral (lower half) (O-7). She was promoted from captain (O-6) to rear admiral (O-8) when she assumed the duties of Deputy Judge Advocate General in 2009.
[215] http://www.navy.mil/navydata/bios/navybio.asp?bioID=609
[216] http://www.navy.mil/navydata/bios/navybio.asp?bioID=626
[217] http://www.navy.mil/navydata/bios/navybio.asp?bioID=221
[218] http://www.navy.mil/navydata/bios/navybio.asp?bioID=83
[219] http://www.navy.mil/navydata/bios/navybio.asp?bioID=122
[220] http://www.navy.mil/navydata/bios/navybio.asp?bioID=243
[221] http://www.navy.mil/navydata/bios/navybio.asp?bioID=151
[222] http://www.navy.mil/navydata/bios/navybio.asp?bioID=363
[223] http://www.navy.mil/navydata/bios/navybio.asp?bioID=362
[224] http://www.navy.mil/navydata/bios/navybio.asp?bioID=393
[225] http://www.navy.mil/navydata/bios/navybio.asp?bioID=496
[226] http://www.navy.mil/navydata/bios/navybio.asp?bioID=387
[227] http://www.navy.mil/navydata/bios/navybio.asp?bioID=486
[228] https://web.archive.org/web/20120323065922/http://www.navy.mil/navydata/bios/navybio.asp?bioID=519
[229] http://www.navy.mil/navydata/bios/navybio.asp?bioID=615
[230] http://www.navy.mil/navydata/bios/navybio.asp?bioID=618
[231] http://www.navy.mil/navydata/bios/navybio.asp?bioID=642
[232] http://www.navy.mil/navydata/bios/navybio.asp?bioID=752
[233] http://www.navy.mil/navydata/bios/navybio.asp?bioID=614
[234] http://www.navy.mil/navydata/bios/navybio.asp?bioID=657
[235] http://www.navy.mil/navydata/bios/navybio.asp?bioID=637
[236] http://www.sameshield.com/hs.html
[237] http://www.navy.mil/navydata/bios/navybio.asp?bioID=382

[238] http://www.navy.mil/navydata/bios/navybio.asp?bioID=499
[239] http://www.navy.mil/navydata/bios/navybio.asp?bioID=528
[240] http://www.navy.mil/navydata/bios/navybio.asp?bioID=601
[241] http://www.navy.mil/navydata/bios/navybio.asp?bioID=515
[242] http://www.navy.mil/navydata/bios/navybio.asp?bioID=652
[243] http://www.navy.mil/navydata/bios/navybio.asp?bioID=660
[244] http://www.navy.mil/navydata/bios/navybio.asp?bioID=634
[245] http://www.navy.mil/navydata/bios/navybio.asp?bioID=704
[246] http://www.navy.mil/navydata/bios/navybio.asp?bioID=714
[247] http://www.navy.mil/navydata/bios/navybio.asp?bioID=705
[248] http://www.navy.mil/navydata/bios/navybio.asp?bioID=729
[249] http://www.navy.mil/navydata/bios/navybio.asp?bioID=708
[250] http://www.navy.mil/navydata/bios/navybio.asp?bioID=741
[251] http://www.navy.mil/navydata/bios/navybio.asp?bioID=715
[252] https://www.disa.mil/NewsandEvents/2018/Change-of-Command
[253] http://www.navy.mil/navydata/bios/navybio.asp?bioID=701
[254] http://www.navy.mil/navydata/bios/navybio.asp?bioID=816
[255] http://www.navy.mil/navydata/bios/navybio.asp?bioID=979
[256] As of 10 April 2017
[257] http://www.au.af.mil/au/aul/bibs/women/womnav.htm
[258] http://www.history.navy.mil/faqs/faq48-2.htm
[259] http://www.usna.edu/LibExhibits/Women_at_USNA/Bibliography_text.html
[260] http://www.womensmemorial.org/H&C/Resources/pdfs/bibliography.pdf
[261] https://web.archive.org/web/20091228134735/http://www.npc.navy.mil/AboutUs/BUPERS/WomensPolicy/
[262] http://www.sealeader.org
[263] http://www.Facebook.com/womenredefined
[264] https://www.flickr.com/photos/unitedstatesnavy/sets/72157623448255090/
[265] http://www.Navyformoms.com
[266] Women of the U.S. Air Force: Aiming High By Heather E. Schwartz, p.14
[267] https://supreme.justia.com/cases/federal/us/411/677/
[268] Technically, the case was decided under the Fifth Amendment's Due Process Clause, not under the Equal Protection Clause of the Fourteenth Amendment, since the latter applies not to the federal government but to the states. However, because *Bolling v. Sharpe*, through the doctrine of reverse incorporation, made the standards of the Equal Protection Clause applicable to the federal government, it was for practical purposes an addition not to due process, but rather to equal protection jurisprudence.
[269] Craig A. Rimmerman Gay rights, military wrongs: political perspectives on lesbians and gays in the military https://books.google.com/books?id=Go9XsJ47GswC&pg=PA249, Garland Pub., 1996 p. 249
[270] Thompson, Mark. (2008-01-28) 'Don't Ask, Don't Tell' Turns 15 http://www.time.com/time/nation/article/0,8599,1707545,00.html. TIME. Retrieved on 2010-11-30.
[271] Richard A. Gittins The Military Commander & the Law https://books.google.com/books?id=ENpnS9KApu8C&pg=PA215, DIANE Publishing, 1996 p. 215
[272] "Women's History Chronology", Women & the U. S. Coast Guard, U.S. Coast Guard Historian's Office
[273] A Preliminary Survey of the Development of the Women's Reserve of the United States Coast Guard, p 3
[274] *A History of Women in the Coast Guard*, by Dr. John A. Tilley
[275] https://supreme.justia.com/cases/federal/us/411/677/
[276] Technically, the case was decided under the Fifth Amendment's Due Process Clause, not under the Equal Protection Clause of the Fourteenth Amendment, since the latter applies not to the federal government but to the states. However, because *Bolling v. Sharpe*, through the doctrine of reverse incorporation, made the standards of the Equal Protection Clause applicable to the federal government, it was for practical purposes an addition not to due process, but rather to equal protection jurisprudence.

[277] http://www.uscg.mil/history/people/StollePAbio.pdf
[278] http://www.uscg.mil/history/uscghist/WomenChronology.asp
[279] Oxford English Dictionary (OED), 2nd Edition, 1989. "five" ... "five-star adj., ... (b) U.S., applied to a general or admiral whose badge of rank includes five stars;"
[280] The Australian insignia for admiral of the fleet, field marshal and marshal of the Royal Australian Air Force, depending on the era, are either identical to, or very similar to, the British insignia. Currently, Prince Philip is the only holder of these Australian ranks. Note that although the highest active New Zealand rank is three-star, (there are *no* New Zealand four-star rank holders), Prince Philip holds five-star ranks in the New Zealand Armed Forces.
[281] With the exception of Thomas Blamey and the Englishman William Birdwood, who both held the rank of field marshal, all other holders of Australian five-star ranks have been ceremonial.
[282] Indian Air Force :: Collar Tabs http://www.bharat-rakshak.com/IAF/Heraldry/Uniform/380-Collar-Tabs.html
[283] Dictionary of Vexillology, Rank Plate https://flagspot.net/flags/vxt-dv-r.html#rankplate
[284] The following Americans have been promoted to five-star rank:

- Fleet Admiral William D. Leahy   15 December 1944
- General of the Army George Marshall   16 December 1944
- Fleet Admiral Ernest King   17 December 1944
- General of the Army Douglas MacArthur   18 December 1944
- Fleet Admiral Chester W. Nimitz   19 December 1944
- General of the Army Dwight D. Eisenhower 20 December 1944
- General of the Army & Air Force Henry H. Arnold   21 December 1944 & 7 May 1949
- Fleet Admiral William Halsey, Jr.   11 December 1945
- General of the Army Omar Bradley   20 September 1950
- General of the Armies George Washington   4 July 1976, with an effective appointment date of 4 July 1776

The timing of the first seven appointments was to establish both a clear order of seniority and a near-equivalence between the Army and Navy services. In 1949, Arnold was honored by being made the first, and to date only, general of the air force. He is the only American to serve in a five-star rank in two of its military services. By a Congressional Act of 24 March 1903, Admiral George Dewey's rank was established as admiral of the navy, a rank which was specified to be senior to the four-star rank of admiral and was equal to admiral of the fleet in the British Royal Navy. Admiral Dewey was the only individual ever appointed to this rank, which lapsed with his death on 16 January 1917. Admiral of the navy was considered superior to fleet admiral during World War II. On 3 September 1919, John Pershing was promoted to the rank of General of the Armies (officially General of the Armies of the United States) in recognition of his service during World War I. He is the only person promoted to this rank during their lifetime.

During the United States Bicentennial year, George Washington was posthumously appointed to the grade of General of the Armies of the United States by the congressional joint resolution Public Law 94-479 passed on 19 January 1976, with an effective appointment date of 4 July 1976 but having rank and precedence over all other grades of the Army, past or present. This restored Washington's position as the most senior US military officer. Between the joint resolution concerning Washington's rank, the fact that Omar Bradley was still alive, and thus still considered to be on active duty, and statements made and actions taken during and after World War II about the relationship between General of the Armies and General of the Army, it appears General of the Armies is superior in rank to General of the Army.

No official law or regulation established exact seniority or reciprocity between Admiral of the Navy Dewey, and Generals of the Armies Washington and Pershing. While Congress clearly indicated that Washington was senior to Pershing, and also all other "officers of the United States Army," and by decades of custom Pershing was considered senior to all 5-star and other 4-star generals of the US Army, nowhere is Dewey's exact seniority established. As Washington was explicitly made senior only to Pershing and other officers of the US Army, ambiguity remains whether Admiral Dewey, with a date of rank as early as 1899 above a 4-star, and senior to all later 5-stars, is not actually senior to Washington by date of rank, and by operation of Naval custom making Dewey senior to all 5-stars. As Dewey died (and his rank died with him) before Pershing was appointed to his final rank, and the Army and Navy were far more independent before the creation of the Department of Defense unified them, this could indicate Admiral of the Navy Dewey, not General of the Armies Washington, is actually the most senior ranking US military officer in US history. By definition, officers of each Armed Force rank amongst themselves by seniority. And when they serve with other Armed Services (Army and Navy, for example), they rank amongst themselves by date of rank notwithstanding their parent Service. In the case of Dewey, he is undisputedly the senior most Navy officer ever to have served in the US Navy, and he had nearly 20 years of seniority over Pershing as a "special rank, above 4-star." Washington's own, revised, date of rank in 1976 does not precede Dewey's date of rank nearly 75 years before, nor did Congress describe in unambiguous wording that Washington was – in fact – senior to all officers of the US Army, as well as all other US Armed Forces including the US Navy. Had Congress chosen to explicitly so state, there would be no ambiguity, but it remains unsettled if – in spite of the desired outcome that Washington be the senior US military officer to have ever served – Congress' ways and means achieved their object.

[285] *Joint Pub 1*, p. GL-11.
[286] Story, p. 2
[287] DefenseLINK - Unified Command Plan
[288] *Joint Pub 1-02*, p. 37.
[289] Joint Pub 1-02
[290] https://www.law.cornell.edu/uscode/text/10/164
[291] *Joint Pub 1*, p. IV-4.
[292] JCS (1985), p. 1
[293] JCS (1977), p. 1
[294] JCS (1977), p. 2
[295] Joint History Office, "History of the Unified Command Plan 1946–1993," 14–15.
[296] JCS (1977), p. 3.
[297] JCS (1977), p. 5.
[298] JCS (1977), p. 6.
[299] Naval Advancement
[300] JCS (1977), p. 4
[301] 10 U.S.C. 161
[302] AFRICOM FAQs
[303] Joint Pub 1, p. V-9.
[304] Holder and Murray, p. 86.
[305] Joint Warfighting Center History
[306] ISO 3166-1 alpha-2
[307] https://www.law.cornell.edu/uscode/text/10/161-
[308] https://web.archive.org/web/20100421182424/http://www.africom.mil/AfricomFAQs.asp
[309] http://www.africom.mil/africomFAQs.asp
[310] http://www.defenselink.mil/specials/unifiedcommand
[311] https://digitalndulibrary.ndu.edu/cdm4/document.php?CISOROOT=/ndupress&CISOPTR=16478&REC=1
[312] https://web.archive.org/web/20100528174827/http://www.dod.gov/pubs/foi/reading_room/268.pdf
[313] http://www.dod.gov/pubs/foi/reading_room/268.pdf
[314] https://web.archive.org/web/20100528175122/http://www.dod.gov/pubs/foi/reading_room/269.pdf
[315] http://www.dod.gov/pubs/foi/reading_room/269.pdf

[316] https://web.archive.org/web/20111027024636/http://www.dtic.mil/doctrine/new_pubs/jp1.pdf
[317] http://www.dtic.mil/doctrine/new_pubs/jp1.pdf
[318] http://www.dtic.mil/doctrine/new_pubs/jp1_02.pdf
[319] https://web.archive.org/web/20061208195931/http://www.jfcom.mil/about/jwfc_history.htm
[320] http://www.jfcom.mil/about/jwfc_history.htm
[321] http://www.tpub.com/content/advancement/14148/css/14148_21.htm
[322] http://www.au.af.mil/au/awc/awcgate/crs/rl30245.pdf
[323] https://web.archive.org/web/20121021051013/http://www.america.gov/st/washfile-english/2007/February/20070206170933MVyelwarC0.2182581.html
[324] http://www.america.gov/st/washfile-english/2007/February/20070206170933MVyelwarC0.2182581.html
[325] https://web.archive.org/web/20130808111417/http://www.centcom.mil/area-of-responsibility-countries
[326] http://www.centcom.mil/area-of-responsibility-countries
[327] https://web.archive.org/web/20130823072510/http://www.eucom.mil/mission/the-region/
[328] http://www.eucom.mil/mission/the-region
[329] https://web.archive.org/web/20140513180226/http://nrt.sraprod.com/nrtconf/reports/040316/USNORTHCOM%20101.ppt
[330] http://nrt.sraprod.com/nrtconf/reports/040316/USNORTHCOM%20101.ppt
[331] https://photos.state.gov/libraries/adana/19452/pdfs/uspacom.pdf
[332] https://web.archive.org/web/20130813044853/http://www.southcom.mil/aboutus/Pages/Area-of-Responsibility.aspx
[333] http://www.southcom.mil/aboutus/Pages/Area-of-Responsibility.aspx
[334] https://web.archive.org/web/20100117005910/http://www.usaraf.army.mil/MAP_INTERACTIVE/INTERACTIVE_MAP.swf
[335] http://www.defense.gov/specials/unifiedcommand/
[336] http://www.globalsecurity.org/military/agency/dod/unified-com.htm
[337] http://www.africom.mil/about-the-command
[338] http://www.africom.mil
[339] *The Economist*, "Policing the undergoverned spaces", 16–22 June 2007, p. 46
[340] Erik Holmes, Official: AFRICOM Will Need Air Force Aircraft http://www.airforcetimes.com/news/2007/12/airforce_africom_standup_071203w/, Air Force Times, 5 December 2007
[341] "TRANSCRIPT: General Ward Outlines Vision for U.S. Africa Command" http://www.africom.mil/getArticle.asp?art=1659 , 18 February 2008
[342] "TRANSCRIPT: AFRICOM's General Ward Interviewed by the BBC's Nick Childs" http://www.africom.mil/getArticle.asp?art=1658 , 18 February 2008
[343] "Bush Says No New U.S. Bases in Africa" https://www.forbes.com/feeds/ap/2008/02/20/ap4674005.html
[344] Stars and Stripes, AFRICOM to depart from J-code structure http://www.estripes.com/article.asp?section=104&article=55606&archive=true, 12 August 2007
[345] Novak, Lisa M., "Italy To Host AFRICOM Headquarters", *Stars and Stripes*, 5 December 2008.
[346] Special Operations Technology, Q & A with Brigadier General Patrick M. Higgins http://www.special-operations-technology.com/sotech-archives/58-sotech-2008-volume-6-issue-6/438-qaa-brigadier-general-patrick-m-higgins.html , Vol. 6, Issue 6, 2008
[347] Lt. Gen. William Grisoli, "The Army has now aligned a brigade with U.S. Africa Command." http://www.army.mil/article/92623/_Fiscal_Cliff__would_challenge_Army_to_maintain_readiness/ accessdate=2012-12-10
[348] SOCOM 2015 Factbook
[349] Ham, Carter. "STATEMENT: AFRICOM Commander on Commencement of Military Strikes in Libya." http://www.africom.mil/getArticle.asp?art=6222 *AFRICOM*, 19 March 2011.
[350] //doi.org/10.1093/afraf/adm084
[351] http://www.africom.mil/
[352] http://www.africom.mil/getArticle.asp?art=4133&lang=0
[353] http://www.usaraf.army.mil/
[354] https://web.archive.org/web/20100117005910/http://www.usaraf.army.mil/MAP_INTERACTIVE/INTERACTIVE_MAP.swf

[355] http://community.apan.org/apcn/default.aspx/
[356] https://www.senate.gov/~armed_services/statemnt/2007/September/Ward%2009-27-07.pdf
[357] https://web.archive.org/web/20080228151516/http://usacac.leavenworth.army.mil/CAC/milreview/English/JanFeb08/McFateEngJanFeb08.pdf
[358] http://usacac.leavenworth.army.mil/CAC/milreview/English/JanFeb08/McFateEngJanFeb08.pdf
[359] http://usacac.army.mil/CAC/milreview/index.asp
[360] https://web.archive.org/web/20041209000230/http://www.ccc.nps.navy.mil/si/#current
[361] http://www.defenselink.mil/home/pdf/AFRICOM_PublicBrief02022007.pdf
[362] http://www.vanityfair.com/politics/features/2007/02/junger200702
[363] http://ww4report.com/node/3154
[364] http://www.esquire.com/features/africacommand0707
[365] http://www.oraclesyndicate.twoday.net/stories/3850265/
[366] https://web.archive.org/web/20080620123253/http://salsa.democracyinaction.org/o/1552/t/5734/content.jsp?content_KEY=3855
[367] http://www.huffingtonpost.com/bryan-maygers/nick-turse-tomorrows-battlefield_b_7480360.html?ir=WorldPost
[368] http://www.truth-out.org/news/item/40385-secret-us-military-documents-reveal-a-constellation-of-american-military-bases-across-africa
[369] //en.wikipedia.org/w/index.php?title=United_States_Central_Command&action=edit
[370] Anthony Cordesman, USCENTCOM Mission and History http://csis.org/files/media/csis/pubs/uscentcom3%5B1%5D.pdf, Center for Strategic and International Studies, August 1998
[371] Harold Coyle's novel *Sword Point* gives an impression of what such planning envisaged, by a U.S. Army officer who would have had some idea of the general planning approach.
[372] Auerswald and Saideman, 2014, 96f
[373] (Army Knowledge Online account may be required.)
[374] http://csis.org/files/media/csis/pubs/uscentcom3%5B1%5D.pdf
[375] http://www.centcom.mil/
[376] http://www.mnf-iraq.com
[377] https://web.archive.org/web/20090605090714/http://www.shurakaal-iraq.com/
[378] http://articles.latimes.com/2007/jan/05/nation/na-generals5
[379] https://foreignpolicy.com/2015/03/30/the-pentagon-ups-the-ante-in-syria-fight-iraq-islamic-state-delta-force/
[380] William Arkin, Code Names, 139, via Al-Monitor.com, If War Comes, Will US Open Its Military Depots In Israel? http://www.al-monitor.com/pulse/security/01/08/open-only-in-case-of-an-emergenc.html, August 20, 2012.
[381] https//web.archive.org
[382] http://www.eucom.mil
[383] http://www.pacom.mil/About-USPACOM/History/
[384] http://www.pacom.mil/About-USPACOM/
[385] http://www.pacom.mil/About-USPACOM/History/
[386] http://www.pacom.mil
[387] In symbolic nod to India, U.S. Pacific Command changes name. https://www.reuters.com/article/us-usa-defense-india/in-symbolic-nod-to-india-u-s-pacific-command-changes-name-idUSKCN1IV2Q2 Retrieved 30 May, 2018.
[388] https://www.state.gov/s/l/treaty/collectivedefense/
[389] "History of the Unified Command Plan: 1946–2012" http://www.dtic.mil/doctrine/doctrine/history/ucp_2013.pdf
[390] In symbolic nod to India, U.S. Pacific Command changes name. https://www.reuters.com/article/us-usa-defense-india/in-symbolic-nod-to-india-u-s-pacific-command-changes-name-idUSKCN1IV2Q2 Retrieved 30 May, 2018.
[391] http://www.pacom.mil/
[392] http://www.northcom.mil/Portals/28/Documents/Supporting%20documents/Historical/NORTHCOM%20History.pdf
[393] http://www.northcom.mil/Newsroom/Fact-Sheets/Article-View/Article/563996/usnorthcom-vision/

[394] http://www.northcom.mil/Newsroom/Fact-Sheets/Article-View/Article/563996/usnorthcom-vision/
[395] http://www.northcom.mil/Leadership/
[396] Informally known simply as "NORTHCOM" or "Northern Command")
[397] 1AF (AFNORTH) National Security Emergency Preparedness (NSEP) Directorate http://www.1af.acc.af.mil/units/afnsep/
[398] United States Northern Command, Advance Questions for Lieutenant General Victor E. Renuart, USAF, Nominee for Commander, U.S. Northern Command (USNORTHCOM) and Commander, NORAD http://www.globalsecurity.org/military/library/congress/2007_hr/070308-renuart.pdf, pre-confirmation hearing on Monday, 19 March 2007. See also https://www.senate.gov/legislative/LIS/executive_calendar/2007/03_19_2007.pdf.
[399] http://www.govtrack.us/congress/bill.xpd?tab=main&bill=h110-4986 Pub.L. 110-181: National Defense Authorization Act for Fiscal Year 2008
[400] http://www.govtrack.us/congress/billtext.xpd?bill=h110-4986 Pub.L. 110-181: National Defense Authorization Act for Fiscal Year 2008 full text
[401] "DOD Needs to Address Gaps in Homeland Defense and Civil Support Guidance GAO-13-128, Oct 24, 2012." http://gao.gov/products/GAO-13-128?source=ra
[402] http://usacac.army.mil/cac2/call/docs/10-16/ch_4.asp
[403] http://www.northcom.mil/
[404] See TITLE 10 > Subtitle A > PART I > CHAPTER 6 > § 164 for assignment, powers and duties.
[405] Martin Edwin Andersen Unpunished U.S. Southern Command role in '09 Honduran military coup https://www.academia.edu/25856284/Unpunished_U.S._Southern_Command_role_in_09_Honduran_military_coup May 24, 2016, Academia.edu
[406] Marisa Taylor and Kevin G. Hall, For years, Pentagon paid professor despite revoked visa and accusations of torture in Chile http://www.miamiherald.com/news/nation-world/national/article16508918.html, Miamiherald.com, March 27, 2015
[407] Robert J. MacLean Band of Brothers: The Whistleblower Remix https://www.academia.edu/28700829/Band_of_Brothers_The_Whistleblower_Remix September 18, 2016, Academia.edu
[408] Merrill's Marauders http://www.marauder.org/
[409] http://www.history.army.mil/books/wwii/Guard-US/index.htm#contents
[410] http://www.southcom.mil
[411] http://www.miamiherald.com/news/nation/story/1114676.html
[412] U.S. Department of Defense, Cyber Command Fact Sheet, 21 May 2010
[413] Chief of Naval Operations, 'Fleet Cyber Command/Commander Tenth Fleet Implementation Plan,' Memorandum, United States Navy, 2009
[414] 24th Air Force - Home http://www.24af.af.mil/. 24af.af.mil. Retrieved on 2014-04-28.
[415] 24th AF becomes AFCYBER https://archive.is/20120720040128/http://www.af.mil/news/story.asp?id=123233993. Archive.is. Retrieved on 2014-04-28.
[416] http://www.armytimes.com/article/20141008/CAREERS03/310080059/Officers-can-apply-go-cyber-voluntary-transfer-program
[417] Air Force Adds Computer Networking Career Field http://usmilitary.about.com/b/2010/11/28/air-force-adds-computer-networking-career-field.htm. Usmilitary.about.com. Retrieved on 2014-04-28.
[418] Career Profile: Marine Cyber Network Operator http://militarycareers.about.com/od/Career-Profiles/p/Career-Profile-Marine-Cyber-Network-Operator.htm. Militarycareers.about.com. Retrieved on 2014-04-28.
[419] DoD Cyber Command is officially online, 21 May 2010, Army Times http://www.armytimes.com/news/2010/05/military_cyber_command_052110/
[420] Cyber Command Achieves Full Operational Capability http://www.defense.gov/releases/release.aspx?releaseid=14030
[421] At the time, Lieutenant Colonel Gregory Conti was a United States Military Academy Professor and Director of West Point's Cyber Security Research Center.
[422] http://www.cybercom.mil/
[423] http://news.cnet.com/8301-1009_3-57610793-83/nsa-chief-may-lose-us-cyber-command-role/

[424] https://arstechnica.com/tech-policy/2013/12/white-house-nsa-and-cyber-command-to-stay-under-one-boss/
[425] https//web.archive.org
[426] https://web.archive.org/web/20110608161026/http://www.defense.gov/home/features/2010/0410_cybersec/docs/USCC_Trifold_2.ppt
[427] https://www.facebook.com/pages/United-States-Cyber-Command/117614808290017
[428] Jeremy Scahill, "The Secret U.S. War in Pakistan" http://www.thenation.com/article/secret-us-war-pakistan, *The Nation*, 23 November 2009.
[429] Emerson 1988, p. 26.
[430] http://www.jcu.mil
[431] USASOC Headquarters Fact Sheet http://www.soc.mil/USASOCHQ/USASOCHQFactSheet.html, from the USASOC official website, last accessed 8 October 2016
[432] Jensen, Finn Robert; Gunnar "Kjakan" Sønsteby Om samhold og innsatsvilje; Pantagruel forlag; Oslo; 2008
[433] USSOCOM Medal recipients https//web.archive.org
[434] https://web.archive.org/web/20090318120640/http://www.ccc.nps.navy.mil/research/theses/kelley07.pdf
[435] http://www.ccc.nps.navy.mil/research/theses/kelley07.pdf
[436] https://web.archive.org/web/20040117084621/http://www.dtic.mil/doctrine/jel/doddict/
[437] https://web.archive.org/web/20080308233658/http://www.foxnews.com/wires/2008Feb27/0,4670,StealthatSea,00.html
[438] http://www.foxnews.com/wires/2008Feb27/0,4670,StealthatSea,00.html
[439] https://www.nytimes.com/2008/02/04/washington/04rules.html?_r=1&scp=3&sq=Army+Rangers&st=nyt&oref=slogin
[440] https://www.nytimes.com/2007/04/27/world/asia/27abuse.html?scp=1&sq=MARSOC&st=nyt
[441] https://www.washingtonpost.com/wp-dyn/content/article/2005/11/01/AR2005110102069.html
[442] http://www.socom.mil/
[443] http://www.soc.mil/
[444] http://www.marsoc.marines.mil/
[445] https://web.archive.org/web/20130514123218/https://www.navsoc.navy.mil/
[446] https://web.archive.org/web/20071231203327/http://www2.afsoc.af.mil/
[447] https://web.archive.org/web/20110529013300/http://www.defense.gov//news/newsarticle.aspx?id=63635
[448] https://wayback.archive-it.org/all/20120913145325/https://jsou.socom.mil/Pages/Default.aspx
[449] http://www.stratcom.mil/
[450] http://www.stratcom.mil/Media/Factsheets/Factsheet-View/Article/960928/e-6b-airborne-command-post-abncp/
[451] http://www.airforce-magazine.com
[452] https://fas.org/spp/military/program/nssrm/initiatives/usspace.htm
[453] http://www.gao.gov/new.items/d06847.pdf
[454] http://www.defense.gov/About-DoD/DoD-101#How%20We're%20Organized
[455] http://www.defense.gov/About-DoD/Biographies/Biography-View/Article/618122/general-darren-w-mcdew
[456] U.S. Transportation Command public website, www.ustranscom.mil, accessed Sep. 14, 2016
[457] Statement of General Darren W. McDew, Commander, United States Transportation Command, Before the House Readiness Subcommittee, On the State of the Command, 15 March 2016 http://docs.house.gov/meetings/AS/AS03/20160315/104661/HHRG-114-AS03-Wstate-McDewD-20160315.pdf
[458] https://web.archive.org/web/20060919184023/http://www.transcom.mil/
[459] http://www.ustranscom.mil
[460] http://www.defense.gov
[461] http://www.msc.navy.mil
[462] http://www.amc.af.mil
[463] http://www.jecc.mil

[464] http://www.dla.mil
[465] http://www.dsca.mil
[466] https://www.marad.dot.gov

Article Sources and Contributors

The sources listed for each article provide more detailed licensing information including the copyright status, the copyright owner, and the license conditions.

United States Armed Forces *Source:* https://en.wikipedia.org/w/index.php?oldid=851916716 *License:* Creative Commons Attribution-Share Alike 3.0 *Contributors:* A D Monroe III, A Great Catholic Person, AFBoomer, Abhishek0831996, Acebulf, Albatross8000, Anotherclown, Aoa8212, BU Rob13, Babymissfortune, BamaBros, Bigggan, BilCat, Bkdotson, Bkusa7, Broadwaygenius, BurritoBazooka, Byteflush, CatcherStorm, Chairhandlers, Charlesaaronthompson, CheChe, ClueBot NG, Clupo1, CogitoErgoSum14, Colonestarrice, Commstec, Coryphantha, Cuprum17, Darylgolden, Davemck, Derek R Bullamore, Diannaa, Eagle4000, El C, Ergo Sum, Excirial, Fnlayson, Foreignshore, GB fan, Garuda28, Glenfarclas, Good Wall of the Pyrenees, Grouchy1, Huberthoff, Hummerrocket, Hwsthl, Ian D 123, Illegitimate Barrister, Imzadi1979, ItsiAvery, Jak525, JasonWikis, Jdcomix, Josve05a, Kbseah, Kfaherty32, KylieTastic, L3X1, LakesideMiners, Lindhe94, Malcolmxl5, Mandruss, Marinella Iv, Materialscientist, Maxman013, Meatsgains, Mechanical Keyboarder, NaBUru38, Neovu79, Nic.Isabel, Nick-D, Nobrchomeever, NutFondler69, Omnipaedista, Operator873, PlyrStar93, Polmandc, Quasar G., RealMadrid11, RolandR, Rural Lyra, Sandiego91, Sasuke Sarutobi, Serols, Shellwood, Simplexity22, Smallchief, Stephenjadhav07, TacticalPepsodent1184, TheFreeWorld, TheGoodBadWorst, Theta Bork, Thewellman, Thewolfchild, Trolley937, TwoNyce, Ultimograph5, Unreal7, Vsmith, Wikilinlin, Willis Hanger, Wrestlingring, Wtmitchell, YSSYguy, 161 anonymous edits 1

Military history of the United States *Source:* https://en.wikipedia.org/w/index.php?oldid=849913493 *License:* Creative Commons Attribution-Share Alike 3.0 *Contributors:* A D Monroe III, Alan Liefting, Altaïr, Alumnum, Anaxial, Anotherclown, BD2412, BUjjsp, Bender235, Berean Hunter, BilCat, BokicaK, CAPTAIN RAJU, Caballero1967, Chris the speller, ClueBot NG, Crispus, Dainomite, Danjeechu, DatGuy, Dawnseeker2000, DemocratiLuntz, Dewritech, Diannaa, Discospinster, Dl2000, Dontie2011, Downthewikiwormhole, Drdpw, Ebrahim, Excirial, Florian Blaschke, Funnyfarmofdoom, GabrielF, Garuda28, Ginsuloft, Grandpallama, Hantsheroes, HazelAB, Hessamnia, Ipodtouchphone5, Iridescent, Italia2006, Jdaloner, Jeancey, Jeff in CA, Jemappelleungarcon, Jojhutton, Jonesey95, Jprg1966, Just the law, JustAGal, KConWiki, Kbh3rd, Kibi78704, Lagrange613, Leventio, LtSpecter, Mark Ironie, Mitchumch, Mogism, Moxy, MusikAnimal, NiD.29, Niceguyedc, Nihiltres, North Shoreman, Numerosori, OJOM, OberRanks, OrenBochman, Orenburg1, PKT, Paintspot, Periglio, Pinethicket, RANDOMSCRANDOM, Racerx11, Ravensfrench, Rcmason, Revent, RightCowLeftCoast, Rjensen, Rorschach, Rrburke, SCOTTPAT64, SajonesUTA, Samf4u, SantiLak, Simishag, SlitherySentinel, Solarra, Sparkgap, Srich32977, Srithikdatta, Stevietheman, Stumink, Super48paul, TeaLover1996, TheFreeWorld, TheSif, TheTimesAreAChanging, Thewolfchild, Timberframe, Tn808, Topbanana, UnbiasedVictory, Vipinhari, Vmavanti, Vrenator, Waacstats, Wikideas1, Wikipelli, XXzoonamiXX, Yahya Abdal-Aziz, Yogottigotti, 168 anonymous edits 23

Organizational structure of the United States Department of Defense *Source:* https://en.wikipedia.org/w/index.php?oldid=837831132 *License:* Creative Commons Attribution-Share Alike 3.0 *Contributors:* Addihockey10 (automated), Antony-22, Blakebs, Buckshot06, ClueBot NG, Codingstream, CommonsDelinker, Da-rb, Dainomite, FFlixx7481, Falcon8765, Feyrauth, Frietjes, Illegitimate Barrister, Jrtayloriv, Just the law, Kndimov, Look2See1, Magioladitis, Mais oui!, Oshwah, R'n'B, Simon Brady, StalwartUK, WereSpielChequers, WikHead, 12 anonymous edits 63

Military budget of the United States *Source:* https://en.wikipedia.org/w/index.php?oldid=850223477 *License:* Creative Commons Attribution-Share Alike 3.0 *Contributors:* 7157.118.25a, Aligzanduh, Anaxial, Anubis90909, Appellative, Ariapaez, Arjayay, Arnapha, AuburnPilot, BabbaQ, Bamyers99, Beland, Besselfunctions, Blaue Max, Bounty42, CRGreathouse, Calebootman, Camdennator11, Cameronjbird, Carrotist2, CherryX, ClaireFanch, ClueBot NG, Coffee, CogitoErgoSum14, Corn cheese, Crosswords, Crystallizedcarbon, Daddy3333, Discospinster, Dismas, Donner60, Dougdoug12, Dragonlord2140, Dream Focus, El C, Enon, Epicgenius, Eric0928, FOARP, Factsearch, Farcaster, Frmorrison, GB fan, Garyalan65, Geraldshields11, Ghbarratt, Giraffedata, GoingBatty, Graham87, Ground Zero, Guest2625, Guy1890, Hardusername, Hcobb, Hmains, Hu12, I am One of Many, Indy beetle, Iridescent, Issyl0, JQF, Jakeaglass, Jarble, Jfmantis, Jim1138, Jimknock, Jjjjjjjjj, Joe Decker, Johnpseudo, Jojalozzo, Jrtayloriv, Just the law, KConWiki, Karaju, Keith D, KierRoyale, Kiwifist, Kndimov, L235, Lachlan.00, Liam.Guevara, MadisonMeredith, Magioladitis, Makyen, Mark Arsten, Mdh0025, Mikael Häggström, Miller714, Mogism, Morgan Wick, Nevfennas, Nightscream, Ninel, Numbermaniac, Oceanflynn, Ohconfucius, OriginalAndCreativeUsernameHere, Oshwah, OuroborosCobra, P2prules, Pharaoh of the Wizards, Philipthegreat88, Pinethicket, Pratyya Ghosh, R'n'B, Rairden, Red-eyed demon, Reinana kyuu, RenamedUser01302013, Rezin8, Rich Farmbrough, Rileeylynn, Rjwilmsi, Robevans123, Rocketrod1960, Rosi3fish, Safehaven86, Shainamarco, Shyamsunder, Silenceisgod, Skr15081997, Skyerise, SloppyG, SnoozeKing, StevenMadden, Sue Rangell, Sunrise, TGCP, Thane, TheDevLee, Tim!, Tkn123456789, Trappist the monk, Trusilver, Tuckerlieberman, Tyrone814, Velella, WIkiderpian, Wallnot, WanderingLost, Wavelength, Widr, Wikideas1, Wikispring, Woohookitty, Wuerzele, XsHoa10pSogRcAVgjAxsVMs1C1BbYUspRh, YSSYguy, Ynyng, Yug, ~riley, 212 anonymous edits 81

United States military deployments *Source:* https://en.wikipedia.org/w/index.php?oldid=852588514 *License:* Creative Commons Attribution-Share Alike 3.0 *Contributors:* Alansohn, Andy120290, Arot0629, Barjimoa, Bathosrex, Bearcat, Bgwhite, Borinquen96, Buck Winston, Buckshot06, C-randles, Carmichael, Ceasar'sGhost, Cerebellum, Citadel48, Clean Copy, ClovisPt, ClueBot NG, Coinmanj, Countakeshi, Cybercobra, DadaNeem, Darkskynet, DavidHeshWalker, Elryacko, Emilfarb, Farolif, Favonian, Frenchgizmo, Gamer112, Ggraham1128, GnuPooh, Gob Lofa, GrapefruitSculpin, Hibernian, Homocidal Surgeon, Howard61313, Jgui~enwiki, Jonesey95, Jrfishe1, Jrquinlisk, Kari Armstron, Kinabrew, Laomeishiwoer, Linguist111, Lotje, Lucasjohansson, Lugia2453, MBlaze Lightning, MJAnders30, Materialscientist, Mrflip, N3tn0, Ncypeters, Neutrality, NewEnglandYankee, Nick Number, Noman200, Prinsgezinde, Rck109d, RightCowLeftCoast, Ryopus, SMcCandlish, Safety Cap, Salamurai, SantiLak, Shibo77, Sjö, SkoraPobeda, Slade, Tentinator, Thehardling, Timsrope, Tresiden, VacationLanegrp, Vivaldi, Wigglejiggle, Wikiedebs, Wing7990, Woohookitty, Wq639, Wrightchr, 232 anonymous edits 103

Women in the United States Army *Source:* https://en.wikipedia.org/w/index.php?oldid=818380861 *License:* Creative Commons Attribution-Share Alike 3.0 *Contributors:* ClueBot NG, Dcirovic, DiscoTent, Elisa.rolle, GrecianEarn, Haakonsson, Hebrides, Hermera34, JaneSwifty, Neutrality, Nick-D, Orenburg1, Precience, Rjensen, SouthernNights, TeriEmbrey, There'sNoTime, 39 anonymous edits 107

Women in the United States Marines *Source:* https://en.wikipedia.org/w/index.php?oldid=848302923 *License:* Creative Commons Attribution-Share Alike 3.0 *Contributors:* *Treker, Another Believer, Drewmutt, GrecianEarn, Hebrides, Heroeswithmetaphors, JaneSwifty, Kelly, Maurreen, Nick-D, Petewarrior, Precience, Tyd7293, Xanzzibar, Zingarese, 37 anonymous edits 113

Women in the United States Navy *Source:* https://en.wikipedia.org/w/index.php?oldid=852360878 *License:* Creative Commons Attribution-Share Alike 3.0 *Contributors:* AdelfoMontanez, Anj610, Aro88, Aussie Evil, Av8r137, Awakko, Bamyers99, Bwolper, Cantab1985, Carreon697, Chris the speller, Christopher Douglas, Cla68, Cookie20, Cremlian, Crystallizedcarbon, Dl2000, Download, Eagle4000, Edward, Frietjes, Frze, GELongstreet, GJWECW, Gamgee, Gobonobo, GrecianEarn, Hebrides, Herb425, Iohannes Animosus, Iridescent, JaneSwifty, Katherinelorio, Kelly, Khazar2, KristyKountz, Kumioko (renamed), Kwamikagami, Lclanglais, LittleWink, MBK004, Maralia, Marc Kupper, Marcd30319, Mccapra, MelanieN, Mhjohns, MonkeyToaster, MrDolomite, Nat965, Neovu79, Nick-D, NortyNort, Ohconfucius, Oluies, Ospalh, Packerfansam, Precience, Rjensen, Seek4thethruth, Silicon retina, Solarra, Thewolfchild, TommyBoy, TuxLibNit, Ukexpat, Vanisheduser00348374562342, WereSpielChequers, Weylin.piegorsch, Wikifan2744, Wolfedc, 236 anonymous edits 118

Women in the United States Air Force *Source:* https://en.wikipedia.org/w/index.php?oldid=818381647 *License:* Creative Commons Attribution-Share Alike 3.0 *Contributors:* Another Believer, Frietjes, GrecianEarn, GünniX, JaneSwifty, Nick-D, Precience, 38 anonymous edits 149

Women in the United States Coast Guard *Source:* https://en.wikipedia.org/w/index.php?oldid=804862929 *License:* Creative Commons Attribution-Share Alike 3.0 *Contributors:* Another Believer, Cuprum17, Flynzy, Precience, WikiDan61, 15 anonymous edits 154

Five-star rank *Source:* https://en.wikipedia.org/w/index.php?oldid=849201913 *License:* Creative Commons Attribution-Share Alike 3.0 *Contributors:* *Treker, 777sms, Adostaler, Andrewa, Aumnamahashiva, Barksmat, BegbertBiggs, Bender235, Blackshod, Bobblewash, Botpankonin, Brandybmm, Bribroder, Chatfecter, Chris the speller, ClueBot NG, CommonsDelinker, Cornellrockey, Cripipper, Dactyle, DocWatson42, DrFrench, DrLuisValdezRicoH, Dwo, EHDI5YS, Eluchil404, Ericfrank94, Evers, F111ECM, Fdewaele, Georgiebest7, Gl359, GoodDay, GraemeLeggett, Greenshed, Gugganij, HHaeckel, Hammersfan, Heralder, Hotspur23, IPAddressConflict, Iamrobholloway, Illegitimate Barrister, Ipankonin, IronGargoyle, Itemirus, Jamesnd, Jayster107, Jdaloner, Jimp, Jmg38, KAP03, Katydidit, Keith o, Kndimov, Koplimek, Kwamikagami, L.smithfield, LukeSurl, MBK004, Magioladitis, Mean as custard, Mesoso2, MrDolomite, Netstar1, Nford24, Notreallydavid, OberRanks, Officer781, Oshwah, PBS, Pdfpdf, Person man345, Pinnerup, PrimeHunter, Prinsgezinde, Qexigator, RA0808, Regulov, Richardguk, Robert A West, Rollingcontributor, Rsrikanth05, Shem1805, Snake bgd, Sodacan, Somervia, Sturmgewehr88, Supertoni123, Ta6513647, Talha, Theonlyedge, Thorkall, Timbouctou, Toda6515, Transphasic, Venqax, Wanderingaroundaimlessly, Whoop whoop pull up, Wikidona, Wikidudeiiininerniner, Woohookitty, Wtmitchell, YSSYguy, Zwerubae, 119 anonymous edits 157

Unified combatant command *Source:* https://en.wikipedia.org/w/index.php?oldid=850397345 *License:* Creative Commons Attribution-Share Alike 3.0 *Contributors:* AdmiralHood, Air Power Geek, Airborne84, Aldis90, Alexander.maitre, Ancheta Wis, Andrew Gray, Apotheosis247, AzureCitizen, BD2412, Bahamut0013, BegbertBiggs, Bender235, BilCat, Brysons77, Buckshot06, CapitalR, Cfuehrer17, Chasetafer0707, Chris the speller, ChrisGualtieri, Chuck Carroll, Claudevsq, Cnwilliams, CommonsDelinker, Corypark, Cybercobra, DOD Updater Private, David Newton, Daysleeper47, Dheitlinger, DocWatson42, Dreish, EF2000HL, Elonka, EpicDream86, EricEnfermero, FM400k, Fairsing, Flyer22 Reborn, Foreignshore, Fredmdbud, Fwbrocks, Gahs, Garuda28, Green Giant, Greenshed, GregorB, GrummelJS, Gwguffey, HJ32, Hackersr4us, HandsomeFella, Harry the Dirty Dog, HolyT, Id447, Illegitimate Barrister, Indianast8, Iridescent, J3nstar, JMTCP, Jbritt31, Jimlemasters, JocularJellyfish, Journalist1983, Jpm2112, Jprg1966, Jredwards, Jrtayloriv, JustJust51, Kevin W., KevinCuddeback, Kwamikagami, LanceBarber, Ldemat, Lightmouse, Lockesdonkey, Lord Pistachio, Los688, LtPowers, MLWilson, Maxaxax, Mezzaluna, Mikebeatty, MilFlyboy, Milprof, Morinao, Neovu79, Nobunaga24, Noclador, Pemslie, Petercorless, Pmsyyz, Polimath, Populus, Preuninger, Rainclaw7, RavenCreeks, Rdingwall, RepSchnell, Rex simiarum, RicJac, Rich Farmbrough, Rjwilmsi, Rougher07,

Rpyle731, Rwalker, SchreiberBike, Searchme, SithLord005, SlitherySentinel, Snakeskinsam, Spartan7W, SpikeToronto, Spoon!, Student7, Tericee, Thewolfchild, Thucydides411, WLior, WhisperToMe, Wolfram.Tungsten, Www06035, Yosy, 120 anonymous edits 173

United States Africa Command *Source:* https://en.wikipedia.org/w/index.php?oldid=850954807 *License:* Creative Commons Attribution-Share Alike 3.0 *Contributors:* 1exec1, Albany NY, All Hallow's Wraith, Ancheta Wis, Basibe, Beland, Bender235, BilCat, Buckshot06, C.Fred, Chas. Caltrop, Chipmunkdavis, Chris the speller, Cla68, Claudevsq, CommonsDelinker, Crito10, D6, Dainomite, Dans, Darrellhab, DavGreg, Daysleeper47, Denniscabrams, Diannaa, Dl2000, DocWatson42, EoGuy, EricSerge, Fillytop, Foreignshore, FritzSoltau, FueGo, GB fan, Gaius Cornelius, Garuda28, Gavbadger, Germina1973, GraemeLeggett, Greensaver, Hcobb, Henryroger1, Holland85, HolyT, Human., Il Dorico, Illegitimate Barrister, Indianast8, Indubitably, InverseHypercube, Jason Quinn, Jdoughe4, Jeffreymcmanus, Jpdulany, Js2081, Jsrawlinson, Jvc341, Krclarke, Ktr101, La Pianista, LanceBarber, Ld80061, Ligunny, Lotje, MBelzer, Magioladitis, Marcd30319, Mathew Roberson, Mattes, Meco, Mnnlaxer, Mr. Guye, Mrjpociask, Mrwojo, Neovu79, Niceguyedc, Nimur, NuclearWarfare, Ohconfucius, Ph.eyes, Phlegat, Pmsyyz, Pociask, Preuninger, Radiantmercury, RicJac, Rich Farmbrough, Rjwilmsi, Rodw, Ryan.opel, Sadharan, Saltine, Scriberius, Senorpepr, SithLord005, Srich32977, SteveStrummer, Student7, Sunwin1960, Super48paul, Tommy2010, Toussaint, Tracer9999, USAfricaCommand, VillaSterne, Vrenator, Werieth, Woohookitty, Www06035, Érico, 115 anonymous edits 187

United States Central Command *Source:* https://en.wikipedia.org/w/index.php?oldid=850515329 *License:* Creative Commons Attribution-Share Alike 3.0 *Contributors:* 786b6364, Abonazzi, Aeh4543, AlmightyDavi, Andrewaranda, Arado, Awakko, AzureCitizen, BDD, Bahamut0013, Bdell555, Bdfrase, Bender235, BiggestSataniaFanboy89, Bobrayner, Bovineone, Buckshot06, Bullmoosebell, C3015530, Caliroan, CapitalR, Chamal N, Chellew620, Chris the speller, Claffey27, Claudevsq, ClueBot NG, Comfr, CommonsDelinker, Courcelles, D6, Dainomite, Dale Arnett, Decoyjames, Dlippman, Dmyersturnbull, DocWatson42, Ed Poor, EmilyGee52, EpicDream86, Ethically Yours, Fakeandhomo, FloridaFox, GJGardner, GabeIglesia, Gladys beck, GrummelJS, Harfarhs, Hmains, How Shuan Shi, Human., Idefix∼enwiki, Illegitimate Barrister, JEB90, Jackie, Jak525, JamezRodriegezEdits, Jaycub912, Jdaloner, Jeffwang, Jonesey95, Jprg1966, Juno, KNVercingetorix, Kaaveh Ahangar∼enwiki, Kent Wang, KevinCuddeback, KimChee, Klemen Kocjancic, Koavf, Ktr101, LanceBarber, Leongbutler, Leszek Jańczuk, Lightmouse, Lord Pistachio, MB298, MBelzer, Mattflaschen, Meco, Michael93555, Mnnlaxer, Moogwrench, Mr. Guye, Mrworldwidedadecounty, Mwinog2777, Namenotek, Ndunruh, Neovu79, Neptune1969, Niceguyedc, Noclador, Nurg, Octoberwoodland, Odessacj, Ohconfucius, Ohnoitsjamie, Oroso, Ottawahitech, Pmsyyz, Purpleturple, Pwforaker, QueenofBattle, R'n'B, RGFI, Reedmalloy, Rejectwater, RicJac, Rich Farmbrough, Richard Arthur Norton (1958-), Rjwilmsi, Rockhead126, Rory096, Rupert Horn, STBotD, SamSennett, Sayerslle, Signaleer, SkonesMickLoud, Sohailstyle, Srich32977, Suedehead 1971, Sundostund, Sunray, TAnthony, TJ Spyke, Teratornis, Tewfik, TexasAndroid, Thelovelyconch, Thewolfchild, Tobby72, Vanished user 9oijnsdfknefijh3tjasfi34, Vijay rath, WilsonjrWikipedia, Woohookitty, Wtmitchell, Wuerzele, YeOldeGentleman, Yitzhak1995, Zbase4, 133 anonymous edits 202

United States European Command *Source:* https://en.wikipedia.org/w/index.php?oldid=850521799 *License:* Creative Commons Attribution-Share Alike 3.0 *Contributors:* Alansohn, Antrim Kate, Archangelsk, Avalon, Bahamut0013, BarabasKid, Bgwhite, BilCat, Billmckern, Bmclaughlin9, Bobo The Ninja, Bobrayner, BrownHairedGirl, Buckshot06, Casonsnow, Chipmunkdavis, Claudevsq, Cntras, CommonsDelinker, Cyberbot II, D.A.Timm, D6, Dainomite, DavGreg, Dewritech, Djharrity, Dl2000, ECCS-H, ELH50, EagleWSO, Emsox, EpicDream86, FieldMarine, Foreignshore, Gaius Cornelius, Gamgee, GeoInfoGeek, Gmred, Grobbs, Ground Zero, H.harder, Henk P51, Howcheng, Hullaballoo Wolfowitz, Human., Ida Shaw, Iridescent, IrishSpook, Jdaloner, Jedi physics, Jinian, JoseREMY, Jpm2112, Jprg1966, JustAGal, KarlsKrazyKusine, Klemen Kocjancic, KocjoBot∼enwiki, LanceBarber, Lightmouse, Ligunny, Lotje, MBelzer, Magioladitis, Maguirej03, Mark Renier, Meco, Midway, Mogism, Monkeybait, Moocha, Morinao, Mr305worldwide, NaBUru38, Neovu79, NerdyNSK, Neutrality, Nobunaga24, Noclador, Ohconfucius, Omerod, Plau, Pmsyyz, President Rhapsody, Preslethe, Preuninger, Purple1993, Resnicoff, Rhillson1, RicJac, Rich Farmbrough, Rifleman 82, Sandstein, Slubbert Slamberti, Smug Irony, Snake bgd, SpikeToronto, Sun Creator, Syrthiss, Thefreemarket, Tom.Reding, Tonster, Ulric1313, Unyoyega, Uusitunnus, Welsh, Werieth, Whpq, WikHead, Woohookitty, YanA, Zaphodia, Δ, 140 anonymous edits 214

United States Indo-Pacific Command *Source:* https://en.wikipedia.org/w/index.php?oldid=851229307 *License:* Creative Commons Attribution-Share Alike 3.0 *Contributors:* 23prootie, Abhikrishna555, Abrio, Alexander.maitre, Amauroni, Amaury, Andrewman327, Arado, Archer1234, Awakko, AzureCitizen, BOT-Superzerocool, Bahamut0013, Bastiaquinas, BilCat, Buckshot06, Camoseleys, CapitalR, Cburris593, Cdhutch, Chekaz, Chinfo, Chris the speller, Claudevsq, ClueBot NG, Cmr08, CommonsDelinker, Connormah, Craig.Scott, D6, Dale101usa, DanMS, Davestanfordjr, Davidbena, Davidcannon, Daysleeper47, Desertsky85451, Dewritech, Dismas, Djharrity, DocWatson42, Doprendek, Dsmorse, EF2000HL, Emaniuz, Enkyo2, EpicDream86, EricSerge, FieldMarine, G0mx, Garberino, Garuda28, GeekChild, Gerald Farinas, Guy Macon, HJ32, Hammersfan, HandsomeFella, Hmains, HolyT, Howard61313, HowlingMadHess, Human., I dream of horses, IComputerSaysNo, IRP, Ida Shaw, Illegitimate Barrister, Indefatigable, Ipankonin, Iskandar21, Jacarandacounsel, Jar789, JayCoop, Jbuckets404, Jigen III, Jks313, JohnEdit21, Jrtayloriv, KConWiki, Kndimov, LanceBarber, Laterose415, Lieutenant of Melkor, Lightmouse, Lockesdonkey, Looper5920, Los688, Lyta79, MARK S., MB, Magioladitis, Makanator, Meco, Monkeybait, Mr305worldwide, Mrsdeleo, Ndunruh, Neovu79, Nobunaga24, Noclador, Ohconfucius, PMDrive1061, Pair O' Dimes, Phd8511, Prodigyman1970, Prvc, RJBurkhart3, RekonDog, RicJac, Rich Farmbrough, Rjwilmsi, RoadDoggFL, Roaddoggfl, Roadrunner, Rogerd, SLi, Signaleer, Smug Irony, Spoon!, Srich32977, Susitenni, Thefreemarket, Thomas.McLaughlin, Tim!, Tonster, USPACOMPAO, Vsmith, W Nowicki, Wbfergus, WereSpielChequers, Zdarnell, Zzsql, 売り塗る塗り□, □, 88 anonymous edits 229

United States Northern Command *Source:* https://en.wikipedia.org/w/index.php?oldid=850579386 *License:* Creative Commons Attribution-Share Alike 3.0 *Contributors:* AHMartin, Aeh4543, Ajonsey215, Arado, BD2412, Bahamut0013, Bender235, BilCat, Billmckern, Blaylockjam10, Buckshot06, CapitalR, Chris the speller, Claudevsq, CommonsDelinker, Cst17, D6, David Barba, Dcirovic, Dl2000, DocWatson42, Dr Gangrene, Ed g2s, Fallsnative01, Fetchcomms, Garuda28, Geogene, Grosscha, Ground Zero, Hajor, Hcobb, Hmains, Human., Ianneub, Ioeth, JJuatai, Jar789, Jatkins, Jigen III, Joehealy, John K, Jpm2112, Jrtayloriv, JubaBear, Kamoranakrre T. Eyaelitenan, KocjoBot∼enwiki, Kujoe, Kwedin, LanceBarber, Lbr123, Lightmouse, Lockesdonkey, Lomn, Longshot14, Lord Pistachio, Los688, LtNOWIS, Luna Santin, MBelzer, Manchurian candidate, Marie26, Martin.Glynn, Meco, Mikebmr, Mr305worldwide, Muhandes, Muzzleflash, Neovu79, Noradnorthcom, NuclearWarfare, OberRanks, Ohconfucius, Phd8511, Phospheros, Pmsyyz, Ppntori, ProprioMe OW, RASPEEGLE, Rcsprinter123, RicJac, Rich Farmbrough, RightCowLeftCoast, Roadrunner, Sammartinlai, ScreaminEagle, Smug Irony, Syrthiss, Tivki, Tom harrison, Tom.Reding, Truth Hawker, Wlegro, 86 anonymous edits 243

United States Southern Command *Source:* https://en.wikipedia.org/w/index.php?oldid=852190176 *License:* Creative Commons Attribution-Share Alike 3.0 *Contributors:* 1990'sguy, 2004-12-29T22:45Z, AHMartin, Aeh4543, Aetheling, Airwags22, Alai, AntiCompositeNumber, Asem18, AzureCitizen, Babelia, Bahamut0013, Bazonka, BilCat, Bruguiea, Buckshot06, C.Fred, Camerong, CaribDigita, ChrisGualtieri, Claudevsq, Cleared as filed, Closedmouth, Connormah, Cubaray, D6, Danberbro, Derek R Bullamore, Dsmorse, Duke Ganote, E.w.bullock, Eagleash, Eleklem, Epolk, FLAHAM, Faizhaider, FelineAvenger, FieldMarine, Garuda28, Giraffedata, Gob Lofa, Grosscha, Ground Zero, Hcobb, Hmains, Human., HumanRightsMatter, Illegitimate Barrister, Janderson23834, Jar789, Jigen III, Jost Riedel, Jpm2112, KConWiki, Kges1901, Khatru2, KocjoBot∼enwiki, LanceBarber, Lightmouse, LilHelpa, Lockesdonkey, Lotje, MARK S., MBelzer, Marcd30319, Mbshaver, McChizzle, Mean as custard, Meatsgains, Meco, Michael Devore, Mike Selinker, Missionary, Mohrflies, Mwilso24, Myheartinchile, Narky Blert, Ndunruh, Neovu79, Niceguyedc, Nobunaga24, Ohconfucius, Oliverhaberdash, Open2universe, Orenburg1, Paul A, Petercorless, Phil Boswell, Pmsyyz, Qwertyus, RUSMCUSA, RayAlt, Redthoreau, Reidgreg, RicJac, Rich Farmbrough, RightCowLeftCoast, RobDuch, SGT141, Shockblaster, Sintaku, SirBob42, SithLord005, Skaboss241, Skapur, Smug Irony, Son of Somebody, Subdolous, Syrthiss, Tabletop, Tatrgel, Tewfik, Thefreemarket, Tom.Reding, Tomcool, Vegaswikian, Viajero, WhisperToMe, WilliamJE, Wimbishmike, ZiaLater, 75 anonymous edits 249

United States Cyber Command *Source:* https://en.wikipedia.org/w/index.php?oldid=852384518 *License:* Creative Commons Attribution-Share Alike 3.0 *Contributors:* Adrian Nicolaiev∼enwiki, Ajaxrocks, Ancheta Wis, Arjayay, Atlas2098, Auntof6, AustralianRupert, Awakko, AzureCitizen, BDONGLI, Bahamut0013, Bejnar, Beland, Bender235, Blaylockjam10, Bobrayner, Botteville, Buckshot06, Cantab1985, CaptainMorgan, Cdiasoh, Certes, Cewlt, Chris the speller, Citationhelper, Compfreak7, Corkythehornetfan, Crosbiesmith, Cyberbot II, Dillpick88, DinosaursLoveExistence, Discospinster, Dl2000, DocWatson42, Doug, Dr Gangrene, Dsamarin, Duttler, Eim2115, Emosy, Ergo Sum, FieldMarine, Fintler, Forcemajeure, FreeWorldGo, Furkaocean, Garuda28, Gderry, Geraldshields11, Gobonobo, Happysailor, Hcobb, How Shuan Shi, Huntscorpio, Hydrargyrum, Iamleeg, Illegitimate Barrister, Inventis, J3nstar, JamesRMeehan, Jatkins, JocularJellyfish, Jogrkim, JonathonReinhart, Jonkerz, Kvng, Lamontap, Look2See1, MaXintoshPro, Magioladitis, Markbassett, MarshalGrant, Maxviwe, Mdupont, Meco, Michipedian, Mikek999, MrDolomite, Neovu79, Nick Moyes, Nonatus99, Northern Muriqui, Ntothe3rd, Nurg, Ohconfucius, Oshwah, Paul Erik, Penguino35, PhilKnight, Pmsyyz, Rambo.rapu, Rbcwa, RicJac, Richard Arthur Norton (1958-), RightCowLeftCoast, Rjwilmsi, Rodw, Ryudo∼enwiki, Sammartinlai, Scottmsg, Scriberius, Sephiroth storm, Sierratangoxray, SithLord005, Skizzik, Skyerise, Sphilbrick, Star72, Swedishcrafter, Tabit Harik, Talbrech, Terrillja, The Anomebot2, The Flying Soda, The PIPE, Toddst1, Tomtom, Tovkal, Verne Equinox, Warrenfish, WhisperToMe, Worldcupnj, Xanzzibar, Xeno, Ylee, Zabanio, 117 anonymous edits 267

United States Special Operations Command *Source:* https://en.wikipedia.org/w/index.php?oldid=852513247 *License:* Creative Commons Attribution-Share Alike 3.0 *Contributors:* 1exec1, 426ca, Aerno, Alpha7248, Apokrif, Archon 2488, Attention whore, Awakko, BEARtruth89, Bender235, Beyond My Ken, Bfranz82, Bgwhite, BilCat, Buckshot06, Bullmoosebell, CAPTAIN RAJU, Cacash refund, ChickenBar, Chris the speller, Citation bot 1, Claudevsq, CommonsDelinker, Cyberbot II, Dainomite, Dewritech, DouglasCalvert, Download, El Felberino, Espfutbol98, Excirial, F111ECM, Frze, Fustos, G913, Garuda28, Giraffedata, Glacialfox, Graham87, Himynameissudip, Howtohandlearope, Human., Il Dorico, Illegitimate Barrister, Iridescent, Jionunez, Jmattthew, Jmg38, JokerAxius, Jprg1966, Jrt989, Just the law, Kahtar, Kapt.Olive, Kencf0618, Khazar2, KylieTastic, LilHelpa, LittleWink, Longhair, Lord Pistachio, LtSpecter, Lugnuthemvar, Mark Arsten, Mark Renier, Mattes, MatthewBurton, McChizzle, Minhquangdo, Momboo, MusikAnimal, Mx. Granger, Neovu79, No parking here, Noclador, Ohconfucius, Oknazevad, Onel5969, Onifpaz, Oranjelo100, PGPirate, Pama73, Passengerpigeon, Pawyilee, Phoenixrod, PiMaster3, Pmsyyz, Poshua.josey, Ptbotgourou, Ramos37, Regulov, RicJac, Rovingardener, Scienz Guy, Scout MLG, Scriberius, Skjoldbro, SkoraPobeda, SlitherySentinel, Srich32977, StAnselm, StayBehind, StillTrill, Swliv, SyriaWarLato, TCN7JM, Tabit Harik, Taudelt, Textpilot22, Thesassypenguin, Thewolfchild, Toddy1, Tom.Reding, TomPointTwo, Trappist the monk, USMCLP, Ulrezaj, WOSlinker, War Machine Alpha, Wavelength, Widr, XxxArcanxxX, 164 anonymous edits 274

United States Strategic Command *Source:* https://en.wikipedia.org/w/index.php?oldid=852681031 *License:* Creative Commons Attribution-Share Alike 3.0 *Contributors:* 5-HT8, A.R., ALCS85, Achmelvic, Ahecht, Airleron, Alphachimp, Amcaja, Ancheta Wis, ArCgon, Arado, Asten77, AzureCitizen, Bahamut0013, Bdriskel, Behun, Beland, Bender235, BilCat, Buckshot06, C7L5N9, CallumDawson, Caltas, Claudevsq, CommonsDelinker, Compfreak7, Connormah, Cornellrockey, Courcelles, D6, DJ Clayworth, DadOfBeanAndBug, DangApricot, Ddelestrac, DenverApplehans, Devnull17, Djbauch,

DocWatson42, Doug, Dr Gangrene, EagleWSO, Fastfission, Florian Adler, Fnlayson, FrozenPurpleCube, Gaius Cornelius, Garuda28, Gbawden, Gbbinning, Glacier109, Goldorn, HJ32, Hcobb, Hmains, Human., Ida Shaw, Illegitimate Barrister, J3nstar, JCO312, Jab843, JamesGraybeal, Jigen III, JocularJellyfish, Jogrkim, Jonverve, Jpm2112, JustAGal, JustBerry, Ken Gallager, Klemen Kocjancic, KocjoBot~enwiki, Kumioko (renamed), LanceBarber, LeyteWolfer, Lightmouse, LilHelpa, MCG, MLWilson, Mais oui!, Mandarax, Marcd30319, Mark83, Marudubshinki, Mdnort, Mhustoft, MrDolomite, Ndunruh, Neovu79, Neutrality, Nick Number, Night Gyr, Nobunaga24, Nohomers48, Ohconfucius, Orenburg1, Pgrote, Phd8511, Pmsyyz, Portkent, Preuninger, PvOberstein, Queso.robusto, Rejectwater, Retanollo, RicJac, Rich Farmbrough, Rodw, Rougher07, Sammartinlai, Scriberius, SeanFromIT, Seitzd, SimonP, SithLord005, Smug Irony, Stevertigo, Student7, Sunray, SweetCanadianMullet, Syrthiss, TCN7JM, TadgStirkland401, Tdrss, Thesmothete, Thewolfchild, Tim!, Tom.Reding, Tourbillon, USSTRATCOM PAO, Uv1234, V and friends, Walker9010, Warrenfish, Woogers, XXzoonamiXX, Xanzzibar, 153 anonymous edits 309
United States Transportation Command *Source:* https://en.wikipedia.org/w/index.php?oldid=852806917 *License:* Creative Commons Attribution-Share Alike 3.0 *Contributors:* AirForceWon, Alinder, AngryBear, Bahamut0013, Beland, Benanhalt, BilCat, Buckshot06, Bullmoosebell, CORNELIUSSEON, Cerabot~enwiki, Claudevsq, Clindberg, Connormah, Copperchair, D6, David Newton, Defleck, EagleFan, Editc, EpicDream86, Epicadam, Faizan, Foreignshore, Garuda28, Giraffedata, HJonas77, Haeinous, Hmains, Human., HurshistanEditor, I dream of horses, Iridescent, Jaraalbe, Jigen III, JocularJellyfish, JonathanFreed, Jpm2112, KocjoBot~enwiki, Kumioko (renamed), LanceBarber, Lightmouse, Mandarax, Marshcmb, Mathew Roberson, Mboverload, Mean as custard, MeltBanana, Molly-in-md, MrDolomite, NE2, Ndunruh, Neovu79, Nobunaga24, Nohomers48, Ohconfucius, Open2universe, Phil Boswell, Pilotofdoom, Prvc, Quadell, RicJac, Rpalme01, SDC, SGT141, STBotD, SalineBrain, SchreiberBike, Scootr71, Scriberius, ShiningTor, SithLord005, Smug Irony, Srich32977, Syrthiss, Tecarr, Thewolfchild, Trappist the monk, USTC CSI, Whitney925, Whoisjohngalt, Wiegandn, Woohookitty, Wyatts, 55 anonymous edits 319

Image Sources, Licenses and Contributors

The sources listed for each image provide more detailed licensing information including the copyright status, the copyright owner, and the license conditions.

Image *Source:* https://en.wikipedia.org/w/index.php?title=File:Seals_of_the_United_States_Armed_Forces.png *License:* Public Domain *Contributors:* Illegitimate Barrister, 2 anonymous edits 1
Image *Source:* https://en.wikipedia.org/w/index.php?title=File:Flag_of_the_United_States_Army_(official_proportions).svg *License:* Public Domain *Contributors:* United States Army 1
Image *Source:* https://en.wikipedia.org/w/index.php?title=File:Flag_of_the_United_States_Marine_Corps.svg *License:* Public Domain *Contributors:* Marine_corps_flag.gif: Himasaram derivative work: Mnmazur (talk) 1
Image *Source:* https://en.wikipedia.org/w/index.php?title=File:Flag_of_the_United_States_Navy_(official).svg *License:* Public Domain *Contributors:* United States Department of the Navy 1
Image *Source:* https://en.wikipedia.org/w/index.php?title=File:Flag_of_the_United_States_Air_Force.svg *License:* Public Domain *Contributors:* United States Air Force 1
Image *Source:* https://en.wikipedia.org/w/index.php?title=File:Flag_of_the_United_States_Coast_Guard.svg *Contributors:* U.S. Army Institute of Heraldry 1
Image *Source:* https://en.wikipedia.org/w/index.php?title=File:Flag_of_the_President_of_the_United_States_of_America.svg *Contributors:* - 1
Image *Source:* https://en.wikipedia.org/w/index.php?title=File:USSecDefflag.svg *Contributors:* - 1
Image *Source:* https://en.wikipedia.org/w/index.php?title=File:Flag_of_the_United_States_Secretary_of_Homeland_Security.svg *License:* Public Domain *Contributors:* User:Offnfopt 1
Image *Source:* https://en.wikipedia.org/w/index.php?title=File:Flag_of_the_Chairman_of_the_US_Joint_Chiefs_of_Staff.svg *License:* Public Domain *Contributors:* United States Department of Defense 1
Image *Source:* https://en.wikipedia.org/w/index.php?title=File:VJCSflag.svg *License:* Public Domain *Contributors:* U.S. Army Institute of Heraldry (design), User:Connormah (vectorization) 2
Image *Source:* https://en.wikipedia.org/w/index.php?title=File:SEACflag.svg *License:* Public Domain *Contributors:* U.S. Army Institute of Heraldry 2
Figure 1 *Source:* https://en.wikipedia.org/w/index.php?title=File:US_National_Command.png *License:* GNU Free Documentation License *Contributors:* User:Nicholas F. in the EnWiki 5
Figure 2 *Source:* https://en.wikipedia.org/w/index.php?title=File:US_defense_spending_1910_to_2007.png *License:* Public Domain *Contributors:* Congressional Research Service 7
Figure 3 *Source:* https://en.wikipedia.org/w/index.php?title=File:US_defense_spending_by_GDP_percentage_1910_to_2007.png *License:* Public Domain *Contributors:* Congressional Research Service 8
Figure 4 *Source:* https://en.wikipedia.org/w/index.php?title=File:Active_duty_end_strength_graph.png *License:* Public Domain *Contributors:* Congressional Research Service 9
Image *Source:* https://en.wikipedia.org/w/index.php?title=File:Flag_of_the_United_States_Army.svg *License:* Public Domain *Contributors:* United States Army 10
Image *Source:* https://en.wikipedia.org/w/index.php?title=File:Flag_of_the_United_States_Navy.svg *License:* Public Domain *Contributors:* United States Department of the Navy 10
Image *Source:* https://en.wikipedia.org/w/index.php?title=File:USCG_Parade_Flag.svg *Contributors:* - 10
Image *Source:* https://en.wikipedia.org/w/index.php?title=File:US_Army_National_Guard_Insignia.svg *Contributors:* - 10
Image *Source:* https://en.wikipedia.org/w/index.php?title=File:United_States_AR_seal.svg *Contributors:* - 10
Image *Source:* https://en.wikipedia.org/w/index.php?title=File:MarforresLogo.jpg *License:* Public Domain *Contributors:* Bahamut0013, Corkythehornetfan, File Upload Bot (Magnus Manske), IngerAlHaosului, OgreBot 2 10
Image *Source:* https://en.wikipedia.org/w/index.php?title=File:United_States_NR_Seal.svg *License:* Public Domain *Contributors:* Keenan Tims 10
Image *Source:* https://en.wikipedia.org/w/index.php?title=File:Air_national_guard_shield.svg *License:* Public Domain *Contributors:* Aloneinthewild, Auntof6, Avron, File Upload Bot (Magnus Manske), IngerAlHaosului, Lineagegeek, OgreBot 2 10
Image *Source:* https://en.wikipedia.org/w/index.php?title=File:Air_Force_Reserve_Command.png *License:* Public Domain *Contributors:* United States Air Force (User:Pmsyyz converted from JPEG to PNG, added transparency, resized to 1000px wide, indexed col 10
Image *Source:* https://en.wikipedia.org/w/index.php?title=File:United_States_Coast_Guard_Reserve_emblem.png *Contributors:* U.S. Coast Guard 10
Figure 5 *Source:* https://en.wikipedia.org/w/index.php?title=File:US_Global_Military_Presence.svg *Contributors:* User:Nagihuin 11
Figure 6 *Source:* https://en.wikipedia.org/w/index.php?title=File:USmilitary.JPG *License:* Creative Commons Attribution-Sharealike 3.0 *Contributors:* Onetwo1 (talk) 12
Figure 7 *Source:* https://en.wikipedia.org/w/index.php?title=File:C-130_-_First_all_female_crew.jpg *License:* Public Domain *Contributors:* ARTEST4ECHO, Acsian88, Afifa Afrin, Akinom, Auntof6, Benchill, Cobatfor, Courcelles, Edward, FieldMarine, File Upload Bot (Magnus Manske), GT1976, Illegitimate Barrister, Infrogmation, Ingolfson, Jan Arkesteijn, Joshbaumgartner, Lineagegeek, LittleWink, Man vyi, Mattes, Morio, PeterWD, Pmsyyz, Rauschenderbach, Rimshot, Rogerd, Snowsuit Wearer, SunOfErat, Thivierr, Wst, 3 anonymous edits 17
Figure 8 *Source:* https://en.wikipedia.org/w/index.php?title=File:Leigh_Ann_Hester_medal.jpg *License:* Public Domain *Contributors:* Specialist Jeremy D. Crisp, United States Army 18
Image *Source:* https://en.wikipedia.org/w/index.php?title=File:Commons-logo.svg *License:* logo *Contributors:* Anomie, Callanecc, CambridgeBayWeather, Jo-Jo Eumerus, RHaworth 20
Image *Source:* https://en.wikipedia.org/w/index.php?title=File:Wikiquote-logo.svg *License:* Public Domain *Contributors:* Rei-artur 20
Figure 9 *Source:* https://en.wikipedia.org/w/index.php?title=File:US_military_personnel_and_expenditures.png *License:* Public Domain *Contributors:* Citynoise 24
Figure 10 *Source:* https://en.wikipedia.org/w/index.php?title=File:Siege_of_Fort_Detroit.jpg *License:* Public Domain *Contributors:* Jibi44, Kevin Myers, Themightyquill, Wmpearl, 1 anonymous edits 25
Figure 11 *Source:* https://en.wikipedia.org/w/index.php?title=File:Bataille_Yorktown.jpg *License:* Public Domain *Contributors:* Anders.Warga, Dr Brains, Hohum, Jeff G., Khaerr~commonswiki, Nyttend, Spellcast, Tom.Reding 26
Figure 12 *Source:* https://en.wikipedia.org/w/index.php?title=File:Washington_Crossing_the_Delaware_by_Emanuel_Leutze,_MMA-NYC,_1851.jpg *License:* Public Domain *Contributors:* AEMoreira042281, Aavindraa, Alex Blokha, Aylaross, Berrucomons, BotMultichill, Bukk, Commons-Delinker, Illegitimate Barrister, Jonkerz, Kelly, Kozuch, Lotje, Lucky For You, Mattes, Morgan Riley, Nanae, Neukoln, Nguyên Lê, Oneam, Patriot8790, Saibo, Savh, Scewing, Shepherd23, Soerfm, Thierry Caro, Trzęsacz, Zeete, 3 anonymous edits 27
Figure 13 *Source:* https://en.wikipedia.org/w/index.php?title=File:Fallen_timbers.jpg *License:* Public Domain *Contributors:* Chowbok, Deadstar, Janneman, Nyttend, Origamiemensch, Taterian, TheCuriousGnome, Thib Phil, Uyvsdi, WFinch 29
Figure 14 *Source:* https://en.wikipedia.org/w/index.php?title=File:Decatur_Boarding_the_Tripolitan_Gunboat.jpg *License:* Public Domain *Contributors:* Painter: Dennis Malone Carter 30
Figure 15 *Source:* https://en.wikipedia.org/w/index.php?title=File:Battle_erie.jpg *Contributors:* Acabashi, Acdixon, AnRo0002, Avron, Barbe-Noire, BoringHistoryGuy, BotMultichill, Bukk, DIREKTOR, Ecummenic, EurekaLott, Jkelly, Mattes, Shauni, Timothy Gu, Wmpearl, Zeete, 1 anonymous edits 31
Figure 16 *Source:* https://en.wikipedia.org/w/index.php?title=File:Battle_of_Chapultepec.jpg *License:* Public Domain *Contributors:* Lithograph by after a drawing by 32
Figure 17 *Source:* https://en.wikipedia.org/w/index.php?title=File:Bodies_on_the_battlefield_at_antietam.jpg *Contributors:* Clindberg, Jpda, Jörg Zägel, Meteor2017, Mtsmallwood, Ras67, Shauni, Timeshifter, Yann, Zaccarias 33
Figure 18 *Source:* https//en.wikipedia.org *License:* Attribution *Contributors:* User:Adam Cuerden 34
Figure 19 *Source:* https://en.wikipedia.org/w/index.php?title=File:Custer_Massacre_At_Big_Horn,_Montana_June_25_1876.jpg *Contributors:* Werner Co. 35
Figure 20 *Source:* https://en.wikipedia.org/w/index.php?title=File:Charge_of_the_Rough_Riders_at_San_Juan_Hill.JPG *License:* Public Domain *Contributors:* AndreasPraefcke, BotMultichill, BrokenSphere, CarolSpears, Daderot, Jim.henderson, Julius Morton, OgreBot 2, Shizhao, SimonATL, Themadchopper, Zzyzx11, 1 anonymous edits 35
Figure 21 *Source:* https://en.wikipedia.org/w/index.php?title=File:Manila646_1899.jpg *License:* Public Domain *Contributors:* Perley Fremont Rockett 36
Figure 22 *Source:* https://en.wikipedia.org/w/index.php?title=File:Straits_of_Magellan,_Chile_-_NH_101483.jpg *License:* Public Domain *Contributors:* Revent 37

Figure 23 *Source:* https://en.wikipedia.org/w/index.php?title=File:Tr-bigstick-cartoon.JPG *License:* Public Domain *Contributors:* William Allen Rogers Courtesy of Granger Collection ... 39
Figure 24 *Source:* https://en.wikipedia.org/w/index.php?title=File:Nogales_Arizona_1910-1920.jpg *License:* Public Domain *Contributors:* United States Army ... 40
Figure 25 *Source:* https://en.wikipedia.org/w/index.php?title=File:AEF_marching_in_France.jpg *License:* Public Domain *Contributors:* Another-clown, Gérald Garitan, Hohum, Palamède, Tomandjerry211 ... 41
Figure 26 *Source:* https://en.wikipedia.org/w/index.php?title=File:The_Conference_on_Limitation_of_Armaments,_Washington,_D.C..jpg *Contributors:* Cobatfor, Moroboshi, Opencooper ... 42
Figure 27 *Source:* https://en.wikipedia.org/w/index.php?title=File:Pearlharborcolork13513.jpg *License:* Public Domain *Contributors:* U.S. Navy ... 44
Figure 28 *Source:* https://en.wikipedia.org/w/index.php?title=File:Douglas_MacArthur_signs_formal_surrender.jpg *License:* Public Domain *Contributors:* United States Navy ... 45
Figure 29 *Source:* https://en.wikipedia.org/w/index.php?title=File:Battle_of_Inchon.png *License:* Public Domain *Contributors:* US Navy ... 47
Figure 30 *Source:* https://en.wikipedia.org/w/index.php?title=File:Foxhole_-_Lebanon_-_Beirut,_-_July_1958.jpg *License:* Public Domain *Contributors:* Thomas J. O'Halloran, U.S. News & World Report Magazine ... 48
Figure 31 *Source:* https://en.wikipedia.org/w/index.php?title=File:Bruce_Crandall_leads_formation_of_UH-1s_of_229th_Aviation_Rgt_ca._1966.jpg *License:* Public Domain *Contributors:* United States Army ... 49
Figure 32 *Source:* https://en.wikipedia.org/w/index.php?title=File:Damage_Done!.jpg *License:* Public Domain *Contributors:* US Army Military History Institute ... 50
Figure 33 *Source:* https://en.wikipedia.org/w/index.php?title=File:CH-53D_HMM-261_Grenada_Okt1983.jpeg *License:* Public Domain *Contributors:* photographer: TSgt. M. J. Creen, USMC ... 52
Figure 34 *Source:* https://en.wikipedia.org/w/index.php?title=File:USF-111_Libya1986.JPG *License:* Public Domain *Contributors:* SSGT Woodward ... 53
Figure 35 *Source:* https://en.wikipedia.org/w/index.php?title=File:Map_of_the_Pentagon's_War_on_Terrorism_strategy_2010.jpg *License:* Public Domain *Contributors:* Major General Darren W. McDew, USAF, Vice Director, Strategic Plans and Policy, J-5, the Joint Staff ... 53
Figure 36 *Source:* https://en.wikipedia.org/w/index.php?title=File:Wisconsin_Shoots.JPG *License:* Public Domain *Contributors:* PH2 JOHN CARNES ... 55
Figure 37 *Source:* https://en.wikipedia.org/w/index.php?title=File:Black_Hawk_Down_Rangers_under_fire_October_3,_1993.jpg *License:* Public Domain *Contributors:* User:"D" ... 56
Figure 38 *Source:* https://en.wikipedia.org/w/index.php?title=File:US_Special_Forces_on_horseback,_Afghanistan,_2001.jpg *License:* Public Domain *Contributors:* Department of Defense employee ... 57
Figure 39 *Source:* https://en.wikipedia.org/w/index.php?title=File:USMarineTankinBaghdad.jpg *License:* Public Domain *Contributors:* Avron, Brnkeet, Chyah, Hohum, Illegitimate Barrister, Innotata, Magog the Ogre, Man vyi, Reguyla, SWAT01, Thine Antique Pen, 2 anonymous edits ... 58
Figure 40 *Source:* https://en.wikipedia.org/w/index.php?title=File:The_Pentagon_US_Department_of_Defense_building.jpg *License:* Public Domain *Contributors:* "DoD photo by Master Sgt. Ken Hammond, U.S. Air Force." ... 64
Figure 41 *Source:* https://en.wikipedia.org/w/index.php?title=File:US_Defense_Agencies.png *License:* Public Domain *Contributors:* US Government ... 72
Image *Source:* https://en.wikipedia.org/w/index.php?title=File:DARPA_Logo.jpg *License:* Public Domain *Contributors:* DARPA ... 70
Image *Source:* https://en.wikipedia.org/w/index.php?title=File:Defense_Commissary_Agency_logo.PNG *License:* Public Domain *Contributors:* File Upload Bot (Magnus Manske), Illegitimate Barrister, Nobunaga24, OgreBot 2, Ricjac∼commonswiki, Sarang, Wikimandia ... 70
Image *Source:* https://en.wikipedia.org/w/index.php?title=File:DCAA_Emblem_2.jpg *License:* Public Domain *Contributors:* Defense Contract Audit Agency ... 70
Image *Source:* https://en.wikipedia.org/w/index.php?title=File:DCMA.PNG *License:* Public Domain *Contributors:* Original artwork made by the Defense Contract Management Agency/Department of Defense ... 70
Image *Source:* https://en.wikipedia.org/w/index.php?title=File:Defense_Finance_Accounting_Services_(DFAS)_Official_Seal.png *License:* Public Domain *Contributors:* James C. Manubay ... 70
Image *Source:* https://en.wikipedia.org/w/index.php?title=File:US-DefenseInformationSystemsAgency-Seal.svg *License:* Public Domain *Contributors:* U.S. Government ... 71
Image *Source:* https://en.wikipedia.org/w/index.php?title=File:US-DefenseIntelligenceAgency-Seal.svg *Contributors:* U.S. Government ... 71
Image *Source:* https://en.wikipedia.org/w/index.php?title=File:Defense_Logistics_Agency.PNG *License:* Public Domain *Contributors:* File Upload Bot (Magnus Manske), Illegitimate Barrister, Imjustmatthew∼commonswiki, Nobunaga24, OgreBot 2, Ricjac∼commonswiki, 1 anonymous edits ... 71
Image *Source:* https://en.wikipedia.org/w/index.php?title=File:DSCA.PNG *License:* Public Domain *Contributors:* Department of Defense ... 71
Image *Source:* https://en.wikipedia.org/w/index.php?title=File:Defense_Security_Service.PNG *License:* Public Domain *Contributors:* Original artwork made by the Defense Security Service/Department of Defense ... 71
Image *Source:* https://en.wikipedia.org/w/index.php?title=File:US-DefenseThreatReductionAgency-Seal.svg *License:* Public Domain *Contributors:* U.S. Government ... 71
Image *Source:* https://en.wikipedia.org/w/index.php?title=File:US-MissileDefenseAgency-Seal.svg *Contributors:* - ... 71
Image *Source:* https://en.wikipedia.org/w/index.php?title=File:US-NationalGeospatialIntelligenceAgency-2008Seal.svg *License:* Public Domain *Contributors:* U.S. Government ... 71
Image *Source:* https://en.wikipedia.org/w/index.php?title=File:NRO.svg *License:* Trademarked *Contributors:* U.S. Government ... 71
Image *Source:* https://en.wikipedia.org/w/index.php?title=File:National_Security_Agency.svg *Contributors:* - ... 71
Image *Source:* https://en.wikipedia.org/w/index.php?title=File:US-CentralSecurityService-Seal.svg *License:* Public Domain *Contributors:* U.S. Government ... 71
Image *Source:* https://en.wikipedia.org/w/index.php?title=File:PFPA_Seal.jpg *License:* Public Domain *Contributors:* Pentagon Force Protection Agency ... 72
Image *Source:* https://en.wikipedia.org/w/index.php?title=File:Defense_Media_Activity_logo.jpg *License:* Public Domain *Contributors:* Nathan Quinn ... 72
Image *Source:* https://en.wikipedia.org/w/index.php?title=File:US-DefenseTechnicalInformationCenter-Seal.svg *License:* Public Domain *Contributors:* U.S. Government ... 73
Image *Source:* https://en.wikipedia.org/w/index.php?title=File:DHRA.PNG *License:* Public Domain *Contributors:* Department of Defense ... 73
Image *Source:* https://en.wikipedia.org/w/index.php?title=File:WHS_Insignia.svg *License:* Public Domain *Contributors:* Keenan Tims ... 73
Image *Source:* https://en.wikipedia.org/w/index.php?title=File:Africom_emblem_2.svg *Contributors:* - ... 75
Image *Source:* https://en.wikipedia.org/w/index.php?title=File:Seal_of_the_United_States_Central_Command.png *License:* Public Domain *Contributors:* Illegitimate Barrister, Sarang ... 75
Image *Source:* https://en.wikipedia.org/w/index.php?title=File:EUCOM_Logo.jpg *License:* Public Domain *Contributors:* GrummelJS, Pmsyyz, Ricjac∼commonswiki ... 75
Image *Source:* https://en.wikipedia.org/w/index.php?title=File:Seal_of_the_United_States_Northern_Command.png *License:* Public Domain *Contributors:* CORNELIUSSEON, Ed g2s, Giggy, Illegitimate Barrister, Mattes, Pmsyyz, Ricjac∼commonswiki, Sarang, 5 anonymous edits ... 75
Image *Source:* https://en.wikipedia.org/w/index.php?title=File:USPACOM_seal.jpg *License:* Public Domain *Contributors:* BukhariSaeed, Claudevsq, FieldMarine, GrummelJS, Pmsyyz, Ricjac∼commonswiki, Tokorokoko, 2 anonymous edits ... 75
Image *Source:* https://en.wikipedia.org/w/index.php?title=File:USSOUTHCOM_emblem.jpg *License:* Public Domain *Contributors:* Chatsam, Pmsyyz, Ricjac∼commonswiki, Sanandros ... 75
Image *Source:* https://en.wikipedia.org/w/index.php?title=File:SOCOM.jpg *License:* Public Domain *Contributors:* CommonsDelinker, GrummelJS, It Is Me Here, Mattes, PS2801, Pmsyyz, Ricjac∼commonswiki ... 76
Image *Source:* https://en.wikipedia.org/w/index.php?title=File:USSTRATCOM_emblem.PNG *License:* Public Domain *Contributors:* Pmsyyz, Preuninger, Ricjac∼commonswiki, Svgalbertian, Ysangkok, 1 anonymous edits ... 76
Image *Source:* https://en.wikipedia.org/w/index.php?title=File:United_States_Transportation_Command_emblem.png *License:* Public Domain *Contributors:* Clindberg, Pmsyyz, Ricjac∼commonswiki ... 76
Image *Source:* https://en.wikipedia.org/w/index.php?title=File:Unified_Combatant_Commands_map.png *License:* GNU Free Documentation License *Contributors:* Lencer ... 76
Figure 42 *Source:* https://en.wikipedia.org/w/index.php?title=File:Wiki_OIG_DOD_Seal.gif *License:* Public Domain *Contributors:* Auntof6, FishInWater, Fry1989, Magog the Ogre, Ricjac∼commonswiki, Wikimandia ... 77
Figure 43 *Source:* https://en.wikipedia.org/w/index.php?title=File:Seal_of_the_National_Guard_Bureau_(US).svg *License:* Public Domain *Contributors:* http://www.ng.mil/resources/photo_gallery/graphics/gal.htm ... 78
Image *Source:* https://en.wikipedia.org/w/index.php?title=File:Defense_Spending_as_a_Percent_of_GDP.png *Contributors:* User:Wikideas1 ... 82
Image *Source:* https://en.wikipedia.org/w/index.php?title=File:Defense_spending.png *License:* Creative Commons Zero *Contributors:* User:Wikideas1 ... 82
Image *Source:* https://en.wikipedia.org/w/index.php?title=File:USA_2010_Military_Budget_Spending.jpg *License:* Creative Commons Attribution-Sharealike 3.0 *Contributors:* User:Carrotist2 ... 85

Image *Source:* https://en.wikipedia.org/w/index.php?title=File:PerCapitaInflationAdjustedDefenseSpending.PNG *License:* Creative Commons Attribution 3.0 *Contributors:* Johnpseudo 87

Image *Source:* https://en.wikipedia.org/w/index.php?title=File:InflationAdjustedDefenseSpending.PNG *License:* Creative Commons Attribution 3.0 *Contributors:* Johnpseudo 87

Image *Source:* https://en.wikipedia.org/w/index.php?title=File:2017_Request_Budget_Breakdown_Fig_1.jpg *License:* Public Domain *Contributors:* Howcheng, Ruff tuff cream puff, ThePatman42 90

Image *Source:* https://en.wikipedia.org/w/index.php?title=File:U.S._Federal_Spending.png *License:* Creative Commons Attribution-Sharealike 3.0 *Contributors:* Apteva, Delphi234, Farcaster, L'amateur d'aéroplanes, Magog the Ogre, Spellcheck, Wieralee, ~riley 95

Image *Source:* https://en.wikipedia.org/w/index.php?title=File:Top_ten_military_expenditures_in_$_in_2013.jpg.jpeg *Contributors:* - 97

Figure 44 *Source:* https://en.wikipedia.org/w/index.php?title=File:Map_of_countries_by_military_expenditure_as_percentage_of_GDP.png *License:* Creative Commons Zero *Contributors:* Mikael Häggström, Sarang 97

Image *Source:* https://en.wikipedia.org/w/index.php?title=File:Flag_of_the_United_States.svg *License:* Public Domain *Contributors:* Anomie, Jo-Jo Eumerus, MSGJ, Mr. Stradivarius 103

Image *Source:* https://en.wikipedia.org/w/index.php?title=File:Flag_of_Alaska.svg *License:* Public Domain *Contributors:* Anime Addict AA, AnonMoos, Cycn, Dbenbenn, DevinCook, Duck that quacks alot, Dzordzm, Fry1989, Homo lupus, Juiced lemon, Juliancolton, MAXXX-309, MGA73, Mattes, Nightstallion, R2D2Art2005, Resident Mario, Serinde, Smooth O, VIGNERON, Wester, Zscout370, 19 anonymous edits 103

Image *Source:* https://en.wikipedia.org/w/index.php?title=File:Flag_of_Cuba.svg *License:* Public Domain *Contributors:* Anime Addict AA, Beao, Benzoyl, Cathy Richards, Cycn, Dbenbenn, Denelson83, DerBorg, EclecticArkie, Emijrp, F l a n k e r, FreshCorp619, Fry1989, Homo lupus, Huhsunqu, J.delanoy, Jdx, Klemen Kocjancic, Ludger1961, MAXXX-309, Madden, Mattes, Neq00, NeverDoING, Persiana, Ricordisamoa, SKopp, Sarang, SiBr4, Spacebirdy, TFerenczy, ThomasPusch, Torstein, Túrelio, Zscout370, 10 anonymous edits 103

Image *Source:* https://en.wikipedia.org/w/index.php?title=File:Flag_of_Honduras.svg *License:* Public Domain *Contributors:* Cathy Richards, D1990, Denelson83, ECanalla, Feydey, FixFixer, Fred J, FreshCorp619, GoldenRainbow, Homo lupus, JMCC1, Klemen Kocjancic, Mattes, Matthew hk, Neq00, Oak27, Pumbaa80, Rocket000, RubiksMaster110, SKopp, SiBr4, Siebrand, Steinsplitter, ThomasPusch, Tocino, Vzb83~commonswiki, Yuval Madar, ZooFari, Zscout370, 10 anonymous edits 103

Image *Source:* https://en.wikipedia.org/w/index.php?title=File:Flag_of_Puerto_Rico.svg *License:* Public Domain *Contributors:* User:Madden 103

Image *Source:* https://en.wikipedia.org/w/index.php?title=File:Flag_of_Greenland.svg *License:* Public Domain *Contributors:* Jeffrey Connell (IceKarma) 104

Image *Source:* https://en.wikipedia.org/w/index.php?title=File:Flag_of_Canada.svg *License:* Public Domain *Contributors:* Anomie, Jo-Jo Eumerus 104

Image *Source:* https://en.wikipedia.org/w/index.php?title=File:Flag_of_Japan.svg *License:* Public Domain *Contributors:* Anomie, Jo-Jo Eumerus 104

Image *Source:* https://en.wikipedia.org/w/index.php?title=File:Flag_of_South_Korea.svg *License:* Public Domain *Contributors:* Various 104

Image *Source:* https://en.wikipedia.org/w/index.php?title=File:Flag_of_Thailand.svg *Contributors:* Achim55, Andy Dingley, Chaddy, Denelson83, Dfddtdt, Duduziq, Emerentia, Fry1989, Gabbe, Giro720, Gurch, Hedwig in Washington, Homo lupus, Illegitimate Barrister, Jo Shigeru, Juiced lemon, Kimjiho2015, Klemen Kocjancic, Mattes, Neq00, Paul 012, Perhelion, Rugby471, Sahapon-krit hellokitty, Siebrand, TOR, Teetaweepo, Xiengyod~commonswiki, Yann, Zscout370, Δ, 28 anonymous edits 104

Image *Source:* https://en.wikipedia.org/w/index.php?title=File:Flag_of_Singapore.svg *License:* Public Domain *Contributors:* Various 104

Image *Source:* https://en.wikipedia.org/w/index.php?title=File:Flag_of_the_Philippines.svg *License:* Public Domain *Contributors:* User:Achim1999 104

Figure 45 *Source:* https://en.wikipedia.org/w/index.php?title=File:US_military_bases_in_Germany.svg *License:* GNU Free Documentation License *Contributors:* Rama 105

Image *Source:* https://en.wikipedia.org/w/index.php?title=File:Flag_of_Germany.svg *License:* Public Domain *Contributors:* Anomie, Jo-Jo Eumerus 104

Image *Source:* https://en.wikipedia.org/w/index.php?title=File:Flag_of_Italy.svg *License:* Public Domain *Contributors:* Anomie, Jo-Jo Eumerus 104

Image *Source:* https://en.wikipedia.org/w/index.php?title=File:Flag_of_the_United_Kingdom.svg *License:* Public Domain *Contributors:* Anomie, Good Olfactory, Jo-Jo Eumerus, MSGJ, Mifter 104

Image *Source:* https://en.wikipedia.org/w/index.php?title=File:Flag_of_Spain.svg *License:* Public Domain *Contributors:* Anomie, Jo-Jo Eumerus, Topbanana 104

Image *Source:* https://en.wikipedia.org/w/index.php?title=File:Flag_of_Belgium_(civil).svg *License:* Public Domain *Contributors:* Allforrous, Andres gb.ldc, Bean49, Cathy Richards, David Descamps, Dbenbenn, Denelson83, Evanc0912, FreshCorp619, Fry1989, Gabriel trzy, Howcome, IvanOS, Jdx, Mimich, Ms2ger, Nightstallion, Oreo Priest, Pitke, Ricordisamoa, Rocket000, Rodejong, Sarang, SiBr4, Sir Iain, ThomasPusch, Warddr, Zscout370, 15 anonymous edits 104

Image *Source:* https://en.wikipedia.org/w/index.php?title=File:Flag_of_the_Netherlands.svg *License:* Public Domain *Contributors:* Zscout370 104

Image *Source:* https://en.wikipedia.org/w/index.php?title=File:Flag_of_Greece.svg *License:* Public Domain *Contributors:* (of code) cs:User:-xfi-(talk) 104

Image *Source:* https://en.wikipedia.org/w/index.php?title=File:Flag_of_Norway.svg *License:* Public Domain *Contributors:* Dbenbenn 104

Image *Source:* https://en.wikipedia.org/w/index.php?title=File:Flag_of_Romania.svg *Contributors:* AdiJapan 104

Image *Source:* https://en.wikipedia.org/w/index.php?title=File:Flag_of_Portugal.svg *License:* Public Domain *Contributors:* Columbano Bordalo Pinheiro (1910; generic design); Vítor Luís Rodrigues; António Martins-Tuválkin (2004; this specific v 104

Image *Source:* https://en.wikipedia.org/w/index.php?title=File:Flag_of_Hungary.svg *License:* Public Domain *Contributors:* SKopp 104

Image *Source:* https://en.wikipedia.org/w/index.php?title=File:Flag_of_Poland.svg *License:* Public Domain *Contributors:* Anomie, Jo-Jo Eumerus, Mifter 104

Image *Source:* https://en.wikipedia.org/w/index.php?title=File:Flag_of_Hawaii.svg *License:* Public Domain *Contributors:* Anime Addict AA, Awg1010, Benzoyl, Clusternote, Cycn, Dbenbenn, Denelson83, Dzordzm, Editor at Large, F. F. Fjodor, Fry1989, Garam, Homo lupus, Hydrargyrum, Jianhui67, KAVEBEAR, Kalathalan, Ludger1961, Manuelt15, Mattes, Mordomo, Nagy, Nightstallion, Ricordisamoa, Serinde, SiBr4, Sinnamon, Svgalbertian, Telim tor, Vonvon, Yaddah, Zscout370, 21 anonymous edits 105

Image *Source:* https://en.wikipedia.org/w/index.php?title=File:Flag_of_Guam.svg *License:* Public Domain *Contributors:* User:Denelson83 ... 105

Image *Source:* https://en.wikipedia.org/w/index.php?title=File:Flag_of_Australia.svg *License:* Public Domain *Contributors:* Anomie, Jo-Jo Eumerus, Mifter 105

Image *Source:* https://en.wikipedia.org/w/index.php?title=File:Flag_of_Bahrain.svg *License:* Public Domain *Contributors:* Source: Drawn by User:SKopp, rewritten by User:Zscout370 106

Image *Source:* https://en.wikipedia.org/w/index.php?title=File:Flag_of_Kuwait.svg *License:* Public Domain *Contributors:* User:SKopp 106

Image *Source:* https://en.wikipedia.org/w/index.php?title=File:Flag_of_Turkey.svg *License:* Public Domain *Contributors:* User:Dbenbenn ... 106

Image *Source:* https://en.wikipedia.org/w/index.php?title=File:Flag_of_Qatar.svg *License:* Public Domain *Contributors:* (of code) 106

Image *Source:* https://en.wikipedia.org/w/index.php?title=File:Flag_of_the_United_Arab_Emirates.svg *License:* Public Domain *Contributors:* Anime Addict AA, Avala, Dbenbenn, Denniss, Duduziq, F l a n k e r, Fry1989, Fukaumi, Gryffindor, Guanaco, Homo lupus, JuTa, Kacir, Klemen Kocjancic, Krun, Ludger1961, Madden, Misisanta97, Neq00, Nightstallion, Piccadilly Circus~commonswiki, Pmsyyz, RamzyAbueita~commonswiki, Ricordisamoa, Schmarrnintelligenz, SiBr4, Zscout370, З.Вукобрат, 5 anonymous edits 106

Image *Source:* https://en.wikipedia.org/w/index.php?title=File:Flag_of_Israel.svg *License:* Public Domain *Contributors:* "The Provisional Council of State Proclamation of the Flag of the State of Israel" of 25 Tishrei 5709 (28 October 1948) 106

Image *Source:* https://en.wikipedia.org/w/index.php?title=File:Flag_of_Saudi_Arabia.svg *License:* Public Domain *Contributors:* Alhadramy Alkendy, Alkari, Ancintosh, Anime Addict AA, AnonMoos, Bobika, Brian Ammon, CommonsDelinker, Cycn, Denelson83, Duduziq, Ekabhishek, Er Komandante, FDRMRZUSA, Fabioravanelli, File Upload Bot (Magnus Manske), Fry1989, Gazimagomedov, Herbythyme, Homo lupus, INeverCry, Itsemurhaja, Jeff G., Klemen Kocjancic, Lokal Profil, Love Krittaya, Love monju, Mattes, Menasim, Meno25, Mnmazur, Mohammed alkhater, Nagy, Nard the Bard, Nightstallion, Palosirkka, Pitke, Pmsyyz, Ranveig, Ratatosk, Reisio, Ricordisamoa, Saibo, Sarang, SiBr4, Wouterhagens, Zscout370, Zyido, 17 anonymous edits 106

Image *Source:* https://en.wikipedia.org/w/index.php?title=File:Flag_of_Egypt.svg *License:* Public Domain *Contributors:* Open Clip Art 106

Image *Source:* https://en.wikipedia.org/w/index.php?title=File:Flag_of_the_British_Indian_Ocean_Territory.svg *License:* Public Domain *Contributors:* Alkari, Benzoyl, CemDemirkartal, Cycn, Cäsium137~commonswiki, David Kernow~commonswiki, Denniss, Fry1989, Gimelthedog, Homo lupus, Hoshie, Leyo, Liftarn, Mattes, Neq00, Nightstallion, Pseudomoi, Pumbaa80, ReconditeRodent, Rodejong, SiBr4, Stefan-Xp, Zaccarias, Zscout370, 2 anonymous edits 106

Image *Source:* https://en.wikipedia.org/w/index.php?title=File:Flag_of_Niger.svg *License:* Public Domain *Contributors:* Made by: Philippe Verdy User:verdy_p, see also fr:Utilisateur:verdy_p. 106

Figure 46 *Source:* https://en.wikipedia.org/w/index.php?title=File:Dunwoody_Gen_Ann_USArmy_2008-11-14-1226691530.jpg *License:* Public Domain *Contributors:* U.S. Army photo 108

Figure 47 *Source:* https//en.wikipedia.org *License:* Public Domain *Contributors:* Fæ, Yann 109

Figure 48 *Source:* https://en.wikipedia.org/w/index.php?title=File:Specialist_Rachel_Carey_prepares_for_a_patrol_from_Towr_Kham_Fire_Base,_Afghanistan.jpg *License:* Public Domain *Contributors:* photo by U.S. Air Force Tech. Sgt. Matt Summers 111

Figure 49 *Source:* https://en.wikipedia.org/w/index.php?title=File:Opha-Mae-Johnson-face.jpg *License:* Public Domain *Contributors:* US Marine Corps ... 114
Figure 50 *Source:* https://en.wikipedia.org/w/index.php?title=File:A_flying_look_into_women's_history_DVIDS80431.jpg *License:* Public Domain *Contributors:* Botteville, Fæ, Kelly, Ruff tuff cream puff ... 116
Figure 51 *Source:* https://en.wikipedia.org/w/index.php?title=File:Admiral_Michelle_J._Howard_VCNO.jpg *License:* Public Domain *Contributors:* Auntof6, GT1976, Illegitimate Barrister, Maliepa, Morio, Neovu79, Senator2029 ... 119
Image *Source:* https://en.wikipedia.org/w/index.php?title=File:Seving_as_a_wave.jpg *License:* Public Domain *Contributors:* United States Navy 121
Image *Source:* https://en.wikipedia.org/w/index.php?title=File:Waves_recruiting_poster.jpg *License:* Public Domain *Contributors:* United States Navy ... 121
Image *Source:* https://en.wikipedia.org/w/index.php?title=File:Team_sweeping_the_seas.jpg *License:* Public Domain *Contributors:* United States Navy ... 122
Figure 52 *Source:* https://en.wikipedia.org/w/index.php?title=File:Change_of_Command_in_New_Orleans_DVIDS195966.jpg *License:* Public Domain *Contributors:* Fæ, Infrogmation, Kelly ... 123
Image *Source:* https://en.wikipedia.org/w/index.php?title=File:Aviation_Ordnanceman.jpg *License:* Public Domain *Contributors:* United States Navy ... 129
Image *Source:* https://en.wikipedia.org/w/index.php?title=File:Quatermaster_Seaman_Apprentice.jpg *License:* Public Domain *Contributors:* United States Navy ... 129
Image *Source:* https://en.wikipedia.org/w/index.php?title=File:Boatswain's_Mate.jpg *License:* Public Domain *Contributors:* United States Navy 129
Image *Source:* https://en.wikipedia.org/w/index.php?title=File:Sonar_Technician.jpg *License:* Public Domain *Contributors:* United States Navy 130
Figure 53 *Source:* https://en.wikipedia.org/w/index.php?title=File:Wolfenbarger_jc4.jpg *License:* Public Domain *Contributors:* US Air Force 150
Figure 54 *Source:* https://en.wikipedia.org/w/index.php?title=File:Esther_Blake.png *License:* Public Domain *Contributors:* Cobysev, 1 anonymous edits ... 151
Figure 55 *Source:* https://en.wikipedia.org/w/index.php?title=File:Kim_campbell_a10.jpg *License:* Public Domain *Contributors:* SSgt Jason Haag, United States Air Force ... 152
Figure 56 *Source:* https://en.wikipedia.org/w/index.php?title=File:US-O11_insignia.svg *License:* Public Domain *Contributors:* Ipankonin ... 158
Figure 57 *Source:* https://en.wikipedia.org/w/index.php?title=File:Australian_Army_OF-10.svg *Contributors:* User:Sodacan ... 158
Figure 58 *Source:* https://en.wikipedia.org/w/index.php?title=File:Royal_Australian_Navy_OF-10.svg *Contributors:* User:Sodacan ... 159
Figure 59 *Source:* https://en.wikipedia.org/w/index.php?title=File:Australia_RAAF_OF-10.svg *Contributors:* User:Sodacan ... 159
Figure 60 *Source:* https://en.wikipedia.org/w/index.php?title=File:AlmiranteMB.png *Contributors:* User:Carlosvicini ... 159
Figure 61 *Source:* https://en.wikipedia.org/w/index.php?title=File:Marechal.gif *License:* Creative Commons Attribution-Sharealike 3.0 *Contributors:* User:Blackcloud11 ... 159
Figure 62 *Source:* https://en.wikipedia.org/w/index.php?title=File:Marechal_ar.gif *License:* Public Domain *Contributors:* Ministry of Defence of Brazil ... 160
Figure 63 *Source:* https://en.wikipedia.org/w/index.php?title=File:Army-HRV-OF-10.svg *License:* Creative Commons Attribution-Sharealike 3.0 *Contributors:* Conquistador ... 160
Figure 64 *Source:* https://en.wikipedia.org/w/index.php?title=File:Rukav_zimske_odore_admirala_flote_HRM.svg *License:* Creative Commons Attribution-Sharealike 3.0 *Contributors:* Conquistador ... 160
Figure 65 *Source:* https://en.wikipedia.org/w/index.php?title=File:Flag_of_the_Marshal_of_the_Air_Force_(India).svg *License:* Creative Commons Attribution-Sharealike 3.0 *Contributors:* User:Jarrad24k ... 161
Figure 66 *Source:* https://en.wikipedia.org/w/index.php?title=File:Field_Marshal_of_the_Indian_Army.svg *License:* Creative Commons Attribution-Sharealike 3.0 *Contributors:* User:Prez001 ... 162
Figure 67 *Source:* https://en.wikipedia.org/w/index.php?title=File:Marshal_of_the_IAF.png *License:* Creative Commons Attribution 3.0 *Contributors:* Sumanch ... 162
Figure 68 *Source:* https://en.wikipedia.org/w/index.php?title=File:IAF_Marshal_of_the_AF_sleeve.png *License:* Creative Commons Attribution 3.0 *Contributors:* Sumanch ... 162
Figure 69 *Source:* https://en.wikipedia.org/w/index.php?title=File:Jenderal_besar_pdh_ad.png *License:* Creative Commons Attribution-Sharealike 3.0 *Contributors:* Bozky ... 163
Figure 70 *Source:* https://en.wikipedia.org/w/index.php?title=File:Laksamana_besar_pdh_al.png *License:* Creative Commons Attribution-Sharealike 3.0 *Contributors:* Bozky ... 164
Figure 71 *Source:* https://en.wikipedia.org/w/index.php?title=File:Marsekal_besar_pdh_au.png *License:* Creative Commons Attribution-Sharealike 3.0 *Contributors:* Bozky ... 164
Figure 72 *Source:* https://en.wikipedia.org/w/index.php?title=File:Rank_insignia_of_generale_of_the_Army_of_Italy_(1973).svg *License:* GNU Free Documentation License *Contributors:* F l a n k e r ... 164
Figure 73 *Source:* https://en.wikipedia.org/w/index.php?title=File:Rank_insignia_of_ammiraglio_of_the_Italian_Navy.svg *License:* Creative Commons Attribution-Sharealike 3.0 *Contributors:* F l a n k e r ... 165
Figure 74 *Source:* https://en.wikipedia.org/w/index.php?title=File:IT-Airforce-OF-10.png *License:* GNU Free Documentation License *Contributors:* F l a n k e r ... 165
Figure 75 *Source:* https://en.wikipedia.org/w/index.php?title=File:Marszalek_m.png *Contributors:* Blackfish, File Upload Bot (Magnus Manske), HHubi, Mateusz War., OgreBot 2, VanWiel ... 166
Figure 76 *Source:* https://en.wikipedia.org/w/index.php?title=File:Marszałek_Polski.svg *License:* Public Domain *Contributors:* Poznaniak .. 166
Figure 77 *Source:* https://en.wikipedia.org/w/index.php?title=File:23ej.png *License:* Creative Commons Attribution-Sharealike 3.0 *Contributors:* User:Supertoni123 ... 167
Figure 78 *Source:* https://en.wikipedia.org/w/index.php?title=File:1arm.png *License:* Creative Commons Attribution-Sharealike 3.0 *Contributors:* User:Supertoni123 ... 167
Figure 79 *Source:* https://en.wikipedia.org/w/index.php?title=File:1a.png *License:* Creative Commons Attribution-Sharealike 3.0 *Contributors:* User:Supertoni123 ... 167
Figure 80 *Source:* https://en.wikipedia.org/w/index.php?title=File:RTA_OF-10_(Field_Marshal).svg *Contributors:* User:Sodacan ... 168
Figure 81 *Source:* https://en.wikipedia.org/w/index.php?title=File:RTN_OF-10_(Admiral_of_the_Fleet).svg *Contributors:* User:Sodacan ... 168
Figure 82 *Source:* https://en.wikipedia.org/w/index.php?title=File:RTAF_OF-10_(Marshal_of_the_Royal_Thai_Air_Force).svg *Contributors:* User:Sodacan ... 168
Figure 83 *Source:* https://en.wikipedia.org/w/index.php?title=File:British_Royal_Navy_OF-10.svg *Contributors:* User:Sodacan ... 169
Figure 84 *Source:* https://en.wikipedia.org/w/index.php?title=File:British_Royal_Navy_(sleeves)_OF-10.svg *Contributors:* User:Sodacan ... 169
Figure 85 *Source:* https://en.wikipedia.org/w/index.php?title=File:British_Army_OF-10.svg *Contributors:* User:Sodacan ... 169
Figure 86 *Source:* https://en.wikipedia.org/w/index.php?title=File:British_Royal_Marines_OF-10.png *Contributors:* User:Hammersfan ... 169
Figure 87 *Source:* https://en.wikipedia.org/w/index.php?title=File:British_RAF_OF-10_(ceremonial_shoulder_board).svg *Contributors:* User:Sodacan ... 170
Figure 88 *Source:* https://en.wikipedia.org/w/index.php?title=File:British_RAF_OF-10.svg *Contributors:* User:Sodacan ... 170
Figure 89 *Source:* https://en.wikipedia.org/w/index.php?title=File:US_Navy_O11_insignia.svg *License:* Public Domain *Contributors:* Ipankonin 171
Figure 90 *Source:* https://en.wikipedia.org/w/index.php?title=File:Army-USA-OF-10.svg *License:* Public Domain *Contributors:* Ipankonin . 172
Figure 91 *Source:* https://en.wikipedia.org/w/index.php?title=File:US_Air_Force_O11_shoulderboard_with_seal.svg *License:* Public Domain *Contributors:* US Air Force ... 172
Figure 92 *Source:* https//en.wikipedia.org *License:* Public Domain *Contributors:* Bahamut0013, BotMultichill, BotMultichillT, Closeapple, Dhfort, Docu, Esrever, Fmjohnson, Gbawden, Manxruler, Neovu79, Reguyla, Ricjac~commonswiki, TCY, 12 anonymous edits ... 174
Figure 93 *Source:* https://en.wikipedia.org/w/index.php?title=File:GCCMAP.png *Contributors:* User:DOD Updater Private ... 174
Image *Source:* https://en.wikipedia.org/w/index.php?title=File:Dagger-14-plain.png *License:* Creative Commons Zero *Contributors:* RexxS .. 174
Image *Source:* https://en.wikipedia.org/w/index.php?title=File:USEUCOM.svg *License:* Public Domain *Contributors:* Not specified ... 175
Image *Source:* https://en.wikipedia.org/w/index.php?title=File:United_States_Pacific_Command.png *License:* Public Domain *Contributors:* US Gov-Military ... 175
Image *Source:* https://en.wikipedia.org/w/index.php?title=File:Seal_of_the_United_States_Southern_Command.svg *License:* Public Domain *Contributors:* Auntof6, Avron, Connormah, Illegitimate Barrister, Vantey ... 175
Image *Source:* https://en.wikipedia.org/w/index.php?title=File:Seal_of_the_United_States_Cyber_Command.svg *License:* Public Domain *Contributors:* United States Cyber Command ... 175
Image *Source:* https://en.wikipedia.org/w/index.php?title=File:United_States_Special_Operations_Command_Insignia.svg *License:* Public Domain *Contributors:* united states army contributor ... 175
Image *Source:* https://en.wikipedia.org/w/index.php?title=File:USSTRATCOM.svg *Contributors:* - ... 175
Image *Source:* https://en.wikipedia.org/w/index.php?title=File:US-TRANSCOM-Emblem.svg *License:* Public Domain *Contributors:* U.S. Government. The original emblem was designed by the U.S. Army Institute of Heraldry. ... 175

Image *Source:* https://en.wikipedia.org/w/index.php?title=File:Seal_of_the_United_States_Africa_Command.svg *License:* Public Domain *Contributors:* Africom_emblem.JPG: n/a derivative work: Bileininger (talk) ... 187
Image *Source:* https://en.wikipedia.org/w/index.php?title=File:United_States_Department_of_Defense_Seal.svg *License:* Public Domain *Contributors:* United States Department of Defense ... 187
Figure 94 *Source:* https://en.wikipedia.org/w/index.php?title=File:Unified_Combatant_Commands_map.png *License:* GNU Free Documentation License *Contributors:* Lencer ... 190
Figure 95 *Source:* https://en.wikipedia.org/w/index.php?title=File:USAFRICOM_United_States_Africa_Command_Map_Draft.jpg *License:* Public Domain *Contributors:* United States Department of Defense ... 191
Image *Source:* https://en.wikipedia.org/w/index.php?title=File:U.S._Army_Africa_Shoulder_Sleeve_Insignia.jpg *License:* Public Domain *Contributors:* Auntof6, Marinaio56, NJR ZA, USarmyafrica ... 194
Image *Source:* https://en.wikipedia.org/w/index.php?title=File:NavyAfrica.png *License:* Public Domain *Contributors:* U.S. Navy ... 195
Image *Source:* https://en.wikipedia.org/w/index.php?title=File:US_Air_Forces_Africa_(emblem).png *License:* Public Domain *Contributors:* U.S. Air Force ... 196
Image *Source:* https://en.wikipedia.org/w/index.php?title=File:U.S._Marine_Corps_Forces_Africa.png *License:* Public Domain *Contributors:* U.S. Marine Corps ... 197
Image *Source:* https://en.wikipedia.org/w/index.php?title=File:SOCAFRICA_Logo.jpg *License:* Public Domain *Contributors:* Jsrawlinson, Sanandros, Wieralee ... 198
Image *Source:* https://en.wikipedia.org/w/index.php?title=File:CJTF-HOA.png *Contributors:* - ... 199
Image *Source:* https://en.wikipedia.org/w/index.php?title=File:General_Kip_Ward_November_2009.jpg *License:* Public Domain *Contributors:* Auntof6, GT1976, Illegitimate Barrister, Magog the Ogre, Neelix, Runningboards, Waldir, ~riley, Érico ... 200
Image *Source:* https://en.wikipedia.org/w/index.php?title=File:GEN_Carter_F.Ham_2011.jpg *License:* Public Domain *Contributors:* United States Department of Defense ... 200
Image *Source:* https://en.wikipedia.org/w/index.php?title=File:General_David_M_Rodriguez_USAFRICOM.jpg *License:* Public Domain *Contributors:* Articseahorse, Danielmendez411, EricSerge, Neovu79 ... 200
Image *Source:* https://en.wikipedia.org/w/index.php?title=File:Waldhauser_Africom_2.jpg *License:* Public Domain *Contributors:* Auntof6, Claudevsq, GT1976, HerrSonderbar, Maliepa, Reguyla, Ruff tuff cream puff, Waldir ... 200
Image *Source:* https://en.wikipedia.org/w/index.php?title=File:Official_CENTCOM_Seal.png *License:* Public Domain *Contributors:* Andrewaranda, Avron ... 202
Image *Source:* https://en.wikipedia.org/w/index.php?title=File:Central_Command_insignia.jpg *License:* Public Domain *Contributors:* U. S. Government ... 203
Figure 96 *Source:* https://en.wikipedia.org/w/index.php?title=File:YPG_and_US_army_Hassaka_1-5-2017.jpg *Contributors:* Tan Khaerr, Themightyquill ... 206
Figure 97 *Source:* https://en.wikipedia.org/w/index.php?title=File:Refueling_the_fight_against_terrorism_170103-F-XF291-0016.jpg *License:* Public Domain *Contributors:* Fæ, Rcbutcher ... 208
Figure 98 *Source:* https://en.wikipedia.org/w/index.php?title=File:Unified_Combatant_Commands_map.png *License:* GNU Free Documentation License *Contributors:* Lencer ... 210
Image *Source:* https://en.wikipedia.org/w/index.php?title=File:General_Robert_Kingston,_official_military_photo,_1984.JPEG *License:* Public Domain *Contributors:* RUSSELL ROEDERER ... 211
Image *Source:* https://en.wikipedia.org/w/index.php?title=File:General_George_Crist,_official_military_photo,_1985.JPEG *License:* Public Domain *Contributors:* James P. Vineyard ... 211
Image *Source:* https://en.wikipedia.org/w/index.php?title=File:NormanSchwarzkopf.jpg *License:* Public Domain *Contributors:* RUSSELL ROEDERER ... 211
Image *Source:* https://en.wikipedia.org/w/index.php?title=File:Joseph_Hoar_official_military_photo.jpg *License:* Public Domain *Contributors:* DoD ... 211
Image *Source:* https://en.wikipedia.org/w/index.php?title=File:General_Binford_Peay,_official_military_photo,_1991.jpg *License:* Public Domain *Contributors:* RUSSELL F. ROEDERER ... 211
Image *Source:* https://en.wikipedia.org/w/index.php?title=File:Anthony_Zinni.jpg *License:* Public Domain *Contributors:* GrummelJS, KTo288, Nobunaga24, Tom ... 211
Image *Source:* https://en.wikipedia.org/w/index.php?title=File:TommyFranks.jpg *License:* Public Domain *Contributors:* Helene C. Stikkel ... 211
Image *Source:* https://en.wikipedia.org/w/index.php?title=File:John_Abizaid.jpg *License:* Public Domain *Contributors:* United States Army ... 211
Image *Source:* https://en.wikipedia.org/w/index.php?title=File:ADM_Fallon_Portrait.jpg *License:* Public Domain *Contributors:* Department of Defense ... 211
Image *Source:* https://en.wikipedia.org/w/index.php?title=File:General_Martin_E._Dempsey.jpg *License:* Public Domain *Contributors:* User:BigBrad21083 ... 211
Image *Source:* https://en.wikipedia.org/w/index.php?title=File:GEN_David_H_Petraeus_-_Uniform_Class_A.jpg *License:* Public Domain *Contributors:* SSgt Bradley Lail, USAF, Official Photographer, US Central Command, Tampa, Florida ... 211
Image *Source:* https://en.wikipedia.org/w/index.php?title=File:LtGen_John_R._Allen_USMC.jpg *License:* Public Domain *Contributors:* United States Marine Corps photo ... 211
Image *Source:* https://en.wikipedia.org/w/index.php?title=File:Mattis_Centcom_2009.jpg *License:* Public Domain *Contributors:* ATX-NL, Athaenara, Gbawden, Infrogmation, MB298, OgreBot 2, Runningboards, ShinePhantom, Wwongbc ... 212
Image *Source:* https://en.wikipedia.org/w/index.php?title=File:Austin_2013_2.jpg *License:* Public Domain *Contributors:* U. S. Central Command 212
Image *Source:* https://en.wikipedia.org/w/index.php?title=File:General_Joseph_L._Votel_(USCENTCOM).jpg *License:* Public Domain *Contributors:* Howard61313, INeverCry, Neovu79, 1 anonymous edits ... 212
Image *Source:* https://en.wikipedia.org/w/index.php?title=File:Streamer_JMUA.PNG *Contributors:* USMC employee ... 212
Figure 99 *Source:* https://en.wikipedia.org/w/index.php?title=File:Unified_Combatant_Commands_map.png *License:* GNU Free Documentation License *Contributors:* Lencer ... 215
Figure 100 *Source:* https://en.wikipedia.org/w/index.php?title=File:EUCOM_Hqdrs_-_IG_Farben_Bldg.,_Frankfurt_(ca_1949-1952).jpg *License:* Public Domain *Contributors:* Charles C Van Cott, U.S. military attaché ... 216
Figure 101 *Source:* https://en.wikipedia.org/w/index.php?title=File:Cold_War_units_in_West_Germany.png *License:* Public domain *Contributors:* Ron Mihalko - Mihalko at en.wikipedia ... 218
Image *Source:* https://en.wikipedia.org/w/index.php?title=File:Matthew_Ridgway.jpg *License:* Public Domain *Contributors:* ArjanH, Benchill, Florival fr, Rmhermen, Yelm ... 226
Image *Source:* https://en.wikipedia.org/w/index.php?title=File:Alfred_W._Gruenther_1946.jpg *License:* Public Domain *Contributors:* United States Navy ... 226
Image *Source:* https//en.wikipedia.org *License:* Public Domain *Contributors:* National Archives and Records Administration. Office of Presidential Libraries. Harry S. Truman Library (04/01/1985 -) ... 226
Image *Source:* https://en.wikipedia.org/w/index.php?title=File:Lyman_L._Lemnitzer.jpg *License:* Public Domain *Contributors:* AusTerrapin, Fæ, GrummelJS, Howard61313, JD554, Jan Arkesteijn, Nobunaga24, Sanandros ... 227
Image *Source:* https://en.wikipedia.org/w/index.php?title=File:Andrew_Goodpaster_portrait.jpg *License:* Public Domain *Contributors:* US Army 227
Image *Source:* https://en.wikipedia.org/w/index.php?title=File:General_Alexander_M._Haig,_Jr.jpg *License:* Public Domain *Contributors:* United States Army ... 227
Image *Source:* https://en.wikipedia.org/w/index.php?title=File:Bernard_W._Rogers.jpg *License:* Public Domain *Contributors:* GrummelJS, Materialscientist, Nobunaga24 ... 227
Image *Source:* https://en.wikipedia.org/w/index.php?title=File:John_Galvin,_official_military_photo,_1991.JPEG *License:* Public Domain *Contributors:* RUSSELL F. ROEDERER ... 227
Image *Source:* https://en.wikipedia.org/w/index.php?title=File:John_Shalikashvili.jpg *License:* Public Domain *Contributors:* Emx~commonswiki, GeorgHH, Nobunaga24, OgreBot 2 ... 227
Image *Source:* https://en.wikipedia.org/w/index.php?title=File:George_Joulwan,_official_military_photo,_1991.JPEG *License:* Public Domain *Contributors:* RUSSELL F. ROEDERER ... 227
Image *Source:* https://en.wikipedia.org/w/index.php?title=File:General_Wesley_Clark_official_photograph,_edited.jpg *License:* Public Domain *Contributors:* General_Wesley_Clark_official_photograph.jpg: United States Army derivative work: Greg A L (talk) ... 227
Image *Source:* https://en.wikipedia.org/w/index.php?title=File:Joseph_Ralston,_official_military_photo.jpg *License:* Public Domain *Contributors:* GrummelJS, Nobunaga24, Ricjac~commonswiki, Tom ... 227
Image *Source:* https://en.wikipedia.org/w/index.php?title=File:James_L._Jones_2.jpg *License:* Public Domain *Contributors:* BotMultichill, BotMultichillT, Dbenbenn, GT1976, Gage, GrummelJS, Illegitimate Barrister, Väsk ... 227

Image *Source:* https://en.wikipedia.org/w/index.php?title=File:Bantz_J._Craddock_EUCOM.jpg *License:* Public Domain *Contributors:* Articseahorse, Auntof6, Cirt, Claudevsq, Flor!an, GT1976, GrummelJS, Illegitimate Barrister, Innotata, Martin H., Nobunaga24, Sandstein, Tom, Vantey, Waldir, Zhuyifei1999, ∼riley 227

Image *Source:* https://en.wikipedia.org/w/index.php?title=File:Stavridis_EUCOM.jpg *License:* Public Domain *Contributors:* U. S. Department of Defense 227

Image *Source:* https://en.wikipedia.org/w/index.php?title=File:Breedlove_2013_HR.jpg *License:* Public Domain *Contributors:* NATO 227

Image *Source:* https://en.wikipedia.org/w/index.php?title=File:Scaparrotti_EUCOM.jpg *License:* Public Domain *Contributors:* Basvb, Claudevsq, GT1976, HerrSonderbar 228

Image *Source:* https://en.wikipedia.org/w/index.php?title=File:Emblem_of_the_United_States_Pacific_Command.png *License:* Public Domain *Contributors:* USPACOM 229

Image *Source:* https://en.wikipedia.org/w/index.php?title=File:USARPAC_insignia.svg *License:* Public Domain *Contributors:* Life of Riley 231

Image *Source:* https://en.wikipedia.org/w/index.php?title=File:Seal_of_the_Commander_of_the_United_States_Pacific_Fleet.svg *License:* Public Domain *Contributors:* US Navy 231

Image *Source:* https://en.wikipedia.org/w/index.php?title=File:Pacific_Air_Forces.png *License:* Public Domain *Contributors:* United States Air Force (User:Pmsyyz converted from JPEG to PNG, added transparency, resized, indexed color) 232

Image *Source:* https://en.wikipedia.org/w/index.php?title=File:Seal_of_U.S._Marine_Corps_Forces,_Pacific.png *License:* Public Domain *Contributors:* U.S. Marine Corps Forces, Pacific 232

Image *Source:* https://en.wikipedia.org/w/index.php?title=File:Seal_of_United_States_Forces_Japan.png *License:* Public Domain *Contributors:* United_States_Forces_Japan.gif: U.S. Government derivative work: Beao 232

Image *Source:* https://en.wikipedia.org/w/index.php?title=File:USFK_Logo.svg *License:* Public Domain *Contributors:* Connormah, Gbarta, Howard61313 232

Image *Source:* https://en.wikipedia.org/w/index.php?title=File:Special_Operations_Command_Pacific_insignia.jpg *License:* Public Domain *Contributors:* Dainomite, JotaCartas, Karlfk, Sanandros 232

Image *Source:* https://en.wikipedia.org/w/index.php?title=File:JIOC_Symbol.png *License:* Public Domain *Contributors:* Cburris593 232

Image *Source:* https://en.wikipedia.org/w/index.php?title=File:Seal_of_the_Center_for_Excellence_in_Disaster_Management_and_Humanitarian_Assistance.png *License:* Public Domain *Contributors:* Auntof6, BotMultichill, Garberino, Howcheng, Illegitimate Barrister 232

Image *Source:* https://en.wikipedia.org/w/index.php?title=File:Seal_of_Joint_Interagency_Task_Force_West.png *License:* Public Domain *Contributors:* User:JIATFWEST 233

Image *Source:* https://en.wikipedia.org/w/index.php?title=File:CINCPAC_ADM_Towers.jpg *License:* Public Domain *Contributors:* USN 239

Image *Source:* https://en.wikipedia.org/w/index.php?title=File:CINCPAC_ADM_Denfeld.jpg *License:* Public Domain *Contributors:* USN 239

Image *Source:* https://en.wikipedia.org/w/index.php?title=File:CINCPAC_ADM_Ramsey.jpg *License:* Public Domain *Contributors:* USN 239

Image *Source:* https://en.wikipedia.org/w/index.php?title=File:CINCPAC_ADM_Radford.jpg *License:* Public Domain *Contributors:* USN 239

Image *Source:* https://en.wikipedia.org/w/index.php?title=File:CINCPAC_ADM_Stump.jpg *License:* Public Domain *Contributors:* USN 239

Image *Source:* https://en.wikipedia.org/w/index.php?title=File:CINCPAC_ADM_Felt.jpg *License:* Public Domain *Contributors:* USN 240

Image *Source:* https://en.wikipedia.org/w/index.php?title=File:CINCPAC_ADM_Sharp.jpg *License:* Public Domain *Contributors:* USN 240

Image *Source:* https://en.wikipedia.org/w/index.php?title=File:CINCPAC_ADM_McCain.jpg *License:* Public Domain *Contributors:* USN 240

Image *Source:* https://en.wikipedia.org/w/index.php?title=File:CINCPAC_ADM_Gayler.jpg *License:* Public Domain *Contributors:* USN 240

Image *Source:* https://en.wikipedia.org/w/index.php?title=File:CINCPAC_ADM_Weisner.jpg *License:* Public Domain *Contributors:* USN 240

Image *Source:* https://en.wikipedia.org/w/index.php?title=File:CINCPAC_ADM_Long.jpg *License:* Public Domain *Contributors:* USN 240

Image *Source:* https://en.wikipedia.org/w/index.php?title=File:USCINCPAC_ADM_Crowe.jpg *License:* Public Domain *Contributors:* USN 240

Image *Source:* https://en.wikipedia.org/w/index.php?title=File:USCINCPAC_ADM_Hays.jpg *License:* Public Domain *Contributors:* USN 240

Image *Source:* https://en.wikipedia.org/w/index.php?title=File:USCINCPAC_ADM_Hardisty.jpg *License:* Public Domain *Contributors:* USN 240

Image *Source:* https://en.wikipedia.org/w/index.php?title=File:USCINCPAC_ADM_Larson.jpg *License:* Public Domain *Contributors:* USN 240

Image *Source:* https://en.wikipedia.org/w/index.php?title=File:USCINCPAC_ADM_Macke.jpg *License:* Public Domain *Contributors:* USN 241

Image *Source:* https://en.wikipedia.org/w/index.php?title=File:USCINCPAC_ADM_Prueher.jpg *License:* Public Domain *Contributors:* USN 241

Image *Source:* https://en.wikipedia.org/w/index.php?title=File:USCINCPAC_ADM_Blair.jpg *License:* Public Domain *Contributors:* USN 241

Image *Source:* https://en.wikipedia.org/w/index.php?title=File:Thomas_fargo.jpg *License:* Public Domain *Contributors:* Cla68, DanMS, Martin H., Nobunaga24 241

Image *Source:* https://en.wikipedia.org/w/index.php?title=File:CDRUSPACOM_ADM_Fallon.jpg *License:* Public Domain *Contributors:* USN 241

Image *Source:* https://en.wikipedia.org/w/index.php?title=File:Timothy_J._Keating_2007_2.jpg *License:* Public Domain *Contributors:* U.S. Navy 241

Image *Source:* https://en.wikipedia.org/w/index.php?title=File:CDRUSPACOM_ADM_Willard.jpg *License:* Public Domain *Contributors:* U.S. Navy 241

Image *Source:* https://en.wikipedia.org/w/index.php?title=File:CDRUSPACOM_ADM_Locklear.jpg *License:* Public Domain *Contributors:* Cpl. Demetrius Munnerlyn, U.S. Marine Corps 241

Image *Source:* https://en.wikipedia.org/w/index.php?title=File:Harris_Jr_PACOM_2015.jpg *License:* Public Domain *Contributors:* U.S. Navy 241

Image *Source:* https://en.wikipedia.org/w/index.php?title=File:Davidson_PACOM.jpg *License:* Public Domain *Contributors:* Claudevsq, Maliepa 242

Figure 102 *Source:* https://en.wikipedia.org/w/index.php?title=File:Unified_Combatant_Commands_map.png *License:* GNU Free Documentation License *Contributors:* Lencer 244

Image *Source:* https://en.wikipedia.org/w/index.php?title=File:Eberhart_re.jpg *License:* Public Domain *Contributors:* GrummelJS, Ricjac∼commonswiki 246

Image *Source:* https://en.wikipedia.org/w/index.php?title=File:US_Navy_041105-D-0000X-001_Adm._Timothy_J._Keating.jpg *License:* Public Domain *Contributors:* BotMultichillT, Sanandros 246

Image *Source:* https://en.wikipedia.org/w/index.php?title=File:Victor_E._Renuart_Jr._2010.jpg *License:* Public Domain *Contributors:* U. S. Air Force 246

Image *Source:* https://en.wikipedia.org/w/index.php?title=File:Winnefeld_2010_2.jpg *License:* Public Domain *Contributors:* U. S. Navy. 246

Image *Source:* https://en.wikipedia.org/w/index.php?title=File:Jacoby_2013.jpg *License:* Public Domain *Contributors:* USNORTHCOM 246

Image *Source:* https://en.wikipedia.org/w/index.php?title=File:Gortney2014.jpg *Contributors:* HerrSonderbar, Maliepa, Neovu79, Ubcwwong 246

Image *Source:* https://en.wikipedia.org/w/index.php?title=File:Robinson_NORTHCOM.jpg *License:* Public Domain *Contributors:* Claudevsq, Corkythehornetfan, HerrSonderbar, Ruff tuff cream puff 247

Image *Source:* https://en.wikipedia.org/w/index.php?title=File:Terrence_J._O'Shaughnessy_NORAD.jpg *License:* Public Domain *Contributors:* Claudevsq, Connormah, Corkythehornetfan, Maliepa 247

Figure 103 *Source:* https://en.wikipedia.org/w/index.php?title=File:Unified_Combatant_Commands_map.png *License:* GNU Free Documentation License *Contributors:* Lencer 250

Figure 104 *Source:* https://en.wikipedia.org/w/index.php?title=File:Southcom_aor.jpg *License:* Public Domain *Contributors:* Auntof6, Avron, Babelia, File Upload Bot (Magnus Manske), GiW, JMCC1, Nachcommonsverschieber, NeverDoING, OgreBot 2, Sanandros, 1 anonymous edits 251

Image *Source:* https://en.wikipedia.org/w/index.php?title=File:United_States_Army_South_CSIB.gif *License:* Public Domain *Contributors:* CORNELIUSSEON, File Upload Bot (Magnus Manske), Illegitimate Barrister, Nobunaga24 252

Image *Source:* https://en.wikipedia.org/w/index.php?title=File:USAF_-_Air_Forces_Southern.png *License:* Public Domain *Contributors:* United States Air Force 252

Image *Source:* https://en.wikipedia.org/w/index.php?title=File:NAVSO_4thFleet_Two_Logo_Image_103116.png *Contributors:* DerBuckesfelder-Sockpuppet, MarcoAurelio, Wimbishmike, ZiaLater 253

Image *Source:* https://en.wikipedia.org/w/index.php?title=File:USMARFORSOUTH.png *License:* Public Domain *Contributors:* Avron, Butko, FieldMarine, MGA73bot2, OgreBot 2, ZiaLater 254

Image *Source:* https://en.wikipedia.org/w/index.php?title=File:SOCSOUTH.jpg *License:* Public Domain *Contributors:* Athaenara, Avron, Butko, Lineagegeek, MGA73bot2, OgreBot 2, Ricjac∼commonswiki, Sanandros 255

Figure 105 *Source:* https://en.wikipedia.org/w/index.php?title=File:Honduran_TIGRES_Commandos_graduate_140619-A-YI554-371.jpg *License:* Public Domain *Contributors:* Fæ, Sanandros 255

Image *Source:* https://en.wikipedia.org/w/index.php?title=File:JTFB_logo.jpg *License:* Public Domain *Contributors:* Avron, Butko, LittleWink, MGA73bot2, OgreBot 2, Ricjac∼commonswiki, Takeaway 256

Image *Source:* https://en.wikipedia.org/w/index.php?title=File:JTFGTMO_logo.png *License:* Public Domain *Contributors:* ZiaLater 257

Image *Source:* https://en.wikipedia.org/w/index.php?title=File:JIATFSOUTH.png *License:* Public Domain *Contributors:* ZiaLater 257

Image *Source:* https://en.wikipedia.org/w/index.php?title=File:GEN_O'Meara,_Andrew_Pick_cropped.jpg *License:* Public Domain *Contributors:* GEN_O'Meara,_Andrew_Pick.jpg: US Army derivative work: Connormah (talk | contribs) 264

Image *Source:* https://en.wikipedia.org/w/index.php?title=File:Robert_W._Porter,_Jr._portrait.jpg *License:* Public Domain *Contributors:* Quibik 264

Image *Source:* https://en.wikipedia.org/w/index.php?title=File:Gen_George_R_Mather.jpg *License:* Public Domain *Contributors:* US Army 264

Image *Source:* https://en.wikipedia.org/w/index.php?title=File:GEN_Underwood,_George_V_Jr.jpg *License:* Public Domain *Contributors:* US Army . . . 264
Image *Source:* https://en.wikipedia.org/w/index.php?title=File:William_B_Rosson.jpg *License:* Public Domain *Contributors:* User:Nobunaga24 264
Image *Source:* https://en.wikipedia.org/w/index.php?title=File:Portrait_gray.png *Contributors:* User:Judicieux, User:ויקיג'אנק . . . 264
Image *Source:* https://en.wikipedia.org/w/index.php?title=File:Wallace_H._Nutting,_official_military_photo_portrait,_1983.JPEG *License:* Public Domain *Contributors:* Russell Roederer . . . 264
Image *Source:* https://en.wikipedia.org/w/index.php?title=File:GEN_Gorman,_Paul_Francis.jpg *License:* Public Domain *Contributors:* US Army 264
Image *Source:* https://en.wikipedia.org/w/index.php?title=File:Frederick_Woerner.jpg *License:* Public Domain *Contributors:* Articseahorse, Auntof6, Cirt, Connormah, File Upload Bot (Magnus Manske), GT1976, Hohum, Illegitimate Barrister, Nobunaga24, OgreBot 2, Waldir, ~riley . . . 265
Image *Source:* https://en.wikipedia.org/w/index.php?title=File:Maxwell_R_Thurman.jpg *License:* Public Domain *Contributors:* U.S. Army . . . 265
Image *Source:* https://en.wikipedia.org/w/index.php?title=File:Barry_McCaffrey.jpg *License:* Public Domain *Contributors:* United States Army 265
Image *Source:* https://en.wikipedia.org/w/index.php?title=File:James_Perkins.jpg *License:* Public Domain *Contributors:* Benchill, GrummelJS, O (bot) . . . 265
Image *Source:* https://en.wikipedia.org/w/index.php?title=File:General_Wesley_Clark_official_photograph.jpg *License:* Public Domain *Contributors:* United States Army . . . 265
Image *Source:* https://en.wikipedia.org/w/index.php?title=File:Charles_E._Wilhelm.jpg *License:* Public Domain *Contributors:* United States Department of Defense . . . 265
Image *Source:* https://en.wikipedia.org/w/index.php?title=File:Peter_Pace_official_portrait.jpg *License:* Public Domain *Contributors:* DoD photo by Monica King, U.S. Army. (Released) — see XMP info attached to original photo, still available at archive.o . . . 265
Image *Source:* https://en.wikipedia.org/w/index.php?title=File:OfficialPhoto_SpeerGaryD_ACU_2006-05.JPG *License:* Public Domain *Contributors:* BotAdventures, GrummelJS, Klemen Kocjancic, Nobunaga24, O (bot) . . . 266
Image *Source:* https://en.wikipedia.org/w/index.php?title=File:James_T_Hill.jpg *License:* Public Domain *Contributors:* U.S. Army . . . 266
Image *Source:* https://en.wikipedia.org/w/index.php?title=File:Bantz_J._Craddock.jpg *License:* Public Domain *Contributors:* Articseahorse, Auntof6, Cirt, Flor!an, GT1976, GrummelJS, Illegitimate Barrister, Innotata, Martin H., Nobunaga24, Tom, Waldir, ~riley . . . 266
Image *Source:* https://en.wikipedia.org/w/index.php?title=File:James_G._Stavridis.jpg *License:* Public Domain *Contributors:* Benchill, Connormah, File Upload Bot (Magnus Manske), GrummelJS, Nobunaga24, ~riley . . . 266
Image *Source:* https://en.wikipedia.org/w/index.php?title=File:DouglasFraserUSAF.jpg *License:* Public Domain *Contributors:* USAF . . . 266
Image *Source:* https://en.wikipedia.org/w/index.php?title=File:John_F._Kelly,_2012.jpg *License:* Public Domain *Contributors:* U.S. Department of Defense . . . 266
Image *Source:* https://en.wikipedia.org/w/index.php?title=File:Tidd_2016.jpg *Contributors:* - . . . 266
Image *Source:* https://en.wikipedia.org/w/index.php?title=File:Ribbon_Bar_of_the_Order_of_Saint_Charles_(Colombia).svg *License:* Creative Commons Attribution-Sharealike 3.0 *Contributors:* User:Angel paez . . . 266
Image *Source:* https://en.wikipedia.org/w/index.php?title=File:General_Keith_B._Alexander_in_service_uniform.jpg *License:* Public Domain *Contributors:* AdamBMorgan, Auntof6, GT1976, Illegitimate Barrister, Morio, Neovu79, OgreBot 2, Stuchka, Waldir, ~riley . . . 273
Image *Source:* https://en.wikipedia.org/w/index.php?title=File:LtGen_Jon_M._Davis,_USMC.jpg *Contributors:* AdamBMorgan, Auntof6, Morio, Neovu79 . . . 273
Image *Source:* https://en.wikipedia.org/w/index.php?title=File:Rogers_2018.jpg *License:* Public Domain *Contributors:* Claudevsq, Neovu79 . 273
Image *Source:* https://en.wikipedia.org/w/index.php?title=File:General_Paul_M._Nakasone_(NSA).jpg *License:* Public Domain *Contributors:* Corkythehornetfan, Neovu79 . . . 273
Figure 106 *Source:* https://en.wikipedia.org/w/index.php?title=File:Barry_Goldwater.jpg *License:* Public Domain *Contributors:* User:Beachanchor, cropped and retouched by Kjetil_r . . . 276
Figure 107 *Source:* https://en.wikipedia.org/w/index.php?title=File:GEN_James_Lindsay_1986.jpg *License:* Public Domain *Contributors:* Russell Roederer . . . 278
Figure 108 *Source:* https://en.wikipedia.org/w/index.php?title=File:MH-60_Blackhawk_landing_on_Hercules.JPG *Contributors:* PHCS TERRY MITCHELL, USN . . . 279
Figure 109 *Source:* https://en.wikipedia.org/w/index.php?title=File:Operation_Nimble_Archer_DN-SC-88-01042.jpg *License:* Public Domain *Contributors:* PH3 Henry Cleveland, USN . . . 280
Figure 110 *Source:* https://en.wikipedia.org/w/index.php?title=File:75th_Ranger_Regiment_Bravo_Company_3rd_Batallion_Somalia_1993.jpg *License:* Public Domain *Contributors:* Articseahorse, Avron, BotMultichill, File Upload Bot (Magnus Manske), FilleDaaahl, Hohum, KTo288, LangerFuchs, Mattes, Multichill, OgreBot 2, Rocket000 . . . 283
Figure 111 *Source:* https://en.wikipedia.org/w/index.php?title=File:Battle_of_mogadishu_map_of_city.png *License:* Public Domain *Contributors:* http://www.army.mil/cmh/ . . . 284
Figure 112 *Source:* https://en.wikipedia.org/w/index.php?title=File:Special_Forces_Medic_in_Afghanistan.jpg *License:* Public Domain *Contributors:* Steve Hebert . . . 287
Figure 113 *Source:* https//en.wikipedia.org *License:* Public Domain *Contributors:* Rupert loup, SantiLak, TheAmerikaner . . . 288
Figure 114 *Source:* https://en.wikipedia.org/w/index.php?title=File:JSOC.png *Contributors:* - . . . 289
Figure 115 *Source:* https://en.wikipedia.org/w/index.php?title=File:US_Army_Special_Operations_Command_SSI.svg *Contributors:* - . . . 292
Image *Source:* https://en.wikipedia.org/w/index.php?title=File:US_Army_Special_Forces_SSI.png *Contributors:* - . . . 291
Image *Source:* https://en.wikipedia.org/w/index.php?title=File:75_Ranger_Regiment_Shoulder_Sleeve_Insignia.svg *Contributors:* - . . . 292
Image *Source:* https://en.wikipedia.org/w/index.php?title=File:U.S._Army_Special_Operations_Aviation_Command_SSI_(2013-2015).png *License:* Public Domain *Contributors:* United States Army Institute of Heraldry . . . 292
Image *Source:* https://en.wikipedia.org/w/index.php?title=File:JFKSWCS_SSI.gif *License:* Public Domain *Contributors:* Avron, CORNELIUSSEON, File Upload Bot (Magnus Manske), Illegitimate Barrister, Nobunaga24, OgreBot 2, Sanandros, Wgn, Wieralee . . . 292
Image *Source:* https://en.wikipedia.org/w/index.php?title=File:US_Army_1st_Special_Forces_Command_Flash.png *License:* Public Domain *Contributors:* The Institute of Heraldry . . . 292
Image *Source:* https://en.wikipedia.org/w/index.php?title=File:1sfg.svg *License:* Public Domain *Contributors:* US Army . . . 292
Image *Source:* https://en.wikipedia.org/w/index.php?title=File:3sfg.svg *License:* Public Domain *Contributors:* US Army . . . 292
Image *Source:* https://en.wikipedia.org/w/index.php?title=File:5th_SFG_Beret_Flash.png *License:* Public Domain *Contributors:* EricSerge, INeverCry, McChizzle, Sanandros . . . 292
Image *Source:* https://en.wikipedia.org/w/index.php?title=File:7th_Special_Forces_Group.svg *License:* Public Domain *Contributors:* US Army 292
Image *Source:* https://en.wikipedia.org/w/index.php?title=File:USA_-_10th_Special_Forces_Flash.svg *License:* Public Domain *Contributors:* US Army . . . 292
Image *Source:* https://en.wikipedia.org/w/index.php?title=File:19sfg.svg *License:* Public Domain *Contributors:* MDragunov . . . 292
Image *Source:* https://en.wikipedia.org/w/index.php?title=File:20sfg.svg *License:* Public Domain *Contributors:* US Army . . . 292
Image *Source:* https://en.wikipedia.org/w/index.php?title=File:U.S._Army_Special_Operations_Command_SSI_(1989-2015).svg *License:* Public Domain *Contributors:* U.S. Army Institute Of Heraldry - Redrawn: McSush . . . 293
Image *Source:* https://en.wikipedia.org/w/index.php?title=File:US_Army_4th_Military_Information_Support_Group_Flash.png *License:* Public Domain *Contributors:* The Institute of Heraldry . . . 293
Image *Source:* https://en.wikipedia.org/w/index.php?title=File:US_Army_8th_Military_Information_Support_Group_Flash.png *License:* Public Domain *Contributors:* The Institute of Heraldry . . . 293
Image *Source:* https://en.wikipedia.org/w/index.php?title=File:95CivilAffairsBdeSSI.jpg *License:* Public Domain *Contributors:* CORNELIUSSEON, Fallschirmjäger, FieldMarine, Kwasura, Monkeybait, Nobunaga24, Perhelion, Sanandros . . . 293
Image *Source:* https://en.wikipedia.org/w/index.php?title=File:95CivilAffairsBdeFlash.jpg *License:* Public Domain *Contributors:* US Army . 293
Image *Source:* https://en.wikipedia.org/w/index.php?title=File:US_Army_91st_Civil_Affairs_Battalion_Flash.png *License:* Public Domain *Contributors:* The Institute of Heraldry . . . 293
Image *Source:* https://en.wikipedia.org/w/index.php?title=File:US_Army_92nd_Civil_Affairs_Battalion_Flash.png *License:* Public Domain *Contributors:* The Institute of Heraldry . . . 293
Image *Source:* https://en.wikipedia.org/w/index.php?title=File:96_Civil_Affairs_Battalion_Flash.png *License:* Public Domain *Contributors:* United States Army Institute of Heraldry . . . 293
Image *Source:* https://en.wikipedia.org/w/index.php?title=File:US_Army_97th_Civil_Affairs_Battalion_Flash.png *License:* Public Domain *Contributors:* The Institute of Heraldry . . . 293
Image *Source:* https://en.wikipedia.org/w/index.php?title=File:US_Army_98th_Civil_Affairs_Battalion_Flash.png *License:* Public Domain *Contributors:* The Institute of Heraldry . . . 293
Image *Source:* https://en.wikipedia.org/w/index.php?title=File:528sb.jpg *License:* Public Domain *Contributors:* Corpusfury, EpicDream86, McChizzle, Sanandros . . . 293
Image *Source:* https://en.wikipedia.org/w/index.php?title=File:US_Army_528th_Support_Battalion_Flash.png *License:* Public Domain *Contributors:* The Institute of Heraldry . . . 293

Image *Source:* https://en.wikipedia.org/w/index.php?title=File:US_Army_112th_SIG_BN_Flash.svg *License:* Public Domain *Contributors:* User:McChizzle ... 293
Image *Source:* https://en.wikipedia.org/w/index.php?title=File:US_Army_SFC_MI_BN_Flash.png *License:* Public Domain *Contributors:* The Institute of Heraldry ... 293
Image *Source:* https://en.wikipedia.org/w/index.php?title=File:JSOC_flash.png *License:* Public Domain *Contributors:* The Institute of Heraldry 293
Image *Source:* https://en.wikipedia.org/w/index.php?title=File:1_Bn_75_Ranger_Regiment_Beret_Flash.svg *License:* Public Domain *Contributors:* Beao (talk), US Army, CORNELIUSSEON ... 293
Image *Source:* https://en.wikipedia.org/w/index.php?title=File:Image5435.gif *License:* Public Domain *Contributors:* Avron, BotMultichill, Kwasura, Monkeybait, Sanandros ... 293
Image *Source:* https://en.wikipedia.org/w/index.php?title=File:Image5436.gif *License:* Public Domain *Contributors:* Avron, BotMultichill, Kwasura, Monkeybait, Sanandros ... 293
Image *Source:* https://en.wikipedia.org/w/index.php?title=File:75thrangerflash.svg *License:* Public Domain *Contributors:* Akinom, Chatsam, VulpesVulpes42 ... 293
Image *Source:* https://en.wikipedia.org/w/index.php?title=File:USASOAC_Flash.png *License:* Public Domain *Contributors:* The Institute of Heraldry ... 293
Image *Source:* https://en.wikipedia.org/w/index.php?title=File:160thflash.png *License:* Public Domain *Contributors:* Ellin Beltz, GifTagger, OgreBot 2 ... 293
Image *Source:* https://en.wikipedia.org/w/index.php?title=File:USAJFKSWCS_flash.gif *License:* Public Domain *Contributors:* US Army ... 293
Image *Source:* https://en.wikipedia.org/w/index.php?title=File:US_Army_Special_Warfare_Training_Group_Flash.png *License:* Public Domain *Contributors:* The Institute of Heraldry ... 293
Image *Source:* https://en.wikipedia.org/w/index.php?title=File:US_Army_Special_Warfare_Education_Group_Flash.png *License:* Public Domain *Contributors:* The Institute of Heraldry ... 293
Image *Source:* https://en.wikipedia.org/w/index.php?title=File:US_Army_Special_Warfare_Medical_Group_Flash.png *License:* Public Domain *Contributors:* The Institute of Heraldry ... 293
Image *Source:* https://en.wikipedia.org/w/index.php?title=File:US_Army_Special_Forces_Warrant_Officer_Institute_Flash.png *License:* Public Domain *Contributors:* The Institute of Heraldry ... 293
Image *Source:* https://en.wikipedia.org/w/index.php?title=File:US_Army_Special_Warfare_NCO_Academy_Flash.png *License:* Public Domain *Contributors:* The Institute of Heraldry ... 293
Figure 116 *Source:* https://en.wikipedia.org/w/index.php?title=File:3rd_Special_Forces_Group.JPG *License:* Public Domain *Contributors:* Department of Defense ... 295
Figure 117 *Source:* https://en.wikipedia.org/w/index.php?title=File:MARSOC_Emblem.jpg *License:* Public Domain *Contributors:* Awg1010, GrummelJS, KTo288, Mattes, Ricjac∼commonswiki, 1 anonymous edits ... 296
Figure 118 *Source:* https://en.wikipedia.org/w/index.php?title=File:AlphaDASR.jpg *License:* Public Domain *Contributors:* SOCOM correspondent 297
Figure 119 *Source:* https://en.wikipedia.org/w/index.php?title=File:NAVSPECWARCOM.logo.gif *License:* Public Domain *Contributors:* File Upload Bot (Magnus Manske), MGA73bot2, OgreBot 2, Thine Antique Pen ... 299
Figure 120 *Source:* https://en.wikipedia.org/w/index.php?title=File:SEALS_wearing_diving_gear.JPG *License:* Public Domain *Contributors:* DoD 299
Figure 121 *Source:* https//en.wikipedia.org *Contributors:* Chief Mass Communication Specialist Kathryn Whittenberger, U.S. Navy ... 300
Figure 122 *Source:* https://en.wikipedia.org/w/index.php?title=File:Shield_of_the_United_States_Air_Force_Special_Operations_Command.svg *License:* Public Domain *Contributors:* en:United States Army Institute of Heraldry ... 301
Figure 123 *Source:* https://en.wikipedia.org/w/index.php?title=File:AC-130U_training.jpg *License:* Public Domain *Contributors:* Senior Airman Andy M. Kin, USAF ... 302
Figure 124 *Source:* https://en.wikipedia.org/w/index.php?title=File:21st_STS_JTACs_CAS_training_mission_at_Nevada_Test_and_Training_Range2.jpg *License:* Public Domain *Contributors:* Dainomite ... 302
Figure 125 *Source:* https://en.wikipedia.org/w/index.php?title=File:USSOCOM_Medal_BAR.svg *License:* Public Domain *Contributors:* User:Mboro ... 307
Image *Source:* https://en.wikipedia.org/w/index.php?title=File:Symbol_support_vote.svg *License:* Public Domain *Contributors:* Anomie, Fastily, Jo-Jo Eumerus ... 308
Image *Source:* https://en.wikipedia.org/w/index.php?title=File:Seal_of_the_United_States_Strategic_Command.svg *License:* Public Domain *Contributors:* Not specified ... 309
Figure 126 *Source:* https://en.wikipedia.org/w/index.php?title=File:Minuteman_III_in_silo_1989.jpg *License:* Public Domain *Contributors:* Arbitrarily0, Balmung0731, Fastfission∼commonswiki, Fæ, Grandy02, Magneticlifeform, Man vyi, Vantey, 2 anonymous edits ... 311
Figure 127 *Source:* https//en.wikipedia.org *License:* Public Domain *Contributors:* Benchill, BotMultichill, BotMultichillT, Huntster ... 311
Figure 128 *Source:* https://en.wikipedia.org/w/index.php?title=File:B-52_and_B-2.jpg *License:* Public Domain *Contributors:* Arado, David Kennedy, FAEP, Lineagegeek, Morio ... 312
Figure 129 *Source:* https://en.wikipedia.org/w/index.php?title=File:USSTRATCOM_hq.jpg *License:* Public Domain *Contributors:* Gbawden, Ligunny ... 315
Figure 130 *Source:* https://en.wikipedia.org/w/index.php?title=File:E-6B_Mercury_flies_over_Solomons_Island_in_November_2014.JPG *License:* Public Domain *Contributors:* Cobatfor ... 315
Figure 131 *Source:* https://en.wikipedia.org/w/index.php?title=File:625th_STOS_maintains_strategic_watch_141003-F-AJ823-045.jpg *License:* Public Domain *Contributors:* Fæ ... 316
Image *Source:* https://en.wikipedia.org/w/index.php?title=File:GEN_George_L_Butler.jpg *License:* Public Domain *Contributors:* USAF ... 317
Image *Source:* https://en.wikipedia.org/w/index.php?title=File:Henry_G_Chiles.jpg *License:* Public Domain *Contributors:* United States Navy 317
Image *Source:* https://en.wikipedia.org/w/index.php?title=File:Eugene_E_Habiger.jpg *License:* Public Domain *Contributors:* File Upload Bot (Magnus Manske), GT1976, Nobunaga24, OgreBot 2 ... 317
Image *Source:* https://en.wikipedia.org/w/index.php?title=File:Richard_W_Mies.jpg *License:* Public Domain *Contributors:* User:Nobunaga24 317
Image *Source:* https://en.wikipedia.org/w/index.php?title=File:James_o_ellis.jpg *License:* Public Domain *Contributors:* USN ... 317
Image *Source:* https://en.wikipedia.org/w/index.php?title=File:James_E._Cartwright.jpg *License:* Public Domain *Contributors:* Anathema, Articseahorse, FieldMarine, Jarekt, Kelly, Mattes, Nobunaga24, Reguyla, Runningboards, Schimmelreiter, 3 anonymous edits ... 318
Image *Source:* https://en.wikipedia.org/w/index.php?title=File:C._Robert_Kehler_2007.jpg *License:* Public Domain *Contributors:* BotAdventures, Gbawden, GrummelJS, Nobunaga24 ... 318
Image *Source:* https://en.wikipedia.org/w/index.php?title=File:Kevin_P._Chilton.jpg *License:* Public Domain *Contributors:* Claudevsq, GrummelJS, Nobunaga24, Väsk, 1 anonymous edits ... 318
Image *Source:* https://en.wikipedia.org/w/index.php?title=File:Kehler_2013.jpg *License:* Public Domain *Contributors:* U. S. Stratcom ... 318
Image *Source:* https://en.wikipedia.org/w/index.php?title=File:Admiral_Cecil_D._Haney_STRATCOM.jpg *License:* Public Domain *Contributors:* Howard61313, Neovu79 ... 318
Image *Source:* https://en.wikipedia.org/w/index.php?title=File:Hyten_STRATCOM_2016.jpg *License:* Public Domain *Contributors:* Claudevsq, E4024, Maliepa ... 318
Figure 132 *Source:* https://en.wikipedia.org/w/index.php?title=File:USNS_Red_Cloud_2.jpg *License:* Public Domain *Contributors:* Mass Communication Specialist 1st Class Joshua Scott ... 321
Figure 133 *Source:* https://en.wikipedia.org/w/index.php?title=File:C-54landingattemplehof.jpg *License:* Public Domain *Contributors:* USAF 322
Figure 134 *Source:* https://en.wikipedia.org/w/index.php?title=File:Simultaneous_operations_no_problem_for_Beaumont_battalion_131212-A-TQ663-773.jpg *License:* Public Domain *Contributors:* Fæ, LUSportsFan ... 324
Figure 135 *Source:* https://en.wikipedia.org/w/index.php?title=File:Exercise_Turbo_Distribution.jpg *License:* Public Domain *Contributors:* Photo by Staff Sergeant Kenneth Norman, 1st Combat Camera Squadron ... 326
Figure 136 *Source:* https://en.wikipedia.org/w/index.php?title=File:USNS_Shughart_gangplank.jpg *License:* Public Domain *Contributors:* Photo by John Pennell ... 329
Image *Source:* https://en.wikipedia.org/w/index.php?title=File:Duane_H_Cassidy.jpg *License:* Public Domain *Contributors:* U.S. Air Force ... 330
Image *Source:* https://en.wikipedia.org/w/index.php?title=File:General_Hansford_Johnson,_official_military_photo,_1990.jpg *License:* Public Domain *Contributors:* Docu, Nobunaga24, Scooter, Tom ... 330
Image *Source:* https://en.wikipedia.org/w/index.php?title=File:Ronald_R._Fogleman.jpg *License:* Public Domain *Contributors:* United States Air Force ... 331
Image *Source:* https://en.wikipedia.org/w/index.php?title=File:Robert_L_Rutherford.jpg *License:* Public Domain *Contributors:* Connormah, File Upload Bot (Magnus Manske), GT1976, Nobunaga24, OgreBot 2 ... 331
Image *Source:* https://en.wikipedia.org/w/index.php?title=File:Walter_Kross.jpg *License:* Public Domain *Contributors:* File Upload Bot (Magnus Manske), GT1976, Nobunaga24, OgreBot 2, Railwayfan2005 ... 331
Image *Source:* https://en.wikipedia.org/w/index.php?title=File:Charles_T_Robertson_Jr.jpg *License:* Public Domain *Contributors:* User:Nobunaga24 ... 331

Image *Source:* https://en.wikipedia.org/w/index.php?title=File:John_w_handy.jpg *License:* Public Domain *Contributors:* File Upload Bot (Magnus Manske), GT1976, Nobunaga24, OgreBot 2 331

Image *Source:* https://en.wikipedia.org/w/index.php?title=File:Norton_A._Schwartz.jpg *License:* Public Domain *Contributors:* BrokenSphere, GrummelJS, Howard61313, Nobunaga24, Pmsyyz, Ricjac~commonswiki, ~riley 331

Image *Source:* https://en.wikipedia.org/w/index.php?title=File:Mcnabb_dj5.jpg *License:* Public Domain *Contributors:* U.S. Air Force 331

Image *Source:* https://en.wikipedia.org/w/index.php?title=File:Fraser_TRANSCOM_HighRes.jpg *License:* Public Domain *Contributors:* Articseahorse, GT1976, Magog the Ogre, Maliepa, OgreBot 2, ProfessorX, Waldir 331

Image *Source:* https://en.wikipedia.org/w/index.php?title=File:Selva_Transcom.jpg *License:* Public Domain *Contributors:* U.S. Department of Defense 331

Image *Source:* https://en.wikipedia.org/w/index.php?title=File:Dew_2015_HiRes.JPG *License:* Public Domain *Contributors:* Claudevsq, Gbawden, Maliepa 332

License

Creative Commons Attribution-Share Alike 3.0
//creativecommons.org/licenses/by-sa/3.0/

Index

.gov, 270
.mil, 270

A-10, 302
A-10 Thunderbolt II, 18
Abdul Haris Nasution, 163
Aberdeen Proving Ground, 112
Aberdeen scandal, 112
Abraham Lincoln, 32, 33
Abu Sayyaf, 58
AC-130, 303
AC-130 Spooky, 303
AC-130U Spooky, 302
Acadia, 25
Accounting, 100
Addis Ababa, 192
Admiral, 235
Admiral Chester W. Nimitz, 234
Admiral flote, 160
Admiral of the fleet, 157, 161, 163, 166
Admiral of the Fleet (Australia), 159
Admiral of the Fleet (Royal Australian Navy), 158, 341
Admiral of the Fleet (Royal Navy), 168, 341
Admiral of the fleet (Thailand), 167
Admiral of the Navy (United States), 16, 157, 171, 341
Admiral (United States), 155, 173, 202, 229, 231, 249, 250, 254, 266, 273, 275
Advanced Extremely High Frequency, 92
Advanced Individual Training, 12
Advice and consent, 15
Aegis Ballistic Missile Defense System, 86
Aeronautical Division, U.S. Signal Corps, 5
AFAFRICA, 195
Afghanistan, 10, 84, 180, 203, 218, 221, 225, 286, 287, 295, 325
Afghanistan-Pakistan Center of Excellence, 207
Africa, 188
African Affairs, 200
African Contingency Operations Training and Assistance, 199
African Union, 192

African Union Mission in Somalia, 188
Africa Partnership Station, 199
AFSOC, 275
AH-6, 284, 294
Air captain general, 167
Aircraft carrier, 45, 46
Air Force Academy, 151
Air Force combat controllers, 285
Air Force Cyber Command (Provisional), 269
Air Force Global Strike Command, 314
Air Force Reserve, 217
Air Force Reserve Command, 10, 301
Air Forces Africa, 195
Air Forces Northern National Security Emergency Preparedness Directorate, 244
Air Force Space Command, 314
Air Force Special Operations Command, 290, 301
Air Force Special Operations Weather Technician, 303, 304
Air Force Specialty Code, 11, 304
Airlift, 327
Air Mobility Command, 320
Air National Guard, 217, 301, 304
Air National Guard of the United States, 10
Air officer, 163
Air power, 44
Air refueling, 327
Air Staff (United States), 74
Airstrikes, 301, 303
Air strikes, 237
Air superiority, 46
Air traffic control, 303
Alaska, 11, 103, 235, 243, 245
Alaskan Command, 176, 178, 234, 245
Albania, 180
Alene B. Duerk, 142
Alene Duerk, 122, 126, 135
Aleutian Islands, 235
Alexander M. Haig, Jr., 227
Alfred Gruenther, 226
Alfred Thayer Mahan, 37
Algeria, 180, 189
Algiers, 220

Al-Hasakah, 206
Allied intervention in the Russian Civil War, 2, 42
Allied invasion of Italy, 45
Allies of World War II, 44, 46
Al-Nusra Front, 59
Al Qaeda, 189
Al-Qaeda, 57, 286
Al Qaida, 205
Al-Shabaab (militant group), 188
Alternate National Military Command Center, 74
Al Udeid Air Base, 203, 208
Ambassadors of the United States, 293
Ambos Nogales, 40
American Bicentennial, 16
American Civil War, 2, 4, 23, 33, 107, 118
American Enterprise Institute, 99
American Expeditionary Force, 41
American Expeditionary Forces, 41
American football, 12
American frontier, 25
American Indian Wars, 2
American Revolution, 26
American Revolutionary War, 2, 5, 23, 25, 26, 28, 107
Anaconda Plan, 33
Ancon, 261
Andorra, 180
Andrew Goodpaster, 227
Andrew Jackson, 31
Andrew P. OMeara, 264
Angels of Bataan, 108, 120
Angola, 180
Anna Der-Vartanian, 126
Ann Agnes Bernatitus, 120
Anna Mae Hays, 110
Ann Dunwoody, 108, 112
Ann E. Dunwoody, 19
Ann E. Rondeau, 136
Annette E. Brown, 138
Ansar Al Islam, 285
Antarctica, 180, 231
Anthony Cordesman, 213, 344
Anthony Wayne, 29
Anthony Zinni, 202, 211
Anti-Gaddafi forces, 60
Antigua and Barbuda, 180
AOCS, 123, 124
Appalachian Mountains, 28
Arapaho, 35
Area of responsibility, 173, 188, 191, 203, 207, 209, 215, 231, 262
Argentina, 180
Arizona, 253
Arjan Singh, 162

Arkhangelsk, 42
Arleigh Burke class destroyer, 86
Arlington County, Virginia, 1, 23, 64
Armed Forces of the Philippines, 58
Armenia, 180
Armistice of 11 November 1918, 41
Armored personnel carriers, 284
Arms control, 42
Army and Air Force Exchange Service, 330
Army Knowledge Online, 344
Army National Guard, 292
Army National Guard of the United States, 10
Army Network Enterprise Technology Command (NETCOM), 268
Army Nurse Corps (United States), 108
Army Special Forces, 286
Arthur W. Radford, 239
Article Two of the United States Constitution, 5
Article X, 43
Aruba, 180
ARVN, 51
Ash Carter, 112, 153, 272
As Sayliyah Army Base, 203
Assistant Secretary of Defense, 66
Assistant Secretary of Defense for Asian and Pacific Security Affairs, 68
Assistant Secretary of Defense for Global Strategic Affairs, 68
Assistant Secretary of Defense for Health Affairs, 69
Assistant Secretary of Defense for Homeland Defense, 68
Assistant Secretary of Defense for International Security Affairs, 68
Assistant Secretary of Defense for Manpower and Reserve Affairs, 69
Assistant Secretary of Defense for Networks & Information Integration, 69, 71
Assistant Secretary of Defense for Nuclear, Chemical & Biological Defense Programs, 67
Assistant Secretary of Defense for Public Affairs, 70, 72
Assistant Secretary of Defense for Special Operations and Low-Intensity Conflict, 68
Associated Press, 263
Atomic bombing of Hiroshima and Nagasaki, 45
Attack on Pearl Harbor, 44, 120
Audit opinion, 88, 100
Australia, 105, 180, 231
Austria, 180
Ayub Khan (Field Marshal), 166
Azerbaijan, 180
Azores, 220

B-52 Stratofortress, 152
Baath Party, 59
Bad date, 308
Bad Tölz, 216
Baghdad, 18
Bahamas, 180
Bahrain, 106, 180, 209, 281
Bakara Market, 283
Banana Wars, 2, 39
Bangladesh, 180
Bantz J. Craddock, 227, 266
Barack Obama, 81, 288
Barbados, 180
Barbara Allen Rainey, 123, 126
Barbara Dulinsky, 115
Barbara E. McGann, 137
Barbary States, 30
Barbary Wars, 2
Barry Goldwater, 275
Barry McCaffrey, 265
Basic Combat Training, 12
Bataan, 108
Battlefield commission, 14
Battle of Antietam, 33
Battle of Baltimore, 31
Battle of Cartagena de Indias, 25
Battle of Chapultepec, 32
Battle of Fallen Timbers, 29
Battle of Germantown, 107
Battle of Gettysburg, 34
Battle of Inchon, 47
Battle of Iwo Jima, 45
Battle of Lake Erie, 31
Battle of Lexington and Concord, 26
Battle of Little Bighorn, 35
Battle of Manila (1898), 37
Battle of Midway, 45
Battle of Mogadishu (1993), 3, 56, 205, 274, 283, 284, 286
Battle of New Orleans, 31
Battle of Okinawa, 45
Battle of Pusan Perimeter, 47
Battle of San Juan Hill, 35
Battle of Saratoga, 27
Battle of Sirte (2016), 200
Battle of Takur Ghar, 286
Battle of the Little Big Horn, 34
Battle of the Philippines (1941–42), 109
Bay of Pigs Invasion, 3
BCT Modernization, 86
Belarus, 180
Belgium, 104, 180
Belize, 180
Bell Boeing V-22 Osprey, 196
Bell UH-1 Iroquois, 49
Ben Gurion Airport, 226

Benin, 180
Benito Mussolini, 43
Berlin Airlift, 322
Berlin Blockade, 322
Berlin Wall, 219
Bermuda, 180, 245
Bernard W. Rogers, 227
Bhutan, 180
Big Stick ideology, 39
Bilateralism, 75
Bill Clinton, 56, 205
Billet, 15
Black Hawk Down (book), 56
Black Hawk Down (film), 56
Black Sea Rotational Force, 220, 224
Blackwater USA, 288
Blue Angels, 128
Bob McDonnell, 66
Boeing C-17 Globemaster III, 327
Boeing KC-46 Pegasus, 327
Boeing P-8 Poseidon, 86
Boko Haram, 188
Bolivia, 180
Bolling v. Sharpe, 338–340
Bolshevik, 42
Bonin Islands, 234
Bonnie Burnham Potter, 137
Booz Allen Hamilton, 205
Border War (1910–19), 40
Border War (1910–1918), 2
Bosnia and Herzegovina, 57, 180
Bosnia-Herzegovina, 325
Bosnian War, 3
Botswana, 180
Boxer Rebellion, 2
Bradley A. Fiske, 38
Brazil, 180, 262
Brigade Combat Team, 248
Brigadier general (United States), 255
British colonization of North America, 24
British Empire, 5, 30
British Indian Ocean Territory, 106
British royal family, 169
British Virgin Islands, 180, 245
Bronze Star Medal, 120
Brown University, 188
Brunei, 180
Bryan D. Brown, 305
Bryan P. Fenton, 232
Budget sequestration in 2013, 263
Bulgaria, 180
Bundeswehr, 217
Burkina Faso, 180
Burma, 180, 235
Burning of Washington, 31
Burundi, 180

C-130 Hercules, 17, 320
C-17 Globemaster, 320
C4ISTAR, 303
C-5 Galaxy, 256, 320
Cambodia, 49, 180
Cameroon, 181
Campaigns of 1793 in the French Revolutionary Wars, 29
Camp Bondsteel, 192
Camp des Loges, 217
Camp E. S. Otis, 261
Camp H. M. Smith, 76, 175, 230
Camp H.M. Smith, 229, 232, 233
Camp Lejeune, 297
Camp Lemonnier, 189, 191, 192, 208
Camp Shelby, 326
Canada, 75, 104, 181, 243, 245
Cannon AFB, 304
Cape Verde, 181, 190
Capitol Hill, 275
Captain (armed forces), 306
Captain general of the Navy, 167
Captain General Royal Marines, 169
Captain general (Spain), 167
Cargo, 325
Caribbean, 249
Caribbean Command, 262
Caribbean Peace Force, 52
Caribbean Sea, 251
Carl Stiner, 305
Carol I. Turner, 144
Carol M. Pottenger, 127, 136
Carter F. Ham, 188, 200
Carter Ham, 193
Casablanca, 220
Cash and carry (World War II), 43
Cayman Islands, 181
Cecil D. Haney, 318
Center for Contemporary Conflict, 189
Center for Excellence in Disaster Management and Humanitarian Assistance, 232
Center for Public Integrity, 258
Center for Strategic and International Studies, 213, 344
Central Africa, 188
Central African Republic, 181
Central America, 249
Central Asia, 75, 209
Central Intelligence Agency, 46, 247
Central Security Service, 70, 71
Chad, 181
Chain of command, 6, 188
Chairman of the Joint Chiefs of Staff, 1, 6, 24, 65, 74, 96, 179, 219, 277, 323
Chakri Dynasty, 168
Chantilly, VA, 71

Chaplain of the United States Marine Corps, 142
Charles Alvin Beckwith, 289
Charles de Gaulle, 217
Charles Erwin Wilson, 236
Charles Evans Hughes, 42
Charles E. Wilhelm, 265
Charles Guthrie, Baron Guthrie of Craigiebank, 170
Charles H. Jacoby Jr., 179, 246
Charles, Prince of Wales, 170
Charles Q. Brown Jr., 202
Charles R. Holland, 305
Charles R. Larson, 240
Charles T. Robertson Jr., 331
Charles Whitehouse, 278
Chemical weapons disposal, 86
Cherokee, 28
Chesapeake Bay, 31
Chester W. Nimitz, 176, 341
Chief Engineer, 261
Chief Management Officer of the Department of Defense, 67
Chief Master Sergeant of the Air Force, 13
Chief of Naval Operations, 6, 20, 65, 134, 176, 254, 275
Chief of Staff of the United States Air Force, 6, 65, 74, 176
Chief of Staff of the United States Army, 6, 65, 73, 176
Chief of the National Guard Bureau, 6, 77
Chief petty officer, 13, 125
Chief Sanitary Officer, 261
Chiefs of Staff Committee, 176
Chile, 181
China, 181, 231, 234
Choctaw, 28
Christine Bruzek-Kohler, 139
Chuck Hagel, 99, 239
CIA, 290
CITEREFMedlicott Jr.1966, 338
CITEREFSafire1997, 335
Civil affairs, 275
Civil Air Patrol, 20
Civil authorities, 243, 245
Civil Defense, 233
Civilian control of the military, 6, 63, 65
Civil Reserve Air Fleet, 320, 327
CJTF-HOA, 189
Classified information, 247
Close air support, 301–303
Coalition of the willing, 59
Coast Guard Academy, 155
Cold War, 2, 4, 46, 204, 219
Colin L. Powell, 219
Colombia, 181

Colonel, 306
Colonel (United States), 246
Colorado, 75, 175, 245
Colorado Springs, Colorado, 243, 245
Combat advisors, 47
Combat Controller, 57, 303
Combat Controllers, 302, 304
Combating Terrorism Fellowship Program, 199
Combat Rescue Officer, 304
Combat search and rescue, 303
Combat service identification badge, 203
Combined Chiefs of Staff, 176
Combined Joint Task Force 180, 208
Combined Joint Task Force – Horn of Africa, 198, 210
Combined Joint Task Force - Horn of Africa, 208
Command and control, 173
Command and control (military), 275
Commandant of the Coast Guard, 6
Commandant of the Marine Corps, 6, 65
Commandant of the United States Coast Guard, 155
Commander-in-chief, 5, 24, 226
Commander-in-Chief of the United States Armed Forces, 3, 5
Commander, Naval Air Forces, 231
Commander Naval Forces Korea, 231
Commander, Naval Surface Force Pacific, 231
Commanding officer, 31
Command (military formation), 173
Command Sergeant Major, 2
Commerce, 320
Commission on Enhancing National Cybersecurity, 272
Commons:Category:Military history of the United States, 62
Commons:Category:Military of the United States, 20
Commons:Category:United States Africa Command, 201
Commons:Category:United States Cyber Command, 273
Commons:Category:United States Department of Defense, 79
Commons:Category:United States European Command, 228
Commons:Category:United States Pacific Command, 242
Commons:Category:United States Special Operations Command, 308
Commons:Category:United States Strategic Command, 318
Commons:Category:United States Transportation Command, 332
Commons:Category:Women in the United States Air Force, 154
Commons:Category:Women in the United States Army, 113
Commons:Category:Women in the United States Coast Guard, 155
Commons:Category:Women in the United States Marine Corps, 118
Commons:Category:Women in the United States Navy, 148
Commons:Unified Combatant Command, 187
Commonwealth of Nations, 157
Communism, 47, 50
Comoros, 181, 190, 191
Confederate States of America, 32
Congressional Budget Office, 95
Congressional Research Service, 99, 186
Congress of the Confederation, 5
Conscription, 41
Conscription in the United States, 4, 33
Constanţa, 220
Consulate, 103
Containment, 48, 50, 51
Contiguous United States, 11, 243, 245
Continental Air Defense Command, 177, 236
Continental Army, 4, 23, 26, 333
Continental Congress, 26
Continental Marines, 4, 23, 26
Continental Navy, 4, 23, 26
Cooperative Security Location, 189
Corregidor, 108
Corregidor Island, 120
Cortina Troubles, 2
Corvée, 39
Costa Rica, 181
Counter-narcotics, 275
Counterterrorism, 189, 288
Counter-terrorism, 275, 292
Craig Deare, 258
Creek War, 31
Croatia, 181
Croatian Armed Forces, 160
Croatian Navy, 161
C. Robert Kehler, 318
Cuba, 38, 103, 181
Cuban Missile Crisis, 3
Curacao, 181
Curtis LeMay, 316
Curtis M. Scaparrotti, 214, 228
Cyber attack, 271
Cyber force, 267
Cyberspace, 267
Cyber warfare, 271, 272
Cyberwarfare in the United States, 267
Cyprus, 181
Czech Republic, 181

Daniel P. Meyer, 258
Daniel Van Voorhis, 261
Dan K. McNeill, 208
DARPA, 67
Darren W. McDew, 319, 320, 332
Dates and numbers, 112
David H. Berger, 232
David M. Rodriguez, 200
David Packard, 333
David Petraeus, 202, 210, 211
Davis-Monthan Air Force Base, 253
D-Day, 16, 45
Deborah Loewer, 144
Deborah Sampson, 107
Declaration of war by the United States, 5
Defense Acquisition University, 67
Defense Advanced Research Projects Agency, 67, 70
Defense Commissary Agency, 69, 70, 330
Defense Contract Audit Agency, 68, 70
Defense Contract Management Agency, 67, 70
Defense Criminal Investigative Service, 76
Defense Equal Opportunity Management Institute, 69
Defense Finance and Accounting Service, 69, 70
Defense Human Resources Activity, 69
Defense Information Systems Agency, 69, 71, 139, 270
Defense Intelligence Agency, 63, 69, 71, 247
Defense Legal Services Agency, 71
Defense Logistics Agency, 67, 71, 330
Defense Media Activity, 70, 72
Defense Policy Board Advisory Committee, 68
Defense Science Board, 67
Defense Security Cooperation Agency, 68, 71, 330
Defense Security Service, 69, 71
Defense Technical Information Center, 67, 73
Defense Technology Security Administration, 68, 73
Defense Threat Reduction Agency, 67, 71
Delayed Entry Program, 11
Delta Force, 209, 275, 283, 292, 294
Democratic Federation of Northern Syria, 206
Democratic Republic of the Congo, 181
Democratic Republic of Vietnam, 49
Denmark, 181
Dennis C. Blair, 241
Dennis P. McAuliffe, 264
Den of Espionage, 275
Department of Defense Dependents Schools, 69
Department of Defense Education Activity, 69, 73
Department of Defense Human Resources Activity, 73
Department of Defense Test Resource Management Center, 73
Department of Homeland Security, 78, 247, 270
Department of the Navy, 124, 135
Deputy Secretary of Defense, 270
Derna, Libya, 30
Desert Crossing 1999, 205
Desert Storm, 324
Destroyers, 280, 281
Destruction, 317
DeWitt C. Ramsey, 239
Dick Cheney, 238
Digital object identifier, 200
Direct action, 292
Direct action (military), 275, 294, 297
Direct commission officer, 14
Director of Administration and Management, 70
Director of Administration and Management (DoD), 71, 73
Director of Cost Assessment and Program Evaluation, 70
Director of the Joint Staff, 74
Director of the National Security Agency, 267
Direct Reporting Unit, 74
Disaster response, 188
Discretionary spending, 95
Disputed statement, 17
Distinguished Flying Cross (United States), 18
Distinguished Service Cross (United States), 16
Division (military), 41
Djibouti, 181, 189, 207
Doha, Qatar, 203
Dominica, 181
Dominican Civil War, 3
Dominican Republic, 38, 181
Donald H. Rumsfeld, 177, 325
Donald Rumsfeld, 190, 226, 238, 317
Donald Trump, 1, 178
Dont Ask Dont Tell, 111, 116, 127, 134, 151
Doral, Florida, 175, 249, 254
Dorothy Stratton, 154
Doughboy, 41
Douglas C-54 Skymaster, 322
Douglas MacArthur, 45, 47, 66, 176, 341
Douglas M. Fraser, 266
Douma chemical attack, 59
Dragoon, 57
Duane H. Cassidy, 323, 330
Due Process Clause, 338, 340
Duke Field, 304
Duncan J. McNabb, 331
Dwight D. Eisenhower, 24, 48, 176, 215, 341

Dwight Eisenhower, 177

Eagle Scout (Boy Scouts of America), 12
East Africa, 191
Eastern Department, 261
Ecuador, 181
Edward C. Meyer, 275
Eglin AFB, 304
Egypt, 75, 106, 181, 188, 190, 207
Eighth United States Army, 231, 232
Eleanor Mariano, 143
Eleanor V. Valentin, 144
Eleventh Air Force, 232
Elihu Root, 38
Elizabeth A. Hight, 139
Elizabeth Hoisington, 110
Elmo Zumwalt, 20
El Salvador, 181
Elwell Otis, 37
Emancipation Proclamation, 33
Embassy, 103
Emblem, 202, 249
Emilio Aguinaldo, 37
End of the Cold War and the Beginning of a New World Order, 316
Enlisted rank, 9
Equal protection, 126
Equatorial Guinea, 181
Eric T. Olson, 306
Eritrea, 181, 207
Ernest King, 341
Esquire (magazine), 201
Esther Hasson, 118
Esther McGowin Blake, 149, 151
Estonia, 181
Ethiopia, 181, 192, 207
EUCOM, 237, 263
Eugene E. Habiger, 317
Europe, 214
European Command, 304
European Theater of Operations United States Army, 214
European theatre of World War II, 44, 176
Evolved Expendable Launch Vehicle, 92
Exercise Bright Star, 207
Exercise Internal Look, 204
Exercise Nifty Nugget, 323
Exercise Nuevos Horizontes, 259
Exercise Reforger, 217
Extremist, 271

F-35 Joint Strike Fighter, 86
Fairchild Republic A-10 Thunderbolt II, 152
Far East Command (United States), 176, 234
Father Rales War, 24
Federal Aviation Administration, 327

Federal Bureau of Investigation, 87, 247
Federal Emergency Management Agency, 233, 247
Federal Government of Somalia, 188
Federal government of the United States, 204
Federal Highway Administration, 321
Federal law, 173
Felix Stump, 236, 239
Field Artillery Branch (United States), 17
Field marshal, 157, 166
Field Marshal (Australia), 158, 341
Field Marshal (India), 161
Field marshal (Thailand), 167
Field marshal (United Kingdom), 168
Field officer, 15
Fifth Air Force, 232
Fifth Amendment to the United States Constitution, 338, 340
Fiji, 181
Finland, 181
Fire support, 303
First Air Force, 245
First Barbary War, 4, 30
First Philippine Republic, 37
Fiscal year, 89, 100
Five-star rank, **157**
Fixed-wing aircraft, 14
Flag officer, 13, 15, 179
Fleet admiral (United States), 15, 170, 176, 234
Flight school, 14
Florence Blanchfield, 109
Florida, 75, 76, 175, 202, 207, 249, 274
Forces committed, 59
Foreign internal defense, 275, 292
Foreign Military Sales, 330
Foreign object damage, 131
Foreign Policy (magazine), 213
Fort Belvoir, 70, 71, 73
Fort Benning, 292, 294
Fort Bragg, 292
Fort Bragg (North Carolina), 216
Fort Campbell, 294
Fort George G. Meade, 71, 175, 267
Fort Jay, 261
Fort Lee (Virginia), 70
Fort Rucker, 14
Fort Sam Houston, 251
Fort Shafter, 231
Fort Sumter, 33
Forward Operating Site, 189
Founding Fathers of the United States, 4
Four-star rank, 170, 171, 173, 270
Fourteenth Amendment to the United States Constitution, 338, 340
France, 181

Frances Shea-Buckley, 142
Franklin Delano Roosevelt, 154
Franklin D. Roosevelt, 38, 43, 125
Fran McKee, 126, 137
Frederick Funston, 37
Frederick F. Woerner Jr., 265
French and Indian War, 25
French and Indian Wars, 25
Friedrich Wilhelm von Steuben, 27
Frontier, 28.
Frontiero v. Richardson, 110, 115, 124, 126, 132, 150, 155
F Super Hornet, 86

Gabon, 181
Gambia, 181
Garmisch, 226
Gary D. Speer, 266
Gary Gordon, 284
Gary Roughead, 254
GAU-17, 300
GCHQ, 272
General, 210
General Atomics MQ-1 Predator, 86
General Atomics MQ-9 Reaper, 86
Generał broni, 306
Generał brygady, 306
General Counsel of the Department of Defense, 70, 71
General Douglas MacArthur, 234
Generał dywizji, 306
Generalissimo, 157
Generalissimus of the Soviet Union, 157
General James Lindsay, 278
General Michael Flynn, 259
General officer, 13, 246
General officers, 15
General of the Air Force, 15, 157, 170
General of the Armies, 16, 157, 171, 341
General of the army, 157, 234
General of the Army (United States), 15, 170, 176
General (United States), 1, 41, 173, 187, 202, 203, 214, 231, 232, 243, 264, 267, 270, 273, 274, 309, 319, 320, 330
George A. Joulwan, 265
George Armstrong Custer, 34, 35
George B. Crist, 211
George C. Marshall European Center for Security Studies, 226
George Dewey, 16, 171, 341
George H. W. Bush, 55, 204, 282
George Joulwan, 227
George Lee Butler, 316, 317
George Marshall, 341
George R. Mather, 264

George VI of the United Kingdom, 158
George V. Underwood Jr., 264
George Washington, 16, 23, 25–27, 171, 341
George W. Bush, 174, 190, 205, 244, 288
George W. Goethals, 261
Georgia (country), 181
Georgia (U.S. state), 292, 294
Gerald R. Ford class aircraft carrier, 86
German Army (German Empire), 41
German Empire, 41
Germany, 10, 75, 104, 175, 181, 187, 188
Ghana, 181
Glenn Fine, 258
Global Information Grid, 309
Global Operations Center, 314
Goldwater–Nichols Act, 7, 173, 177
Goldwater-Nichols Act, 219, 277, 316, 323
Goldwater-Nichols Department of Defense Reorganization Act of 1986, 65
Gorget patches, 163
Government Accountability Office, 88, 100, 291
Governor of Virginia, 66
Governors Island, 261
Grace Hopper, 142
Grafenwoehr, 225
Grand Admiral, 159
Greater Miami, 249
Greatest Generation, 46
Great White Fleet, 37
Greece, 104, 181
Greenland, 104, 214
Grenada, 52, 182
Gretchen S. Herbert, 145
Gross domestic product, 97
Ground-Based Midcourse Defense, 86
Ground Launched Cruise Missile, 218
Guam, 11, 36, 105
Guantanamo Bay Naval Base, 103
Guantánamo Bay Naval Base, 36
Guatemala, 182
Guerrilla warfare, 27
Guinea, 182
Guinea-Bissau, 182
Gulf of Aden, 237
Gulf of Guinea, 188, 189
Gulf of Mexico, 245
Gulf of Oman, 237
Gulf of Tonkin Resolution, 50
Gulf War, 3, 17, 53, 111, 202, 204, 214, 220, 274
Gulf War Syndrome, 54
Gunnar Sønsteby, 306
Guyana, 182

Haiti, 38, 182, 260, 325

Hansford T. Johnson, 330
Harbor Defense Command, 261
Harold Coyle, 344
Harrisburg International Airport, 304
Harry B. Harris Jr., 239, 241
Harry D. Felt, 240
Harry S. Truman, 17, 66, 176, 262
Harry Truman, 48
Hawaii, 11, 44, 105, 175, 229, 231
Hawaii Emergency Management Agency, 233
Hay–Bunau-Varilla Treaty, 261
Head of the Royal Thai Armed Forces, 168
Headquarters Marine Corps, 74
Heads of state, 157
Heidelberg, 217
Henry G. Chiles, Jr., 317
Henry H. Arnold, 171, 341
Henry H. Shelton, 305
Herzliya Pituah, 226
Hessian (soldier), 27
Hezbollah, 263
High-value target, 294
Hiroshima, 45
History, 20
History of slavery in the United States, 32
History of the Democratic Party (United States), 32
History of the United States, 4
History of the United States Republican Party, 32
Ho Chi Minh Trail, 50
Holy See (The Vatican), 182
Homeland defense, 75
Homestead Air Reserve Base, 254
Honduras, 103, 182, 255
Honeypot (computing), 271
Honorary rank, 157
Horn of Africa, 206
Howard A. Craig, 235
H.R. 5122 (2006), 248
Humanitarian assistance, 188
Humanitarianism, 325
HUMINT, 290
Hungary, 104, 182
Huntingdonshire, 226
Huntington Hardisty, 240
Hurlburt Field, 301, 305
Hurricane Stan, 260

Iceland, 182, 220
Iceland Defense Force, 224
IFOR, 57
IG Farben Building, 216
III Marine Expeditionary Force, 232
Illinois, 76, 175, 319, 320
I Marine Expeditionary Force, 232

Imperial German Navy, 41
Impressment, 30
Incirlik Air Base, 214
Incorporation (Bill of Rights), 338–340
India, 182, 231
Indian Air Force, 163
Indian Armed Forces, 8
Indian Ocean, 200, 231, 235
Indonesia, 182
Indo-Pacific, 229
Industrial College of the Armed Forces, 75
Information Resources Management College, 75
Infrared, 54
Initial operating capability, 244
Insurrection Act, 248
Intelligence agency, 247
Intelligence analysts, 207
Intelligence (information gathering), 207
Intelligence Star, 282
Intelligence Support Activity, 290
Inter-American Defense Board, 75
Intermediate-Range Nuclear Forces Treaty, 219
Intermediate scrutiny, 126
Intermodal container, 321
International Military Chiefs of Chaplains Conference, 219
International Security Assistance Force, 208, 210
International Standard Book Number, 60, 61, 79, 148, 306, 307
Invasion of Grenada, 3, 51
Invasion of Poland, 44
Iran, 54, 182, 280
Iran Ajr, 280
Iran–Iraq War, 204, 279
Iran hostage crisis, 203, 275
Iraq, 53, 59, 84, 182, 203, 225, 325
Iraq disarmament crisis, 59
Iraqi no-fly zones, 55
Iraqi security forces, 286
Iraq War, 3, 59, 99, 112, 117, 153, 155, 202, 203, 221, 274, 285
Iraq War order of battle, 208
Ireland, 182
Ironclad, 34
ISIL, 59, 263
ISIS, 207
Islamic Extremism, 57
Island nation, 52
ISO 3166-1 alpha-2, 342
Isolationism, 43
Israel, 75, 106, 182, 214, 218, 220
Israeli Air Force, 226

ISR (Intelligence, surveillance and reconnaissance), 317
Isthmian Canal Commission, 261
Italian Air Force, 165
Italian Army, 164
Italian Navy, 165
Italy, 10, 104, 182, 193
Ivory Coast, 182

Jacqueline O. (Allison) Barnes, 143
Jamaica, 182
James A. Winnefeld, Jr., 246
James B. Perkins (admiral), 265
James C. Vechery, 188
James E. Cartwright, 318
James G. Stavridis, 221, 227, 266
James J. Lindsay, 279, 305
James L. Holloway III, 275
James L. Jones, 227
James Mattis, 1, 202, 212
James O. Ellis, 317
James T. Hill, 266
JAMRS, 69
Janes Defence Weekly, 200
Jane Skiles ODea, 123
Janet C. Wolfenbarger, 19
Jan E. Tighe, 128
Janet Wolfenbarger, 150, 153
Japan, 104, 182, 231, 232, 234
Japanese Instrument of Surrender, 45
Japanese invasion of Manchuria, 43
Japanese offensives, 1941–42, 44
Jay Treaty, 29
Jean-Bertrand Aristide, 56
Jeanne Holm, 148
Jeanne M. Holm, 150
Jean Zimmerman, 133, 148
Jeffersonian political philosophy, 28
Jenderal besar, 163
Jerry P. Martinez, 232
Jerzy Gut, 306
J. H. Binford Peay III, 211
Jim Mattis, 239
Jimmy Carter, 203
Joan Marie Engel, 137
Jock Stirrup, Baron Stirrup, 170
John Abizaid, 202, 211
John Adams, 29
John B. Bellinger III, 288
John C. Aquilino, 231
John E. Hyten, 309, 318
John F. Kelly, 266
John F. Kelly (Marine), 263
John F. Kennedy Special Warfare Center and School, 292, 296
John Galvin (soldier), 227

John Henry Towers, 235
John H. Towers, 239
John J. Broadmeadow, 319
John J. Pershing, 16, 40, 41, 171
John McCain, 66
Johnnie Phelps, 109
John O. Brennan, 288
John O. Marsh, 278
John Pershing, 341
John R. Allen, 210, 211
John R. Galvin, 265
John Shalikashvili, 227
John Sirica, 122, 126
John S. McCain, Jr., 240
John W. Handy, 331
John W. Troxell, 2
Joint Base Anacostia-Bolling, 71
Joint Base Pearl Harbor-Hickam, 232
Joint Chiefs of Staff, 6, 74, 176, 177, 186, 234, 262, 323, 325
Joint Combined Exchange Training, 189
Joint Communications Support Element, 322
Joint Communications Unit, 290
Joint Enabling Capabilities Command, 321
Joint Force Command Naples, 224
Joint Force Headquarters National Capital Region, 246
Joint Forces Staff College, 75
Joint Functional Component Command for Global Strike and Integration, 313
Joint Functional Component Command for Integrated Missile Defense, 313
Joint Functional Component Command for Intelligence, Surveillance and Reconnaissance, 313
Joint Functional Component Command for Space, 313
Joint Functional Component Command – Network Warfare, 270, 317
Joint Improvised Explosive Device Defeat Organization, 67
Joint Intelligence Center, 207, 232
Joint Intelligence Operations Center Europe Analytic Center, 226
Joint Interagency Task Force West, 233
Joint Meritorious Unit Award, 212, 229, 243, 330
Joint Multinational Command Training Center, 225
Joint Operational Support Airlift Center, 321
Joint Professional Military Education, 178
Joint Region Marianas, 231
Joint Requirements Oversight Council, 74
Joint Special Operations Command, 209, 289, 293, 294

Joint Special Operations Task Force Trans – Sahara, 197
Joint Staff, 177
Joint Task Force Aztec Silence, 189, 224
Joint Task Force-Civil Support, 246
Joint Task Force East, 220
Joint Task Force for Global Network Operations, 270
Joint Task Force-Global Network Operations, 317
Joint Task Force North, 246
Joint warfare, 250
Joint Warfare Analysis Center, 313
Jon M. Davis, 273
Jordan, 182
Joseph D. Kernan, 254
Joseph Dunford, 1
Josephine Beatrice Bowman, 118
Joseph P. DiSalvo, 249
Joseph P. Hoar, 211
Joseph Prueher, 241
Joseph Ralston, 227
Josephus Daniels, 119, 125
Joseph Votel, 202, 203, 207, 210, 212, 306
Joseph William Martin, Jr., 66
Joy Bright Hancock, 126, 148
JSOC, 285
Judge Advocate General of the Navy, 136
Judith Neuffer, 123
Junior officer, 15

Kadena AB, 305
Kaiserslautern Military Community, 225
Kandahar Province, 287
Karen A. Harmeyer, 138
Karen Flaherty, 139
Katharine L. Laughton, 143
Katherine L. Gregory, 141
Kathleen L. Martin, 138
Kathleen Paige, 138
Kazakhstan, 182
KC-10 Extender, 320
KC-135 Stratotanker, 320
Keith B. Alexander, 269, 273
Kelley Barracks, 75, 175, 187, 188, 191, 220
Kelly Flinn, 152
Kentucky, 294
Kenya, 182, 205
Kevin P. Chilton, 318
Key West, 257
Key West Agreement, 176
Khobar Towers bombing, 205
Kibibyte, 201
Killed in action, 36
Killing of Osama bin Laden, 286, 287
Kim Campbell (pilot), 18, 152

Kingdom of Bahrain, 208
Kingdom of Great Britain, 25, 26
King Philips War, 24
Kiribati, 182
Kirstjen Nielsen, 1
Kodandera Madappa Cariappa, 161
Korea, 234
Korean DMZ Conflict (1966–69), 3
Korean War, 3, 9, 17, 46, 66, 110, 115, 149, 154, 229, 235, 322
Kosovo, 182, 219, 325
Kosovo Diplomatic Observer Mission, 223
Kosovo Force, 57
Kosovo War, 3, 57
Kristen Marie Griest, 112, 113
Kristin Beck, 306
Kurt W. Tidd, 249, 250, 266
Kuwait, 53, 59, 106, 182, 204, 209, 279
Kuwait City, 281
Kyrgyzstan, 182

Lakota people, 35
Landstuhl Regional Medical Center, 225
Laos, 49, 182
Laotian Civil War, 49
Larry Freedman, 282
Las Cuevas War, 2
Latvia, 182
Laura M. Cobb, 120
Lauris Norstad, 226
Law enforcement, 244
Lawrence Korb, 100
League of Nations, 43
Lebanon, 48, 51, 182, 206, 217, 218, 220
Lebanon crisis of 1958, 48
Legion of Merit, 120
Legion of the United States, 29
Leigh Ann Hester, 18
Lenah Higbee, 118
Lend-Lease, 43, 44
Leon Panetta, 112, 117, 128, 153
Les Aspin, 111, 116, 152, 282
Lesotho, 182
Liberia, 182, 192, 200
Libya, 52, 182, 188, 192, 200
Liechtenstein, 182
Lieutenant General, 210
Lieutenant general (United States), 202, 229, 232, 243, 249, 264, 273, 306, 319, 333
Lillian E. Fishburne, 127, 143
Limited Duty Officer, 15
Lincoln Laboratory, 207
Linda J. Bird, 138
Lisa Jaster, 112
List of countries by military expenditures, 2, 4, 7, 97

List of countries by number of active troops, 8
List of countries by number of military and paramilitary personnel, 2
List of landmark court decisions in the United States, 110, 115, 124, 126, 132, 150, 155
List of Major Commands of the United States Air Force, 74, 301
List of Military Sealift Command ships, 320
List of United States Air Force Field Operating Agencies, 74
List of United States Army installations in Germany, 10
List of United States Coast Guard enlisted ranks, 3
List of United States Coast Guard ratings, 12
List of United States defense contractors, 2
List of United States Navy enlisted rates, 3
List of United States Navy ratings, 11
List of United States Supreme Court cases, volume 411, 110, 115, 124, 126, 132, 150, 155
List of United States Supreme Court cases, volume 419, 126
List of wars involving the United States, 3
List of wartime cross-dressers, 107
Lithuania, 182
Littoral combat ship, 86
Lloyd Austin, 210, 212
Lockheed AC-130, 282
Lockheed C-5 Galaxy, 327
Lockheed EC-130, 304
Lockheed MC-130, 285, 303
Logistics, 58
Loophole, 43
Lords Resistance Army, 198
Loretta Perfectus Walsh, 119, 125
Lori Robinson, 19, 247
Los Angeles Times, 213
Louise Currie Wilmot, 143
Louis E. Denfeld, 239
Louis Ludlow, 43
Loyalists (American Revolution), 27
Lucy Brewer, 114
Ludlow Amendment, 43
Luxembourg, 182
Lyman Lemnitzer, 227
Lyndon B. Johnson, 50

M1 Abrams, 58
MacDill Air Force Base, 75, 76, 175, 191, 202, 203, 207, 274, 275, 322, 323
Madagascar, 183, 191, 237
Maghreb, 188
Mainland invasion of the United States, 244
Major general (United States), 229, 232, 265

Malaria, 261
Malawi, 183
Malaysia, 183
Malaysian Army, 284
Maldives, 183
Mali, 183, 189
Malta, 183
Manbij, 207
Mandatory spending, 95
Manifest Destiny, 32
Manila, 36
Manta Air Base, 257
Manuel Noriega, 52
Marcus Luttrell, 287
Margaret A. Rykowski, 145
Margaret Craighill, 108
Margaret D. Klein, 140
Margaret G. Kibben, 142
Mariana Islands, 234
Marianne B. Drew, 143
Mariann Stratton, 143
Marine barracks bombing, 52
Marine Corps, 297
Marine Corps Cyberspace Command, 269
Marine Corps Forces Strategic Command, 314
Marine Corps Womens Reserve, 115
Marine Forces Reserve, 114, 115
Marine Intelligence Battalion, 298
Marine Rotational Force – Darwin, 232
Marine Special Operations Regiment, 297
Marine Special Operations Support Group, 298
Mark V Special Operations Craft, 281
Marsha J. Evans, 127, 137
Marshal, 159
Marshall Islands, 183
Marshal of France, 157
Marshal of Poland, 166
Marshal of the air force, 157, 162, 163
Marshal of the Royal Air Force, 168
Marshal of the Royal Australian Air Force, 158, 341
Marshal of the Royal Thai Air Force, 167
MARSOC, 275, 297
Martial law, 244
Martin Dempsey, 211
Maryanne T. Gallagher Ibach, 143
Mary F. Hall, 143
Mary Joan Nielubowicz, 142
Maryland, 112, 175, 267
Massachusetts Institute of Technology, 207
Master Chief Petty Officer of the Coast Guard, 13
Master Chief Petty Officer of the Navy, 13
Materiality (auditing), 88, 100
Matthew Ridgway, 216, 226
Maurice E. Curts, 236

Maurice F. Weisner, 240
Mauritania, 183
Mauritius, 183, 191
Maxine Conder, 142
Maxwell R. Thurman, 265
Mayotte, 183
McLean, Virginia, 205
MD5, 268
Measurement ton, 321
Medal of Honor, 284, 287
Mediterranean, 216, 224
Meles Zenawi, 192
Melissa Rathbun-Nealy, 111
Merchants of death, 43
Merrills Marauders, 262
Mexican–American War, 2, 32
Mexican Revolution, 39
Mexico, 183, 243, 245, 250
MH-47, 294
MH-6, 280, 283, 294
MIA Accounting Agency, 68, 72
Miami, Florida, 76
Miami Herald, 258
Michael P. Murphy, 287
Michael S. Rogers, 273
Michelle J. Howard, 119, 128, 135, 136
Micronesia, 183
Middle East Force, 204
Mihail Kogălniceanu International Airport, 220
Mike Mullen, 96
Mildred H. McAfee, 126
Military, 3
Military Assistance Command, Vietnam, 237
Military attaché, 103
Military budget, 81
Military budget of the Peoples Republic of China, 97
Military budget of the United States, 7, **81**
Military Commissions Act of 2006, 248
Military discharge, 126
Military exercise, 323
Military history of the United States, **23**
Military intervention against ISIL, 3
Military officers club, 14
Military of the Confederate States of America, 4
Military of the United States, 243
Military operation, 275
Military recruitment, 11
Military reserve force, 272
Military Sealift Command, 320, 321
Military Staff Committee, 75
Military supply chain management, 173
Military Times, 134, 339
Militia, 26
MIM-104F .28PAC-3.29, 86

Minority Leader of the United States House of Representatives, 66
Missile Defense Agency, 67, 71, 86
Missing Personnel Office, 68
Mississippi River, 28
Mobile Army Surgical Hospital, 17
Mogadishu, 205, 283
Mohamed Farrah Aidid, 56, 282, 285
Moldova, 183
Monaco, 183
Monarchy of Spain, 167
Monarchy of Thailand, 168
Mongolia, 183, 231
Mons, Belgium, 217
Montenegro, 183
Morocco, 183, 189
Mozambique, 183
Muammar Gaddafi, 59
Multi-National Corps – Iraq, 221
Multinational Force in Lebanon, 3, 51
Munich massacre, 217
Muslim Filipino, 39
Mutually assured destruction, 46
MV-22 Osprey, 116
MV Sea Isle City, 281
Myanmar, 183

Nagasaki, 45
Namibia, 183
Nancy A. Fackler, 143
Nancy Elizabeth Brown, 136
Nancy J. Lescavage, 138
Nanette M. DeRenzi, 136
Naples, 193, 225
Napoleonic Wars, 30
Napoleon I of France, 31
Nathanael Greene, 27
Nathaniel Coverly, 114
Nathaniel Hill Wright, 114
National Airborne Operations Center, 74
National Capital Region (United States), 64
National Command Authority, 6, 177, 299, 323
National Communications System, 78
National Defense Authorization Act for Fiscal Year 2010, 330
National Defense Authorization Act for Fiscal Year 2018, 89
National Defense University, 75, 258
National emergency, 244
National Geospatial-Intelligence Agency, 69, 71, 247
National Guard Bureau, 219
National Guard (United States), 263
National Highway System (United States), 321
National interest, 244

National interests, 243
National Military Command Center, 74
National Network for Manufacturing Innovation, 92
National Planning Scenarios, 247
National Reconnaissance Office, 70, 71, 144
National Security Act of 1947, 4, 6, 46, 149
National Security Advisor (United States), 6
National Security Agency, 63, 69, 71, 178, 247, 267
National War College, 75
Native Americans in the United States, 24, 27
NATO, 54, 59, 63, 157, 170, 171, 214, 217, 323
NATO Military Committee, 75
NATO School, 226
Nauru, 183
Naval Amphibious Base Coronado, 298
Naval Construction Battalion Center (Gulfport, Mississippi), 128
Naval Flight Officer, 124
Naval Forces Japan (United States), 231
Naval gunfire support, 237
Naval Institute Press, 148
Naval Medical Center San Diego, 139
Naval Network Warfare Command, 268
Naval Postgraduate School, 189
Naval Reserve Officers Training Corps, 124
Naval Special Warfare Development Group, 283, 290
Naval Special Warfare Group 2, 198
Naval Station Mayport, 253
Naval Station Norfolk, 321
Naval Station Pearl Harbor, 231
Naval Support Activity Bahrain, 208
NAVSPECWARCOM, 275
Navy, 4
Navy Expeditionary Combat Command, 139
Navy Expeditionary Logistics Support Group, 139
Navy Nurse Corps, 125, 126
Navy Recruiting Command, 123
Navy Region Hawaii, 231
Navy SEALs, 285
Navy Warfare Development Command, 139
Nazi Germany, 45
Near East, 10
Nebraska, 76, 175, 309
Nelson A. Miles, 38
Nepal, 183
Netherlands, 104, 183
Neutrality Acts of 1930s, 43
Newburgh conspiracy, 28
New Look (policy), 24
New Mexico, 304
Newport, RI, 124

New York City draft riots, 2
New Zealand, 183, 231
Nicaragua, 38, 183
Niger, 106, 183, 189
Nigeria, 183, 189, 192
NOAA Commissioned Officer Corps, 333
Noel Gayler, 240
Non-commissioned officer, 13, 293
NORAD, 233
Nora W. Tyson, 127, 128, 136
Norman Schwarzkopf, 202, 204, 209
Norman Schwarzkopf, Jr., 211
North American Aerospace Defense Command, 63, 75, 245
North Atlantic Treaty Organization, 215
North Carolina, 292
NORTHCOM, 238
Northern Cheyenne, 35
North Korea, 183, 231, 235, 272
Northrop Grumman RQ-4 Global Hawk, 86
North Vietnamese Army, 50
Northwest Indian War, 28, 29
Northwest Ordinance, 28
Northwest Territory, 28
Norton A. Schwartz, 331
Norway, 104, 183, 306
NROTC, 126
NSA, 87
Nurse Corps, 108
Nurse Corps (United States Army), 107
Nye Committee, 43

Oahu, 76
Oberammergau, 226
Oceanography, 14
Office of Economic Adjustment, 73
Office of Net Assessment, 70
Office of the Chief of Naval Operations, 74
Office of the Inspector General, U.S. Department of Defense, 76, 88
Office of the Secretary of Defense, 66, 70, 72
Office of the Secretary of the Air Force, 74
Office of the Secretary of the Army, 73
Office of the Secretary of the Navy, 74
Officer (armed forces), 7, 9, 14
Officer Candidate School, 14, 124
Officer Candidate School (United States Navy), 124
Officer corps, 28
Officer Training School, 14
Offutt Air Force Base, 76, 175, 309
Okinawa, 305
Oliver Hazard Perry, 31
Olmsted Air Force Base, 304
Oman, 183, 209
Omar Bradley, 171, 341

Operation Active Endeavour, 224
Operation Allied Force, 3, 223, 325
Operational Test and Evaluation Directorate, 67
Operation Anaconda, 286
Operation Blue Bat, 48
Operation Continuing Promise, 249
Operation Deliberate Force, 3
Operation Deny Flight, 3
Operation Desert Fox, 205, 223
Operation Desert Shield, 115, 151, 155
Operation Desert Shield (Gulf War), 324
Operation Desert Storm, 115, 151, 155, 219
Operation Desert Thunder, 325
Operation Dragon Rouge, 218
Operation Eagle Claw, 3, 275, 289
Operation Eagle Eye (Kosovo), 223
Operation Earnest Will, 204, 274, 279
Operation Enduring Freedom, 3, 58, 99, 223, 325
Operation Enduring Freedom – Horn of Africa, 3
Operation Enduring Freedom – Philippines, 3, 58
Operation Enduring Freedom – Trans Sahara, 3, 197
Operation Enduring Freedom - Horn of Africa, 189, 200
Operation Enduring Freedom - Trans Sahara, 189, 200, 224
Operation Essential Harvest, 223
Operation Golden Pheasant, 3
Operation Gothic Serpent, 3, 274, 282
Operation Husky, 45
Operation Inherent Resolve, 203, 274
Operation Joint Endeavor, 325
Operation Joint Endeavour, 57
Operation Joint Guardian, 325
Operation Looking Glass, 314
Operation Neptune Spear, 290
Operation New Horizons, 249
Operation Nimble Archer, 281
Operation Northern Watch, 214
Operation Ocean Shield, 200
Operation Odyssey Dawn, 200
Operation Onward Liberty, 200
Operation Overlord, 45
Operation Praying Mantis, 281
Operation Provide Relief, 205, 281
Operation Red Wings, 286
Operation Resolute Support, 203
Operation Restore Hope, 282, 325
Operation Rolling Thunder, 49
Operation Silk Purse, 217
Operation Support Hope, 325
Operation Torch, 45

Operation Unified Protector, 59, 200
Operation Unified Response, 249
Operation Uphold Democracy, 274, 325
Operation Urgent Fury, 277
Opha May Johnson, 114, 115
OPLAN 5027, 209
Order of San Carlos, 266
Ordnance Corps (United States Army), 17
Organizational structure of the United States Department of Defense, 6, **63**
Organization for Security and Co-operation in Europe, 68
Organization of the United States Marine Corps, 74
Osama bin Laden, 205, 291
Ovda air base, 226
Oxford University Press, 228

Pacific Air Forces, 230
Pacific Ocean, 231
Pacific War, 44, 45, 108, 176, 234
Pakistan, 183, 206, 209, 231
Pakistan Army, 166, 284, 285
Pakistan–United States skirmishes, 3
Palau, 183
Palestinian people, 217
Panama, 38, 183, 260, 275
Panama Canal, 235, 249
Panama Canal Company, 260
Panama Canal Department, 261
Panama Canal Treaty, 262
Panama Canal Zone, 38, 52, 261
Panama City, 261
Panamanian, 260, 261
Panamanian Isthmus, 260
Panama Railroad, 260
Pancho Villa, 40, 261
Pancho Villa Expedition, 40
Pandemic Response Program, 199
Pan Sahel Initiative, 189
Panzer Kaserne, 198, 224–226
Papua New Guinea, 183
Paraguay, 183
Pararescue, 303
Pararescuemen, 304
Paris, 217
Partnership for Peace, 219
Patch Barracks, 175, 214, 217, 224
Pathfinders (military), 303
Patricia Ann Tracey, 136
Patricia Horoho, 112
Patricia Tracey, 127
Patriot (American Revolution), 26
Patriot War, 2
Paul F. Gorman, 264
Pauline Hartington, 142

Paul J. Selva, 2, 331
Paul M. Nakasone, 267, 273
Peace and Security Council, 192
Peacekeeping, 188
Pearl Harbor, 16, 44, 235, 236
Pen name, 114
Pennsylvania, 304
Pennsylvania Air National Guard, 304
Pentagon Force Protection Agency, 64, 70, 71
Peoples Liberation Army, 8, 66
Pequot War, 24
Pershing II, 218
Persian Gulf, 75, 204, 279, 280, 325
Persian Gulf War, 203, 286
Peru, 183
Pescadores, 236
Peshmerga, 59, 285
Peter J. Schoomaker, 305
Peter Pace, 179, 265
Peterson Air Force Base, 75, 175, 243, 245
Petty officer, 13
Philip M. Breedlove, 227
Philippe-Jean Bunau-Varilla, 260
Philippine–American War, 2, 36, 37
Philippines, 36, 39, 104, 183, 234
Philippine Scouts, 37
Philip S. Davidson, 229, 239, 242
Philip Sheridan, 34
Piotr Patalong, 306
PLO, 51
Poland, 104, 184, 306
Polar Bear Expedition, 42
Polish Army, 166
Politico, 100
Pontiac (Ottawa leader), 25
Port of Beaumont, 324
Port of Port Arthur, 324
Portugal, 104, 184
Posse Comitatus Act, 244, 248
Post-Soviet states, 10
Potomac River, 64
Power projection, 4, 173
Prague Spring, 217
President of the United States, 1, 3, 5, 24, 64, 65, 173, 179, 230, 245
President Truman, 235
President Trumans relief of General Douglas MacArthur, 48
Prime Minister of Ethiopia, 192
Prince Harry, Duke of Sussex, 169
Prince Philip, 341
Prince Philip, Duke of Edinburgh, 158
Principal Deputy Under Secretary of Defense for Personnel and Readiness, 73
Privateer, 29
Private military company, 94

Program Executive Officer, 144
Province of Georgia, 25
Province of Massachusetts, 26
Province of South Carolina, 25
Proxy war, 46, 50, 54
Psychological operations (United States), 293
Psychological warfare, 275
Public domain, 332
Public Law 80-557, 20
Public Works Administration, 43
Puerto Rican Nationalist Party Revolts of the 1950s, 3
Puerto Rico, 11, 36, 103, 243, 245

Qatar, 106, 184, 209
Quarantine Speech, 43
Quarry Heights, 261
Quasi-War, 29
Queen Annes War, 25
Q:United States Armed Forces, 20

RAAF, 159
RAF, 170
RAF Mildenhall, 224, 304
RAF Molesworth, 191, 226
Raid at Los Baños, 120
Railroad car, 321
Ralph Eberhart, 245
Ralph E. Eberhart, 246
Ralph Puckett, 306
Ramstein Air Base, 193, 195, 224, 225
RAND Corporation, 19
Randy Shughart, 284
Ranger School, 112
Ranks and insignia of NATO, 157
Rapid Deployment Forces, 203
Rapid Deployment Joint Task Force, 203
Ray Mabus, 125
Raymond A. Thomas, 274, 306
Raymond C. Smith, Jr., 305
Ready Reserve Force, 329
Rear Admiral, 190
Rear Admiral (United States), 233, 254, 265
Reconnaissance, 294
Recruit training, 11
Red Army Faction, 217
Red Brigades, 217
Referendum, 43
Reform War, 2
Refueling and Complex Overhaul, 86
Regimental Reconnaissance Company, 290
Republic of China, 44
Republic of Ireland, 219
Republic of Korea, 10
Republic of Macedonia, 182
Republic of the Congo, 184

Republic of Vietnam, 49, 50
Reserve components of the United States Armed Forces, 9
Reserve Officers Training Corps, 14
Reserve Officer Training Corps, 124
Réunion, 184
Revenue Cutter Service, 5
Revolt of the Admirals, 66
Revolutionary France, 29
Rhonda Cornum, 111
Richard C. Macke, 241
Richard M. Nixon, 51
Richard Scholtes, 277
Richard W. Mies, 317
Richmond, Virginia, 33
Rifled musket, 34
Roberta L. Hazard, 137
Robert Brooks Brown, 231
Robert E. Lee, 33
Robert F. Hale, 88, 100
Robert F. Willard, 241
Robert Gates, 98, 174, 190, 330
Robert J. Papp, 155
Robert Kingston, 211
Robert L. J. Long, 240
Robert L. Rutherford, 331
Robert M. Gates, 100
Robert Moeller, 190
Robert W. Merry, 334
Robert W. Porter Jr., 264
Robin Braun, 123, 128, 136
Rocket-propelled grenade, 283
Rollback, 48
Roll-off, 328
Romania, 104, 184
Ronald J. Hays, 240
Ronald Reagan, 52, 279, 323
Ronald R. Fogleman, 331
Ronne Froman, 137
Rosemary Bryant Mariner, 123
Rough Riders, 35
Royal Navy, 27, 30, 169, 341
Royal Thai Air Force, 167
Royal Thai Army, 167
Royal Thai Navy, 167
Royal United Services Institute, 192
Russia, 184, 194, 214, 220
Russian Revolution of 1917, 42
Ruth Cheney Streeter, 115
Rwanda, 184, 325
Ryukyus, 234

Sadaam Hussein, 291
Saddam Hussein, 55, 59, 205, 286
Sahara, 189, 219
Sahel, 188, 189

Saint Helena, Ascension and Tristan da Cunha, 184
Saint Kitts and Nevis, 184
Saint Lucia, 184
Saint Pierre and Miquelon, 184
Saint Vincent and the Grenadines, 184
Sam Manekshaw, 161
Sam Nunn, 276
Samoa, 184
Samuel J. Locklear, 241
Samuel V. Wilson, 306
Sandra Stosz, 155
Sandy Daniels, 140
San Marino, 184
Sao Tome and Principe, 184
São Tomé and Príncipe, 190
Saratoga campaign, 27
Saudi Arabia, 54, 98, 106, 184, 204, 271
Schlesinger v. Ballard, 126
School of the Americas, 259
Scot J. Paltrow, 89
Scott Air Force Base, 76, 175, 319, 320
SCPO, 306
Scud, 285
SEAL Delivery Vehicle Teams, 300
Sealift, 320, 328
SEAL Team Six, 300
Sebastian Junger, 201
Secession, 32
Second Barbary War, 4, 30
Second Continental Congress, 5, 20
Second Italo-Ethiopian War, 43
Second Sino-Japanese War, 43
Secretary of Defense, 135, 177, 188, 276, 279, 296, 317, 323
Secretary of Defense of the United States, 230
Secretary of Homeland Security, 6
Secretary of the Army, 278
Secretary of the Navy, 123, 134
Selective Service System, 4, 8
Senate Armed Services Committee, 190, 275, 276
Senator Barry Goldwater, 276
Senator Patrick Leahy, 258
Senegal, 184
Senior Enlisted Advisor, 13
Senior Enlisted Advisor to the Chairman, 2, 13
Senior Foreign Service, 193
Seoul, 232
September 11, 2001 attacks, 57
September 11 attacks, 244
September 11 terrorist attacks, 205
Serbia, 184
Sergeant Major, 229, 243
Sergeant Major of the Army, 13
Sergeant Major of the Marine Corps, 13

Seventeenth Air Force, 193, 195
Seventh Air Force, 232
Sexual assault, 112
Seychelles, 184, 191
Shaba II, 218
Shah-i-Kot, 286
Shaw Air Force Base, 207
Shawnee, 28
Shaye Lynne Haver, 112
Sheila Widnall, 152
Shelter in place, 233
Shoulder sleeve insignia, 292
Siege of Fort Detroit, 25
Siege of Port Royal (1710), 25
Siege of Yorktown, 26, 27
Sierra Leone, 184
SIGINT, 290
Sikorsky UH-60 Black Hawk, 294
Silver Star, 18
Singapore, 104, 184
Sino-African relations, 189
Sioux, 35
SIPRI, 81, 228
Six-star rank, 16
Slovakia, 184
Slovenia, 184
Solomon Islands, 184
Somalia, 56, 184, 205, 281, 325
Somali Civil War, 3
Soto Cano Air Base, 256
South Africa, 184
South America, 76, 249
South Carolina, 207
Southeast Asia, 231
Southern European Task Force, 193
Southern theater of the American Revolutionary War, 27
Southern United States, 32
South Korea, 104, 184, 231, 232, 272
South Sudan, 184
South Vietnam, 50, 237
Soviet–Afghan War, 203
Soviet Ground Forces, 204
Soviet Navy, 224
Soviet Union, 44, 54, 204, 215, 216, 219
Space-Based Infrared System, 86
Spain, 104, 184
Spanish Air Force, 167
Spanish Army, 167
Spanish Civil War, 43
Spanish Florida, 25
Spanish–American War, 2, 36
Spanish Navy, 167
SPAWAR, 144
Special Activities Division, 281, 286
Special Air Service, 289

Special Boat Teams, 279, 298
Special forces, 274, 275, 285
Special Forces (United States Army), 291
Special Mission Unit, 289, 294
Special operations, 173, 250
Special Operations Command Central, 208
Special Operations Command, Europe, 226
Special Operations Command Korea, 230, 232
Special Operations Command-North, 245, 246
Special Operations Command Pacific, 230, 232
Special Operations Command South, 254
Special Operations Craft – Riverine (SOC-R), 300
Special Operations Forces, 206
Special Purpose Marine Air-Ground Task Force - Crisis Response - Africa, 196
Special reconnaissance, 275, 292, 297
Special Relationship, 46
Special Tactics Squadrons, 304
Special Warfare Combatant-craft Crewmen, 300
Springfield, VA, 71
Spring Offensive, 41
S:Public Law 94-479, 16
Sri Lanka, 184
SS-20, 218
SSBNs, 124
SSGN, 124
STA-21, 124
Staff college, 15
Staff (military), 38
Staging area, 59
Standing army, 28
Stanleyville mutinies, 218
Stars and Stripes (newspaper), 343
State Partnership Program, 199, 219
St. Clairs Defeat, 29
Stealth aircraft, 54
Stephen Decatur, 30
Stožerni general, 160
Strait of Hormuz, 204, 238
Straits of Florida, 245
Straits of Gibraltar, 224
Straits of Magellan, 37
Strategic Air Command, 235, 237, 316
Strategic bombing, 45, 49
Strategic Insights, 201
Strategic Support Branch, 290
Stryker, 329
Stuttgart, 75, 175, 187, 188, 191, 210, 214, 224
Stuttgart, Germany, 217
Stuttgart-Vaihingen, 224
Subordinate Unified Commands, 207
Sub-Saharan Africa, 10, 188
Sudan, 184, 191, 207

Sudirman, 163
Sue Dauser, 126
Suffolk, Virginia, 322
Suharto, 163
Sulu Archipelago, 58
Superintendent (education), 155
Superpower, 23, 46
Supreme Allied Commander, 170, 171
Supreme Allied Commander Europe, 75, 215
Supreme Allied Commander, Europe, 214
Supreme Allied Commander Transformation, 136
Supreme Headquarters Allied Expeditionary Force, 176
Supreme Headquarters Allied Powers Europe, 215
Surface Deployment and Distribution Command, 320
Suriname, 10, 184
Sveto Letica, 160
Swaziland, 184
Sweden, 184
Switzerland, 184
Syria, 184, 207, 219, 220

Tailhook scandal, 115, 127
Taiwan, 185, 236
Tajikistan, 185
Takur Ghar, 286
Taliban, 58, 286
Tampa, Florida, 202, 203, 207, 275
Tampico Affair, 40
Tanker War, 204
Tanzania, 185, 205
Task Force 11, 209, 291
Task Force 121, 291
Task Force 145, 291
Task Force 60, 195
Task Force 6-26, 291
Task Force 73, 231
Task Force 88 (anti-terrorist unit), 209
Tecumsehs War, 31
Tempelhof Airport, 322
Terminal High Altitude Area Defense, 86
Terrence J. O'Shaughnessy, 243
Terrence J. OShaughnessy, 247
Territory of Hawaii, 235
Terrorism, 57
Tet Offensive, 50, 51
Texas Revolution, 32
Thailand, 104, 185
Thai language, 167
Theater (military), 203
The Bahamas, 243, 245
The Economist, 343
The Joint Staff, 74

Thelma Bendler Stern, 120
The Marine Special Operations School, 298
The Nation, 288
Theodore Roosevelt, 37, 39, 261
The Pentagon, 1, 23, 64, 112, 116, 152, 270
The Sacred Twenty, 118
The Special Mission Training Branch—East, 298
Third Air Force, 224, 225
Thirteen colonies, 26
Thomas B. Fargo, 241
Thomas Blamey, 158, 341
Thomas D. Waldhauser, 179, 187, 200
Thomas Jefferson, 29
Thomas T. Handy, 216
Three-star rank, 13
Timor-Leste, 185
Timothy J. Keating, 241, 246
Timothy Ray, 214
Title 10 of the United States Code, 7, 65, 66, 70, 72, 173, 177, 185, 271, 333
Title 14 of the United States Code, 333
Togo, 185
Tokyo, 232
Tomahawk (missile), 59
Tommy Franks, 202, 211
Ton, 325
Tonga, 185
Tongo Tongo ambush, 187
Tonnage, 4
Total war, 34
Transgender, 117
Trans-Saharan Counterterrorism Initiative, 189
Treaty of Alliance (1778), 29
Treaty of Paris (1783), 5, 28
Treaty of Paris (1898), 36
Treaty of Versailles, 43
Trench warfare, 34
TRICARE Management Activity, 69
Trinidad and Tobago, 185
Tropical Storm Gamma, 260
Tunisia, 185
Turkey, 75, 106, 185, 207
Turkey shoot, 54
Turkmenistan, 185
Turks and Caicos Islands, 245
Turks & Caicos Islands, 185
Tuvalu, 185
Twenty-Fourth Air Force, 269

Uganda, 185
UH-60 Black Hawk, 283
Ukraine, 185
Ulysses S. Grant Sharp, 240
Unconventional warfare, 275, 292
Under Secretary of Defense, 66

Under Secretary of Defense Comptroller, 70
Under Secretary of Defense (Comptroller), 68, 88, 100
Under Secretary of Defense for Acquisition and Sustainment, 67
Under Secretary of Defense for Acquisition, Technology and Logistics, 70, 71, 73
Under Secretary of Defense for Intelligence, 69, 71
Under Secretary of Defense for Personnel and Readiness, 69, 70, 73
Under Secretary of Defense for Policy, 68, 71–73
Under Secretary of Defense for Research and Engineering, 67
Unified Combatant Command, 7, 19, 63, 65, 75, 103–105, **173**, 187, 188, 192, 202, 203, 208, 214, 229, 234, 243, 249, 267, 274, 275, 309, 316, 319
Unified Command Plan, 177, 218–220, 244, 262
Unified Task Force, 274
Uniformed services of the United States, 4
Uniformed Services University of the Health Sciences, 69
Union (American Civil War), 4, 33
United Arab Emirates, 106, 185, 209
United Kingdom, 104, 185, 215
United Nations, 47, 54, 75, 235, 330
United Nations Command, 235
United Nations Command (Korea), 47
United Nations Operation in Somalia II, 56
United Nations Security Council Resolution 1199, 223
United Nations Security Council Resolution 1973, 59
United Nations Security Council Resolution 678, 204
United States, 1, 9, 52, 103, 177, 185, 214, 243, 249, 309, 319
United States Africa Command, 75, 76, 175, 177, 185, **187**, 203, 208, 210, 220, 224, 317
United States Agency for International Development, 193
United States Air Force, 1–3, 5, 10, 12, 23, 46, 52, 53, 63, 74, 81, 103–106, 188, 193, 210, 214, 229, 243, 246, 250, 266, 269, 305, 309, 317, 319, 320, 330
United States Air Force Academy, 14, 19
United States Air Force Basic Military Training, 153
United States Air Force Basic Training scandal, 153
United States Air Force Combat Control Team, 290
United States Air Force enlisted rank insignia, 3
United States Air Force officer rank insignia, 3
United States Air Force Pararescue, 290
United States Air Forces Central Command, 207
United States Air Forces in Europe, 195, 224, 225
United States Air Force Special Operations School, 305
United States Air Force Tactical Air Control Party, 290, 304
United States Armed Forces, **1**, 43, 64, 119, 188, 229, 268, 275
United States Armed Forces nude photo scandal, 117
United States Army, 1–3, 5, 10, 12, 23, 63, 73, 81, 103–106, 112, 200, 202, 211, 214, 229, 243, 246, 249, 250, 264, 267, 268, 273, 274, 294, 305, 320
United States Army Africa, 187, 201
United States Army Air Forces, 5, 20
United States Army Alaska, 231
United States Army Central, 207
United States Army Coast Artillery Corps, 261
United States Army Cyber Command, 268
United States Army enlisted rank insignia, 3
United States Army Europe, 224, 225
United States Army Forces Strategic Command, 314
United States Army Intelligence and Security Command, 268
United States Army, Japan, 231
United States Army officer rank insignia, 3
United States Army Pacific, 230, 231
United States Army Rangers, 291
United States Army Research, Development and Engineering Command, 271
United States Army Reserve, 10
United States Army South, 251
United States Army Space and Missile Defense Command, 314
United States Army Special Forces, 293, 295
United States Army Special Operations Command, 289, 291
United States Atlantic Command, 219
United States Bicentennial, 341
United States Cabinet, 6, 46, 63
United States Central Command, 75, 175, 178, 188, 189, 191, **202**, 219, 324
United States Coast Guard, 1, 3, 5, 10, 23, 63, 103–106, 193, 233, 250
United States Coast Guard Academy, 14, 19
United States Coast Guard Auxiliary, 20
United States Coast Guard officer rank insignia, 3

United States Coast Guard Reserve, 10
United States Coast Guard Womens Reserve, 154
United States Code, 63
United States Congress, 5, 23, 100, 189, 271
United States Constitution, 5, 43, 64, 95, 177
United States Cyber Command, 175, 178, **267**
United States Declaration of Independence, 4
United States declaration of war upon Japan, 44
United States Department of Commerce, 193
United States Department of Defense, 3, 4, 6, 23, 63, 81, 88, 100, 103, 173, 185, 187, 189, 193, 201, 202, 207, 214, 229, 243, 249, 267, 268, 274, 275, 309, 319
United States Department of Homeland Security, 3, 23, 63, 87, 262
United States Department of State, 186, 193
United States Department of the Air Force, 4, 6, 63, 66, 74, 86
United States Department of the Army, 6, 63, 66, 73, 86
United States Department of the Navy, 6, 63, 66, 74, 86
United States Department of the Treasury, 63
United States Department of Transportation, 63
United States Department of Treasury, 193
United States Department of Veterans Affairs, 84, 87
United States Deputy Secretary of Defense, 66, 67, 333
United States dollar, 2, 63
United States Embassy, Saigon, 50
United States European Command, 75, 175, 189, 191, 209, **214**
United States federal budget, 81
United States federal executive departments, 4
United States fiscal cliff, 100
United States Fleet Forces Command, 245, 314
United States Forces – Iraq, 208
United States Forces Japan, 10, 230, 232
United States Forces Korea, 10, 178, 230, 232
United States Fourth Fleet, 254
United States House Armed Services Subcommittee on Readiness, 276
United States House Committee on Appropriations, 100
United States House Committee on Armed Services, 269
United States House of Representatives, 66, 100
United States Indo-Pacific Command, 175, 178, **229**
United States invasion of Iraq, 206
United States Invasion of Panama, 3, 17, 52, 249, 274, 275

United States Joint Forces Command, 75, 177, 186, 225, 291
United States Life-Saving Service, 5
United States Marine Corps, 1, 3, 5, 10, 12, 23, 52, 63, 74, 81, 86, 103–106, 187, 210, 211, 229, 250, 265, 269, 273, 282, 319
United States Marine Corps Forces, Europe, 193, 218, 224, 225
United States Marine Corps Forces Pacific, 232
United States Marine Corps Forces, Pacific, 230
United States Marine Corps Forces Special Operations Command, 296
United States Marine Corps rank insignia, 3
United States Marine Corps Reserve, 10, 245
United States Marine Corps School of Infantry, 12
United States Marine Corps Womens Reserve, 16
United States Marine Forces Central Command, 207
United States Marines, 114
United States Maritime Administration, 329
United States Merchant Marine, 20
United States Merchant Marine Academy, 14, 19
United States military, 214, 226
United States Military Academy, 14, 19, 38, 345
United States military deployments, **103**
United States military occupation codes, 11
United States Military Railroad, 34
United States Military Sealift Command, 320
United States National Guard, 24
United States National Security Council, 4, 6, 46
United States Naval Academy, 14, 19, 124, 126, 127
United States Naval Forces Central Command, 208
United States Naval Forces Europe, 224, 225
United States Naval Observatory, 78
United States Naval Reserve, 119
United States Naval Special Warfare Command, 290, 298, 299
United States Naval Special Warfare Development Group, 294
United States Navy, 1, 3, 5, 10, 12, 23, 52, 63, 74, 81, 103–106, 118, 119, 210, 211, 229, 246, 249, 250, 265, 268, 273, 294, 305, 317, 320
United States Navy Nurse Corps, 16, 108, 118
United States Navy officer rank insignia, 3
United States Navy Reserve, 10, 136
United States Navy SEALs, 290, 298, 299

United States Northern Command, 75, 175, 178, **243**
United States of America, 3
United States Pacific Air Forces, 232
United States Pacific Command, 76, 176, 189, 191, 247, 305
United States Pacific Fleet, 230, 231
United States Permanent Representative to NATO, 68
United States Principal Deputy Under Secretary of Defense, 68
United States Public Health Service Commissioned Corps, 333
United States Readiness Command, 279
United States Reports, 110, 115, 124, 126, 132, 150, 155
United States Secretary of Defense, 1, 6, 24, 64, 65, 67, 98, 99, 173, 179, 245, 330
United States Secretary of Energy, 6
United States Secretary of Homeland Security, 1, 6
United States Secretary of State, 6
United States Secretary of the Air Force, 6, 65, 66, 74, 179
United States Secretary of the Army, 6, 65, 66, 73, 179
United States Secretary of the Navy, 6, 65, 66, 74, 179
United States Secret Service, 263
United States Service academies, 14
United States Seventh Fleet, 231
United States Sixth Fleet, 195, 216, 225
United States Southern Command, 76, 175, 203, **249**
United States Space Command, 317
United States Special Operations Command, 76, 175, 197, 208, **274**
United States Special Operations Forces, 276
United States Strategic Command, 76, 175, **309**
United States Supreme Court, 110, 115, 124, 126, 132, 150, 155
United States Tenth Fleet, 268
United States Third Fleet, 231
United States Transportation Command, 76, 175, **319**
United States Under Secretary of the Air Force, 74
United States Uniformed Services Oath of Office, 15
United States usage, 57
United States Virgin Islands, 245
Unity of effort, 271
University of North Texas Press, 148
Unmanned aerial vehicle, 60
Unrestricted submarine warfare, 41
Uruguay, 185

U.S. 1st Marine Division, 58
USAF, 202
USAFRICOM, 180–185
U.S. Air Forces in Europe, 215
U.S. Ambassador, 188
U.S. Army, 203, 210
U.S. Army Africa, 194
US Army NATO Brigade, 225
U.S. Army Reserve, 217
U.S. Army Special Forces, 57
U.S. Army Special Operations Aviation Command (USASOAC), 292
U.S. Army War College, 38
USASOC, 275
U.S. Atlantic Command, 176, 179
U.S. Atlantic Fleet, 176
US Caribbean Command, 264
USCENTCOM, 180–186, 191
U.S. Central Command, 218, 291
U.S. Coast Guard, 210, 328
U.S. Code, 173
US Code, 177
U.S. Department of Defense, 203
U.S. Department of Defense Military Health System, 69
U.S. Department of State, 188
USEUCOM, 180–186, 191
U.S. federal budget, 81
U.S. Fifth Army, 245
U.S. Fleet Cyber Command, 268
U.S. Forces Japan, 236
U.S. Forces Korea, 236
USINDOPACOM, 180–185
U.S. Joint Forces Command, 220, 262, 320
U.S. Marine Corps, 200, 210
U.S. Marines, 260
U.S. Military, 134
U.S. Military Telegraph Corps, 34
U.S. National Security Council, 259
U.S. Naval Forces, Eastern Atlantic and Mediterranean, 215
U.S. Naval Forces Europe - Naval Forces Africa, 194
U.S. Naval Forces Southern Command, 254
U.S. Naval Station Guantanamo Bay, 256
U.S. Navy, 190
U.S. Navy SEALs, 224
USNORTHCOM, 19, 180, 181, 183–185
U.S. Northeastern Command, 176
USNS Shughart (T-AKR-295), 329
U.S. occupation of Veracruz, 1914, 39
U.S. Pacific Fleet, 235
USPACOM, 186, 191
U.S. Readiness Command, 204
USS Arizona (BB-39), 44
USS Benfold, 127

USS Cape Cod (AD-43), 133
USS Cole bombing, 205
USS Constitution, 114
USS Dolphin (PG-24), 118
U.S. Secretary of Defense, 226
U.S. Senate Committee on Armed Services, 201
USS Hopper (DDG-70), 142
USS Jarrett (FFG-33), 280
USS Maine (SSBN-741), 125
USS Mayflower (PY-1), 118
USS Michigan (SSGN-727), 125
USS Ohio (SSGN-726), 125
USS Opportune (ARS-41), 127
USSOUTHCOM, 180–186
USS Philadelphia (1799), 30
USS Samuel B. Roberts (FFG-58), 281
USS Spearfish, 120
USS Stark (FFG-31), 204
USS Stark incident, 204
USS Wisconsin (BB-64), 55
USS Wyoming (SSBN-742), 125
U.S. territory, 11
U.S. uniformed services pay grades, 9
Utah War, 2
Uzbekistan, 185

V-22 Osprey, 86
Valedictorian, 111
Vanity Fair (magazine), 201
Vanuatu, 185
V Corps (United States), 221, 224
Venezuela, 185
Venustiano Carranza, 40
Veracruz (city), 39
Vice admiral (United States), 333
Vice Chairman of the Joint Chiefs of Staff, 2, 6, 74, 179
Vicenza, 193
Victor E. Renuart Jr., 246
Victoriano Huerta, 40
Victory in Europe Day, 45
Viet Cong, 50
Vietnam, 54, 185
Vietnam War, 3, 9, 15, 17, 46, 49, 98, 110, 115, 150, 154, 217, 229, 237, 285, 322
VII Corps (United States), 219, 220, 224
Vincent K. Brooks, 232
Vincent R. Stewart, 273
Virginia, 23, 64
Virginia class submarine, 86
Virginia Hall, 16
Virginia Pilot, 134, 339
Volcano Islands, 235
Volunteer military, 4

Wallace H. Nutting, 264
Walter Kross, 331
War, 157
War crimes, 256
War in Afghanistan (2001–2014), 203, 274
War in Afghanistan (2001–present), 3, 58, 112, 117, 153, 155, 202, 286
War in North-West Pakistan, 3
War of 1812, 2, 30, 31
War of Austrian Succession, 25
War of Jenkins Ear, 25
War on Terror, 3, 274, 275
War on Terrorism, 4, 57, 256, 286, 325
Warrant Officer Candidate School (U.S. Army), 14
Warrant officer (United States), 3, 9, 14, 293
Warsaw Pact, 54, 217
Washington, DC, 71
Washington, D.C., 33, 64
Washington Headquarters Services, 70, 73
Washington Naval Conference, 42
Washingtons crossing of the Delaware River, 27
Washington Times, 339
WAVES, 16, 120, 126
W. A. Worthington, 265
Wayne A. Downing, 305
Weapon trafficking, 189
Weimar Republic, 41
Wendi B. Carpenter, 139
Wesley Clark, 227, 265
Western Confederacy, 29
Western Front (World War I), 41
Western Hemisphere, 10
Western Sahara, 185
West Point, 110
West Virginia Air National Guard, 326
Whiskey Rebellion, 2
White House, 288
Wiesbaden, 225
Wikipedia:Citation needed, 81, 84, 95, 176, 179, 193, 195, 208, 209, 285, 306
Wikipedia:Citing sources, 177
Wikipedia:Link rot, 21, 201
Wikipedia:Please clarify, 193
Wikisource:Public Law 94-479, 341
Wikt:posthumous, 306
Wild weasel, 54
William Allen Rogers, 39
William Arkin, 209, 225
William Birdwood, 1st Baron Birdwood, 341
William B. Rosson, 264
William C. Gorgas, 261
William Cohen, 276
William D. Leahy, 341
William Eaton (soldier), 30
William E. Gortney, 246

William E. Ward, 190, 200
William Fallon, 202
William Halsey, Jr., 341
William H. McRaven, 306
William J. Crowe, 240
William J. Crowe Jr., 277
William J. Fallon, 179, 211, 241
William J. Lynn, 270
William J. Perry Center for Hemispheric Defense Studies, 258
William M. Fraser III, 331
William Tecumseh Sherman, 34
William Westmoreland, 50
Wilma Leona Jackson, 120
Winfield Scott, 32
Winifred Collins, 126
Winifred Quick Collins, 148
Wireless Emergency Alerts, 233
Włodzimierz Potasiński, 306
Women Airforce Service Pilots, 16
Women's Army Corps, 149
Women in the Air Force, 149
Women in the United States Air Force, **149**
Women in the United States Army, **107**
Women in the United States Coast Guard, **154**
Women in the United States Marines, **113**
Women in the United States Navy, **118**
Womens Armed Services Integration Act, 16, 110, 115, 149
Womens Army Corps, 16, 108
Woodrow Wilson Center, 259
Worlds largest arms exporters, 81
World War I, 2, 41, 108, 115, 118, 119, 341
World War II, 2, 4, 7, 23, 63, 99, 108, 115, 120, 154, 170, 171, 176, 322
World War II and recovery, 44
Wounded in action, 36
WP:NOTRS, 209

Yalu River, 47, 66
Yamasee War, 24
Yellow fever, 261
Yemen, 185
Yeoman (F), 119
Yokota Air Base, 232
Yongsan Garrison, 232

Zachary Taylor, 32
Zagros Mountains, 204
Zaire, 218
Zambia, 185
Zimbabwe, 185

www.ingramcontent.com/pod-product-compliance
Lightning Source LLC
Chambersburg PA
CBHW030517230426
43665CB00010B/651